ETHICS

"Clear explanations, aimed at laity in everyday language, concerning the moral task, the moral life, why it is important, and how it is necessary today —Maguire's *Ethics* is indeed a complete method for moral choice, perfectly fitted for university text or adult discussion groups. Incorporates treatment of a multitude of the most contemporary moral dilemmas with the wisdom of the finest moral thinkers of the ages."

CHRISTINE E. GUDORF
Professor of Ethics and Chair of Religious Studies,
Florida International University

"Daniel Maguire has been a courageous and creative interpreter of the moral life over many decades. This is a thoughtful and provocative work that combines practical wisdom with spiritual insight. It deserves to be read by anyone who is wrestling with the big moral questions of our day."

LINDA HOGAN
Professor of Ecumenics, Trinity College

"Doing ethics, for Maguire, is not just a rational exercise but fully engages the emotions and passions. This lively written book is both profound and accessible and reflects the wisdom and wit of the author."

NORMAN FARAMELLI
Boston University School of Theology

"An enticing invitation to the vast field of ethics written in crystal clarity. This book, more than any other, offers you understanding of ethics, yourself, and and your moral life."

KELLY JAMES CLARK
Professor of Philosophy, Calvin College

ETHICS

A Complete Method for Moral Choice

Daniel C. Maguire

Fortress Press / Minneapolis

ETHICS
A Complete Method for Moral Choice

Cover image: copyright © SuperStock RF / SuperStock
Cover design: Paul Boehnke
Book design: Zan Ceeley / Trio Bookworks

Library of Congress Cataloging-in-Publication Data

Maguire, Daniel C.
  Ethics : a complete method for moral choice / Daniel C. Maguire.
       p. cm.
  Includes bibliographical references.
  ISBN 978–0–8006–6443–5 (alk. paper)
  1. Ethics—Methodology. I. Title.
  BJ37.M26 2010
  170—dc22   2009032324

The paper used in this publication meets the minimum requirements of American National Standard for Information Sciences — Permanence of Paper for Printed Library Materials, ANSI Z329.48-1984.

Manufactured in the U.S.A.

14   13   12   11   10   1   2   3   4   5   6   7   8   9   10

CONTENTS

Part Two
The Theory of Ethics

6. From Awe to Strategy: The Art and Science of Ethics   65

Part Three

Asking the Right Questions: Introducing the "Wheel Model"

7. The Subject of Ethics: Defining the Model of the Wheel   79

8. Deepening the Probe: Why? How? Who? When? Where? 93

9. Foreseeable Effects, Viable Alternatives: The Link to the Future 109

Part Four

The Moral Mind in Action

10. Trusting Our Feelings and Emotions 129

11. Creativity and Surprise   145

12. Principles and Their Limits   165

16. Conscience and Guilt: The Agenbite of Inwit 225

PART FIVE

Hazards of Moral, Political, and Economic Discourse

17. The Power of Myth 247

18. Obstacles to Right Thinking 261

19. Epilogue: Religion, Ethics, and the Social Sciences 277

PREFACE

Most students of moral philosophy, coming to the subject for the first time,
are disappointed by the remoteness of the subject from the practical
problems they expect it to illuminate. They find that instead of dealing with urgent
problems . . . moral philosophers are usually preoccupied with . . . arguing over the definition of
words (such as "good" and "right") or debating the merits of very general theories (such as utilitarianism).
If practical problems of conduct are mentioned at all, it is only by way of illustrating some more
theoretical point. It is easy for students to conclude that, contrary to their expectations,
moral philosophy has little relevance to actual moral problems.

—James Rachels

Moral Problems: A Collection of Philosophical Essays (New York: Harper & Row, 1971), ix

THIS BOOK WILL NOT do to students what Rachels describes above. This book offers—what other books do not—a full method for doing ethics and a full definition of what ethics as a field of study is. It shows how you get to moral truth in three steps: (1) by asking the relevant questions; (2) by tapping all of our intellectual, emotive, and aesthetic powers; and (3) by facing the hazards and pitfalls that can trip us on our way to judgment.

A Complete Method for Moral Choice

Moral problems are ubiquitous in human life. This method shows how to *address* them. A method is not a straitjacket; it does not compel you to one conclusion. Not everyone using this method will come to the same answer, but the method ensures thoroughness and sensitivity to the subtle differences and pitfalls of the ethical quest. When I discuss particular issues to illustrate the method, it will be clear, for example, that I favor a form of single payer health care, but this method can be used to critique single payer plans. I will criticize the overuse of war, but the method can be used by both sides in debates on the use of force. I will not pretend to have no opinions on issues—no ethicist is neutral on moral issues—but the main purpose of the book is to give a method that does justice to all sides in a debate, a method that will bring clarity and form to both *pro* and *con* positions on any debated issue.

The questioning part of ethics asks the following, often neglected questions: *What? Why? How? Who? When? Where?* and *What are the foreseeable effects and the viable alternatives?* Most errors in ethics come from ignoring one or more of these questions.

Having asked all the essential questions, the second phase of ethics calls on all the ways that the human mind can get to truth. Our knowing powers are pluriform. We make cognitive contact with reality in many ways, none of which ethics can neglect. Thus, this method, using a wheel model, will put all the questions in the hub of the wheel and then have nine spokes focusing on what the questions have revealed, each spoke representing a mode of evaluation. These nine ways are *affectivity, reason and analysis, principles, creative imagination, individual experience, group experience and comparison, authority, comedy,* and *tragedy.* Too often ethics texts sin by neglecting most of these modes of reality contact.

The Wheel Model

The following graphic illustrates the innovative device, which I call the "wheel model," that I am using in this book to help readers make sense of the complete method:

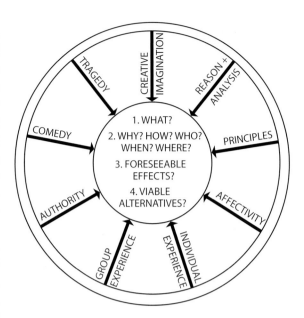

Once readers engage with the various components of the model (beginning in part 3, chapter 7, and running through to part 4, chapter 15), the wheel model appears at the beginning of the chapter with that part of the model that is under investigation. So, for instance, as the component "Principles" is being discussed in chapter 12, the model will appear with this emphasis:

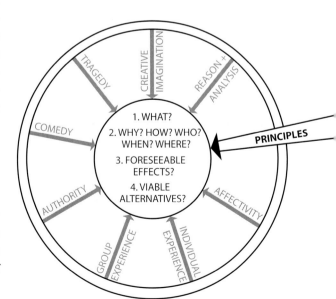

Note that the complete model's elements are always included so that readers know at any given time where they are in working through the method. It is hoped that this model will be a useful, convenient, and visual reminder of how the method effects sound moral thinking.

The third phase of ethics deals with the fact that a number of personal and socially constructed obstacles and filters impede our quest for moral truth. To be unaware of these obstacles and filters is to be unaware of how it is that we really *know*. It is an epistemological mortal sin. Ethics is not done in a vacuum but in the maelstrom of emotion, bias, and socially constructed myths and narratives. Here we will look at *myth, forbidden memories, archaic and false analogies, abstractions, selective vision, role,* and *banalization.* Each of these, if ignored, can befuddle moral judgment.

In 1978, Doubleday published my book *The Moral Choice.* It was my first effort to fill a gaping hole by offering what I dared to tout as a complete method for doing ethics. Most reviews were kind. Some called it "a landmark," "the most important contribution made to ethics for a long time," "a masterpiece," and "light years away from practically everything philosophers have been turning out recently in this field." The *Los Angeles Times* went a bit overboard in emphasizing my point on the decline and neglect of ethics as a distinct intellectual field, headlining its review "The Rediscovery of Morality." That was all very nice. Now I amplify that method and build a new book on it, one that I could not have written thirty years ago, one that takes account of the new literature and new problems that have engaged ethics since that time.

Ethics seeks wisdom wherever it is to be found, in philosophy, in the social sciences, in the arts, as well as in those storehouses of hard-won experience that we call the world religions. Ethics, thus, is not sectarian. The method developed in this book can be used by philosophers and theologians, by scientists, by economists and other social scientists, by atheists and agnostics, by the theistic religions such as Judaism, Christianity, and Islam or by nontheistic religions such as Taoism, Buddhism, and Confucianism. In treating theistic religion I capitalize all references to Gods and Goddesses, eschewing debate on upper- or lowercase deities. Ethics must not be blind to the ethical content of religious as well as nonreligious moral traditions.

Everyone brings to ethics a background of cultural and personal experience and insight, but the ethical quest is ultimately one. We are in this quest together. Ethics is the systematic effort to discover what befits us and what befits this good earth that is our generous host. It is the prime challenge for the human mind. One way or the other, all humans in all cultures and times are at the work of ethics. Ethics will be done either haphazardly and by impulse or by the use of a thorough, skillful, holistic method. It is just such a method that this book offers. Ethics is the way that we can serve a humanity that thus far has proved itself more clever than wise.

Content Overview

As explained, this book presents a complete method for dealing with all ethical problems. It shows how ethical theory connects to politics, economics, science, health care, ecology, warmaking and peacemaking, death and dying, and other issues such as sexuality and reproductive choice. Applications will be made to issues of sexism, racism, classism, and militarism. Unapplied ethical theory that floats on high like a wispy cloud far removed from the problems of life on earth is little more than a magnificently contrived irrelevancy. Approaching ethics in such a way is also downright boring. Life is certainly not boring, and ethics that is boring has failed in its calling. At the same time, a series of ethical quandaries without any theoretical framework or method is a stumble in the dark. This book treats all the usual ethical categories—utilitarianism, emotivism, relativism, intuitionism, deontology, teleology—but it lets these tools make their claims within a full method for doing ethics. This book converses with philosophers and social theorists ancient and modern and in between, but it does so without drowning the reader in a pedantic sea of names.

Part One faces head-on the question, *Is there such a thing as moral truth?* Humans are the only species with the talent to totally wreck the earth or to turn it into a garden. Ethical choices will decide that. Yet in the face of this awesome responsibility, with militarism and ecocide rampant, there is widespread confusion about what ethics is. It is not only postmodernists who wonder if truth statements can be made about basic categories like justice and the common good.

Part Two faces the fact that ethics is not identical with science or with art but that it involves elements of both. The first task of ethics is to define itself. Moral intelligence is pluriform, and realistic ethics must neglect none of the routes to moral truth. Moral reasoning and moral truth are grounded in an affective appreciation of life and its privileged setting on this planet. Justice is the first articulation of moral knowledge. It is justice, Aristotle said, that holds societies together, and defining it is the initial challenge of ethics.

Part Three shows that ethics rests on the art of questioning. The unasked (or poorly framed) question is the bane of the ethical inquiry, leaving us at the whim of the "hype" and "spin" that befog many ethical debates. Placed at the center of the wheel model of ethics, this is the "hunting and gathering" phase of ethics. Framing the issue, promoting harmony between ends and means, assessing effects, and reaching for alternatives are the tasks of dependable ethical method.

Part Four acknowledges that not by reason alone do we arrive at moral truth. Moral reason is never severed from emotion. There are at least nine ways our intelligence operates in doing ethics. These are the nine spokes of the wheel model of ethics presented in this book. Ethics involves the discovery of principles and the limits of those same principles. But ethics also requires imagination, foresight and hindsight, as well as personal intuition and good antennae to hear what others think. Tragedy and comedy often function as solvents of illusion. Ethics must take account of all this as it works to shape conscience and explore that painful reality that is healthy guilt.

Part Five faces the fact that the best ethical method we devise is not applied in a chaste vacuum. The moralscape is a muddle with tugs and pulls from within and without. The grip of myth and mood as well as false analogies and untested assumptions can fetter the mind. Class, race, and gender biases hold secret sway, and the comforts of familiarity can banish questions and numb the awe that animates moral consciousness. Ethics that does not address all of that fails in its mission and suffers from a fatal naïveté.

The Epilogue addresses the sibling relationship of philosophical ethics, religious ethics, and the social sciences. Religions are powerful culture-shapers and inveterate ethics-doers. At their best they are classics in the art of cherishing; at their worst they are the epitome of mischief, rife with false claims of divine illumination. In either role their ubiquitous influence cannot be ignored. Religious ethics explicitly critiques the moral content of religions while doing all the things that good philosophical ethics does; the two should be on speaking terms. Philosophical ethics loses a lot by absenting itself from this fruitful dialogue. Social sciences under false pretenses of neutrality are neck high in moral evaluation and unexamined moral assumptions. They need a reunion with systematic ethics.

Features in the Book

In order to assist instructors and students who will use this introductory textbook, I have developed numerous headings and subheadings for easy navigation through each chapter, to ensure that readers will know where they are within this "complete method." These headings and subheadings form the *Chapter Outlines* at the beginning of each chapter for a quick overview.

To enhance each chapter, I offer helpful excerpts in the form of text boxes labeled *Thinking Critically*. I invite readers to consider and reflect on these sometimes provocative examples as they relate to the broader themes under examination in the given chapters. These text boxes can even serve as sources for writing assignments, should instructors be so inclined.

A variety of end-of-chapter study aids are included as well. Following the completion of each chapter, a *Summary of Key Themes* highlights that chapter's most important themes and contents. A listing of *Key Terms* follows, enumerating the most important terms used in that chapter (and sometimes repeated in other chapters). To assist readers further, many key words are included in the glossary at the end of the book. For further reflection and class discussion and as possible writing topics, a set of questions labeled *Questions for Discussion* is included following each set of key words. These questions are particularly thought-provoking and require comprehension of the chapter's contents as they seek to urge readers to critically analyze themes and topics in full, critical detail. Finally, a set of *Suggestions for Further Reading* is included for each chapter, which will permit readers to extend their study and understanding of ethics in substantial and meaningful ways.

At the end of the book, readers will find an extensive glossary of key words; a thorough index of names, titles, and key concepts; and a substantial set of chapter notes for reference. Additionally, the publisher, Fortress Press, and I have collaborated to support this textbook with a companion website, *www.fortresspress.com/maguire*, which contains myriad resources, including the following:

For students: a study guide; a research guide, including instructions on writing papers; additional Web resources; and a searchable glossary.

For instructors: instructional notes, including how to use this book in courses; author videos that help explain the book and its contents and organization; sample syllabi; a premade test; additional Web resources; and research topics.

These many elements are combined to offer both students and instructors a rich pedagogy to extend and enrich their studying and teaching of ethics. I hope you find them valuable as you engage in this complete method of ethics.

The Real Stuff of Ethics

Some philosophers and theologians confuse obscurity with profundity. That leads to "unnecessary roughness" with students. A serious study of ethics in all of its ramifications need not look on clarity as offensive and intellectually suspect. There is, of course, a clarity wrought of superficiality and suitable, in Kant's phrase, only for "shallowpates." But there is a clarity that comes from knowing what you are talking about and not emitting half-digested thoughts or wallowing in obscure jargon.

Ethics is also not alien to passion. Adam Smith, the Scottish moral philosopher, took a dim view of unfeeling teachers of ethics. "None of them tend to animate us to what is generous and noble," he lamented. Instead, they befuddle us "by their vain subtleties" and eventually distract us from our "most essential duties."[1] That is unforgivable. Morality is born of ecstasy. It springs from the passionate discovery of the beauty and goodness of this privileged and generous earth and all the life that abides therein. As the German philosopher Arthur Schopenhauer said, the moral and the beautiful "mutually presuppose each other." Only when seen together "do they complete the explanation of things as they really are."[2]

Good scholarship in ethics knows how to think, to analyze, to remember, as well as to celebrate the miracle of our privileged existence in this universe, and to scream when it is profaned.

PART ONE

The Challenge of
Thinking Ethically

Ethics, the Renaissance

Introduction

TO FOLLOW THE FATE of ethics in the modern Western world, take a trip to the library of Amherst College. If you open the 1895 catalog of courses, you will discover that **ethics** held an honored primacy in the curriculum. The entire first page of the "Course of Study" is devoted to the course on ethics. It was taught by the president of the college (!) to seniors, and you can see by the grand prose used in describing the course that it was enshrined as the capstone of the entire educational process: "The aim of the course is by the philosophic study of the social and political relations of the individual to his fellow citizens and to the State, to promote that moral thoughtfulness . . . which is the strongest element in true patriotism."[1]

In the thinking of that time, no one who was not sophisticated in moral-value questions could wear the cap and gown. This was faithful to a long tradition. Probing the mysteries and intricacies of **morality** was long seen as the supreme challenge for the giants of genius. Arthur Schopenhauer wrote in 1848 that "all philosophers in every age and land have blunted their wits on the question of the moral."[2] So the 1895 Amherst catalog was heir to a distinguished tradition.

But wait! Back to Amherst we go. By 1905, just ten years later, ethics had been dethroned from its front-page billing and was relegated to the nether regions of the catalog as an elective for sophomores . . . and thus even lowly sophomores could avoid it.

Ethics, Science, and Values

Ethics is simply defined as the study of what is good or bad for people and for the rest of nature. The unseating of ethics was not just limited to this one venerable college in Massachusetts. This revolution and denigration of the study of ethics was the symptom of a cultural pandemic in which moral evaluation yielded place to an intoxicated trust in science as savior. As science and social science were unearthing greater and more intractable moral-value questions, the systematic study of values (i.e., ethics) was moving into oblivion. A chimeric quest for **value-free objectivity** opened the door to a world where upstart cleverness thrived and wisdom waned.[3]

Science and "Scientism"

Poor ethics. Even those who stubbornly plied this path took to calling their books something like *The Science of Ethics* in a brave effort to be taken seriously. The devil here, of course, is not science. Science is a noble enterprise of human genius that gives us gifts of comfort, ease, and longevity that would make the Caesars of ancient Rome green with envy. *Scientism* is the culprit. "-ism" is a nasty suffix. *Legal*, for example, is a wholesome word, referring to the conscientious effort to sort out the conflicts and possibilities of life in a fair way. *Legalism*, however, would signal a deterioration into needless bickering and nitpicking.

So, too, *scientism* is the freighting of science with burdens it cannot bear and should not try to carry. Science is strong on whats and hows, but weak on whys and oughts. Science gives awesome powers, but it does not tell how to use them or whether they should be used at all. An ethics that humbly and sensitively searches out the whys and oughts of our gargantuan talents is the natural spouse of science. When the two are divorced, the separation is bloody. Take a look at the record of this fatal estrangement.

It has been said that the prodigious powers of science have created the end of the world and stored it in our nuclear silos while stuffing our soils and foodstuffs with a hundred thousand chemicals. Most of these chemicals have not been tested for safety, and it is estimated that as many as half of them are toxic to humans.[4] As we are out jogging for health, the groundwaters below may contain the ingredients of our bodily undoing. Human breast milk often contains more toxins than are permissible in milk sold by dairies. And take note! Toxins are so ubiquitous and permeating that some are even permitted by dairies. Human bodies at death often contain enough toxins and metals to be classified as hazardous waste, and sperm counts worldwide have fallen by 50 percent since 1938. Whales and dolphins and birds and little fungi are among our victims.[5] Only science could double-baste the planet in CO_2, melting mighty glaciers and ancient ice caps.

Environmental scientist Duane Elgin predicts that in this twenty-first century, if current trends continue, we might drive 50 percent of the world's plant and animal species to extinction.[6] (And recall that death is the end of life; extinction is the end of birth.) The planet is now a coal mine with all kinds of canaries dropping. Elgin also compares our wiping out of other species on whom we depend to rivets popping out of the wings of an airplane. How many rivets can a plane lose before it crashes? Twenty-five percent of the drugs prescribed in the United States derive from wild organisms.[7] Science has discovered cures hidden in nature and enhanced our lives and longevity. An obscure fungus found in the mountains of Norway produces a powerful suppressor of the human immune system, allowing transplants to take hold.[8] As we destroy our natural environment, are we not behaving like a stupid fetus devouring the womb that bears us?

New Determinants of Ethical Thinking

What a dear companion ethics would have been on the long march of science. Ethics can be more formally defined as *the effort to bring sensitivity and method to the discernment of moral value.* More simply yet, it is the struggle to figure out what is good and bad for us and for this generous host of an earth, tucked away in this privileged little corner of the universe. Ethics is not a dictator. It is a mind-expanding, questioning art that brakes the blind momentum fueled by unasked questions and untested assumptions.

Wonder. This big-brained species with its humongous promise becomes deadly when we lose the ability to stop and look and see and say "Wow!" And "Wow," after all, is the very first step of ethics; wonder is the beginning of wisdom. Healthy ethics champions our essential capacity for awe. Done well, ethics is the cure for squinting, narrowed eyes fixed on texts and tasks while losing the ecstasy of wide-eyed wonder. It is the cure for an arid technopolis, where the prizing of beauty withers and where art and poetry lose their saving, life-expanding allure. The perception of beauty may be the crown jewel of human intelligence.

Surgeon and author Leonard Shlain argues that as we grew in technical skills, culture lost its balance, opting for "left brain" accents rather than "right brain," the *yang* over against the *yin.* That makes sense since left-brain talents are in analysis,

ordering, balancing, and organizing. But the right brain is where compassion, kindness, nurturing, a synthesizing sense of the whole, intuition, metaphor, and, yes, humor and laughter flourish.[9] The left brain, says Shlain, reasons, gives us speech and order, but it hugs less and laughs less. An overly left-brained culture is lamed. It is less equipped to do effective ethics since ethics involves both right- and left-brain powers and becomes insipid or worse if either dimension of human cognition is slighted.

Practical Wisdom. To put this talk of ethics differently, and in the way Aristotle would, ethics is nothing less or more than practical wisdom. Anyone who finds that description off-putting should remember that the alternative would be impracticality and stupidity! Ethics is no more threatening to science and human progress than is a lighthouse to a mariner. The dumb things we do when moral questions are not asked is proof of their necessity. Human affairs do not unfold in a moral vacuum. Yet even an intelligent, serious scholars like Arthur Schlesinger Jr. could write an article some years ago entitled "The Necessary Amorality of Foreign Affairs."[10] Why would a serious and sensitive scholar like George Kennan warn against making "constant attempts at moral appraisal" in international politics and warn against "making ourselves slaves of the concepts of international law and morality"? The problem is not that these are immoral men; the problem is that they show confusion about the nature of morality and the role of ethics. In the half century following such confused references to morality and ethics, we have, while avoiding serious "attempts at moral appraisal" and "the concepts of international law and morality," started brutal and unwinnable wars in Vietnam, Afghanistan, and Iraq; blocked international efforts to heal the environment; and failed to address world poverty seriously.

Carol Bly compares our long-time aversion to discourse on morality and the **common good** to sexual suppression and notes how our literature mirrors this eerie emptiness:

> If an American were to turn out a novel or story . . . in which men and women characters consorted together without one mention of physical desire, we would wonder in reviews and at lunch why the author suppressed sexuality. Yet hundreds of novels and stories offer us American characters who live out their lives without any political and ethical anxiety. We ought to be calling it suppression, because we are as much political and moral creatures as we are sexual creatures.[11]

Religion. Throughout history, those conglomerations known as the world's religions have been moralcentric in their concern. Amid all of their myths and stories, their mission has been twofold: to figure out what this world is and what our role in it should be. Religions have been the loudest and most influential voices in issuing "Thou shalts" and "Thou shalt nots." As Buddhist philosopher David Loy points out, the "traditional religions are fulfilling this role less and less, because that function is being supplanted—or overwhelmed—by other belief systems and value systems."[12] He is not yet ready to label the world's major religions "moribund," but he doesn't shy from saying that "it is somewhat ludicrous to think of conventional religious institutions as we know them today serving a significant role in solving the environmental crisis. Their more immediate problem is whether they, like the rain forests we anxiously monitor, will survive in any recognizable form the onslaught of this new religion."[13] That new major religion, he says, is our current economic system. It is the **market** that is telling us what this world is and how we should behave in it. It is the market that is issuing the modern "shalts" and "shalt nots."[14]

Loy continues, saying that "the discipline of economics is less a science than the theology of that religion, and its god, the Market, has become a vicious circle of ever-increasing production and consumption by pretending to offer a secular salvation." With communism faded away, says Loy, "the Market is becoming the first truly world religion, binding all corners of the globe into a worldview and set of values whose religious role we overlook only because we insist on seeing them as 'secular.'"[15] If philosophical and religious ethics stand aside, the vacuum will be filled.

In a word, ethics doesn't go away. We are never unconcerned with the questions of what is good for us or bad. Historian Arnold Toynbee observed that "the distinction between good and evil seems to have been drawn by all human beings at all times and places. The drawing of it seems, in fact, to be one of the intrinsic and universal characteristics of our common nature."[16]

THINKING CRITICALLY

The character Gordon Gekko in Oliver Stone's movie *Wall Street* famously made a defense of greed: "Well, in my book you either do it right or you get eliminated. . . . Thank you. I am not a destroyer of companies. I am a liberator of them! The point is, ladies and gentleman, that greed, for lack of a better word, is good. Greed is right, greed works. Greed clarifies, cuts through, and captures the essence of the evolutionary spirit. Greed, in all of its forms—greed for life, for money, for love, knowledge—has marked the upward surge of mankind. And greed, you mark my words, will not only save Teldar Paper, but that other malfunctioning corporation called the USA. Thank you very much." (Oliver Stone and Stanley Weiser, *Wall Street*, 1987. http://www.imdb.com/title/tt0094291/ [May 18, 2009])

1.1

But if ethics is not done openly and honestly, it will be done surreptitiously, as is happening with the economic system and the naïve faith that *scientific = good*. The value judgments of this new religion are influential but the ethics it contains stays under wraps. If economic dogma dismisses the claims of the environment as an irrelevant "externality" and sees human rights and essential needs as categories that do not compute, moral and political choices will be made and made badly on these issues, and the earth and its beleaguered poor will perish. A thing called **globalization** will be hailed like the return of Elijah or the second coming of Jesus Christ, and the dynamics of the market will be seen to be as natural and unchallengeable as the law of gravity. With ethics thus supplanted, and with science giving us daunting new power, earth-wrecking can proceed apace and the accumulating debris becomes the price of "doing business." And so indeed it has come to pass.[17]

Regaining Our Ethical Sense

Something is happening. Ethics is making a comeback, and the door to it has been opened by our most basic emotion, fear. Respected voices are crying, "Apocalypse now!" "Development" itself, as well as "progress," is being questioned. The *more = good* axiom is being dashed with vigorous critique. If we were to return to tenth-century Europe, we would find the belief that the *aetas aurea*, the golden age, had ended and culture was spiraling down. Citizens of that age believed that we were born too late with nought but gloom and doom our destiny. Eight centuries later, that myth did a total reversal as we got smarter with our toys and tools and suddenly the "golden age" moved from past to future. "We ain't seen nothing yet" became our myth and faith. It was morning in the world. But now, all of a sudden, in our day, the sun is dipping and the shadow of night is falling upon us.

Dire Consequences in the Absence of Ethics

Finnish philosopher Georg Henrik von Wright says with chilling calmness:

> One perspective, which I don't find unrealistic, is of humanity as approaching its extinction as a zoological species. The idea has often disturbed people. . . . For my part I cannot find it especially disturbing. Humanity as a species will at some time with certainty cease to exist; whether it happens after hundreds of thousands of years or after a few centuries is trifling in the cosmic perspective. When one considers how many species humans have made an end of, then such a natural nemesis can perhaps seem justified.[18]

Playwright and former Czech Republic president Vaclav Havel warns that if we endanger the earth, she will dispense with us in the interests of a higher value—that is, life itself. Evolutionist Lynn Margulis joins the grim chorus, saying that the rest of the earth's life did very well without us in the past and will do very well without us in the future.

New York University physics professor Marty Hoffert adds to this gloom boom: "It may be that we're not going to solve global warming, the earth is going to become an ecological disaster, and somebody will visit in a few hundred million years and find there were some intelligent beings who lived here for a while, but they just couldn't handle the transition from being hunter-gatherers to high technology. It's entirely possible."[19]

A dire conclusion presses in on us: *If current trends continue, we will not.*

Contemporary **apocalypticists** indict us with this judgment: that the two greatest disasters to hit this generous planet have been (1) the asteroidal pummeling of sixty-five million years ago that extinguished the dinosaurs and other life-forms and (2) the arrival of the rogue species that calls itself (all too prematurely) the ***animal rationale***, the rational animal.

The Good News

The good news, in a hedged sort of way, is that some say it is not too late. Christopher Flavin of Worldwatch Institute (which has led the wise worriers for years) greeted 2007 with an article entitled "It May Not Be Too Late." That's about as reassuring as the pilot announcing: "This plane may not crash." But it does signal an opportunity to ask, "What's wrong?" and to invite in that discipline called ethics, which specializes in such questions and in the task of awakening consciences.

Spirituality is often the code word for ethical awakening. Interest in it is suddenly in vogue. Indeed, spirituality is more popular than religion. People who would not darken the door of a church, temple, or mosque are open to discussion of spirituality. The left-wing investigative magazine *Mother Jones* devoted a whole issue to spirituality, with the cover title "Believe It or Not: Spirituality Is the New Religion."[20] Books and articles appear on spirituality in the workplace. There are many definitions and notions of what spirituality is, but the phenomenon signals a hunger for the clear thinking that ethics is charged with providing. The modern mind is also being focused on because of the ongoing demythologization of war.

War, Terrorism, and Globalization

I write now at a time when the state-sponsored violence we call "war" is simultaneously rampaging and getting embarrassed. Even though there were 149 wars between 1945 and 1992, with more appearing since as groups of humans bang "against one another with no more plan or principle than molecules in an overheated gas"[21]—still, with all of that, realists, not just idealists, are now challenging the inevitability of **war**. War has reached a moral turning point where it can no longer do more good than harm, the basic test of every moral choice. The reasons offered for war cannot be truthful; it can never deliver what it promises.

The old principle of "non-combatant immunity" has become infeasible. Science has ended the possibility of limiting the horrors of war to uniformed combatants. If we take as a rock-solid ethical principle—and we should—that what is good for children is good and what is bad for children is ungodly, the new data are grim. According to journalist Chris Hedges, "More than 2 million children were killed in wars during the 1990s. Three times that number were disabled or seriously injured. Twenty million children were displaced from their homes in 2001 alone."[22] In the wars of the 1990s, civilian deaths constituted between 75 and 90 percent of all war deaths. That makes war and terrorism convertible terms and takes away the respectability of the havoc we euphemistically call "war." Nuclear weapons have moved war from thinkable to unthinkable. We have prepared the end of the world and packed it away in our arsenals.

Terrorism, by definition, means the deliberate killing of civilians to achieve your political goal.

War has transmogrified into terrorism, bringing the human race to a crossroads. Science has re-written the medieval script. The new choice for humankind is this: find alternatives to war—or accept terrorism as your only defense. Europe, that military tinderbox of yore, now exemplifies the alternative to war: *economic and political interdependence.* In the European Union, they don't go to war with each other anymore; they bargain and they negotiate.

The United Nations Charter proposed an idea that may have seemed idealistic in the ashes of World War II but now has become sheer practicality. As international law expert Richard Falk writes:

> World War II ended with the historic understanding that recourse to war between states could no longer be treated as a matter of national discretion, but must be regulated to the extent possible through rules administered by international institutions. The basic legal framework was embodied in the UN Charter, a multilateral treaty largely crafted by American diplomats and legal advisers. Its essential feature was to entrust the Security Council with administering a prohibition of recourse to international force (Article 2, Section 4) by states except in circumstances of self-defense, which itself was restricted to responses to a prior "armed attack" (Article 51), and only then until the Security Council had the chance to review the claim.[23]

This policing paradigm is not **pacifism** that says that all killing is evil. It stipulates, rather, that any nation planning to attack another militarily must face not only that nation but all nations coordinated—police style—into an international security force. This would be an impressive deterrent. Of course, nations, and especially the United States, have trashed this historic initiative and returned to the vigilante approach to warring. "Like a dog returning to its vomit is a stupid man who repeats his folly" (Prov. 26:11). Yet, ironically, the American dogs of war have given a lesson to the world on the wisdom of the United Nations Charter. Witness the United States' fatal follies in Vietnam, Iraq, and Afghanistan. None of these killing adventures passes the elementary "more good than harm" test. The United States while in militaristic heat has been the unwitting witness to the inutility of traditional war.[24] That opens the door to a new ethical critique of state-sponsored violence, a bloody invitation to clarity of thought.

Globalization of commerce adds clout to the lesson. A Chinese official was quoted on television shortly after the American invasion of Iraq as saying to Americans: "You people invade countries that are rich in oil. We simply buy the oil. It's cheaper and no one gets hurt." He could have added: "If you insist on warring, we will lend you the money to do so at handsome interest and then we will use that interest to buy oil." It is a lovely thing for our species when doing good and doing well happily coincide. Such is the case now as nonviolent modes of power are proving more efficient and enriching.

The new lesson we are learning is that intelligent economics and diplomacy trump bludgeoning as policy. It is promising that we live in an age when empire, too, is becoming anachronistic. Empire is the exploitation of the weak by the powerful. Its tools are military and economic might. The United States has been having a go at it, but its empire is cracking at the seams. Environmental professor Vaclav Smil, writing three years before the 2008 financial collapse, predicted that within a short time "there will be a profoundly altered United States: economically weaker and technically less competent, with an impotent currency, rampant corruption, and distant memories of superpower glory."[25] Anyone who has exchanged dollars for euros will know that that collapse is well begun. Declining empires are dangerous. They go not gently into night. They require ethical intensive care.

Reinvigorating Ethics

Practicality invites a reinvigorated ethics to fresh analysis of the use of collective force and to investigate the multiple modes of power overlooked by the military mind. This book will address the neglected art of peace-making and present a power chart showing the ethical alternatives to kill-power.

Human knowledge is pluriform; there are multiples ways by which we achieve reality contact. To bring that reality into analytical focus, I employ an architectonic tool, a wheel model that includes a hub of diagnostic questions to guard against the hazard of incomplete information and then develops nine ways in which human intelligence makes contact with reality. The wheel model will be discussed in detail starting in chapter 7. Some of those cognitive modalities are obvious and not neglected in most standard treatments of ethics; some are less obvious, like tragedy, comedy, affect, and creative imagination. This method stresses creativity as our supreme moral faculty and show its relationship to **courage** since timid minds stray reluctantly from the miring pastures of the tried and the familiar. History is a maelstrom and our knowing

THINKING CRITICALLY

Morality is not just a matter of the customs of the tribe you happen to be in. Some moral insights are remarkably resonant throughout very different cultures.

The Golden Rule, "Do unto others as you would have them do unto you," is one of humankind's highest and nearly universally held ideals, and it can be found in essence in all the great religions of the world. Religions, with all their faults, are the repositories of some of the most important sensitivities of humankind.

- Good people proceed while considering that what is best for others is best for themselves. (Hitopadesa, Hinduism)
- Thou shalt love thy neighbor as thyself. (Leviticus 19:18, Judaism)
- Therefore all things whatsoever ye would that people should do to you, do ye ever so to them. (Matthew 7:12, Christianity)
- Hurt not others with that which pains yourself. (Udanavarga 5:18, Buddhism)
- What you do not want done to yourself, do not do to others. (Analects 15:23, Confucianism)
- No one of you is a believer until he loves for his brother what he loves for himself. (Traditions, Islam)

1.3

takes place there. Many are the forces that boggle the mind on the road to truth. These have to be dealt with. Hence, this method has a chapter on "the hazards of moral, political, and economic discourse." These include such things as myth, strategic forgetfulness, momentum and mood, false analogues and seductive abstractions, and more. At every point the method here developed fights the TINA (There Is No Alternative) temptation. The TINA syndrome paralyzes social ethical discourse like a collective cerebral stroke.

Justice, Class, and the Common Good

Justice requires special handling and I will give it special stress. Studies of justice list more than fifty forms of justice. I will argue that all these are reducible to three: commutative (or inter-individual) justice, social justice, and distributive justice. I will present a model that illustrates how every society labors to find a balance between individual good and the common good (see p. 56). I'll accept the challenge of defining "the common good," a slippery term that is often used and rarely tied down. I will argue that all systems of law with more or less success are operating within this trinity of justice forms. Traditional economics often slights the core significance of essential human need and the relationship of need to human rights. Healthy justice theory does not. I will illustrate this justice theory by application to thorny issues like preferential affirmative action, the distribution of limited resources including organs for transplant, debt cancellation in response to poverty crises, and taxation of international money exchanges. I will also argue that basic health care is a human right like the right to literacy or the right to vote, not a consumer item to be gotten if you can afford it. Justice theory is at the heart of all those issues.

Ethics has to put major stress on the category of *class*, working on the thesis that if you show me your zip code, I will usually get a good peek into your conscience as well as your wallet. Moral judgments often gush forth from our perceived interests, with little intervening reflection or critique. "People go after what they perceive to be in their own interests," said the apostle Paul to the Philippians, sounding almost like a member of the Chicago School of Economics. Transcending narrowly conceived self-interest in ways that favor community and the common good, and, at the same time, guarding a sensible self-interest, is a perennial ethical challenge, and we'll wrestle with it here.

Power, Affluence, and Fertility

Vaclav Havel put it this way:

> I think there are good reasons for suggesting that the modern age has ended. Today, many things indicate that we are going through a transitional period, when it seems that something is on the way out and something else is painfully being born. It is as if something were crumbling, decaying and exhausting itself, while something else, still indistinct, were arising from the rubble.[26]

In the United States where I write, the halcyon euphoria that followed World War II and lingered for two decades was pregnant with illusions and false hopes. Thomas Aquinas sagely observed that young people and drunks are most liable to false hopes.[27] Post–World War II America was a drunken youngster. The shedding of illusions and the pains of maturing are upon us. Our now ongoing value quake compares well to what happened in Japan more than a century ago. Commodore Perry in 1853 opened eyes and ports when his ships steamed into Yedo Bay. Japan had been hiding from reality and its unavoidable tumults. Now, we in this slowly humbling nation are meeting our Yedo Bay as new realities and our limits meet a new day of rapid change.

Ethics to a large extent is a study of power, and power in our day is mutating (as I will show in a graph of the multiple modes of power that operate in society) Following the Treaty of Westphalia in 1648, sovereignty was attributed to the individual nation-state, and all laws and wars accepted that arrangement as a law of nature. Slowly and without fanfare the nation-state has been shorn of its hegemony. Behemothic entities, called corporations, have arisen, displacing the power of states. While taking little note of it, we have arrived at the point where "of the world's one hundred largest economies, fifty are now corporations—not including banking and financial institutions."[28] Corporate lobbies muscle out the voice of the ***demos***; democracy becomes lobby-ocracy. When sheer power acts without ethical reflection, the people perish, and the earth with them.

For two hundred years, the affluent part of the world has been on orgy mode. I've never attended an orgy, but I can't imagine they end on a happy note. This one is not ending merrily, as the time of normalized excess slowly crashes. When I was born, there were some two and a half billion people on the planet. There are triple that number now with no date certain for a cap on growth. It all depends on those more than one billion adolescents who dwell among us. Half the people on the planet are under twenty-five. There are more young fertiles on the planet now than there were people in 1960. Their reproductive behavior is unpredictable. Poverty as well as orgiastic excess lead to over-reproductivity. As our numbers swell, a terrible formula looms:

$$H + A + A = A$$

Hyperfertility + Affluence + Appetite = Apocalypse. As a colleague from India said to me, "We are intent on making all the mistakes you made but making them faster." If everyone were to live as North Americans and Europeans live, the planet could not sustain more than three billion of us. It would require several supplementary planets to keep the party going. But as people "develop" into affluence, their appetite grows accordingly, and therein lies the road to apocalypse. The apocalypse has already started but is only dimly impinging on our collective awareness. Hunger has replaced war as the most efficient killer. Some forty million people die every year from hunger and poverty-related causes—the equivalent of three hundred jumbo jet crashes daily, with half of the passengers being children.[29]

It is a rule of nature for any species: we limit our numbers, or nature will do it for us. We, the ethical animal, are the only species that can make that decision reflectively and freely. Family planning is not a luxury. It is essential and will always be so: family planning means contraception with access to safe abortion as an option when necessary.[30] But not by condoms alone shall we be saved. As ethicist James Martin-Schramm writes, there must also be a redistribution "of land and income, improvement in access to education and employment, the elimination of discrimination based on race or sex, and substantial improvement in access to affordable housing, food, and health care."[31] And that agenda is the very stuff of ethics and justice theory, especially that painful word *redistribution*.

The Urgency for Ethical Action

So there is much that is harshly new in this time, but there is also something that is not new. The human race has always teetered between barbarity and morality, with morality only slowly establishing its claims. This dialectic continues with new tones. The stakes, of course, are higher now. Technological barbarians are more dangerous. But the gateway to an alternative to barbarism is, as it always has been, ethical reflection. The ancients said: "He who reflects not in his heart is like the beast that perishes." That really is not true. The beasts are better off. Even without reflection, they have instinct that imbues them with the wisdom of survival.

Some years ago I spoke on demographic issues to a group of Ford Foundation program officers at a meeting near Athens, Greece. When we stopped for a twenty-minute break, they urged me upon return to explain better the terms *ethics* and *the common good*. I headed down a dirt path leading to the sparkling Aegean Sea. Ahead of me I saw what looked like a black ribbon stretched across the path. As I neared it, I saw it was two rows of black ants, one row carrying something and the other row obviously returning for a load. A real estate move was in process. I stepped over the columns reverently and went down to feast on the beauty of the waters. On my return the ants were gone, their mission accomplished. What a splendid example they gave me to bring back to the Ford Foundation people. All those ants were committed to the common good. There were no divisive special-interest groups, no shirkers from the mission. This commitment to the common good was inscribed in their genes.

Our genes, it seems, are a mixed bag with an inbuilt tilt toward **egoism**. They definitely do not propel us generously toward the common good. For our species, genetic inscription doesn't fill the bill. For us, the alternative is ethics, that delicate activity of moral beings. We will neither survive nor flourish by instinct, but only by the activation of our moral consciousness.

If ethics seems dull, and often it does when it is reduced to a rehearsal of the unapplied thoughts of long-ago dead men—and a few women—it is ethicists who have made it so. I have strived not to join them in that sin. Ethics is about life with its tragedy and comedy, its variety and its shocks, its conundrums and its dreams. None of that should be boring.

Summary of Key Themes

- Ethics provides insight into how we should or ought to live our lives in concert with nature, as science provides insight into what is possible and how it might be achieved—two disciplines that need to work in tandem.
- The limits of science and economic reasoning to address ethical implications of human behavior—notably, the threat and practice of war and terrorism—demand a renewed ethical sense of all people.
- Dire consequences exist for human and animal populations unless power relationships and the excesses of affluent lifestyles are transformed.

Key Terms

Animal rationale
Apocalypticists
Common good
Courage
Demos
Egoism
Ethics
Globalization
H + A + A = A
Hyperfertility

Justice
Market
Moral/morality
Noncombatant immunity
Pacifism
Policing paradigm
Practical wisdom
Redistribution
Religion
Scientism
Spirituality
Value-free objectivity
War

Questions for Discussion

1. Explain the new way of going to war according to the United Nations Charter (see p. 9). Why is this called the "policing" way of war? How would it deter prospective invaders?
2. Advertisers say that if they know your zip code, they can say what you wear, drive, and eat. Does one's zip code signal one's "class" and therefore also tell something of one's conscience? Does your economic class control conscience or just influence it?
3. What moral questions were ignored as the ongoing ecological crisis unfolded? What moral questions should have been asked?

4. Gordon Gekko in *Wall Street* said that greed is good. Aristotle said that justice holds human community together. Could greed do that? If not, why not?

Suggestions for Further Reading

Elliot, Robert, ed. *Environmental Ethics.* Oxford Readings in Philosophy. New York: Oxford University Press, 1995.

Hedges, Chris. *What Every Person Should Know about War.* New York: Free Press, 2003.

Nash, James A. *Loving Nature.* Nashville: Abingdon, 1991.

Worldwatch Institute. *Vision for a Sustainable World.* 2008. http://www.worldwatch.org (July 2009). Visit this website to see what issues are being discussed today on the global environment.

Is There Such a Thing as Moral Truth?

"WHAT IS TRUTH?" Pilate asked Jesus, and it really was a good question, perhaps the most philosophical question in the entire Bible (John 18:38). Truth is the oxygen of the mind. We say "true" when we are convinced that reality and our minds match. True knowledge is the stored record of our reality contact. That is quite straightforward. The problem is that reality is not a seamless garment; it is jumbled and diverse, and, accordingly, so are our experiences of truth.

Proof of Truth-Claims: Scientific and Moral

Sometimes proof of truth, that is, proof of reality contact, is easily achieved. Let me illustrate. If I told a group of listeners that water boils at 212 degrees Fahrenheit and they doubted me, I could give them a Revere Ware copper-bottomed soup kettle and a thermometer and send them to the adjacent kitchen to verify it. If we were at the right altitude, what I told them would happen—the water would boil at 212 degrees—and my statement would stand as *true*. Verifiability here is very easy. If they hungered for more truth and I told them that water would freeze at a certain temperature, I could send them back to the kitchen—and *voila*—right again! To extend my streak of verifiable truth-statements, I could announce that metal expands when heated. The same kettle in the same kitchen would back me up. Put that kettle on without water, and the lovely copper base would expand, destroying the kettle but making my point: metal, when heated, does expand. (I've done all these things myself, so I know they are true.)

Clearly, by this point my listeners would be impressed, and since truth can stimulate a hunger for more of the same, I could then offer them yet another truth-claim requiring verification. I could say: "Promises made to persons who are now dead should normally be honored and kept!" If my listeners headed back to the kitchen to check that out, I would have to recall them. My earlier statements were about scientific truth that can be verified in a kitchen or laboratory. I just shifted gears into moral **truth-claims**. Here **verifiability** is tougher and more mysterious.

Moral Language

Verifying moral truth-claims requires a different approach than scientific experimentation. Thus, I would then turn to Socrates and to his method of intellectual midwifery, drawing truth out of the womb of the mind where

it reposes in untapped implicitness. A story would do it.

Your son has become a billionaire. He is visiting his old friend Joe who is near death. They speak of times past when they were together. Your billionaire son then says to Joe: "Joe, we both know you are not doing well. Is there anything an old friend like me could do for you at this time?" Joe hesitates and then confesses that months ago when he was well, he cheated a poor old man out of $400. He hates to go into death with that burden on his conscience. Joe is now penniless and he asks your son to pay the old man that money. Your son rises to the occasion and says, "Joe, in honor of our great friendship, I promise you this: I will give that old man a windfall of four thousand dollars in your name." Joe beams, smiles, but slowly slips away into a deep sleep and dies. Your son looks around and muses, "Well, nobody heard that and poor old Joe is as dead as a doornail, so I think I'll just forget about it."

Now the test: If you were the billionaire's parent, would your breast swell with pride and would you say, "That's my boy! He's everything I ever hoped for"? Or would some word like *sleazy* come to mind? And notice, *sleazy* is a moral term. We've moved into moral language. Moral language is *ought talk*. It refers to what humans ought or ought not to be. Most people would judge almost reflexively that the promise made to poor old Joe should be kept even though Joe is now a corpse. You'll never prove that obligation or moral burden in a lab or kitchen, but the truth of it tugs at us nevertheless. The billionaire's breach of faith is not admirable or decent or good. It really is sleazy.

Verifying Moral Truth

But how to verify that claim to moral truth?

Let me, Irish style, add to the dilemma with another story. J. Glenn Gray, in his thoughtful book *The Warriors: Reflections on Men in Battle*, tells of an incident in World War II. The occupied Dutch had been shooting German soldiers. To stop them, the commander rounded up some citizens and ordered their execution as an example to other Dutch rebels. His message: Shoot another German soldier, and we will randomly execute another group of you. He ordered several of his soldiers to be the firing squad. When the poor, terrified hostages were lined up before him, one soldier assigned to the firing squad looked at them and suddenly walked away, refusing to shoot. This was treasonous disobedience on the battlefield, punishable by instant death. The young soldier was stripped of his gun, lined up with the hostages, and shot dead by his erstwhile companions.

The incident had become fabled among the Dutch who related it to Gray. Amid the dark horrors of war, Gray said the incident "cannot fail to be inspiring . . . and a revelation of nobility."[1]

Question: If that young soldier were your son (instead of that sleazy billionaire), would you not in your grief say that the manner of his death proved how precious he was? If you had had a bad impression of that young soldier, would you not now have to say you were wrong since his death revealed depths of nobility and courage and integrity that merit the encomium *heroic*?

Yet think of it. The hostages still died in spite of the soldier's dissent. His action had a glaring futility about it. His refusal was not "cost efficient"; there was more, rather than less, death. All the

good that could have come of his good life after the war in a healing nation was cut short, never to be realized. And yet—and yet—it stubbornly remains admirable. Again, if someone did this whom we had always thought of as ruthless, egoistic, and self-serving, we would have to change our estimate of his character. Is it not true to our deepest experience to say that we would hope that in a similar situation we or our children would have the courage not to stand there like the other soldiers and obediently blast lead into the quivering flesh of innocent and desperate hostages? Indeed, if we were among those hostages and knew that we would die anyhow, would we not still have experienced something in this young soldier that was beautiful and good, even if not useful to us? Would not his sacrifice seem to represent the fullest flowering of humanity? Was not his choice what the Greeks would call *kalon*, an adjective that denotes both moral goodness and beauty?

One thing we do know empirically is that this physical life of ours is the matrix of all the good things we experience. When we become a cadaver, that matrix is gone. Many people believe that when we become a corpse, that matrix perdures in some other form and our personal life continues in a new mode. However, those who affirm an afterlife *believe* it, *hope* for it. They do not *know* it with the irrefutable immediacy of here-and-now lived experience.[2] Approval of "the supreme sacrifice" is, admittedly, an extreme example of moral truth, one we hope never to be tested on in our own lives. But it does introduce us to the mysterious, almost ineffable, even enigmatic profundity that moral truth can entail. Our classical literature is full of testimony to the moral meaningfulness of such honored self-sacrifice.

Other moral truths, generally accepted and encoded in our laws, seem less dauntingly problematic, such as the moral duty not to cheat or rape or kill without warrant. But these moral demands also put our reasoning to the test, and some fine minds have staggered in responding to that test.

We all like tidy explanations, and that is fine, but when reality is messy, our tidy talk may miss the point. Simplism results, and simplism abounds when people have underestimated the difficulty of explaining the "shalts" and "shalt nots" that are at the heart of morality and culture. Let's look at some of these abortive shortcuts.

Custom and Morality: The Relativist Temptation

The word **moral** derives from the Latin *mores,* which means "customs." Aha! says the relativist. That explains it *tout court,* or "simply enough"! Moral obligations are simply the socially approved customs of our tribe. Early anthropology was tempted in this direction. As more and more variety was found in the customs and practices of other societies, it seemed there was no "natural law" or universal blueprint for morality and it seemed like the tribes were making it up as they went along. As anthropologists Abraham and May Edel said when they saw that what other societies called good or bad often contravened our attitudes, "We know that such contraventions of our attitudes—to adultery, or truth-telling, or killing or toward virtually any role we accept—are extremely common among the peoples of the different cultures of the world."[3]

Anthropologist Ruth Benedict took it to this blunt conclusion:

We do not any longer make the mistake of deriving the morality of our own locality and decade directly from the inevitable constitution of human nature. We do not elevate it to the dignity of a first principle. We recognize that morality differs in every society, and is a convenient term for socially approved habits. Mankind [*sic*] has always preferred to say, "It is

morally good," rather than "It is habitual," and the fact of this preference is enough to a critical science of ethics. But historically the two phrases are synonymous.[4]

This gives academic expression to "do-your-own-thing-ism," but it crashes on the same rocks. It shrinks ethics to customs-cataloguing, and as for criteria, it leaves us naked. If the customary equals the good, how do we critique evil customs? And we do. The history of law is a history of critiquing and changing customs. Slavery was for a long time a socially approved custom and legal, and in some of its modern forms it still is. Critics of it have obviously found some higher ground from which to judge. Sexism has been a persistently "socially approved habit," even to the point of denying women the right to vote. Social blessings have been given for racism, the "divine right of kings," and the preference for violent modes of conflict resolution. All of this has been challenged, and pure **relativism** offers no grounding on which to base that challenge.

Even Benedict, after her unnuanced conflating of custom and morality, conceded that "it is quite possible that a modicum of what is considered right and what wrong could be disentangled that is shared by the whole human race."[5] That contradicts her previous statement. If cultural customs are always a variable and if even a "modicum" of morality is transculturally invariable, then morality and custom are not one and the same. The United Nations Universal Declaration of Human Rights in 1948 actually spelled out a "modicum of morality" for all human beings. That heroic effort made "human rights" the accepted vernacular for international ethical discourse and inspired an ongoing flood of "human rights" declarations on topics such as genocide, racism, sexism, and freedom from torture.[6] The ratifying nations of the UN were not going to say that those things were just interesting alternative folkways immune to a firm *j'accuse!* (French for "I accuse you (of wrongdoing)!").

The Role of "Choking" in Moral Intelligence

Relativism is an indefatigable tempter, not just because of its simplicity, but also because it sounds so democratic and the human race is at least infatuated with democracy if, on the ground, only haltingly committed to it. "Cultural relativism" seems so democratic as we bend over backwards to respect all the differing "customs" of other societies. As democracy-loving, multicultural people, we do that with all our liberal might until we try to ingest something and we choke. Take female genital mutilation, or, as it is euphemized, "female genital cutting." This custom, which grew up mainly in Africa, performs crude forms of clitoridectomy on young girls as a rite of passage, leaving them maimed for life.[7] An interesting cultural variation? Or a violation of a basic moral right to bodily integrity? Consensus is happily veering to the latter conclusion. It may be "socially approved custom," but it is a human disaster that is increasingly recognized as such. Girls fleeing this assault are now often accepted as legitimate refugees. Instead of going relativistic and tolerant on that cruel mutilation, we are instead *doing ethics*

THINKING CRITICALLY

On December 10, 1948, in what was a moral breakthrough for the human race, the United Nations passed The "International Bill of Human Rights." Its preamble includes these statements:

"Whereas recognition of the inherent dignity and of the equal and inalienable right of all members of the human family is the foundation of freedom, justice and peace in the world.

"Whereas the peoples of the United Nations have reaffirmed their faith in fundamental human rights, in the dignity and worth of the human person and in the equal rights of men and women . . .

"Now, Therefore, THE GENERAL ASSEMBLY proclaims THIS UNIVERSAL DECLARATION OF HUMAN RIGHTS as a common standard of achievement for all peoples and all nations. . . ."

This is followed by thirty articles spelling out the basic rights that every human being is entitled to, regardless of race, creed, nationality, or gender.

2.2

on it, that is, making the distinction between harmless cultural variants and moral crimes.

National sovereignty has been international dogma since the Treaty of Westphalia in 1648 and could be and has been relativistically understood to permit every nation simply to do its own thing, however gross and abusive its "thing." At the level of theory, and often in practice, that leniency has not been allowed to stand. Governments committing "crimes against humanity" (a term pure relativism could not fathom) are treated as illegitimate. Just as parents who abuse their children can lose the right to retain those children or even to see them, punitive action is justified to stop crimes against humanity and genocidal acts of governments. Though there is usually insufficient political will to follow through on it, the Charter of the United Nations allows for this.[8] This proves again that although relativism is tempting, you can't live with it. (Of course, I have not yet given my theoretical answer as to why you can't live with it. Relativism does not explain what I will call the foundational moral experience. That challenge I will assume in the next chapter.)

Relativism *No*, Relational *Yes*

With all my critique of wishy-washy relativism, the fact stands tall that morality (and therefore ethics) is *relational*. "Human actions," as Thomas Aquinas said, "are good or bad according to their circumstances."[9] What is moral for one person may be **immoral** for another because of the diversity of circumstances. The moral meaning of behavior depends on circumstances and how those circumstances relate to one another. It may seem morally unpromising to put a bullet through the head of a man unless it is the only way to stop that man from gunning down a schoolyard of children. In those circumstances, with no other alternative available, that lethal act is moral and good. Tragic? Yes. But because of the circumstantiality that is our moral lot, the act is ethically defensible. The tragic is not always wicked.

Moral judgments are like the judgment of a detective. The goal is to see how all the facts (clues) connect and relate. When you see how they all connect, you have (if you got it all right) moral insight. The moral decider cannot escape the "it depends" that is indigenous to human affairs. In that sense ethics is relational. That does not open the door to the mush of relativism. What it does do is make the artlike work of ethics a permanently questing process requiring sensitive, out-stretching antennae and appropriate tentativeness when we encounter circumstantial blur. It makes ethics humble and firm in its resistance to the human penchant for unfurling false absolutes.

In looking for the foundational moral experience, rela-

tivism falls on its face. There are other efforts that also do not stay standing.

The "Ask God" Fallacy: The Fundamentalist Temptation

It is a shame that the term **fundamentalism** has been perversely co-opted. After all, getting down to the fundamentals of things is the goal of all research and thought. The term, however, has come to describe those theistic religionists who think that God wrote a book and, in so doing, did our ethics for us. Whether it is the Qur'an or the Bible, fundamentalists see the book that God dictated as the ultimate "What to Do and How to Do It" book. Of course, not all religions are text based and not everyone in the text-based religions is a fundamentalist. Sophisticated religionists find in their sacred literature the experience and wisdom of many lives. Such scriptures are complicated records requiring skilled interpretation. They are not magical texts that foresaw problems that did not exist when they were written; they are not feats of magical prescience. Along with a lot of terrible stuff that is merely descriptive of how folks lived back then, biblical writings are replete with insights into human needs and foibles, and their insights when reappropriated and applied can lend light, as do all the ancient classics. The classical religious texts have a place

---

THINKING CRITICALLY

On the problems of relativism, Alasdair MacIntyre writes: "In different cities there may be different conceptions of the virtues. What is taken to be just in democratic Athens may be different from what is taken to be just in aristocratic Thebes or in military Sparta. The sophistic conclusion is that in each particular city the virtues are what they are taken to be in that city. There is no such thing as justice-as-such, but only justice-as-understood-at-Sparta. This relativism . . . involves its adherents in a number of related difficulties."

—Alasdair MacIntyre, *After Virtue*

2.3

at the ethical table, but they cannot replace the table.

Economic Fundamentalism

Religious foibles, however, are human foibles, and they show up all over the place. The illusion of certitude is the common failing of those who say "God told me so" but also of those secularists who say "the market told me so." Economics likes to present itself as a science, though increasingly it can be seen to have a religious mission, a theology, and a priesthood. (I am addressing here the dominant capitalistic model, but the sacralizing of economic theory affects all economic systems, as we saw in Soviet Communism.) Indeed, University of Maryland economics professor Robert Nelson hailed the religious character of his discipline in his 2001 book *Economics as Religion.* He says that his fellow economists want to think of themselves as scientists but they are really "more like theologians." In times past religions conferred legitimacy in society. Not anymore. "Economic efficiency has been the greatest source of social legitimacy in the United States for the past century," he writes approvingly, "and economists have been the priesthood defending this core social value of our era."[10] He does not hesitate to say that the laws of economics are "the new word of God."[11]

Nelson is not alone. As Harvard Divinity School's Harvey Cox says, in criticism of this trend, the market and its dynamics and demands have come to resemble the Yahweh of the Hebrew Bible, "not just one superior deity contending with others but the Supreme Deity, the only true God, whose reign must now be universally accepted and who allows for no rivals."[12]

Now that is downright scary. Economists are doing our religious and ethical thinking and thus are the official experts on values in our society? Economist Theodore Levitt hoists a panoply of red flags aloft when he says, "Organized business has been chronically hostile to every humane and popular reform in the history of American capitalism."[13] And ethicist Larry Rasmussen writes: "No American corporation has supported a single major piece of progressive environmental legislation while most all of them have rushed to congressional offices to help write deregulative legislation. . . . Privatizing profits while socializing costs to vulnerable human and other communities is a deeply ingrained capitalist practice, and a very bad one."[14] With the broad, unchecked influence they have in our market-driven world, economic fundamentalists can be just as, if not more, dangerous than religious fundamentalists.

Constitutional Fundamentalism

And then we have our constitutional fundamentalists. "Strict constructionist," "original intent" interpreters of the U.S. Constitution are also fundamentalists. They share the error of thinking reality and all of its tortuous paths and corners can be mapped and jammed into the pages of a text. Life would be simpler if that were true, and that's the lure that drives the hunt for gurus, oracles, sacred answer books, markets, and constitutions that will do all your thinking for you.

Fundamentalists flee the changes that mark a reality in flux; they resist the flow of life with all its disconcerting surprises and inconsistencies. They are relentless blueprint hunters who will excise what does not fit on their chosen pages. Unfortunately for them, but fortunately for a lively ethics, reality is not that simple because life is not that dull. Fear of change makes religious fundamentalists reject evolution. It makes constitutional fundamentalists fear the evolution of law. Constitutional fundamentalists want to believe that a group of eighteenth-century fellows said the last word on how a democracy should adjust to life. The authors of that classic offered many good principles, but they could not apply them to circumstances they did not foresee, nor were they able to come up with all the needed principles. Love those authors we do, thank them we must, but deify them? Let's not.

Fundamentalism is simplistic and anything that is simplistic gives good cover to meanness. Thus, Justice Antonin Scalia of the Supreme Court can claim to be an "originalist," searching faithfully for the answers that are precontained in the text of the Constitution. Yet I would argue that his decisions show a different agenda when he denies prisoners held on American soil the right to a lawyer, signaling that his passion has a controlling political purpose. When these "originalists" write, the poor, racial minorities, women, and prisoners all tend to be the losers. Alleged fidelity to the framers covers another agenda. Ethics must be alert to the fact that one of the characteristics of any fundamentalism is the covering up of hidden agendas.

Religious Fundamentalism

Similarly, religious fundamentalists with stark consistency countenance the subordination of women to men, capital punishment, and the liberal use of that state-sponsored violence we call "war" while treating reasonable tolerance as a villain. The alleged commitment to "the word of God" houses a right-wing mission that is—in telling irony—regularly contradicted by the sacred texts they worship.

God-talk is not a substitute for thinking clearly about morality. Indeed, it can be a distraction. Throughout history too many atrocities have been rationalized by alleged commitment to "the will of God." Crusades and jihads drown morality in blood with the cry of *Deus vult*—"God wills it." Hitler's soldiers had

Gott mit uns—"God is with us"—stamped on their buckles. Empires always see themselves as divine missionaries, often dressing their dominative ideology in explicitly religious language. "The worst of madmen is a saint gone mad," said the poet Alexander Pope, and the misuses of God-talk prove his point.

Belief in a personal God is an inference from other experiences, including moral experience. Primary cognitive experience is within the world we can see and touch. Theistic or atheistic conclusions are possible inferences from that experience. Some world religions, like Buddhism, Taoism, and Confucianism, are nontheistic. As professor Chun-fang Yu writes of the Chinese religions, "there is no God transcendent and separate from the world and there is no heaven outside of the universe to which human beings would want to go for refuge."[15] It is a Western parochial habit to think of religion only in theistic terms. The point is that moral experience originates in the tangible visible world of flesh and rock and dirt. It is prior to religious judgments and conclusions, though healthy religion can enrich and advance moral experience, and to that I shall return.

In a final word, fundamentalist oracularism (i.e., forecasting the future with certainty and special insight) in church, state, business, or academe is an avoidance mechanism that shuns the demanding work of ethics. It is a mind-shutting failure.

> ### THINKING CRITICALLY
>
> "Abortion has fractured a nation, threatened the rule of law, disrupted religious communities, divided families, decided elections, spurred violence, and presented women—and couples—with unwanted pregnancies with difficult personal decisions. No medical definition could explore these ramifications, much less explain them . . . abortion is a topic of interpretive conflict. What is in dispute is not medical meaning but moral meaning."
>
> —Lloyd Steffen, *Life/Choice: The Theory of Just Abortion*
>
> 2.4

Is Enlightened Self-Interest Enough? The Survivalism Temptation

Is enlightened self-interest really enough? Ayn Rand thought so. She had no time for a relativism that would reduce "good" to "habitual." She knew that if torture became habitual, it would not thereby become good. She was out to find some objective validation for our moral judgments. She saw Aristotle as the greatest of the philosophers, but she said his ethics was based on what the good and wise men (not women) of his day chose to do, but did not attend enough to the question of why they chose to do what they did—or why old Aristotle had decided that they were good and wise in the first place.[16]

Survival as Ethical Tool

Rand hungered after objective validation of moral judgments; she looked for the ethical tool that can make the proper incision between right and wrong. She chose as that tool *survival*. It is elementary, she says, that the life of an organism constitutes its standards of value. What promotes and enhances that life is good, and what destroys or threatens that life is evil. Figuring out what survival requires is the work of ethics.

Rand seems to have moved onto some solid ground here. Anthropologists have long since cited the remarkable amount of agreement among all peoples about those moral values that aid survival. So maybe Rand has found the ground zero of all morality: *That is good which promotes survival; that is evil which does not.* As a matter of clear fact, this principle does operate in a lot of ethics. It dominates ecological ethics, the most in-crisis area of contemporary ethics. Those who justify police violence base their view on the need for survival in society. Marital ethics focuses on the things necessary for the survival of the marriage.

The Problems with Survivalism

Now comes the big "however."

Rand's **survivalism** assumes that survival is an absolute good, and it is not. People call non-survivors heroic when they make the "supreme sacrifice" for the good of others. People who risk their lives working for refugees in troubled lands are admired, not thought of as fools. Generous people shorten their lives caring for sick children and loved ones and we don't call them nutty. Terminal patients in unbearable, unrelievable pain might reasonably decide that death is preferable to survival.

When the survivalist tire hits the road, it skids. Survival is only a relative good. It can become undesirable or even ignoble in certain circumstances.

Also, survival is a free-floating concept. Its ambiguity screams out for adjectives. Thirteen billion people on this limited planet with dwindling supplies of nonrenewable natural assets might "survive." But is survival without thrival (new coinage) really surviving? Rand acknowledged that she was not advocating the survival of thugs, so no one could couple her with, say, organized criminals who are very keen on surviving.[17] But Rand's survivalism and its enlightened self-interest is not helpful or realistic when the survival needs of persons collide. Being told that you are simply acting out of enlightened self-interest and as an exercise in "the virtue of selfishness" triggers the choke reflex. Would enlightened selfishness (or maximizing your utility, as some economists put it) really explain why, for instance, you rise for the umpteenth time in the night to aid a sick and regurgitating child with diarrhea, even though you have to go to work the next morning? Survivalism does not know the inner being of compassion or the spontaneity of heartfelt love.

Finally, the hollowness of the survival concept allows for some crude content. It can slip into a chilly **utilitarianism** where the survival of the group, however conceived, would become the absolute, and the survival of the individual would be subordinated. The thrust of this would be to-talitarian. As with fundamentalism, Rand's theory of life allowed for a very rugged and damaging individualism. She carried a lot of unexamined freight, made easy by the mischievous simplism of her single rubric. Despite her above-mentioned criticism of Aristotle's noble and wise men, Rand has her own wise men. It is those wise men's conception of what kind of survival befits humans as humans that she takes as self-evident, taking too little account of the class and gender interests that shape and define "enlightened self-interest." After all, in times past those who presumed to call themselves "nobles" and "gentlemen" (!) chose these moral encomia to cover their class-based purloined privileges.

Show me your children, Ms. Rand, and I will tell you what you are. Rand's influential enlightened egoism infused a lot of what came to be called "neoconservative" and "neoliberal" economic theory, which theory is liable to serious criticism in terms of class bias and fairness.

So, Again: Is There Such a Thing as Moral Truth?

Law is witness to the ubiquity of ethics and the human search for moral truth since law is the embodiment of the ethics on which we agree. We call "moral" what befits and enhances human and terrestrial life, and we make laws to insist on it and not allow whim or meanness to rule. Figuring out what's good for us and our earth is called ethics, and everybody and every society is at it. Hattie McDaniel as Mammy in *Gone with the Wind* spoke a judgment *homo moralis* is making all the time: "It ain't fittin'. . . . It ain't fittin', it jes' ain't fittin'." And when we figure out what ain't fittin' we outlaw it, and as we get better at doing this human ethical task, civilization has a chance to advance.

So now, after lambasting the inadequacies of other attempts, my burden is to explain the basis of moral truth-statements. What experience underlies our "shalts" and "shalt nots"? Why is moral language meaningful and not just noise? How do you verify moral claims? What is the foundational moral experience? The next chapter will dare to try to answer all of those questions.

Summary of Key Themes

- We must learn to distinguish scientific from moral truth-claims and to develop a way to verify moral truths.
- The relativist temptation in accepting moral differences is perennially appealing but cannot be sustained in the face of the commission of absolute moral crimes.
- Avoiding the impulse toward fundamentalism in economics, constitutional law, and religion will circumvent simplistic, nonethical thinking.

- Objective moral validation consists in more than enlightened self-interest in survival.

Key Terms

Fallacy
Fundamentalism
Immoral
Moral
Relativism
Survivalism

Truth-claims
Utilitarianism
Verifiability

Questions for Discussion

1. Give examples of socially approved customs and laws that were once accepted but we now see as uncivilized and totally immoral.
2. Explain this sentence: "The tragic is not always wicked." Give examples of actions that are tragic but not immoral.
3. Jacques Thiroux in his book *Ethics: Theory and Practice* writes that "there are those who would argue that morality stems strictly from within human beings. This is, they believe that things can have values and be classed as good, bad, right, or wrong if and only if there is some conscious being who can put value on these things. In other words, if there are no human beings, then there can be no values." If there were no human beings, would birds and roses and sunsets have value?

Suggestions for Further Reading

Elgin, Duane. *Promise Ahead: A Vision of Hope and Action for Humanity's Future.* New York: William Morrow, 2000.

Rand, Ayn. *The Virtue of Selfishness: A New Concept of Egoism.* New York: New American Library, 1961. See esp. pp. 15, 17, 22.

United Nations. "The Universal Declaration of Human Rights." New York: United Nations, 1948. http://www.un.org/en/documents/udhr/ (May 19, 2009).

PART TWO

The Theory
of Ethics

A delicate marvel made a surprising appearance
on the surface of the earth. Photo: NASA/courtesy of nasaimages.org

The Roots of Moral Meaning

The Foundational Moral Experience

IT IS PRECARIOUS and fragile and weight-wise almost insignificant since it is less than a billionth of the weight of the whole planet. Many things militate against the survival of this precious cosmic rarity, and that concerns us, because the name we give to this phenomenon—perhaps the only manifestation of it in all the folds of this universe—is *life*. What enhances and protects life, we call **moral**, what damages it, **immoral**; and the systematic effort to cherish and make sense of this life and the privileged earth that is its setting is called *ethics*.

That makes morality serious business, and getting to the root of it is not just an "academic" exercise but the supreme challenge to human intelligence. The fate of the world is in our hands, because with the arrival of humans, life on earth got a mind. As the wise scientist Edward O. Wilson says: "Because all organisms have descended from a common ancestor, it is correct to say that the biosphere as a whole began to think when humanity was born. If the rest of life is the body, we are the mind. Thus our place in nature, viewed from an ethical perspective, is to think about the creation and to protect the living planet."[1]

That said, I am on the spot. I have dismissed a number of thinkers who, I allege, suffered a short circuit on the way to the big question: *What is the foundation of morality*, the experience that gives moral talk meaning without which it would be babble? The terms *moral, sacred,* **the sanctity of life** are meaningful across cultures. We call moral that which befits persons and this good earth. Our deeper experiences of the preciousness of life we call sacred. *Sacred* is the superlative of *precious,* and we invoke that word when preciousness dips into mystery and strains our powers of description. The concept of *the sanctity of life* undergirds all the laws of all peoples. The deep-felt solemnity of that term explains why our courts are set up with the rituals and grandeur of temples to show the reverence due their mission.

The Foundational Moral Experience (FME)

What's at the root of it all? A grand question that. In offering my answer I am impelled to register an immediate plea that you not be put off by the apparently excessive simplicity of my position. Defensively I note that it is the simplest and most basic truths that we are often most prone to ignore. And it is often the simplest truths that invite us to the deepest penetration.

That said, here goes: *The **foundational moral***

THINKING CRITICALLY

"It is important for ethicists to draw on any and all data and on valid results of experiments from the natural, physical, and social sciences. . . . But it seems to me even more crucial for ethicists to contribute something toward helping all human beings to live with each other more meaningfully and more ethically. If philosophy cannot contribute to this, then human ethics will either be decided haphazardly by each individual for himself or by unexamined religious pronouncements."

—Jacques P. Thiroux, *Ethics: Theory and Practice,* 9th ed.

3.1

experience is the experience of the value of persons and their earthly home in this universe. This profound value-experience is the distinctively human and humanizing experience and the gateway to personhood. It is this experience that marks us as human. It is the primordial "Wow!" from which all moral theory and all healthy law, politics, and religion derive. This experience is the seed of civilization, the root of culture, and the badge of unique human consciousness. Without immersion in this experience, moral language would be senseless noise. If human activities, institutions, educators, and religions do not enhance this experience, they are negligible and indeed objectionable, for they are failing at the essential and distinctly human talent of moral evaluation.[2]

Every discussion of every moral issue—from war to capital punishment, from mercy death to same-sex marriage, from human rights to the rights of the rest of nature; every ethical argument that roils us in medicine, politics, business, and law—is an attempt to apply the meaning of this foundational moral experience to concrete and specific cases.

Moral debate takes place because persons and life itself are perceived as valuable in such an exquisite way that a world of awe and oughts is born in response. When we work to discover what is good for us and the rest of nature to which we are kith and kin, we are probing into the mysterious chemistry of life and human personhood.

The Good/Sacred Nexus

This foundational moral experience is also the foundational religious experience. Religion is, definitionally, a response to the sacred, however that sacred is explained—again, theistically or not. Ethics and religion are twinned. What enhances life and its milieu we call moral; its mysterious and awe-filled grandeur we call holy. Some religions presume one or many divinities at the root of this grandeur; others say theistic conclusions truncate our sense of wonder and detract from the miracle that is life itself. Whatever the explanations of sacrality, theistic or not—and on this humans will never agree—the fact remains that the experiences of the good and the holy are concentric. More simply put, the sacred is the nucleus of the good. If nothing is sacred, human life becomes absurd, and ethical discourse—as well as law—is rendered inane.

Can I *prove* this? Of course not. The experience does not fall into the simpler zone of the provable. Like all of our deeper experiences, it can only be illustrated. That offends tidy reductionist rationalists, to whom I say: Live with it! You cannot *prove* that a poem or a sunset or a rose or a painting or a melody is beautiful. At most you can educate someone's tastes to open that person to aesthetic ecstasy. Ecstasy, like democracy, cannot be imposed. The same is true for the experience of moral truth. It is no surprise that the word *fair* is as at home in aesthetics (*My Fair Lady*) as in ethics (fair trade), because there is a beauty in the morally good. We don't all have the foundational moral experience (FME) to the same degree, any more than we all are equally alive to beauty. But when it comes to the FME, we incarcerate those who have too little of it. Morality is too serious to be trifled with.

So I face a task more daunting than mere proof. I invite the reader to take a walk into the mysteries of moral awareness—into the unchartable but somewhat discoverable roots of moral intelligence. I'll start by returning to the strangest part of morality: our stubborn conviction about the moral beauty of what is called the **supreme sacrifice.**

The Oxymoron Called Supreme

Education floats on the hope that reality can be captured. It operates on the principle that the unfathomable can be fathomed. Sometimes it can't. At that point we have two choices: we can avoid it, or we can press into it to see what light is lent by pushing our eyes to the limits of visibility. Such is the case when we have to live with the anomaly that we are drawn to admire those who give life up altruistically in certain sacrificial situations with no guarantee of any sequel and with the distinct possibility that they are giving up existence for nonexistence. Descartes' main failure might have been his belief that clarity is the mark of truth. For truths of lighter weight, that may be so. But heavier truths seem better signaled by paradox.

The Supreme Sacrifice

I am stressing the supreme sacrifice here because no one who does ethics can ignore this persistent paradox in human experience. Ethics cannot ignore it because it shows in the most dramatic and outstanding form the depths of the experience of the sacredness of persons that grounds all of ethics. The boldest manifestations of any experience reveal more of what that experience is. Of course, pathological acts of self-destruction are universally condemned, but the insistent and ever-recurring theme is that at certain times self-sacrifice can be humanity at its noblest.

I do not imply that admiration for the supreme sacrifice is universal. There are persons and cultures that do not esteem heroic self-sacrifice. But there are persons and societies that do not esteem justice or gratitude or the sense of beauty either, and that does not undercut the claim that there is a precious validity in the esteem of these values.

Skinner's Mechanistic Moral Behaviorism

An age drunk on science and technology in which everything seems measurable will have trouble with moral knowledge. It is so disconcertingly full of paradox. B. F. Skinner, a mechanistic psychologist who enjoyed a brief time of faddish popularity, is an example of a technically obsessed mind in flight from the paradoxical mysteries of real life. He managed to console many who relished simplism, who wanted a world that is simpler than the one in which we live. Skinner is dead, but his kind of thinking is not. According to the principle *de mortuis nil nisi bonum* ("speak only good of the dead"), I should let him rest, but I won't. He is too useful as a caricature. (Also, it will be a convenient illustration of what will follow later in this book on good exceptions to good principles.)

Skinner's message was that people are puppets and the conditioning environment is the puppeteer.[3] Had he stuck to the data of his animal experiments, his data would be of solid interest, but he leapt into philosophy and broke both legs. He looked at the moral history of humankind and tried to squeeze it into tiny boxes. And if you do not see things his neat way, you are "prescientific," which, in Skinner's lexicon, is worse than being wrong. Somehow he missed the fact that a qualitative leap is involved when you move from the behavior of pigeons to the behavior of people. He did allow that pigeons are not people, but the unwritten premise of his work was that people are pigeons.

Once upon a time, says Skinner, simple, prescientific folks tried to explain physical events by attributing human qualities of will and emotion to things. So ancient physics taught that a falling body accelerates because it grows more jubilant as it finds itself nearer home. Good scientific physics stopped attributing human qualities to inanimate objects. Likewise, psychology will advance if we stop attributing human motives to intentions, purposes, aims, and goals. As philosopher Peter Caws summarized **Skinner's psychology**, scientific progress will follow in psychology "if we could stop attributing human characteristics to human beings."[4] So there it is: it is good physics to depersonalize inanimate things (we can only agree); it is good psychology to depersonalize persons (we can only gasp!).

Skinner's vision is useful as a caricature, but a caricature that tellingly drew a crowd. Ethics gets shrunken to "a technology of behavior." In this he is the sibling of Ayn Rand because their ethical theories melt down into a raw egoism. The reason you should not steal or lie is because it will cause you trouble. "You ought not to steal" could be translated, "If you tend to avoid punishment, avoid stealing."[5] Stealing will eventually inconvenience you; that's why you should not do it. If you treat others well and beneficently, it is not because of any "loyalty or respect" for them, or any great experience of their value, but because "they have arranged effective social contingencies."[6] Love, too, is evacuated of personal meaning. Skinner says, "We should not attribute behaving for the good of others to a love of others." Such seemingly altruistic behavior "depends upon the control exerted by the social environment." Likewise, "a person does not support a religion because he is devout; he supports it because of the contingencies arranged by the religious agency." Neither does he "support his government because he is loyal but because the government has arranged special contingencies."[7]

One wonders where Skinner found either governments or religious agencies organized enough to organize all those contingencies!

Skinner, Rand, and the Supreme Sacrifice

The Skinnerian world, and those who indulge in it in less crude forms, is, to shift a phrase of Shakespeare's, "sicklied o'er with the pale cast of technology." There is no room for generosity, nobility, or mysticism, or for the marvelously unpredictable movements of the human spirit. Indeed, in this narrow-eyed view, admiration of noble deeds proceeds from ignorance: "We are likely to admire behavior more as we understand it less." A hero is someone who is addicted to and controlled by the reinforcements of praise and adulation. Thus reinforced, the hero "takes on more and more dangerous assignments until he is killed." (Implicit here is the conception of hero as ass.) Heroic behavior is not unlike the phototrophic behavior of a moth whose proclivity for light "proves lethal when it leads into flame."[8] (The hero as moth.)

Skinner and altruism-deniers cannot understand heroism because they have no room for the mysterious fact that people actually do discover in the world of persons values so great, so precious to the point of "sacred," that when they're at issue, people will die to all "reinforcements" and banish all "contingencies," including life, to defend them—or at least we will admire those who have the courage to do so. Again, Ayn Rand. For her, love is a personal and selfish value and a reaction to one's own value discovered in another person. The goal and yield of love is one's own selfish well-being and happiness. To risk your life for a stranger would be immoral unless it involved minimal risk. It could be moral and rational to risk all to save someone you love dearly for the simply selfish reason that you could not bear to live without this person. Sacrifice is not sacrifice in this view. It is just another investment in the ego itself. Rand was overreacting to those philosophers and theologians who say that self-love is morally bad. They are, of course, in error, as is she in overreacting to them. Because we do and must love ourselves, the fact that we admire and perhaps feel drawn to imitate the supreme sacrifice of one's life in certain cases becomes all the more a mystery.[9]

Such "true mechanics" approaches to human psychology are also unable to address the nether side of life, the mystery of evil. Dietrich Bonhoeffer, the German theologian who was killed by the Nazis for his heroism, lamented the inability of reasonable people to comprehend the depths of evil. Skimming at the surface does not work in ethics or in any serious probe of human personality and consciousness.

The Dangers of Reductionism

My concern here is to stress the reductionism and shrinkage practiced in the realm of values. I see it as despair, a classical and very modern despair rooted in disappointed pride. Eric Voegelin refers to "the Positivistic conceit that only propositions concerning facts of the phenomenal world [are] 'objective,' while judgments concerning the right order of soul and society [are] 'subjective.'"[10] **Positivism** was part of the quest for the illusory grail of "value-free science" that made its debut in the middle of the nineteenth century. Marvelous scientific progress was a heady wine. The first intoxicating glimmers of what could happen in the measurable world of the sciences were stunning. Less precise modes of intellectual inquiry were left in the shadows before the thrilling advent of this new great light. And ethics is, admittedly, not precise. It moves from muddied waters to cloud-covered peaks. It encounters paradox and cases where contradictory answers seem equally defensible . . . and they are! All of this could be unattractive to the scientific mind of the new age, which had not absorbed the news that relativity is a fact of life and probability is often the best we can get.

Now, back to that which altruism-deniers would banish and which I insist has to be faced to understand ourselves. Like a leitmotif that finds ingeniously new expression multiple times in a great symphony, the supreme sacrifice has infused history, literature, and religion. Is it always in healthy form? Nothing human ever is. Human sacrifice to placate the gods, even when accepted freely by deluded victims, belongs in the tragic trash heap of the human story.

"It Is a Far, Far Better Thing . . ."

Charles Dickens knew he had a winner as he penned some of the most quoted lines in all of literature. He ends his book *A Tale of Two Cities* with a stirring instance of supreme sacrifice. Sydney Carton substitutes himself for the noble Charles Darnay and goes to the guillotine in his stead. Carton's famous appraisal of his deed on the way to his death is that "it is a far, far better thing that I do than I have ever done. . . ." The novel endorses Carton's act in terms of high heroism, and millions of readers since have thrilled to it. A similar use of this kind of heroic ending is in Arthur Miller's play *Incident at Vichy*. The German Von Berg explains to the Jewish LeDuc that "there are people who would find it easier to die than stain one finger with this murder." Thereupon he presses his exit pass upon LeDuc, allowing him to escape, while he himself assumes the risk of death as the play ends.

The philosopher Albert Camus witnesses to the same conviction when, during the French-Algerian crisis in 1958, reprisal raids against civilian populations were being used, and torture had become established policy, as it still does when fear controls the collective mind. He wrote at that time that "it is better to suffer certain injustices than to commit them even to win wars."[11] In this he echoes Socrates: "It is better for a man to suffer injustice than to commit it."[12] All this says it is better to be killed than to kill unjustly. Better, in other words, to be tortured than to torture! The acceptance of this could only be traceable to what could be called a mystical perception of the inviolable sanctity of human life, a perception that undergirds every moral ought. Those who are totally alien to it (a sociopathic rarity) are alien to moral consciousness.

R. L. Bruckberger, a French Roman Catholic priest, writes that there are times when death is preferable to continued living, when the voice of conscience and integrity outweighs the urgency of self-preservation. Is it not true, he asks, that we can say

that the individual conscience transcends political obligation, that there is something in [humankind] which dominates society; that this something which dominates society also transcends life and earth, since people are willing to die in order to preserve that integrity and refuse to live if life is to be preserved at the expense of it? Yes, these are indeed the essential features of martyrdom: death to bear witness to what exceeds life, to place its seal on what death cannot touch.[13]

In cases of unjust executions, he asks, "If one had to choose between the victims who die and the executioners who survive, who would not be on the victims' side?"[14]

The Humanities and Self-Sacrifice

The world's religions, which all are absorbed in confronting the potentially fatal lure of egoism, all treat self-sacrifice as the supreme triumph over egoism. A revered saying in Buddhist literature states: "As a mother even at the risk of her own life watches over her own child, so let everyone cultivate a boundless love toward all beings."[15] Hindu literature recognizes the value of loving self-sacrifice in sayings such as, "People without love think only of self, but the loving strip themselves to the bone for others."[16] In Judaism, laying down one's life for friends is esteemed as a high act of virtue, and in Jewish thought it could be mandatory to lay down one's life for the nation.[17] In Islam, self-sacrifice, even in the form of martyrdom, is admired when it is in the cause of justice. (It is a distortion of Islam to see it as a tactic of war.) In Christianity, the idea of dying for others as the supreme moral action attains classical expression: "There is no greater love than this, that you will lay down your life for your friends" (John 15:13).

Aristotle joins in saying of "the good man" that

"he does many acts for the sake of his friends and his country, and if necessary dies for them; for he will throw away both wealth and honors and in general the goods that are objects of competition, gaining for himself nobility. . . . Now those who die for others doubtless attain this result; it is therefore a great prize that they choose for themselves."[18]

Adam Smith, in his book *The Theory of Moral Sentiments*, written in 1759, said: "A brave man ought to die rather than make a promise which he can neither keep without folly nor violate without ignominy."[19] The psychologist Abraham Maslow, notwithstanding his stress on self-actualization, laments "the widespread 'valuelessness' in our society, i.e. people having nothing to admire, to sacrifice themselves for, to surrender to, to die for." The experience of human values and readiness to die when these values are at issue is, for Maslow, healthy and not a contradiction to the quest for self-actualization. Witness again the booming paradox that is part of this experience. And sociologist Richard L. Means condemns the vacuity of dying for abstractions or for material things, saying, "Only dying for human beings . . . is moral." He notes that Socrates said he was dying for the youth of Athens.[20]

The Wonder of the FME

Why am I dunning so on the sacrifice that all of us hope never to have to make? Because it unearths the wonder that lies at the depths of the FME. It speaks to what persons are perceived to be worth, and that is where ethics plants its roots. It sends a message to those who would do ethics, or any of the social sciences that started out as branches, or at least as relatives, of ethics. The message is that the study of the moral cannot be adequately served by mathematical or merely scientific models. It is stubbornly *sui generis.*

When technology is the cultural monarch, the fallibility and limits of certainty in ethics could be offensive. A chastening word from Aristotle is apposite and helpful: "It is a mark of the educated person and a proof of his culture that in every subject he looks for only so much precision as its nature permits."[21] Many heated arguments are stoked by the desire for more precision, more certainty than is available.

The more common (quotidian) applications of the FME—truth telling, promise keeping, debt paying, heeding the demands of justice and the call of compassion and respecting the needs of the rest of nature—are all explainable only by the perception that people and life are worth all of that. Similarly, our indignant objections to torture, biological or nuclear warfare, ecocide, the neglect of starving peoples, rape, racism, sexism, or heterosexism would be stripped of meaning were it not for this value-experience whereby the term *moral* comes to life.

If I say that the FME is the experience of the worth of persons and the rest of life in this gifted corner of the universe, I am making a truth-claim. Paleontologist and philosopher Teilhard de Chardin dares to offer the two tests for any truth: *coherence* and *fruitfulness*. A statement is true if it coheres with our other experiences of reality *and*

THINKING CRITICALLY

"Ethical theory has enormous practical benefits. It can free us from prejudice and dogmatism. It sets forth comprehensive systems from which to orient our individual judgement. It carves up the moral landscape so that we can sort out the issues in order to think more clearly and confidently about moral problems. It helps us clarify in our minds just how our principles and values relate to one another, and, most of all, it gives us some guidance on how to live."

—Louis P. Pojman, *Ethics: Discovering Right and Wrong*, 5th ed.

3.2

if it works. Incoherence and chaos would be the yield of a denial of the sanctity of life and the dignity and integrity of the rest of nature. Proof negative of this is that our weak immersion in the FME is allowing us to wreak chaos on this planet and making history, as Lenin said, "a butcher's bench." The lack of appreciative awe in the face of life explains why some say that the two greatest disasters to hit this planet are (1) the pummeling of the planet sixty-five million years ago, the catastrophe that ended the tenure of the dinosaurs (whose two-hundred-million-year tenure we well might envy and never match), and (2) the arrival of the species that would call itself *sapiens.* Moral errors and insufficient penetration into the FME are not just sad: they are lethal failings. Hence the dread seriousness of what we are about in ethics.

Enough Said?

It is not enough to stop here. We need to delve into the psychology of the FME to get a surer grip on what it is, to see how it works. Knowing how we know is the gateway to wisdom. This probe into the psychology of ethics brings us to a study of the three dimensions of the FME in action.

Summary of Key Themes

- Moral knowledge is grounded in the experience of the value of persons and this generous and fruitful earth.
- This experience is deep and elicits terms like *the sanctity of life.*
- The foundational moral experience (FME) wrestles with the mysteries of self-sacrifice and altruism without erasing all that is mysterious and ineffable about the preciousness of life.

Key Terms

Altruism
Foundational moral experience (FME)
Immoral
Moral
Positivism
Sanctity of Life
Skinner's psychology
Supreme sacrifice

Questions for Discussion

1. When economists speak of "acceptable levels of unemployment," does this raise any moral questions?
2. There is an old saying: "All is fair in love and war." Is that true?

Suggestions for Further Reading

Orr, David W. *Earth in Mind: On Education, Environment, and the Human Prospect.* Washington, D.C.: Island, 1994.

Skinner, B. F. *Beyond Freedom and Dignity.* New York: Knopf, 1971.

Swimme, Brian, and Thomas Berry. *The Universe Story: From the Primordial Flaring Forth to the Ecozoic Era.* San Francisco: HarperSanFrancisco, 1992.

Wilson, Edward O. *The Future of Life.* New York: Knopf, 2002.

The Elements of Moral Thinking
Affectivity, Faith, and Process

Affectivity

Contrary to the thinking of rigorous rationalists, it is in the swirling pools of **affectivity** (symbolized by the heart) that morality has its birth. The ethical brain moves on to confirmatory reason, debate, and theory, to demonstrations of the coherence and fruitfulness (and thus truthfulness) of one's claims, but it is in *feeling* that the roots of morality are found and nourished. The **foundational moral experience** (FME) is an affective and emotive reaction to value. It is not primordially a metaphysical or logical or religious experience, though it has implications for all of that. It is not a conclusion to a syllogism, though syllogisms can be mustered into ethical service. The value of persons and of life cannot be "taught" or "proved" as we usually use those terms.

Where Computers Dare Not Tread

What's more—and this is a blow to modern Cyberman—such valuing can't be computerized.

Computers can play chess, but they can't do ethics or write poetry. We may try to personalize them, as when *Time* magazine famously granted the personal computer its "Man of the Year" award in 1992 (though it renamed the honor "Machine of the Year"). Journalists write articles on artificial intelligence, telling us how computers can "think," but life they are not. The so-called "thinking computer" is no match for what Edward O. Wilson calls "the white-hot core of activity we call the conscious mind."[1]

As cognitive scientists work on the nature of the mind, they conclude that the working human brain is not just a physical entity but "more specifically a flood of scenarios."[2] Neuroscientist Paul MacLean writes of the human brain as triune, saying the brain evolved in three parts. The more primitive brain, called the *R-complex*, we have in common with reptiles. It controls basic functions like muscle movement and breathing. Next is the *limbic system*, which evolved in early mammals to control emotive fight-or-flight responses and reactions to pleasure and pain. The third part is the *neocortex*, which controls reasoning and speech and is the latest arrival in the evolutionary process. The brain of *homo moralis* involves both limbic and neocortical activity, with emotion and reasoning interweaving and sometimes competing to form moral consciousness. Computers can serve that "white-hot" conscious dynamism called "mind," but they cannot replace it.

Ask a "thinking" computer to match the poetry of an Adrienne Rich or a Seamus Heaney, or ask it to fathom the fire that stirs human-rights claims, and a truly thinking computer would reply: *nolo contendere.*

Human Responsiveness, Not Emotivism

The FME springs from the discovery that all life, whether it be in leaf, flower, bird, or beast, is awe inspiring, a kind of miracle of energy and organization, with personal life being even more dazzling. Humans, in response to such a discovery, can transcend everything, including their own lives. Not only can they perceive what is and react to it, but they can also imagine what is not but could be and bring it about. We are the *animal creativum* more impressed (when we're at our best) by horizons than by the terrain on which we stand. We can find and create beauty. We can speak and sing and laugh and be merciful. (Some medievals defined us as the *animal risibile*, the one animal that can laugh. The hyena seems to laugh, but our best information is that they don't have a smidgeon of an idea as to what they are laughing about.)

With all this, even a modicum of sensitivity drives us to superlatives like *sacred* to voice our awe and appreciation of the evolutionary marvel that we are.

In locating the FME in the affections, I am, of course, not thereby lapsing into the stupidity of "emotivist" ethicists who said that moral judgments about particular issues are only emotional noises, *oohs* or *aahs* or *ughs*, that cannot be classified as true or false. To which one could reply: Yuck! A negative response to the Nazi Holocaust and a warm response to alternative, nonpolluting energy sources are emotional mental responses that can be evaluated in terms of true or false. What arises in the emotions is to some degree expressible in the mind and in reason. Pure **emotivism** would throw us back into mindless relativism and should be buried with the silly philosophers who conjured it.

Ethics is not just a matter of arbitrary taste. It is a hunt for truth by argument, comparison, analysis, and all nine evaluational modes I will submit as pertaining to ethical method and the flowering

> ### THINKING CRITICALLY
>
> "As human beings our greatness lies not so much in being able to remake the world—that is the myth of the 'Atomic Age'—as in being able to remake ourselves."
>
> —Mahatma Gandhi
>
> 4.1

of moral intelligence. The dilemma of the Persian emperor Darius I is a symbol of the perennial human problem. He found that some of his Indian subjects ate their fathers' corpses while his Greek subjects burned them. The pollution of holy fire was as shocking to the Indians as cannibalism was to the Greeks. And so, we Greeks and Indians today, right wingers and left wingers, conservatives and liberals and radicals too, though united in reverence for life, are forever diverging on what does or does not befit that life. Intelligent, sensitive, and heated ethical debate is the human response to this divergence, and is indeed the spice of life, to be embraced, not mourned.

Redeeming the Mystical

Superficial is not always a dirty word. We have superficial likes and dislikes and may be amused at times by ditties and doggerel and silly little jokes; no harm done. That's part of our affectivity too. But our love power can also leave these little mounds and go for the mountaintops. Affectivity has shallow and peak experiences, but it is in the latter that morality is founded. The medievals had a name for peak affectivity. They called it **mystical**.

Mystical—now there is a word in need of help in our time. Words are like people; they have relatives and friends that they pick up over time, and often those friends are not nice. And so it has come to pass that the concept of mysticism is mired in disrepute. The press often referred to the Ayatollah Khomeini, that spooky leader of Iran, as a mystic. That didn't help. Even Christian hagiographers piled on. St. John of Alcantara was so intent on practicing meditation that he took that practice of *custodia oculorum* to extremes. Thinking that with eyes closed he could best contemplate the mysteries, he bumped into monastery walls and had trouble finding the dining room. Clearly he needed therapy, but instead they called him a mystic. Ouch!

Better the medieval usage that reserved the term for affectivity at its most profound, ineffable levels. *Mystical* comes from the same Greek root as *mystery*, *mueo*, meaning "to lie hidden."

It is a word that deserves redemption. The existentialist philosopher Jean-Paul Sartre spoke once of an experience he had while taking a walk in Paris. He met some former students walking with their new infant. The baby was still at that early stage of loving and smiling at everyone with a face. She smiled with the inimitable sweetness of a baby's smile as Sartre held her in his arms.

Here was a man deemed by many the greatest philosopher of his century, his work translated into a myriad of languages, but suddenly the thought-feeling struck him. If one were to take all of his life's works and put them on a balancing scale and put the smiling baby on the other side of that scale, he sensed that all his work would weigh as nothing compared to the preciousness he held in his arms. Sartre could not prove that this baby was worth more than the accumulated cells and chemicals in its body, but he *knew* it affectively with unmatchable intensity.

That powerful experience is something with which we can identify. It deserves a special word, cleansed and resurrected for modern use. That word is *mystical*. If Sartre honored us with the confidence that he really, really liked Chicklets, we might appreciate his sharing that news, but it would not be big news. If he then shared the story of his emotive response to the baby, the leap would be not quantum but qualitative. The prizing of that baby is a mystical experience, and we all know it unless some horrid sociopathy has destroyed it in us. My son Danny died at age ten of Hunter syndrome. As he neared death and I held his dwarfed and withered body in my arms, I felt all the reverence I used to feel when I was a priest handling the Eucharist, believing as I then did that I had divinity itself in my hands.

Neither my experience nor Sartre's can be captured with ordinary words. Words like *wonder*, *awe*, *sacred* come to mind, and all these are encapsulated in *mystical*. It is in those rich regions that the FME resides, and neither we nor our species will survive if our minds are not bathed and refreshed there. In trying to describe this reach of our love-power, the word *mystical*, reenfranchised, may be the best we can do.

The Emergence of Cherishing

We like to think back to "firsts" in our planetary history, like when the dense cloud covering of early earth broke open enough for sunlight to first sparkle on the waves of the sea. We treasure the first signs of *homo faber* making simple tools. Finding the beginnings of art in ancient caves understandably thrills us. And of course, the early signs of technology and art are more easily found and chronicled, but a greater historical event had to be the first appearance of cherishing in our species.

Loren Eiseley, the anthropologist with the soul of a poet, pondered this and tied it to the discovery of the one-armed skeletal remains of a Neanderthal man. Eiseley knew that in that world the lack of an arm was a drastic handicap, one that would seem to ensure quick death. But the skeleton showed that this crippled creature lived for a long time. He could not have done it without being cherished. The sun of moral cherishing had broken through the clouds, and humanity was crossing the threshold into moral humanhood. The talent of caring was in tiny bud.

In Eiseley's own words:

Forty thousand years ago in the bleak uplands of southwestern Asia, a man, a Neanderthal man, once labeled by the Darwinian proponents of struggles as a ferocious ancestral beast—a man whose face might cause you some slight uneasiness if he sat beside you—a man of this sort exists with a fearful body handicap in that ice-age world. He had lost an arm. But still he lived and was cared for. Somebody, some group of human things, in a hard, violent, and stony world, loved this maimed creature enough to cherish him.[3]

Caring and loving started somewhere back there in the harshest of times. Concern appeared and with it morality. Eiseley compares its emergence to "a faint light, like a patch of sunlight moving over the dark shadows of a forest floor."[4] The "faint light" is also visible in the start of ceremonial burying of the dead, something that began before the extinction of the Neanderthals.[5] The funeral impulse signals grief, which is the pain of frustrated love. In our time, with the planet in deadly mounting peril, openness to that "faint light" is crucially needed for survival. We are in danger that it is receding just when it is so necessary.

Spiritual Anorexia and Autism. As the twentieth century dawned with big-binge modernity ebulliently and promisingly rising, some sober heads refused to reel. The sociologist Max Weber in 1904 wondered whether the technical capitalistic culture aborning was not building "an iron cage" to trap us all. He lamented the "disenchantment" of the world that would leave us spiritually anorexic, "specialists without spirit" and "sensualists without heart." He feared the coming boom was "a nullity."[6]

Earth scholar Thomas Berry (he called himself a geologian) worries about our growing "autism," our speciesism that leaves us cut off from our geobiological matrix. We have lost "our intimacy with the natural world," and it happened, he says, in three phases. First, he indicts the influential Christian sell-out to an unbalanced anthropocentrism when Christians bedded down with Greek humanism. This led to a *fuga mundi* ("flight from the world"), *mortuum mundo* ("dead to the world"), ethereal, otherworldly spirituality that no longer lets the "grace and mystery of life wash our grimy souls," to use ethicist Larry Rasmussen's phrase.[7]

The second phase of alienation from the rest of nature, according to Berry, traces to the Black Death in Europe in the period from 1347 to 1349. People had no explanation as half or more of them died. They concluded that the world had become wicked and God was punishing it. This augmented the spirituality of detachment from and hatred of the world. The third and deciding move was from an agricultural economy to an "industrial non-renewing extractive economy." With all this, the planet "lost its wonder and majesty, its grace and beauty, its life-giving qualities. The planet became an object of use."[8]

A remarkable book by Rita Nakashima Brock and Rebecca Ann Parker, *Saving Paradise: How Christianity Traded Love of This World for Crucifixion and Empire*,[9] indicts Christianity for falling out of love with the earth in favor of a spiritual beyond. Their quest is the recovery of the beauty of an earth-loving Christianity lost for a thousand years beneath dry creeds and formulae and poisonous myths of sacralized violence. Our capacity for ecstasy was stifled, and otherworldly religions contributed to renewing our love for the earth in the West.

Nature Shocks. It is not merely a donnish exercise or intellectual nicety to stress that the FME is grounded in feeling and in affectivity. Ignore this fact of life and the current human plight on a planet wracked by militarism and ecocide cannot be diagnosed or cured. Jewish theologian Abraham Heschel wrote that humankind "will not die for lack of information but it may perish for lack of appreciation."[10] If we continue with our destructive ways, "Blasé" may be our epitaph.

When the child in us dies, wonder dies; and wonder, as Aristotle said, is the beginning of wisdom. And wonder is lost when we forget whence

> ## THINKING CRITICALLY
>
> When it comes to fussing with nature, a warning comes to us from the eighteenth century: "In New England they once thought blackbirds useless, and mischievous to the corn. They made efforts to destroy them. The consequence was, the blackbirds were diminished; but a kind of worm, which devoured their grass, and which the blackbirds used to feed on, increased prodigiously; then finding their loss in grass greater than their saving in corn, they wished again for their blackbirds."
>
> —Benjamin Franklin
>
> 4.2

we came and thus what we are. As Rasmussen says, "'Humans,' as all things of earth, are of 'humus,' that organic residue of roots, bone, carrion, feces, leaves, and other debris mixed with minerals and organized as a community for life."[11]

It helps haughty human eyes to remember that all life on this earth probably started from a single cell. As theologians Charles Birch and John Cobb put it:

> The evolution of a living cell from organic molecules may have happened more than once on the earth. But probably only one original cell gave rise to all the rest of life on earth. This seems to be the only possible explanation of the basic similarity of the cells of all living organisms. All use the same DNA code and similar amino acids. The doctrine of evolution holds that from one beginning all the diversity of life on earth, its two billions of species (of which two million known species are alive today), and the many varieties within these species, have arisen. Life is like a great branching tree with one central stem.[12]

To be fully conscious is to be stunned, unless, of course, our affect is like a dead battery. We walk on and breathe mysteries, but because we are unmindful of these mysteries, we can trash them. Writer Annie Dillard tells what biologists find in one square foot of topsoil in an inch-deep pan. Contained there are "an average of 1,356 living creatures, . . . including 865 mites, 265 springtails, 22 millipedes, 19 adult beetles, and various numbers of 12 other forms."[13]

Included also are billions of bacteria and millions of fungi, protozoans, algae, and other creatures that make topsoil the miracle it is. We should bow our heads before that pan of soil because our lives totally depend on it, but more so, just because it *is*; to be fully alive means being mindful of it. Buddhist meditation stresses our need to cultivate *mindfulness*. It doesn't seem to come to us naturally. Our affectivity has poor antennae, and so, the Buddhists say, build those antennae and thus build awareness through gentle, focusing meditation. Awareness is a gentling thing, and the rest of nature hopes we get there.

Curative Anger

Anger in a therapeutic culture gets a bad rap. We are more aware of anger as a vice than as a virtue. Some old and forgotten wisdom can restore it to an honorable respectability. Anger can indeed be a virtue. We can go back seventeen centuries to John Chrysostom, who said, "Whoever is not angry when there is cause for anger, sins!" Thomas Aquinas, eight centuries later, repeated that and explained why. Reasonable anger, he said, is a virtue for one clear reason: anger looks to the good of justice. Whoever is not angry in the face of injustice loves justice too little. The "faint light" of moral awareness is too dim in them. Thomas then embarked on a discussion of how anger was in disrepute even in his time. He liked the Pythagorean axiom *virtus in medio stat*—"virtue stands in the middle between too much and too little, between excess and defect." So, for example, courage is a virtue, but if you have too much of that stuff we call courage, it is no longer a virtue but the vice of foolhardiness. If you have too little, it is the vice of cowardice. But just the reasonable amount of it is the virtue of courage.

THINKING CRITICALLY

"I went to the woods because I wished to live deliberately, to confront all of the essential facts of life, and see if I could learn what it had to teach, and not, when I came to die, to discover that I had not lived. . . . I wanted to live deep and suck out all of the marrow of life."

—Henry David Thoreau, *Walden*

4.3

Now Thomas, having decided that anger is a virtue, and seeing it in action in his biblical heroes like Jesus and the other prophets of Israel, examined his Latin language and found that there was no name for the virtue of anger. Tellingly, there is only a name for too much of it, *iracundia*, but no name for just enough or too little! The virtue, he lamented, remained "unnamed," and so it does to our day. This is wrong, said Thomas, because the absence of just anger is a vice, and, he added, anger is in no way opposed to the virtue of gentleness.[14]

Applying this to the FME, the absence of anger would be a defect in one's appreciation of the value of persons and this good earth. If we do not feel anger when life is profaned, we love life too little. The lack of indignation could kill off our species and much of nature with us. If there is no anger while more than a billion people are in absolute poverty (i.e., starving slowly), while wars are waged without reason and cluster bombs are dropped where farmers farm and children play, while money is wasted on weapons as children wither, while nature is ruined beyond its power to heal—if we bear all that with easy calm and untroubled sleep, the FME is ill.

German Catholic philosopher Josef Pieper faults a society that displays a kind of "lazy inertia incapable of generating anger." This, he says, "is the sign of complete and virtually hopeless degeneration. It appears whenever a caste, a people, or a whole civilization is ripe for its decline and fall."[15] He wrote those words a half century ago. Fair warning. Revving up anger, appropriate anger fueled by a love of justice, is a moral exercise. It helps us do ethics. In the sixth century Gregory the Great said, "Reason opposes evil the more effectively when anger ministers at her side."[16] Anger is one of the integral passions of the FME.

Faith

Next in our parade of disparaged words that are essential to the foundation of morals, that is, to the FME, is *faith*. Faith sounds like such an affront to our "show me" empiricism. "Taking it on faith" sounds flimsy. Religious people often call themselves "people of faith." For people who eschew organized religion "people of faith" is the opposite of "people of reason." The word is often associated with superstition and with anti-scientific and anti-intellectual bias. That's a bad set of relatives.

Self-Evidence

Now to the facts of epistemology (the study of how we know): Faith is a normal and basic way of knowing. And not just any old way of knowing; it's the way we know our most essential truths, the ones we live for and some would die for.[17] **Faith-knowledge** can be so strong that we think its claims self-evident. America's founding fathers made this mistake when they proclaimed, "We hold these truths to be self-evident, that all men are created equal, that they are endowed by their Creator with certain unalienable Rights, that among these are Life, Liberty, and the Pursuit of Happiness." Not a bit of that is "self-evident," and most people in most of history saw none of it as true. Aristotle was a smart fellow, but he did not see slaves and women and non-Greeks as endowed by a Creator with equal and unalienable rights. If Aristotle missed it and if most people in history missed it, it's not self-evident. It is, however, believable.

The Declaration of Independence was a faith proclamation and the beginning of a country founded on faith. The Declaration went on to tick off a long list of abuses and usurpations committed by the British crown, denying freedoms that the signers thought were self-evident rights even though so many of the bright people through most of history never even dreamed of them. In the same genre is the United Nations Universal Declaration of Human Rights, noted earlier. These beliefs had to be solemnly proclaimed and insisted on precisely because they are not self-evident.

Sir William David Ross, the British ethicist, made the same mistake our Declaration signers did: "To me it seems as self-evident as anything could be, that to make a promise, for instance, is to create a moral claim on us in someone else."[18] Not so fast, Sir William. Such moral obligations are not self-evident to everyone at every level of moral development. Life would be lovelier if such were the case. These duties can be called primal moral experiences that are *discoverable* and *believable* in mature persons. They make sense only as derivatives of the FME. It does not weaken their claim to truth to say they are faith-statements, *beliefs* that persons are worth fidelity and truth and justice.

Heart-Knowledge

Truth can be known affectively. As Blaise Pascal put it, "We know truth, not only by the reason, but also by the heart. . . . The heart has reasons

> **THINKING CRITICALLY**
>
> Showing how moral knowledge is processual, the *Dred Scott v. Sanford* decision of the U.S. Supreme Court in 1857 declared that at the time of the Declaration of Independence, and when the Constitution of the United States was framed and adopted, "[blacks] had no rights which the white man was bound to respect."
>
> 4.4

which reason does not know."[19] The French philosopher Henri Bergson said we have a "genius of the will" as well as a genius of the intellect, and it is the geniuses of the will who draw us after them and must move moral evolution forward.[20] And as Scottish theologian John Macquarrie puts it, "All affective and conative experience has its own understanding."[21] But if these witnesses seem too ponderous, consult the lover in you who knows well that love knows more than it can say. The lover cannot explain or justify with reasons the insights of her heart, but she calmly believes that these insights make supreme sense. The lover is surer of this belief-knowledge than of many other things she *grasps with her senses* or *can prove*. Never has there been generous love that was not an adventure in the heart-knowledge called faith.

Thomas Harris, in his once-popular psychology book *I'm OK—You're OK*, put it this way: "The idea that persons are important is a *moral* idea without which any system of understanding people is futile. . . . We cannot prove they are important. We have only the faith to believe they are, because of the greater difficulty of believing they are not."[22]

Contrary to the common wisdom, seeing is not believing. Believing is knowing what you cannot see or prove but what you still accept and hold with firmness. Life is full of faith-knowledge, the kind of knowing that has its source in affectivity.

Thomas Aquinas was quite at home with all of this. He said that faith lends a kind of certitude that is "in the genre of affection." It is knowledge and it brings us into contact with reality, but it does so through feeling and affectivity.[23] Notice that faith is not just of the religious variety. Sir William David Ross was writing as a philosopher when he voiced his *belief* that promises create a moral claim. Immanuel Kant famously averred that "every rational being exists as an end in himself and not merely as a means to be arbitrarily used for this or that will. . . . Rational beings are designated 'persons' because their nature indicates that they are ends in themselves, i.e., things which may not be used merely as means."[24] What the philosopher is saying here is that the perceived value of persons leads us to conclude that persons are too valuable to be reduced to exploitable means. That's not a provable fact. It is a belief.

Essayist Jonathan Schell, writing about the ongoing reevaluation of nonviolent power in history, says that his authorities on this subject rest their case on faith:

> What Gandhi, Havel, and most of the others who have won nonviolent victories in our time believed and made the starting point of their activity was a conviction—or, to be exact, a faith—that if they acted in obedience to certain demanding principles, which for all of them included in one way or another the principle of nonviolence, there was somewhere in the order of creation a fundament, or truth, that would give an answering and sustaining reply.[25]

So there it is: philosophers, theologians, social scientists, and everyone else—when they make moral statements, they do so in terms of affective faith-knowledge.

Verifying Faith-Knowledge

"But," some may worry, "Look at some of the weird things people believe!" This is a worthy concern. Faith-knowledge, like all claimed knowledge, can be dead wrong. We can and often do believe nonsense. But, of course, "factual" and supposedly proved knowledge has often fallen to better proof or new experience. That means that verification is a constant necessity. All knowledge is to be distrusted and tested, imperfect knowers that we are, but no form of knowledge, faith-knowledge or empirically tested knowledge, is to be dismissed without a hearing.

Even in science faith is involved in every probe.

It is the push of faith that keeps the researcher going even when the goal might seem on its face to be absurd. And yet it appears even more absurd not to believe. We "hang in there" with what we believe because the alternative is unbearable and we could make no sense of it. And sometimes researchers will find that the clouds disappear and the sun of evidence shines on what they felt and believed all along.

The FME is belief. We cannot see or prove that persons are sacred in their worth. We cannot prove that the Jewish philosopher Martin Buber is right when he says that a human being "is *Thou* and fills the heavens."[26] But we believe it, and so morality is born.

What is often lost in an age of technical wizardry is the art of contemplation. Reaching for the core of moral awareness admits the weakness of reason. This doesn't mean that knowledge fails, but that primal moral knowledge unfolds in a mystical and contemplative form. At its base, ethics is contemplative. Its foundations lie in what Thomas Carlyle called those "quiet mysterious depths" that exist in the center of personality "underneath the region of argument and conscious discourse."[27] This is an admission of the limits of reason in constituting the foundations of morality, but not of the impossibility of reliable knowledge.[28]

Process

Moral truth admits of more or less. Some have more of it, some less, though it is difficult to imagine someone identifiably human being utterly untouched by it. To be touched by moral truth is to start a process that admits of growth—and also of decline. The move of our species into the FME was precarious and slow. The gentle forays of moral awareness were retarded by **egoism** and tribalism (collective egoism). Concern spread slowly, spilling out first only on those who

were near and thus somewhat dear. As anthropologist Ralph Linton wrote, "At the primitive level the individual's tribe represents for him the limits of humanity and the same individual who will exert himself to any lengths in behalf of a fellow tribesman may regard the non-tribesman as fair game to be exploited by any possible means, or even as a legitimate source of meat."[29] Though focused on the distant past, Linton's observation has contemporaneity. Tribalism today is called "nationalism," and through the powerful mechanisms of political economy, we are still eating nontribesmen. Our cannibalism is indirect now, operating through such things as "the terms of trade" and the widening structured gaps between rich and poor. But in our newly efficient globalized fashion, we are still at it. In what must be the greatest stacking feat of history, we have arranged income on this little earth of ours so that 82.7 percent of it goes to the top 20 percent of humankind, leaving the remainder to the bottom 80 percent, with the poorest 20 percent receiving only 1.4 percent of world income.[30] To say this is just the way things are, the way the cookie crumbles in life, is wrong. No, this is the way the cookie was baked. Such massive maldistribution is no accident; only a strategically naïve faith could believe otherwise.

Thus, the FME, the experience of the value of persons and our natural environment, has historically meant the value of only certain persons. The history of tribalism, racism, sexism, ethnic rivalries, and slavery all witness to the fact that the civilizing advance of fairness and compassion is slow. In ancient Greece, even murder did not always conflict with social respectability. We find there that "outside the circle of the dead man's kinsmen and friends, there is no indication of any popular sentiment against ordinary homicide."[31] Homicide at that point of moral evolution was an accepted means of conflict resolution. Dueling was socially blessed for a long time for the same purpose. We could be superciliously shocked at that if in our day mass hunger, death, and the spoliation of the planet were not borne with such eerie equanimity.

"Man of Humanity" — or of Depravity?

If we draw a circle and label it "human moral concern," we can ask how filled that circle is today. That question has attracted many minds who have tried to do a kind of moral inventory on the species. Adam Smith, the ethicist who became a founding father of economics, proposed in 1759 some hypotheticals as a test. He wanted to see how "a man of humanity," his term for a good and apparently decent person, would react to tragic news.

> Let us suppose that the great empire of China, with all its myriads of inhabitants, was suddenly swallowed up by an earthquake, and let us consider how a man of humanity in the world, would be affected upon receiving intelligence of this dreadful calamity. He would, I imagine, first of all express very strongly his sorrow for the misfortune of that unhappy people, he would make many melancholy reflections upon the precariousness of human life, and the vanity of all the labours of man, which could thus be annihilated in a moment. He would, too, perhaps, if he was a man of speculation, enter into many reasonings concerning the effects which this disaster might produce upon the commerce of Europe, and the trade and business of the world in general. And when all this fine philosophy was over, when all these humane sentiments had been once fairly expressed, he would pursue his business or his pleasure, take his repose or his diversion, with the same ease and tranquility as if no such accident had happened.[32]

That is slightly damning of this "man of humanity," but Smith presses the hypothetical. He goes on to wonder what would happen if this person were to face a comparatively slight misfortune himself. Would his thin veneer of decency be further thinned? Smith thinks it would.

> The most frivolous disaster which could befall himself would occasion a more real disturbance. If he was to lose his little finger tomorrow, he would not sleep tonight; but provided he never saw them, he will snore with the most profound security over the ruin of a hundred million of his brethren, and the destruction of that immense multitude seems plainly an object less interesting to him than this paltry misfortune of his own.[33]

As Smith concludes this dour reflection, he does pull up short of judging his "man of humanity" as totally depraved. One more hypothetical: he asks what this imperfect man would do if he were in a position to prevent "this paltry misfortune of his own" in exchange for consigning a hundred million unseen Chinese to their death. Smith finally chokes. "Human nature startles with horror at the thought, and the world in its greatest depravity and corruption, never produced such a villain as could be capable of entertaining it."[34] Really? Smith may have been overly kind.

Egoism and Righting Moral Wrongs

With close to two billion people destitute on the planet and many of them in advanced states of starvation, James Tobin, winner of the 1984 Nobel Prize for economics, proposed a simple plan. Trillions of dollars whirl around the globe in foreign-exchange transactions, all of it untaxed. Tobin proposed a 0.5 percent tax that would help dampen speculative international financial movements but would be too small to deter commodity trade or serious international investments. This money could be used to pay the crushing debts of poor nations to give them sound footing, to finance the operations of the United Nations, to stamp out illiteracy, and to support nongovernmental organizations

(NGOs) that are a major force for good but always short of cash.[35]

A slight diminution of military budgets worldwide would bring food to all the hungry and drink to the thirsty, would replenish topsoil and save the oceans. We could do all that and still keep our little fingers. And we don't.

Tobin's suggestion fell with a dull thud. Contemporary "men of humanity" rolled over and went back to sleep. Societal progress into the FME may be more stalled than we dare admit. To cast even more dismal shadows on our collective moral character, I turn to the gloomy Russian philosopher Vladimir Solovyev. Writing in 1895, he argued for the overwhelming hegemony of rank egoism in our species. "Egoism is a force not only real but fundamental, rooted in the deepest centre of our being, and from thence permeating and embracing the whole of our activity—a force functioning uninterruptedly in all departments and particulars of our existence." A dire diagnosis indeed, but he doesn't stop there. Perhaps he was writing in the fierce frost of a Siberian winter, but he sees love itself as chimeric and illusory. It could develop in us (thank you, Vladimir), but it hasn't.

> It would be entirely wrong to deny the possibility of realizing love merely on the ground that hitherto it never has been realized: you must know that many another thing was once found in the same position, for instance, all science and art, the civic community, our control of the forces of Nature. Even the rational consciousness itself, before being a fact in man, was only a perplexed and unsuccessful aspiration in the world of animals. . . . Love is as yet for man the same as reason was for the animal world: it exists in its beginnings, or as an earnest of what it will be, but not as yet in actual fact.[36]

Solovyev does allow that in the early moments of erotic love there may be a transcendence over egoism, but, he says, this doesn't last. Even though his book is promisingly entitled *The Meaning of Love*, it seems unsuitable as a Valentine's Day gift.

Human Moral Possibility

Let's concede that Solovyev got a bit carried away. It is hard to believe that our achievements in science, art, and civic community have issued forth without at least some rudimentary emergence of the power of love. Indeed, heroic moral influences have been with us urging the process on, pushing us more deeply into the foundational moral experience. "Pioneers in morality," as Bergson calls them, have warmed us with a vision of human moral possibility. We have heard the Buddha, Lao-tse, Confucius, Jesus, Muhammad, Karl Marx, Mahatma Gandhi, Mary Wollstonecroft, Katie Stanton, Dorothy Day, and Martin Luther King Jr. Theirs was a love-heated vision and we saw that "life holds for them unsuspected tones of feeling like those of some new symphony, and they draw us after them into this music that we may express it in action."[37]

Still, our attitude toward the rest of nature is indicting. Like relatives who became rich, we have trampled on our familial earth-roots with little sign of reverence or affection.

Again, Loren Eiseley:

> It is with the coming of man that a vast hole seems to open in nature, a vast black whirlpool spinning faster and faster, consuming flesh, stones, soil, minerals, sucking down the lightning, wrenching power from the atom, until the ancient sounds of nature are drowned in the cacophony of something which is no longer nature, something instead which is loose and knocking at the world's heart, something demonic and no longer planned—escaped, it may be—spewed out of nature, contending in a final giant's game against its master.[38]

Tragically, at this moment we seem to be winning that "game," even as we behave like a rebellious fetus attacking the womb that bears us. So the FME is still a perilously young and precarious *process*. With that said, the self is worthy of love and it is for ethics to probe the nature of healthy **self-love**.

Self-Love

Healthy self-love, where you respond appropriately to your own value, has proved a strange challenge for both philosophers and theologians. Their stumbling there is another case of yielding to the lure of unavailable clarity rather than dealing with the less clear reality of paradox. In the other-love vs. self-love contest, Ayn Rand made self-love the whole and only enchilada. Altruism is just a masked investment in the self. That's nice and tidy—and, like most things nice and tidy when it comes to human psychology, wrong.

Vaulting to the other extreme was philosopher Arthur Schopenhauer, who alleged that moral worth can only be ascribed to behavior that has no "self-interested motives." Pressing his point, he wrote, "The absence of all egoistic motives is thus the criterion of an action of moral value." Self-love and morality have, in his blunt view, irreconcilable differences. If you act with an eye to your own "weal and woe," you are egotistical, not moral.[39] So, in effect, any appreciation for yourself and your legitimate interests is a no-no.

In theology, Martin Luther disparages love of self. He was reacting against Catholic Christianity, which found love of self compatible with love of God. Not at all, said Luther; self-love has to be plucked out by the roots. Citing the biblical Paul's statement, "Love seeks not its own" (1 Corinthians 13:5), Luther called self-love "crooked" and said it "is not made straight unless it ceases to seek what is its own, and seeks what is its neighbor's." Luther confronts the obvious difficulty and common sense in the biblical text that says you should love your neighbor *as you love yourself* by saying—

contortedly—that this means self-love should be diverted and transferred to the neighbor and thus be set straight.[40] This twisted reasoning is all the more remarkable since Martin Luther had to have had a prodigious amount of self-respect and, yes, self-love to confront papal abuses so powerfully and with such zest. Self-respect is a synonym for self-love. After all, the Luther with whom the pope had to deal was no self-despising little fellow. He loved himself and respected himself enough to know that he had a right to think for himself, to shake off religious tyranny, and to find joy in marriage if he so chose.

These attacks on self-love are scattershot. The enemy they fail to target is egoistic self-love that gives self a hierarchical and hostile prominence over all other values and claimants. In fact, the recognition of one's own value is the only feasible base from which to reach out and love others. Only the experience of our own lovability can release us from a cringing self-centeredness and empower us to love and reach out. Humanity is a shared glory, and not to know that we are part of it would be psychologically crippling and, quite simply, wrong.

The Mystery of Self-Sacrifice. The personal life that is glorious is no less so for being one's own. There is a mind-shocking pain in paradox from which we shrink and flee to the caves of simplism. But out in the light, paradox remains, and so, out of love, I may sacrifice myself for another as that person might also for me. Such sacrifice is not caused by low self-esteem but is rather a mysterious response to the person-related values that at times can merit such an absolute gift. To claim that life is sacred does not mean that continued existence in life is an absolute obligation. Indeed, since death is as natural as birth, it is an impossibility. Life is more than any single embodiment of it, and sometimes death serves that *more* better than continued living. Life-shortening service to others is a fact of daily living, and we are all the beneficiaries of it. Medical workers and police officers take risks with their health and survival as a matter of course, and there is nothing sick about those professions.

The paradox is heightened by the fact that it is from persons who have achieved a high degree of self-actualization and confidence, born of well-nourished self-love, that heroic self-sacrifice can be anticipated. (Obviously, a morbid self-sacrifice is possible from a number of psychiatric causes. These cases, when understood, would not be classified as heroic.)

Moral Behavior as Self-Serving. Sensible ethics has another major point to make here, and Schopenhauer, even with all his disdain of self-love, will help us make it. Self-love is legitimate and unavoidable because of the unique nature of moral values. Moral values, as philosopher John Dewey says, determine "what one will be, instead of merely what one will have."[41] If we are clumsy, poor at mathematics, nonaffluent, or ugly by common standards, that's a pity. We lack certain "values." It does not, however, make us bad people. If, however, someone is a genius with championship athletic skills and enviable good looks, but is somewhat prone to fraud and murder, that is a human disaster. Moral values are constitutive. They make us what we are as persons. Failure here is drastic, not just unfortunate.

And here, at the happy underside of all this, is where Schopenhauer comes on board. To be moral by being benevolent, fair, and just to others is, in a good sense, self-serving. Schopenhauer wrote, "Conduct having real moral worth . . . leaves behind a certain self-satisfaction which is called the approval of conscience."[42] That makes sense since it is normal (in the normative sense) to be moral, and that has its own built-in satisfactions and sense of self-fulfillment. The moral also has its own beauty; the good has its own loveliness. The moral sense and the aesthetic sense are not unrelated. Right to the point is Schopenhauer once again: "The metaphysics of nature, the metaphysics of morals, and the metaphysics of the beautiful mutually presuppose each other, and only when taken as connected together do they complete the explanation of things as they really are, and of existence in general."[43]

Conversely, that literally biting word *remorse* is our lot when in destructive behavior the *do* of us contradicts the *is* of us. With Lady Macbeth, guilt draws from us an agonized, "Out, damned spot!"—at least if we are free from sociopathy and are not mired in numbing habituation to evil.[44]

Summary of Key Themes

- One does not have to be an "emotivist" to know the role of emotion in moral knowledge.
- We too easily grow deadened to the beauty and mystery of biological and personal life.
- Faith and belief can be deluded or wise.
- Moral sensitivity ranges in degrees from barbaric to heroic.
- Self-love and generosity are not incompatible.

Key Terms

Affect/affectivity
Egoism
Emotivism
Faith/faith-knowledge

Foundational moral experience (FME)
Mystical
Self-love

Questions for Discussion

1. Ethicist Holmes Rolston, in his book *Environmental Ethics*, says, "Chemicals, unlike persons, are not innocent until proven guilty, but suspect until proven innocent." Since modern life is awash in chemicals, many of which are not tested for human toxicity, how do you assess his statement? Can certain material realities be "suspect"?

2. The belief that growth is always good is a deeply embedded myth in Western culture, but it has been called a "grand illusion." Kenneth Boulding, an economist, chided his colleagues, saying that anyone who believes we can have infinite growth on a finite planet is either a madman or an economist (see his "The Economics of the Coming Spaceship Earth," in Jarrett, ed., *Environmental Quality in a Growing Economy* [Baltimore: Resources for the Future/ Johns Hopkins University Press, 1966], 3–14). Give examples of growth as a problem in the economic and political world.

Suggestions for Further Reading

MacIntyre, Alasdair. *After Virtue.* Notre Dame, Ind.: University of Notre Dame Press, 1984.

Polanyi, Michael. *Personal Knowledge: Towards a Post-Critical Philosophy.* Chicago: University of Chicago Press, 1962.

Swimme, Brian, and Thomas Berry. *The Universe Story: From the Primordial Flaring Forth to the Ecozoic Era.* San Francisco: HarperSanFrancisco, 1992.

5

Theories of Justice

What's So Good
about the Common Good?

THERE'S A WORD that is not in the dictionary, and more's the pity. The word is ***socialindividual***. Type it and your computer will underline it as an error. But it is no error; *socialindividual* is what we are. *Individual* is a misnomer; it only gets a part of us. That's the word the computer should underline. In so saying I simply mean what Aristotle meant when he said a person "is a political animal."[1] He was not using that term as we often do, referring to cunning maneuvering. Rather, his reference was to the Greek word *polis*, meaning "people" or "community." *We are social beings as well as private, public as well as personal, interrelated as well as unique, communitarian as well as individual.*

Neglect either dimension of us and you have distorted both personhood and society. Once again, it is a Scylla-and-Charybdis challenge, where you are unable to avoid one or another unpleasant option: Overstress the communitarian, social side of us as Maoist Communism did by force and violence, and the private individual perishes. The government, the prime caretaker of the **common good**, becomes all-powerful, swallowing up individuals and individual initiatives and genius. Overstress the individual side of us, as the dominant U.S. culture does, and you have individualism with insufficient stress on sharing for the common good. The government, as Ronald Reagan put it, becomes the "problem," not a positive part of the solution. Acquisitive individuals are king, and the weak and the poor are losers. What gets lost in individualism is the recognition that human life is a shared glory. A society with insufficient sharing withers like a brain following a massive stroke. Individualism is not enforced as rigid collectivism was in Maoist China, but its effects are far-reaching in American policies.

Between these two extremes—communism and individualism—is a balanced society, with privacy and common good concerns both getting their due. This does not mean that all sharing is good sharing or that we have to share everything we have, but it does mean—and here's the rub—that our privately and fairly made **entitlements** and possessions are not absolute or immune to demands from the common good. This all may sound unbearably abstract, but it is not. Every April 15 the government reminds us that we will contribute to the common good, or we will go straight to jail. If we were only individuals (and not socialindividuals), they couldn't put a hand on us, but because we are in and of society, some sharing is necessary and therefore mandated. The hundreds of nations on the earth all know this and recognize that to be born is to be in debt. There are social debts as well as interpersonal debts, and those debts have to be paid.

Justice as Key

As Aristotle said, it is **justice** that holds the city together.[2] Without it, society disintegrates. All laws are efforts to do justice, and governments are legitimate only inasmuch as they serve justice. "An unjust law is not law at all"—*lex mala lex nulla.* Justice is everyone's passion. Every policymaker and every litigant claims it. In talking justice we are talking about what persons are and what society is, and we are trying to find the right balance between individual rights and social obligations. May individual interests be sacrificed for social goals? Are state interests and social concerns always to be preferred to individual interests, or do individuals have some sacred turf upon which even Caesar may not tread?

Basic as justice is, we rarely pause to ask the most fundamental question of our life together: *What is justice?* That's an important question since most injustice rises from a botched theory of justice. You can do a lot of work with electricity without knowing what the essence of electricity is, but that's not how it is with justice. If the idea of justice we have is twisted, good decisions will be made only by accident. Of course, there is a way in which the handling of justice and the handling of electricity are the same. In both cases mistakes can be lethal.

In talking justice we are reaching for the foundations of human existence, since justice is not merely one virtue among the lot. It is the cornerstone of human togetherness, the first breath of the FME, the foundational moral experience. It's our starter response to what persons are worth. Without the experience of what persons are worth, justice talk would sound like gibberish.

If we do not give people justice, we have declared them worthless and we might as well incinerate them as Hitler did to those he found worthless.

Love and Rights

We can do better than justice. We can love, and that is why Aristotle says friends have no need of justice.[3] In friendship—that is, in love—a higher, more generous dynamism is operative. Justice-talk in a love relationship is repugnant. You wouldn't tell ecstatic newlyweds that they have an obligation in strict justice to show some signs of affection to one another. The fervor of love makes justice-talk irrelevant. If love fails, justice-talk arises—usually in a courtroom. You wouldn't tell a thrilled new mother that she owes at least minimal cherishing to her baby. However, if parents do not love their children and treat them accordingly, justice claims will be made in the halls of justice.

Love does not make the political or economic order go around. Only a mad romantic would think so. You don't go into a corporate boardroom or into the U.S. Department of State and say, "Have you folks tried love?" In politics and economics only justice stands between us and barbarity. At this point in the moral evolution of the species, justice is the bulwark of the social order.

Since we are part of nature, and perhaps the most dangerous part of it, we can't limit rights to human rights. Rights-talk can be used analogously of nature. We owe it filial respect, and not just out of self-interest. Aside from utility, the bird on the wing, the budding rose, the air, and the life-filled oceans voice moral claims to us if we have the moral ears to hear.

Suum Cuique: To Each His or Her Own

The definition of justice begins in deluding simplicity. In fact, in Latin the definition is only two words long: *suum cuique*, "to each his or her own." That is the persistent core formula for justice that has spanned the literature from Homer through Aristotle, Cicero, Ambrose, Augustine, and Roman law, and is still the reigning axiom in our time.[4] Simple as it may appear, it is a loaded

THINKING CRITICALLY

Norwegian prime minister Gro Harlem Brundtland reported to the Oslo Symposium on Sustainable Consumption that "if 7 billion people were to consume as much energy and resources as we do in the West today, we would need 10 worlds, not one, to satisfy all our needs."

5.1

formula. As we peel away, we find many layers of reality coming to light.

Justice is the first assault on **egoism**. Egoism would say: "To me my own!" Justice says: "Cool it! There are other selves whose value commands respect." The ego has a tendency to declare itself the sun and center of the universe. Justice breaks the news to the ego that there are no solar Gods in the universe of persons. Our legitimate interests are related to other interests in the web of life.

The Words of Justice

The unfolding of justice theory brings these words to the fore—*worth, owe, **right**, need*—and the trinity of justice forms. Because persons are *worth* justice, we *owe* it to them and they have a *right* to it. A right is a claim you can insist on with others. There are two sources of rights: *earned entitlements* and *need*. With that last word, a problem arises. Since classical economics moved far from its original home in ethics, the *n* word, *need*, is not prominent, to put it mildly. Your rights are based on deserts. Deserts and entitlements come from your own achievements or as gifts from other achievers. Fine. But here is the bone that sticks in the throat of individualists shy about the common good. You also *deserve* what you essentially need. (Superficial needs are not the issue here. Nobody needs a Lexus or Rolex.) Essential needs give entitlement. There is a sting in that. "To each according to his/her essential needs" is a solid dictate of justice, so solid that it can at times override the entitlements based on achievement. You might have to give what you have earned because of the essential needs of others.

Needs and Rights

Permit my retarded son Danny to drive home the message of rights generated by needs. For several years Danny went to Gaensalen School, a school in Milwaukee for children who are physically or mentally disabled. He received extraordinary benefits from the American political community, particularly the city of Milwaukee. He had door-to-door transportation to school by bus and, when necessary, by taxi. He rode in heated comfort through Wisconsin winters while other children walked. He was often in an almost one-to-one teacher/student situation. Skilled specialists attended to his many needs.

There was no public utility in any of this. Danny had Hunter syndrome, an incurable, degenerative disease that was slowly ravaging his central nervous system and would end his life at age ten. When he was going to this school, his mental age was no more than two to three years. Danny could lay no claim to distinctive merits, works, rank, or earned entitlements. He was delighted with the efforts of his teachers and passionately reached out for what they tried to offer. He wanted to be part of this world, and his teachers were a medium for contact with the world and some portion of its meaning. His abilities were slight and diminishing, but his need for the stimulation of school was real and insistent. He would look for the school bus even on holidays and weekends. When he could still manage such a sentence, he would announce to people on the street: "I go school!" His human need to be with us as much as he could was essential, not frivolous. School was one essential link.

Yet with all of that, the fact was that he was learning less and forgetting what he knew. His physical problems were alleviated by the physical therapy the school provided, but that, too, was a losing battle. The polity invested enormously and would never get a productive citizen. With some conditions like Down syndrome, education can help to make these persons more independent. There is some payback for this investment. With

Danny there would be none. He would progressively deteriorate and then die, which at age ten he did.

Danny's story raises critical questions: Who paid for all that care he got, and was the cost borne out of justice or out of charity? My taxes didn't cover it. Through law-based taxation, the people of the political community paid. Some of those who paid were childless and still had to pay. Some had children in school who did not get the benefits Danny got and still they had to pay. Danny would never give any calculable return to any of his anonymous benefactors, most of whom never knew of his coming or his passing, and still they gave of their earned monies for his care.

Remarkably, even amid tax revolts and lamentations, such aid to the handicapped is not in principle threatened. The ruling perception seems to be that this little boy with blighted mind but exquisite affections deserved suitable though expensive care from the community, and the community made it a matter of enforced law, not of optional charity. Calling it a matter of charity would make it **supererogatory** and therefore dispensable. Neglecting it in that case would be ungenerous but not morally wrong. The care Danny needed that I could not afford to give him was given by the community as an expression of **social justice**. The "his own" part of "to each his own" included his needs. The *essential* needs of both the productive and the unproductive generate rights.

Not a Contract

Summarily: Danny's need-based right to develop the little potential he had for as long as he had it was not based on a deal he struck with the community. It was not a reward, for he was without "merits." It was not reparation, since the community had not harmed him; and it was not an investment, for he would make no return. It was based on his worth. Helping him to do as much as he could for as long as he could was his minimal essential need. Essential needs are those without which self-respect and hope could not endure, and even the retarded have such needs. *Basic needs issue into rights when their neglect would effectively deny the human worth of the needy.*

This introduces a big agenda for a justice theory. Can you feel respected and have any hope if you have no access to a job, no way of getting basic health care, no chance to develop your talents through education, no access to legal representation, no pension to support you in your old age, no opportunities for leisure, no access to beauty if you are buried in rural poverty or in a decaying ghetto or barrio? Healthy governments and all those with distributive power in a society aside from government have moral obligations to work to meet the essential needs and to see that no one lacks them.

When Practice Is Wiser than Theory

Even though economic theory has not paid its dues to *need*, we all assume that needs can generate rights and that we ought to pay up. Handicapped persons whose ailments were self-induced by drug use, for example, have needs to which society is and ought to be responsive. If they are rendered incompetent, we don't gas them and incinerate them, which we could do if they had no rights. (In practice, we may indeed slowly starve them of the care they need as a result of an undeveloped health-care system, but we would not openly admit that.) Likewise, it is generally seen as unjust to use criminals, even those condemned to death, as guinea pigs in medical experiments. This is another reason why capital punishment is unjust, since it implies that the person, who may indeed have lost his right to freedom, has lost all his rights and is therefore worthless. This is a gratuitous assertion that bears a burden of proof it cannot meet. Personal worth is not negated by the loss of some rights. No one can judge any human being completely worthless.

We also in practice endorse needs-based justice with corporations that sink into financial distress.

Sometimes we judge that the mismanaged corporation should be allowed to die, but sometimes for considerations of the common good we judge that unbearable harm would come to the economy, and a rescue operation is undertaken at public expense. If well advised and truly promotive of the common good, this is an act of justice, since at issue here is the good of persons. All valid claims are traceable to the breeding ground of every right and entitlement—the perceived preciousness of persons. That's the bottom line.

As we evolve out of tribal nationalism, we will more and more see that the needs of others everywhere on the planet must be honored. If subsidies to American cotton growers are suffocating Brazilian cotton farmers, there is a justice issue here since humanity transcends tribe. We tribalists are not yet ready to admit that. As **speciesists** we are not yet ready to honor the rest of nature. Progress in the FME is slow.

The Three Sides of Justice

Like Caesar's Gaul, all of justice is divided into three parts. There are three ways in which we give "to each his/her own." To miss out on even one of these is to be unjust. The three forms of justice are ***commutative***, ***social***, and ***distributive***. Insisting that there are three modes of justice may seem like a professorial scheme. Professors like to divide things into three for convenience. No professorial games here. This is life. There are three forms of justice because persons relate to persons in three different ways. We relate on a one-to-one basis (commutative justice); individuals relate to the social whole (social justice); and the representatives of the social whole relate back to individuals (distributive justice). When we talk about fulfilling contracts or repairing injuries done to discrete individuals, we are speaking of commutative justice. When we speak of indebtedness to the social whole and the common good exemplified by such things as taxes, voting, jury duty, and eminent domain, we are speaking of forms of social justice. And when we speak of distributing the goods and bads of society fairly (largely but not exclusively through the instrumentality of government), we are speaking of distributive justice. Social and distributive justice both relate to the common good and are thus coordinates. It is an act of distributive justice for the state to collect and use tax money; it is an act of social justice to pay fairly allocated taxes.[5]

Rather than a teaching gimmick, the model below is being used knowingly or unknowingly by every one of the some two hundred nations on planet Earth. Inasmuch as they have some success at acting on this tripartite model, they each survive as a nation. Depart from this model and one will be classified as a "failed nation," and be so treated by other nations.[6] This is theory of the most practical sort.

Commutative Justice

Commutative justice (from the Latin *commutatio,* exchange) could be called interindividual justice. It is quite simple in its concept, and in an individualistic society like the United States, you had better take it seriously since there are a million lawyers out there ready to insist on it. If I contracted to cut your lawn, I owe you a lawn cut; if I stole your lawn mower, I owe you a lawn mower's worth of restitution. Justice at this level is so simple it can often be captured in terms of mathematical equality. If my lawn cutting and your cash are seen as equal, it's a square deal. Also, adding to the simplicity of this form of justice is the fact that it is limited to the two persons (or corporations) who are interacting. Social and distributive justice are much messier, as we will see. On top of that, commutative justice is marked by freedom. If I am too lazy to cut your lawn, I need not deal with you. If Ford does not want to trade with Mitsubishi, it is free to choose to deal with Toyota. So, in commutative justice, *freedom* and **equality** reign,

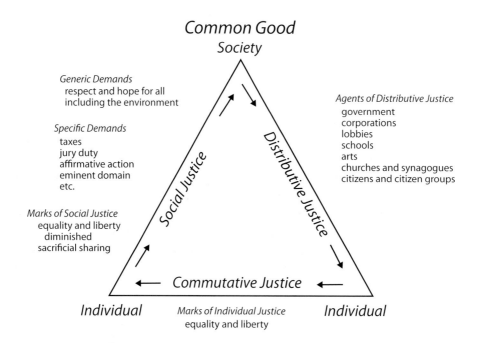

The Three Sides of Justice

which gives it a kind of red-white-and-blue attractiveness. These qualities do not reign in social or distributive justice, where needs are treated and unequal demands can be justly made. It's enough to make red-blooded individualistic Americans wince, and they do.

Social Justice

Social justice concerns individuals' debts to the common good. What is the common good? *Common good* is a descriptive term with normative clout. That is to say, it describes conditions where human life and the rest of nature can flourish, where the basic needs of life are met. The normative part says that we all have to contribute to it (normative = ought). For human life to flourish, two things are needed, and only two. You might stop me there and say: Wrong. We need many more than two things: water, food, oxygen, friends, opportunities to express our talents and to play and enjoy beauty. The list could go on. Still I insist: we absolutely need only two things—*respect* and *hope*. Many things we can do without; those two we cannot do without. Understood properly, respect and hope entail a big social-justice agenda that will include all the needs just listed, food, jobs, and so forth.

Sometimes basic concepts are best understood by their opposite. Thus, the meaning of love is illumined by its opposites, indifference and hate; to explain hope, take a look at despair. The opposite of respect is insult, and insult is the root of all rebellion. In a context of respect, we can bear with suffering and even do so gladly. In a context of disrespect, the slightest slight is galling, searing, and unbearable. If we are caught in social arrangements concocted by empire, class, or gender monopolies, arrangements that keep us hungry, thirsty, unemployed, demeaned, and without beauty in our lives, we cannot feel respected. Such disabling arrangements insult our humanity. Dismantling them is a demand of social justice.

Hope couples with respect. The opposite of

hope is despair, and there is nothing more disabling. Some psychologists find traces of despair in all the maladies of our emotions and minds. Without hope we cannot move. Hope is the motor of the will. Even Sisyphus had to be hoping for something or he would have left that silly rock where he found it and gone fishing. And he wouldn't have gone fishing if he had no hope for a catch. Deprive people of hope by the powerful social structures of evil, and you have broken their limbs.

And here is the selfish payload from a full understanding of the common good: the common good is the matrix of all private good. If we have large populations of insulted humanity in our cities or elsewhere on this shrinking planet, our own private good is imperiled. Injustice comes home to visit us, so increasingly knit together are we all. Gated communities and tariffs will not isolate the infections of poverty. The pollution of poverty will come home to us in the rainfall, in the air, and in the strawberries and the beef. Speaking to those who ignore the injustices in which they are complicit by their indifference and neglect, the prophet Jeremiah asserted: "Do you think that you can be exempt? No, you cannot be exempt" (Jer. 25:29).

What Social Justice Requires. In 1992 I wrote these words with a dash of foresight:

> Can we sit now in our First World comfort at a table with a view of the golf course, and ignore starvation in the Third World and joblessness and homelessness in our own cities? The prophets of Israel would answer: "No, you cannot be exempt." Injustice will come home to roost, whether in wars of redistribution (the most likely military threat of the future), or in crime and terrorism, or in far-reaching economic shock waves. The planet will not forever endure our insults. If the prophets' law is correct—and the facts of history endorse it—we will not be exempt.[7]

As in the model, the generic demands of social justice are to contribute to the creation of a context where all have access to respect and hope, those nonnegotiable needs without which human life turns foul. The specific requirements of social justice are such things as taxes, voting, obedience to just laws, **affirmative action** to break up unjust monopolies, jury duty, eminent domain, and the like.

Now notice what is missing in social justice—those two lovely qualities of equality and freedom that grace commutative justice. No nation puts its monetary needs for public works on a voluntary basis. Governments do not say: "We would really, really appreciate it if you would chip in 20 to 40 percent of all your earnings to meet public needs. We thank you in advance for your kindness." Instead, all of them with remarkable unison say: "Hand it over when we tell you and as much as we demand or we will put you behind bars." A summons to jury duty does not arrive as a genteel invitation. It arrives as a command. No freedom here: the needs are too serious. Voting and joining citizens' lobbies are free acts of social justice, and in an individualistic society like the United States, voting rates will be revealingly low and anti-tax movements fervid.

Equality also takes a big hit. Once need enters the equation—and needs are never equal—equality departs. Some are taxed more, some not at all. Some like my son Danny take funds and never pay back. Some are drafted; some are not. Some drafted into military service pick up new skills and return to civilian life richer; some return dead or maimed. In affirmative action to break up the American white male monopoly, not every white male suffers lost opportunity. *Unequal* is not *unjust* when we come to social justice.

Sacrifice and Society. So what do we get when we lose equality and see liberty drastically diminished? We get *sacrifice*. Equality goes but sacrifice stays. A viable society is built on a broad sacrificial base. Here is the question: May individual rights be sacrificed for the common good? Does it make any sense to say that individuals who have done no wrong or who have assumed no contractual obligations should, at times, be required in a just society to sacrifice their privileges, rights, possessions, and career goals and even to risk their lives for the broader social good? The answer is yes. And no society that does not have this readiness for sacrificial sharing will endure. Any society that survives does so by living with this enigmatic fact of life—however many monuments that society may build to individual rights.

The pervasive assumption that the common good can command sacrifice is assumed even by pragmatic, nonreflective persons. The assumption is housed in terms like "the national interest," "the public interest," "national security," or "eminent domain." Obviously those terms can be abused by despotic governments in flawed democracies and in dictatorships. Convictions about the need to yield to the necessities of a common life are so strong that it has been necessary to draw up and doggedly insist upon bills of rights to protect the legitimate claims of individuals from being swallowed up in group concerns. Historically the rights of the individual were only gradually even acknowledged. Public power was absolutized. The "divine right of kings" was proclaimed and "executive privilege" was used as a pretext for a return to tyranny. But even while critiquing such abuses, we live with the recognition that the state has rights to make demands—even ultimate demands in the cases of common defense.

We can try to offer an earnest defense of all of this sacrificing for the common good. We might say that since we are all born in debt to the common good and to those who conceive and nourish us in family and society, sacrificing is a partial repayment and therefore just. Those who would say that egoism is the only motivating force in our personalities might say sacrificing for the common good is smart and self-serving, since the common good is the supportive context for private good.

Try using that argument with the white male who could not get into medical school because of affirmative action. Tell him his sacrifice is a triumph of egoism. Tell that to the hero who risks her life for others. Tell her that this is just an exercise in self-aggrandizement. Such efforts are out of joint. As with the supreme sacrifice our minds cannot exhaust the meaning of all of life's mysteries, and yet we have to live with them. Somehow there is dying commingled in living, not only at the organic level, but also in the social order. We can fight this law of our nature but we cannot banish it. A little pragmatic humility helps when our minds meet mountains whose peaks elude us. Our minds, as impressive as they are, cannot fully measure the real.

Distributive Justice

Distributive justice completes the triangle. Power and wealth accumulate in a society, as do needs and obligations. How all of those burdens and goods get distributed fairly back down to individuals and groups is the work of distributive justice. In dictatorships all distributive power is claimed by the king and the royal court. Democracy developed as an antidote to this monopolism. Actually, there never has been pure democracy or pure dictatorship. Power seekers are always struggling to get their hands on the helm, and to some degree they succeed. In modern "democracies," lobbies, special-interest groups, and corporations work full-time to wrest control, often with notable success. Social theorists coin words like "lobbyocracy" and "**corpocracy**" to show who's really in charge in supposedly democratic societies. No one calls it "the divine right" of corporations and lobbies to rule, but the passion of these powers matches that of the pharaohs and kings of yore. Distributive justice fights this permanent human passion for *coup d'etat*. It is a mistake to think of a *coup d'etat* as an isolated, sometime event that

happens "over there." It is a permanent strategic thrust in all supposedly democratic states, professional organizations, corporations, churches, universities, and so forth. An oligarchic few always seek to control the many.

The Need for Democracy. Democracy is a demand for a sharing of distributive power. The government, by its access to carrot and stick, will be the prime distributor, but it must not be the only one. The citizens of a society are also agents of distributive justice, for it is they who give legitimacy to the government. Eight hundred years ago, at a time when kings had undue power, Thomas Aquinas faced the objection that distribution is the prerogative of the "prince," the view insisted on in royal courts. Not at all, said Thomas. The prince gets the power from the people, and in that sense the people, the "subjects" (*subditi*, in Thomas's wording), are part of distributive justice because their acquiescence allows the patterns of distribution to go on. If the citizens are, in Thomas's word, *contenti*, satisfied, not making a fuss, they are responsible for the distribution and are agents of distributive justice.[8] When they are not *contenti*, crowned heads sleep uneasily. What this says is that for citizens political detachment is a sin of injustice, distributive injustice.

Since justice is the least you can do to claim moral standing, this thickens the plot considerably. Practicing commutative justice, being fair and square in all your one-to-one dealings, does not make you decent if you wallow in contentment since you are getting yours while shirking your citizen's responsibility to keep a check on government and other social distributors of power and privilege. There is a devious and ignoble infantilism involved in citizen inertia. It permits "democratic" neodespotism. Voting does not end the citizen's duty toward the elected: eternal vigilance is the necessary moral follow-up. Groups like Common Cause give citizens the muscle they need to make their presence and views felt and heard.

Agents of Distributive Power. Other agencies and entities have a perfect right to influence distribution and voice their needs and perspectives. A principle has arisen in Catholic social theory called "the principle of subsidiarity," which says that not all initiative should be left to government. Thomas Jefferson spoke good sense to early America when he urged that the object of government "is to bring into action that mass of talents which lies buried in poverty in every country."[9] It is in the public interest to harvest the genius of all citizens and citizen groups. To do less is to shrink the public mind.

Not to understand distributive power is sociologically naïve. For a primer on social power, look at dictatorships: their agenda of suppression tells the tale. Everything they suppress would limit their claim to total control. With infallible instinct they go after the press, schools, religious organizations, and even the arts. How wise they are in their perversity. Journalism is an agent of distributive justice and among the noblest of callings when it does its job and doesn't just recycle propaganda. Religious groups have enormous power if they awaken their political consciences and speak loudly. Small wonder Hitler wanted a concordat to silence the Roman Catholic Church. Universities and schools are major "distributors." Professional schools have been called "the gateways to power." When they limited their cohorts to white males, they created the white male aristocracy that has long controlled the United States and other countries. Dictators also go after the arts, and wise they are to do so. When the arts awaken imagination and creativity, citizens are no longer manipulable pawns. The arts are not sideshows. They make us fully alive, and fully alive, imaginative citizens are a threat to despots.

What this says is that none of these actors in a society exists in a moral vacuum. They are all agents of distributive justice in their distinct fashion. The corporate boardroom is an ethics lab where decisions are made daily that affect the good of individuals and the common good of all. It is never "just business" when business is done. The "military industrial complex," which President Eisenhower indicted, was a coup against the common good leading to the neglect of the life-sustaining infrastructure in favor of the accumulation of arms and political power. Its immoral effects: a preference for kill-power and neglect of the art of **diplomacy**. The militarization of American foreign policy is a miscarriage of distributive justice.[10]

Government: A Necessary Evil?

The divide between right wing and left wing, between liberal and conservative, always involves competing definitions of what government is. Thomas Paine spoke for the early American spirit when he called government a necessary evil. Having inflicted genocide and banishment on the Native Americans, we found ourselves in the land of milk and honey. The skies were dark with bird life, the rivers jammed with fish, the fields hungry for crops or grazing. Who needed government?

Early America was phobic toward government. Horatio Alger was the true father of the country. He was never on welfare. He never asserted rights based on needs but only on his earned deserts. He was a self-made man. Early America, drunk on its pristine abundance, spawned the myth of a nation of self-made men (it was never too keen on self-made women). The glorification of the self-made man was quintessential Americana. In an epochal leap of illogic, we decided that the private good is the common good: what is good for Horatio Alger or General Motors is good for the nation.

The American Faith

Senator Chauncey M. Depew, praising Commodore Vanderbilt at Vanderbilt University, summed up the American faith:

> The American Commonwealth is built upon the individual. It recognizes neither classes nor masses. . . . We have thus become a nation of self-made men. . . . Commodore Vanderbilt is a conspicuous example of the product and possibilities of our free and elastic condition. . . . He neither asked nor gave quarter. The same open avenues, the same opportunities which he had before him are equally before every other man.[11]

We can assume that these empirically unsupportable assertions produced no winces or quizzical grimaces among his audience. No one asked what the senator was smoking. What he said was American dogma. "The same opportunities . . . equally before every other man." Every person had the same chance, be that the person white or black, slave or free, healthy or crippled, brilliant or retarded, male or female. The good senator was at one with the well-received nineteenth-century assurance of the popular Herbert Spencer that "each adult gets benefit in proportion to merit, reward in proportion to desert."[12] If you are rich, you have earned it; if you're poor, that is your self-made lot.

In all of this shines forth what Richard Hofstadter called "the ideology of self-help, free enterprise, competition, and beneficent cupidity upon which Americans have been nourished since the foundation of the Republic."[13] Beneficent greed

is our savior; we shall not want. This dogma has never wanted for gospelers. Robert Nozick was strikingly unoriginal and right in the mean stream of American thinking when he wrote that

> a minimal state, limited to the narrow functions of protection against force, theft, fraud, enforcement of contracts, and so on, is justified; that any more extensive state will violate persons' rights not to be forced to do certain things, and is unjustified. . . . There is no justified sacrifice of some of us for others. . . . The state may not use its coercive apparatus for the purpose of getting some citizens to aid others.[14]

He doesn't flinch at carrying this all the way to an anathema against taxes: "Taxation of earnings from labor is on a par with forced labor." (Since Nozick did not end up in jail, we may conclude he paid taxes on his Harvard earnings. Academics can get away with that. Consistency be damned.)

Events like the Great Depression and the economic collapse of 2008 took much but not all of the steam out of this puerile faith. Mighty corporations that skin their shins come running to government as to their mom for comfort and rescue. Government is the "necessary evil" . . . until you need it. Still, the lure of that purblind individualistic faith continues to draw and grip too many in the political sphere.

Government against Greed

Definition to the rescue: Government can be defined as *the prime caretaker of the common good with a particular concern for the poor.* That may sound like an idealistic definition, but it is pure practicality and it is empirically verifiable. If it is justice that holds the city together, as Aristotle saw, if the pursuit of justice knits the community into a kind of unity, the absence of justice causes political unraveling. Widespread poverty is the sure signal of injustice, and it tears a society apart.

Again Aristotle: "Poverty is the parent of revolution and crime."[15] This is an insight that should be congenial to conservatives and liberals alike. You cannot be tough on crime if you are soft on poverty.

And here is that *sharing* word again. Poverty exists because of insufficient sharing. The name for insufficient sharing is *greed.* It can be said that the main purpose of government is to ensure sufficient sharing to make life possible. Strangely but truly, it is in our self-interest to share. As Buddhist scholar David Loy says, "A society where people do not feel that they benefit from sharing with one another has already begun to break down."[16] Treating taxes as an evil from which we require "relief" is a sure symptom of greed run amuck.

As Thomas Jefferson said, when there are many unemployed poor, "it is clear that the laws of property have been so far extended as to violate natural right."[17] Violation of natural rights breeds discontent. In the same vein, the ancient Greek Thales said, "If there is neither excessive wealth nor immoderate poverty in a nation, then justice may be said to prevail."[18] What Jefferson and Thales both saw was that there is a thrust in society toward excess in both directions, immoderate wealth and immoderate poverty. Power blocks form and gobble up immoderate wealth, precipitating immoderate poverty. It is ever so. And poverty gnaws at peace and eventually undoes it.

Distributional patterns are created directing the flow in one direction and blocking its movement elsewhere. "It will trickle down," the gobblers say as they assiduously plug any leaks that would allow a trickle. This is dumb as well as unhealthy.

It is as though certain organs in the body could effect a bypass so they would receive a surfeit of blood while other organs would be left desiccated. It is the role of government to direct the flows of goods and burdens so that as in the prophetic vision of the biblical book of Deuteronomy, "there shall be no poor among you" (15:4). Note that the world's religions are at root philosophies of life and its economics. They are also probes into social psychology. And every one of them targets greed and the need to eliminate poverty by appropriate modes of sharing. Quite simply, the elimination of poverty is the prime role of government.

Contrary to self-serving, upper-class myths, studies show that an overwhelming majority of the poor want to work, and their lack of access to it is the painful center of their poverty.[19] Government policies should be directed at job creation, and not just jobs that "make stuff," but jobs that serve the social economy in areas of ecology, care of the sick and aged, and treatment of the addicted as well as areas that serve the arts and the creation of beauty. There is ample work to be done, and there are many human needs to be met. Job creation is not mission impossible. It cannot be done by government alone or by industry alone. As economist Alice Rivlin says: "It does not seem, from an analytical point of view, that there is any magic number below which we cannot push unemployment. It is a question of the will and of choosing the right mix of politics."[20] Quite simply, it is an issue of justice, and it is an issue of justice that need not divide conservatives and liberals, since both want and strive for a society without discord.

Summary of Key Themes

- Persons have a private and a public, a personal and a social dimension, leading to the three forms of justice—commutative, social, and distributive.
- Communism overstresses the social dimension; individualism overstresses the private.
- Needs as well as earned entitlements produce rights.
- The need for justice is rooted in our nature and not just from an agreement or "contract."
- The common good is the matrix of all private good.
- Justice is not the same as equality.
- Government is not the only agent of distributive justice.

Key Terms

Affirmative action
Common good
Commutative justice
Corpocracy
Diplomacy
Egoism
Entitlement
Equality/egalitarianism
Justice
Need
Rights
Social justice
Socialindividual
Speciesism/speciesists
Supererogatory
Suum cuique

Questions for Discussion

1. Though we differ on what a minimum-wage law should be, the concept is broadly accepted. A maximum wage law would stipulate that a 100 percent tax would apply for any income over X million dollars. What are the arguments for and against a maximum-wage law?
2. Basic human rights are rights without which persons could not survive in a decent and humane manner. The right to literacy and the right to vote are considered basic human rights. Could guaranteed universal health care be considered a basic human right?
3. Can social needs trump individual claims as in affirmative action where previously excluded groups are preferred over equally qualified candidates to end an unjust monopoly?
4. Can minimal-risk medical experiments be done on infants inasmuch as infants also have debts to the common good?

Suggestions for Further Reading

Del Vecchio, Giorgio. *Justice: An Historical and Philsophical Essay.* Edinburgh: University Press, 1952.

Pieper, Josef. *Justice.* New York: Pantheon, 1955.

Plato, *The Republic.*

Rawls, John. *A Theory of Justice.* Cambridge: Harvard University Press, 1971.

From Awe to Strategy

The Art and Science of Ethics

START WITH THE SELF-EVIDENT. Clearly there is a real, not an imaginary difference between Adolf Hitler and Francis of Assisi, between Attila the Hun and Albert Schweitzer, between Oliver Cromwell and Florence Nightingale, between a sycophant and a prophet, a hero and a conniving coward. We know we are saying something real when we describe certain conduct as contemptible, disgusting, demeaning, or when we call someone a thief or a liar. Such language is moral language embodying ethical judgments. In such speech, we are describing what persons ought or ought not to be. If we did not agree that persons ought to be truth tellers, there would be nothing wrong with being a liar. If human life ought not to be respected, murder would be as innocent as cribbage and rape would be as guiltless as masturbation.

Anyone who is even slightly alert knows the terms *moral* and *immoral* are meaningful. Ought talk is morals talk, and we're all at it. **Ethics** is the effort to refine our moral consciousness. A lot of our moral ideas have been foisted on us by society. Ethics is an effort to see through the hype and get better reality contact.

At first blush, the task of ethics might look simple. If we agree that killing and thieving and lying are immoral, then let us simply cease and desist from them and persuade or constrain others to do likewise. Why tax the mind with ethical inquiry? The problem is that we don't agree. There is a wide range of opinions on almost every moral issue. As we meet other cultures, we are jarred to discover that our way is not the only way.

In parts of Africa, prior to the arrival of Christian missionaries, young people were allowed to engage in free but supervised sexual experimentation. Rosemary Ruether describes it this way:

> In the traditional societies of the region the grandmothers supervised a group of huts where the young people were allowed to come and engage in free sexual experimentation. The older women taught them how to satisfy each other sexually and how to avoid pregnancy. After this period of sexual experimentation, young people married and were expected to be faithful to one partner. But the key was that they went into marriage experienced in how to give one another pleasure and equipped to elect or avoid pregnancy.[1]

Then the Christian missionaries arrived and were horrified at what they saw as sexual license and promiscuity. Their belief was that all sexual activity outside a monogamous, heterosexual marriage was evil, and so they got to work teaching this to the natives in the name of God. They were good

THINKING CRITICALLY

The late prime minister of Canada, Lester Pearson, observed: "No planet can survive half slave, half free; half engulfed in misery, half careening along toward the supposed joys of an almost unlimited consumption. . . . Neither ecology nor our morality could survive such contrasts."

6.1

teachers, and the result was a disaster. Sexual experimentation by the young did not stop—another triumph of gonads over ideology—but the supervision did. The result was a rash of unintended pregnancies and less sexual compatibility in marriage. Missionary zeal is not limited to missionaries. The U.S. government under President George W. Bush allocated billions of dollars to bring "abstinent-unless-married" programs to Africa.

Once again, in moral matters of great importance we tend to want more certitude than is available. President Bush and the Christian missionaries were convinced that their ethics of sex was the right one, even though it had never really worked in their culture and led to a lot of hypocrisy and double standards. Ethics fights this false dogmatism and is open to exploring the possibility that maybe the traditional Africans had it right—or at least they had it right for them. We need ethics to challenge the tyranny of false but dominant consensus and the hype that forces it into our minds so successfully that we don't even know we have been hyped. Getting over hype is tough. The "divine right of kings" was hype and it took us eons to get over it. Indeed, we are still not fully cured.

There are other reasons why we need a method to figure out morality. Even when some moral obligations seem clear, we find that they collide with other obligations. Truth telling is good, but it would not be good if the Nazis asked you where Anne Frank and her family were hiding. Truth telling then would be lethal. Someone who always tells the truth would be a source of chaos and could never be confided in. And that illustrates the problem of ethics. After discovering what we think are real moral values, it is often a delicate task to see how they apply or which of them applies when two or more compete. To be moral is to love well. How to love well amid conflicting value claims is the problem. Love needs a strategy and that strategy is ethics.

Ethics: Daring to Define It

Ethics, that bruised discipline, is misunderstood to mean everything from etiquette to the study of customs. Here, I submit, is what it really is: *Ethics is the art/science that seeks to bring sensitivity and method to the discernment of moral values.* I call it an art/science even though it is not simply art and not simply science, but it is art-like and social-science-like. It is best, though imperfectly, described as art/science. First to the art-like part of ethics:

Art

Ethics is like art in one sense of that term as defined by *Webster's Third New International Dictionary*: Art is "the conscious use of skill, taste, and creative imagination in the practical definition or production of beauty." The focus of ethics is not primarily on aesthetic values but on moral values. But it, too, involves imagination, intuition, and taste. Just as sensitivity to beauty cannot really be taught, just as a sense of the exquisite cannot be packed into logical formulae or reduced to mathematics, so, too, the good or the moral cannot be spelled out or efficiently captured in the jejune processes of "reason." Ethics, like art, is not just a work of uninvolved intellectuality but is, rather, immersed by its nature in feeling, in a sense of fittingness, of contrast, and even in a sense of the macabre. It involves an intuitive sense of correspondence that can be cultivated only in lived experience. At times it will body forth appreciations that have been stirring inarticulately in group consciousness. At times it will resonate from the unrepeatable uniqueness of a heroic soul. Always, ethical evaluation will involve us at many levels of our psyche and in ways that are only partially chartable. Whether we are talking sex, or business, or politics, or mercy death, or late-term abortion, or chemical or psychosurgical manipulation of personality, or even simpler matters, evaluation will have many psychic dimensions and will not be simply a syllogism unfolding tidily.

The comparison of ethics to art is redemptive since ethics has been done too rationalistically in the main. Ethics is comparable to art because art that is really worthwhile is to some degree unexplainable. There is no way of giving an account of all that makes art genuine or great. Even what artists say about their own work is not all that important. If they are successful as artists, they have achieved more than they can say or even conceptualize. If the art is good, its value verges on the inexhaustible. It can be improved upon, as later performances of masters like Beethoven have shown.

In a sense, moral insight is an inexhaustible work of art. No principle or no ethicist can exhaust it. This is a caution to the overly wise that should be built into the very definition of ethics. Since ethics is so serious, we rush to closed and safe-seeming dogmatism when we should be spreading out our antennae in quest of other insights.

And, again, the beauty of moral health is another contact point between ethics and art. When we find vice ugly and virtue attractive, our reaction has roots, as John Dewey says, "in esthetic sentiment."[2] A culture with a dulled aesthetic sense will not be ethically bright. I have noted the double meaning of "fair" in ethics and in art, and Dewey says that the Greek *sophrosyne*, imperfectly translated as "temperance" or "moderation," actually implies a harmonious blending of affections into a beautiful whole. This, says Dewey, is essentially an artistic idea. Justice also can be seen as closely allied to the sense of symmetry and proportion. And the Greek identification of virtue with the proportionate mean is an indication of "an acute estimate of grace, rhythm, and harmony as dominant traits of good conduct." Dewey concludes: "The modern mind has been much less sensitive to esthetic values in general and to these values in conduct in particular. Much has been lost in direct responsiveness to right. The bleakness and harshness often associated with morals is a sign of this loss."[3] If Dada is our art, moral wisdom will not be our forte.

To be sensitive to the beauty of the moral, however, should not push us to conflate the two categories. Some of the Nazi planners had a high sense of the aesthetic, and Tolstoy speaks of the women who wept at the beauty of the symphony but had no care for their coachmen who were freezing outside. A sense of beauty and a sense of morality are not as one. This, however, need not impede our recognizing that the good has its own loveliness and that moral awareness evokes our aesthetic sense. This is why the philosopher Gottfried Leibniz could speak of the beauty of virtue and why Schopenhauer could link the metaphysics of morals and the metaphysics of the beautiful.[4]

Science

In comparing ethics to art (and it is a comparison, not an identification), there is no effort to consign ethics to a normless subjectivity. (The theory of art would accept no such consignment for art either.) To stress this, I compare ethics to science, particularly to social science. Like science, ethics weighs, assesses, analyzes, and studies relationships of empirical data. Ultimately, moral values are rooted in the earth with its people, its animals, its vegetation, rock, and soil. Like a scientist bent on hunting, gathering, and analyzing amid that data, the ethicist has an inductive fact-gathering and analytical task.

Instant analysis is not the norm when dealing with ethical quandaries. Even Thomas Aquinas, living in a simpler time, pointed out that in moral matters there is an infinity of diverse data to con-

sult (*quasi infinitae diversitates*), that no one person can do it all, and certainly could not do it in a hurry.[5]

If someone asks about the morality of gay couples adopting children, the answer will not come from simple intuition. You need data, and since such adoption is not infrequent today as heterosexism begins to wane, there is data galore. Like a social scientist, the ethicist has to gather and sort through that data to see how and in what circumstances such adoptions are beneficial and healthy. If you tackle the morality of affirmative action in the United States, you have to analyze all the effects of the white male monopoly that has reigned for so long in this land and then face all the objections that rise when you try to dismantle it. There is a lot of sweat work involved in doing ethics in a complicated world. Another example would be that most intensely moral enterprise, the formation of a national budget. No "ideal observer" sitting on a distant mountaintop will do the needed analysis of sprawling and competing claims on national monies.

The goal of the ethicist, like the goal of the scientist, is to get to the objective truth. A realistic ethicist or a realistic scientist has no illusions about the ease of the task. As philosopher Eugene Fontinell writes: "It is now being suggested that even scientific knowledge is symbolic in that we no longer have a one-to-one correspondence between mind and reality but rather a continuing transaction in which a person's knowledge is a pathway to a more adequate relationship with reality."[6] Similarly, Hannah Arendt observed that "the allegedly absolute objectivity and precision of the natural scientists, is today a thing of the past."[7] Paul Knitter notes that "sound data" are not "readily available" in the field of economics, and that (in spite of its pretensions) it cannot lay a claim to being "hard science."[8] The "impartial spectator" and the "ideal observer" theories of ethical knowledge are inadequate when they represent an outmoded hunger for absolute objectivity. They represent a false passion for clean, intellectually pure knowledge that bypasses the illumination that comes from affective and existential immersion in the gritty realities of the moral order.

In doing ethics, in probing into moral questions, there is something of the scientist at work, but there is also the artist, the believer, and the mystic. It is very taxing work but unavoidable, since the alternative to ethics is chaos.

Sensitivity

Our definition of ethics says that it seeks to bring "sensitivity and method to the discernment of moral values." Stress on sensitivity is needed since no conscience is perfect and every conscience has blank spots. The sociopathic personality that can hurt and even murder people without compunction is the extreme in moral blindness. There are more common ways whereby the moral dimension is submerged. When we hear that something is "a political, not a moral matter," or "an economic, not a moral matter," or even "a practical, not a moral matter," pernicious mischief is afoot, since the onus of moral responsibility is being effectively avoided. Part of the role of ethics is to reassert the moral dimension of *all* deliberate human behavior, whether private or collective, so that the civilizing presence of conscience will not anywhere be lost.

Not all persons or cultures are equally morally sensitive. Native American cultures tend to be much more aware of the rights of animals, trees, and other vegetation, and to express this in ritual and mythic language. As Native American scholar Daisy Sewid-Smith writes, the Kwagiutl people "were taught to express gratitude to all species of life for giving up their own lives so homo sapiens could live. When a Kwagiutl hunter killed a bear he would give praise to the bear for his sacrifice." There were similar rituals for thanking salmon. When he had to cut down a hemlock tree to make his otter trap, the hunter would say: "Thank you, my friend, that I have found you, for I have come to ask for your assistance, my friend. I would like you to work for me and be an instrument to kill the intelligent land otter when he enters my trap. You must be careful to help one another, you and the deadfall. Do not let the otter escape and be sure he dies instantly (not to suffer)."[9]

As quaint as these hunting practices may seem to modern sophisticates, Sewid-Smith says they reminded the Kwagiutl "that they were not the only important species on this planet. . . . It also helped to remind them that one must live within certain boundaries: otherwise, one must pay the consequences." Such cultures would seem better equipped to hear the pain of nature and to be more responsive to its beauty and its needs.

Since moral intelligence relies on sensitivity, it varies from person to person and even from male to female. There are certain debits and assets that come when you are born with a male or a female body. I have argued elsewhere that among male debits are a propensity to violence, a hierarchical instinct, a seducibility by abstractions, a bias for consequentialist, bottom-line thinking, and a generous dose of misogyny. All that lies in wait on the blue

> ## THINKING CRITICALLY
>
> The Dalai Lama says that "compassion is the connective tissue of the body of human life. . . . Without it children would not be nurtured and protected, the slightest conflicts would never be resolved, people probably would never even have learned to talk to one another. Nothing pleasant that we enjoy throughout our lives would come to us without the kindness and compassion of others. So it does not seem unrealistic to me: compassion seems to be our greatest power."
>
> 6.2

blanket, though happily not all men succumb to these proclivities.

The pink blanket is not without its rips and wrinkles, but on the positive side women tend to have a better integration of mind and affect, more at-home-ness with bodily existence, and more association with children. As children need parenting, adults need childing, and women tend to be better childed. The long history of alienation also lends light to the pink-blanket people. Draw a circle and cut me out of it, and I will become intensely aware of what is going on inside that circle. Alienation may lend a certain immunity to hype.[10]

The conclusion for ethics is that it should not be monogendered or monocultured, because neither gender and no culture has a monopoly on sensitivity and sensibility.

Method

Ethics is like breathing, in the sense that everyone is already doing it. Unlike with breathing, we do not all do ethics the same way; neither is our doing it blessed with the same instinctive efficiency. We can make a mess of it, and that is serious, since ethical errors can be cruel or even fatal. So it's a case of mess or method. The role of an ethics method is to bring balance and completeness to the quest for moral wisdom.

There are two looming roadblocks to effective ethical discernment: one is at the level of personality development, and the other comes from a lack of theoretical clarity regarding the nature of ethical inquiry. Sophisticated studies in developmental psychology have shown that we may grow from one way of doing ethics to another. At early stages of development we may antisocially conclude that good is whatever we want it to be. We are likely to be impulse ridden, opportunistic in evaluating, with little ability to distance ourselves from our own interests or to relate properly to moral authorities. Some people may grow old and die at these early levels. Others go on to develop an ability for more sensitive judgment and can respond to principles and ideals in a way that shows a maturely integrated awareness of the value of self and others, and the links between self-love and other-love.[11]

The second roadblock to which method is antidotal is the lack of clear theory on how we should go about judging and discerning moral values. This is the problem of method. We persons are valuing animals who are willy-nilly involved in concocting our own homegrown method of making ethical judgments. If you present moral quandaries and cases to people of any educational level, their answers would reveal in broad outline the ethical method with which they are operating. Probably these people have never paused to evaluate the method they are using almost instinctively. Probably, too, they are locked into a number of opinions that, if they became critically reflective, they would alter. Instead, they just lumber along, thinking and evaluating in the way into which they have fallen through a number of uncoordinated and unexamined influences.

Without a well-critiqued method, you and your conscience may be sailing through life with a broken compass. Programmed into certain set ridges of thought, you might say you are morally programmed but not morally educated and not enjoying the freedom of personal judgment. Those with an unexamined conscience do not even suspect the horizons that are open to the free and are likely to feel threatened by those who are being freed through critical reflection. They are in a box that impedes their growth and befuddled by those not similarly confined.

Without a good ethical method, some persons will have an unrealistic confidence in authority or tradition: "My Bible or my Qur'an or my constitution will tell me everything I need to know. . . . Don't bother me with the facts." Others will rely on an almost vertical intuition into the immediate facts but will lack breadth of vision or any sense of continuity or history. Others will trust firmly in principles and group expectations and be unequipped to handle exceptional cases or to trust their own intuitions. In all these cases the problem is a limited grasp of the epistemological dimensions of moral evaluation, that is, how we go about *knowing*.

The plot thickens when these partial approaches to ethical inquiry occur not just in practice but also in theory. Those who think and write about ethics, the professionals, often lend authority to limited ethical approaches. The method I offer here promises not to bypass any of the personal or cultural routes to insight. It's a leave-nothing-out method. It is not limited to reason and the use of principles, though it includes both. It doesn't ignore the usefulness of authorities and classical texts, but neither does it divinize them. It is open to personal genius and intuition, even among the unlettered, and respects the lessons of history, since without memory our ethics is amnesiac. It looks to harvest the wisdom of other cultures that may seem alien but are rich variants on the theme *human*. It includes the wisdom found in comedy and acknowledges the sad fact that sometimes it is only tragedy that teaches us moral lessons, as may be happening right now in ecological ethics and in the continued reliance on state-sponsored violence, that is, war.[12]

The Wheel Model. To do all this, I use a **wheel model**.

The wheel model shows the two phases in ethics: (1) the questioning, hunting-and-gathering phase and (2) the evaluational processes. The questions in the hub of the model are akin to the "fact sheet" lawyers assemble prior to the actual legal argumentation. The spokes of the model represent the nine evaluational processes, the nine ways our multidimensional minds make contact with reality with full recognition of the social roots of knowing. All

of this, however (and the foundational moral experience itself), has its beginnings in the empirical order where persons, animals, and things dwell in uneasy community. It is the questioning mind in its fullness that achieves discernment here.

A Disclaimer. It should be conceded from the outset that every intellectual model limps. A model justifies itself only if it gives significant form and consistency to thought. Theoretically we ask all the questions in the hub of the wheel and then move on to evaluation. In reality evaluation does not stay obediently in abeyance while we run through the expository, questioning phase. What the model does do, as I shall attempt to show, is call attention to the pluriform possibilities of evaluation that are available to us. The mind is not a single-lane highway. I hope through this method to provide a systematic framework for moral inquiry, whether in private and interpersonal matters or in collective or political situations.[13]

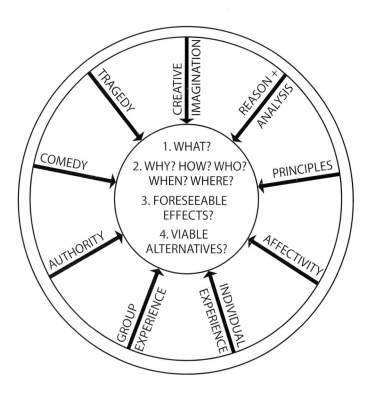

Beware the Lazy Mind

In any field of study, the method (smart-talking people like to call it "methodology") is a quest for realism. Laziness is the enemy in any field of study. It is easier to bask in generalities than it is to plunge into the gritty world of empirical experience where no two things or persons are exactly the same and where meaning-giving relationships are crisscrossing and shifting. Asking all the questions taxes the mind and calls it to make distinctions where there are real differences. The mind easily shrinks from this and prefers false generalization to true and individuated discernment. I'll give an example:

Some years ago when gay couples were more closeted, I polled a class on whether they approved of homosexual couples adopting children. The approval response was only 7 percent. I then told them the true story of two lesbians known to me. When I first met them, they were each completing their studies in special education, which was training them to teach handicapped children. They considered themselves married and had even solemnized their union in a private religious ceremony with friends. When they completed their studies, they planned to adopt one or two children whose disabilities made them unlikely candidates for adoption and whose lives would probably be lived mostly in institutions. With the strength of their mutual relationship and with the skills they had in special education, these two women felt they could bring more happiness and development to these children than could be found even in a good institution.

After telling this story, I asked how many would approve of this particular case of adoption by homosexual persons. Approval rose to 80 percent. The change in approval rates indicates that when first asked the question, the respondents were thinking of homosexuals stereotypically and mythically—in other words, in a falsely generalized, unindividuated fashion with the necessary

questions unasked. The proper answer to the original question should have been: "It depends," or "Generally yes," or "Generally no," followed by the necessary questions. Beware the unasked question. It will trip you every time.

Principles

There are good generalizations: we call them principles. It is fair to say that both killing and using heroin are generally bad. But this limited generalization allows for individuated differences. A terminal cancer patient who uses heroin for pain relief may be acting quite morally. Likewise, killing in self-defense may be morally good.

The point of ethics we are making here is that "human actions are good or bad according to the circumstances,"[14] as Thomas Aquinas put it, and the center of the wheel model is the search for the relevant circumstances. There is another reason why circumstantial analysis is eschewed. This "good or bad according to the circumstances" thing could seem to open the door to complete ethical relativism and to a rather flaccid and normless "situation ethics." If it all depends on the circumstances, then there is no solid ground in ethics, for circumstances are always changing.

Aquinas and all the philosophers of history knew that circumstances constitute moral meaning. That doesn't mean that what Lola thinks is good for Lola is necessarily good; it means that what is good for Lola depends on the circumstances.[15]

Insight

The ethicist, after all, is a bit like a detective in search of clues. If we miss one clue in its relationship to all the others, we don't solve the case. Finding them all and seeing how they relate is what Roman Catholic theologian Bernard Lonergan called insight:

In the ideal detective story the reader is given all the clues yet fails to spot the criminal. He may advert to each clue as it arises. He needs no further clues to solve the mystery. Yet he can remain in the dark for the simple reason that reaching the solution is not the mere apprehension of any clue, nor the mere memory of all, but a quite distinct activity of organizing intelligence that places the full set of clues in a unique explanatory perspective.[16]

Insight is a relational judgment about how things connect into a meaningful whole. That's precisely the business of ethics.

The Taboo Block

The moral tabooist, while granting that most things are right or wrong according to their circumstances, holds that certain actions are wrong *regardless of the circumstances.* People, for example, have considered as wrong *regardless of the circumstances* gambling, contraceptive intercourse, remarriage after divorce, interracial marriage, conscientious objection to civil authority, flag burning, same-sex intimate relationships, and a thousand other things. If they judged that all of these things were likely to be bad precisely because of the circumstances that attend them, then we might agree or disagree with their assessment of the circumstances, but we could not fault their ethical method. The error in method arises from proclaiming certain activity wrong with no perceived need to consult the essential circumstances that constitute its moral meaning.[17]

This tendency to judge preter-circumstantially is typical of children and of those who don't grow up. Psychologist Jean Piaget pointed out that young children do not evaluate intentions and other circumstances in their value judgments. A type of action has a fixed meaning *regardless of the circumstances,* to use the language of taboo. Thus, a child will not see any moral difference in breaking a cup accidentally or out of spite. The cup got

broken; that is all that really counts. As the child matures—or, we might better say, *if* the child matures—he or she will see the essential difference circumstances make.[18]

Jean-Paul Sartre, with his existentialist's aversion both to false generalization and to the lack of specific awareness, can be instructive here even though he oversteps a bit. Sartre says that the greatest evil of which man is capable is to treat as abstract that which is concrete. That is a great statement when you think of the evils perpetrated in the name of abstractions like "national interest" or "profitability" or "free enterprise." What he rightly fears is blurring unique persons and unique situations into ill-fitting, abstract categories, ignoring the empirical specifics of every person and every case. Sartre's press for specific acuity even leads him to say that there is no such thing as "human nature." Of course, the "human nature" he denies is one that is "abstract, an essence independent of human beings or anterior to their existence" in concrete reality. In fact, Sartre says that "there is no such thing as a human condition in general," so concerned is he to avoid losing concrete and individual reality in the fog of abstract conceptualization.

With all this said, of course, we can still say that certain things are generally wrong. Indeed, when fully described, they may be seen as so negative, disruptive, and neglectful of creative alternatives that no circumstance could be imagined in which they might be justified. I have argued elsewhere that capital punishment is in this category.[19] I did not so argue, however, on the grounds that an intuitive perception of the moral implications of human nature issues inexorably into a judgment of the moral infeasibility of penal killing. Rather, it is because there are alternatives to it and because an analysis of what this kind of killing is, when viewed in all of its historical roots and foreseeable effects, supports the conclusion that it cannot be justified. I establish it as wrong by argument, not by edict or purported intuition.

Cognitive Modesty and Booming Certitudes

In stressing the need for energetic questioning in the pursuit of moral truth, there is no suggestion here that the quest will lead to the perfect possession of the quarry. Simplicity will often enough elude us, and limpid clarity will be rare. The ethical system called "naturalism," which attempts to force moral inquiry into a scientific model of detached observation, is symptomatic and symbolic of Western myopia. It wants to get morality wrapped up with scientific tidiness. As Joseph M. Kitagawa writes, "By and large, the Westerner's mindset has been conditioned by strong emphases on reason, judgment and discrimination." There is nothing wrong with reason and judgment, he concedes, but he insists that the profound gulf between East and West is provided by the word *system*, which denotes the task of getting things together in a rational order. This is the keynote of the West. The Easterner is more contemplative, more receptive, more modest in taking the measure of things, less in need of a "postmodern" revolt.[20]

Paradox and Humility

A bit of that Eastern modesty befits the doer of ethics. Whoever would think ethically must be reacquainted with the untidy notion of paradox. The

> ## THINKING CRITICALLY
>
> "The soundness of moral standards depends on the adequacy of the reasons that support or justify them. Fashion standards are set by clothing designers, merchandisers, and consumers; grammatical standards by grammarians and students of language; artistic standards by art critics and academics. . . . In every case, some authoritative body is the ultimate validating source of the standards and thus can change the standards if it wishes. Moral standards are not made by such bodies. . . . The validity of moral standards depends not on authoritative fiat but on the adequacy of the reasons that support or justify them."
>
> —William H. Shaw, *Social and Personal Ethics*
>
> 6.3

Western passion to get everything squared away with a neatness unattainable in a messy world is a hazard in ethics. Often we are left with perceptions that seem separately true but contradictory. In practical cases of ethics, we will find contradictory answers to the same question defensible and well braced by reason. I once spoke to a group of pediatric neurologists who had presented me with a number of difficult cases in their practices and wanted to know the best solution morally speaking. In some of those cases I said contradictory alternatives were equally defensible. They were not pleased. They wanted a simplicity these harrowing decisions did not allow. Ethics at times does not offer the alleged precision of "precise science." Sometimes it can only lighten the darkness slightly but not dispel it, leaving us with an only partially guided leap in the dark. This is disconcerting to those who look for a neat code of dos and don'ts. The desire for this, of course, is understandable. It is a desire to escape from the disturbing responsibility of having to decide when wracked by unbanishable doubt. This responsibility, however, is part of the burden and challenge of being both free and finite.

Great thinkers can surprise us with their humility. Medievals praised what they called *docta ignorantia*, a learned ignorance, knowing the limits of our knowing. Noonday clarity is not available at dusk, and there are many dusks in matters moral. Surprisingly for those who do not know him, Thomas Aquinas supplies an epistemological approach that is marked by this humility. One might conclude inaccurately that one who wrote a massive *Summa* is a prime example of getting it all together into a closed system. Thomas, however, believed, as one of his commentators summed it up, that "truth cannot be exhausted by any [human] knowledge; it remains therefore always open to new formulation."[21] Thomas has some very humbling things to say about our capacity to understand. He says, for example, that "the essential grounds of things are unknown to us."[22] He also says we do not know the "essential differences" or the "substantial forms" of things as they are in themselves.[23]

And Thomas the theologian, and a very determined theist, says that the highest form of knowledge of God is the knowledge of God "as the Unknown."[24] (A learned agnosticism?) Thomas did not see human knowledge as ever complete, but always imperfect and struggling to contain a light that exceeds our capacity. As knowers, we are always unprofitable servants of truth. In fact, Thomas himself illustrated the experience of this by giving up the writing of his magnum opus, his *Summa*, with the announced conviction that all that he had ever written was "nothing but straw." His reminder of the straw quality of our best understanding is a chastening valedictory. (Was the medieval Thomas "postmodern"?) Given the ex-cessive certitudes that abound in moral discourse, we need that message.

Seeking Solid Ground

Are we to greet all this with a wail of despair? Is there no solid ground in ethics? There is indeed, and the human family has been getting better at finding that ground with its rock-solid certainties. The United Nations has led the way, making the term *human rights* the vernacular of international ethical discourse. Its 1948 Universal Declaration of Human Rights was only the start. To see some fifteen hundred pages of human-rights claims, consult the two volumes of *Human Rights: A Compilation of International Instruments.*[25] The condemnations of torture, slavery, and discrimination; the treatment of prisoners; the rights of refugees; the special needs of women and of children; the obligation to eliminate hunger and malnutrition; and hundreds of other issues are all presented with unequivocal prophetic certainty. There are basic values we can be sure of without a hint of ambiguity. All of the world's major and indigenous religions are storehouses of human-rights claims expressed in varying idioms but bristling with urgency. All of this bears witness that we can know what promotes the good of the earth with its life-forms and what trashes it. We can *know*. The main problem is in the *doing*.

Summary of Key Themes

- Ethics is the systematic effort to refine our moral consciousness, to critique our consciences.
- Ethics is a unique discipline, in some ways similar to art and to science without being precisely either.

- Instant analysis of complex moral issues is rarely successful.
- We often look for more certitude in moral debates than is available.
- Without ethics, bias rules.
- Right and wrong are determined circumstantially.

Key Terms

Deontology
Ethics
Ethics as art
Ethics as science
Situation ethics
Wheel model

Questions for Discussion

1. Why can ethics not be properly called a science? Why can we not design a computer program that would give us perfect answers to what is right and what is wrong?
2. Are all cultures morally equal, or are some cultures more morally sensitive on certain issues?

Suggestions for Further Reading

Facione, Peter A., Donald Scherer, and Thomas Attig. *Ethics and Society.* 2nd ed. New York: Prentice-Hall, 1991.

Maguire, Daniel C., and A. Nicholas Fargnolli. *On Moral Grounds: The Art/Science of Ethics.* New York: Crossroad, 1991.

Thiroux, Jacques P., and Keith Krasemann. *Ethics: Theory and Practice.* 10th ed. Upper Saddle River, N.J.: Pearson, 2009.

PART THREE

Asking the
Right Questions

Introducing the "Wheel Model"

The Subject of Ethics

Defining the Model of the Wheel

"What's in a name?"
—William Shakespeare, *Romeo and Juliet*

To answer Juliet's question: *ownership* and *power*! You name it, you own it. You have framed it and set its meaning, and if other people buy into your framing, you control them. The hub of the wheel model is packed with the reality-revealing questions: *What? Why? How? Who? Where? When? Foreseeable effects? Alternatives?* All the questions are important—they save us from miss-

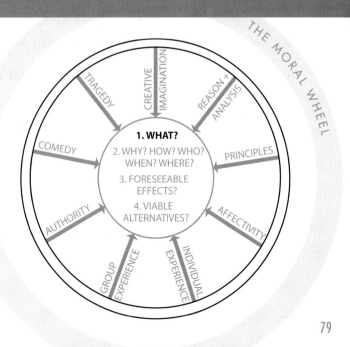

79

ing the obvious (though sometimes one question will be more important than the others). But none is more important than that simple question *What?* The *what* question refers to our first cognitive contact, our first picturing or characterization of the issue at hand, our first "fix" on the topic. If that first fix is skewed, we have committed the original sin and the rest of our analysis will be off-kilter. In asking the *what* question, our target is the prima facie facts that lie beneath the figments and arbitrarily imposed meanings with which society and culture drape things.

THINKING CRITICALLY

"Frames are mental structures that shape the way we see the world. As a result, they shape the goals we seek, the plans we make, the way we act, and what counts as a good or bad outcome of our actions. In politics our frames shape our social policies and the institutions we form to carry out policies. To change our frames is to change all of this. Reframing *is* social change."

—George Lakoff, *Don't Think of an Elephant! Know Your Values and Frame the Debate*

7.1

and a reliever who removes the affliction and is therefore a hero."[1] Anyone against "tax relief" is a villain. Taxes become an evil to be fought. Lost from view, given the mesmerizing power of this reframing, are all the good and essential things that taxes do: provide courts and police and fire protection, fund basic science that keeps us healthy, educate children, build libraries, provide for the enforcement of laws in banks and businesses, conduct oversight of food industries to keep us from being poisoned, and the list goes on and on. Taxes well used make life livable and give the gift of healthy longevity. Clearly we don't want relief from all of that.

Defining the *What*

Examples to the rescue, and I will use many in this chapter, devoting the entire chapter to the single question *What?*—all to show the importance of initial diagnosis. Linguist George Lakoff is a good starter. He has popularized parts of cognitive science with telling examples. He credits President George W. Bush with effectively redefining the term *taxes* by giving us a different *what.* From the start of his first term, Mr. Bush canonized the phrase *tax relief.* The expression showed up everywhere in presidential addresses and thence in the news media and even in the Democratic Party's treatment of taxes. In Lakoff's terms he reframed the word *tax*; in my sense he altered the definition of *what* taxes are. As Lakoff puts it, "For there to be relief there must be an affliction, an afflicted party,

Words Matter

Whenever there is a redefinition of a key term, especially in the influential world of politics and economics, the scent of mischief is in the air. Misnaming is the first refuge of scoundrels. In the case at hand, providing tax breaks for some but not for others was the real agenda, and the success of that agenda required a subversive new picturing of *what* taxes are. Words matter. They frame our understanding, for good or for ill. Words can pack a lot of hidden wrong. Dig deeper into something like "taxes" and you can find even more of that wrong. Assumptions about whether taxes are fair are riddled with self-serving delusions. A little honesty shows that the rich do not ever pay a fair share. The honest rich man Warren Buffett admits that his social setting is responsible for much of his wealth. "If you stick me down in the middle of Bangladesh or Peru," he said, "you'll find out how much this talent is going to produce in the wrong kind of soil."[2] The Nobel Prize–winning economist and social scientist Herbert Simon estimates "that 'social capital' is responsible for at least 90 percent of what people earn in wealthy societies like those of the United States or Northwestern Europe."[3] By "social capital" Simon is referring not only to the natural resources of the country in which one works, but also to the skills in technology and the educational level of the community along with effective government. On those gifts the wealthy can build their fortunes. Knowing that the idea is quite infeasible, Simon nevertheless says one could argue on moral grounds for a flat income tax of 90 percent. Underlying all this is the lie that the rich get what they have through hard work and through their talent alone with no reference to the massively supportive context. And on the underside, those who are not rich lack either talent or pluck.

Lakoff also talks about the successful reframing of the term *family values*. It has been redefined narrowly as referring to sexual and reproductive matters but with no reference to ongoing ecocide and unnecessary wars—neither of which is good for families.

The *Is* and the *Ought*

To put this another way: the *is* is the parent of the *ought*. If we miss contact with what really is, our oughts are messed up. All the questions in the hub of the wheel model help here, but *what* is the critical first step in coming into contact with the *is*. Knowing what really is, therefore, is the goal of ethical inquiry. If our judgment of the prima facie facts is skewed, the brilliance of subsequent discussion and analysis will be victimized by this bad start. What we say may be impressive, but we will not know *what* we are talking about. The first step toward *prescribing* what ought to be is *describing* what is. Description is the beginning of prescription. Description, of course, is not the end of

prescription. True ethics is creative and is as concerned with what might be as it is with what now is. However, we will never know what might be if our first contact with the issue is blurred. The possible emerges from the actual. The creative mind is always well informed.

What Are We Talking About?

Many, if not most, ethical debates result from ignorance of what is being discussed. In fact, you could say the hotter the debate, the likelier it is that the participants to some large degree don't know what they are talking about.

A good deal of discussion of capitalism and **socialism** is lamed from the start by a failure to identify what it is that is meant by capitalism and socialism. Economics historian Robert L. Heilbroner points out that in much that is said about capitalism, the explicit assumption is that the United States is the most typical capitalist nation. Thus, Paul Sweezy, the American Marxist critic, says that "the United States is a capitalist society, the purest capitalist society that ever existed." And French Marxist Roger Garaudy sees the United States as the capitalist system in its most typical expression.[4] If so, it is bad news for capitalism.

The definition of the *what* here contains what Heilbroner calls "the assumption that certain contemporary attributes of the United States (racism, militarism, imperialism, social neglect) are endemic to all capitalist nations."[5] Could it not be better argued that the United States is not a pure realization of capitalism but rather "a deformed variant, the product of special influences of continental isolation, vast wealth, an eighteenth-century structure of government, and the terrible presence of its inheritance of slavery—the last certainly not a 'capitalist institution'"? "Indeed," Heilbroner continues, "could we not argue that 'pure' capitalism would be best exemplified by the economic, political, and social institutions of nations such as Denmark or Norway or New Zealand?"[6] Obviously, the latter assumption would affect all subsequent analysis of the political, economic, or moral dimensions of capitalism. We would start with a different *what*.

Going beyond Heilbroner, you might say the countries he mentions—the Scandinavian countries and New Zealand—are best understood as examples of both capitalism and socialism. National health-care systems can be described as a form of socialism. So could public schools and the public library. Are the Green Bay Packers, owned by the city of Green Bay, a socialist football team? If 40 percent of health-care costs are covered by Medicare and Medicaid in the United States, is this country 40 percent socialist? Social Security was criticized as a form of socialism when it was proposed in the 1930s. Misdefinition is the gateway to confusion—and roguery.

Heilbroner's caution applies equally to the conservative critics of anything named "socialist" who would single out the old Soviet Union or Maoist China as the paradigms of socialism. The argument might be made that Russia, strapped as it was with some tragic historic legacies, and China, recovering from invasion and war, just happened to be the wrong places for the best ideals of socialism to flourish. It might also be said that the United States was not the best place for a healthy capitalism to be born.

Many of the heated discussions of capitalism and socialism in the past century took place with the discussants not knowing *what* they were talking about. The terms *capitalism* and *socialism* are not univocal, and if you take them as such, you miss a world of nuance. Not all conclusions there-

after would necessarily be wrong. As an old axiom of logic puts it: *Ex falso sequitur quidlibet* ("from false premises, anything can follow"). Still, the odds are poor.

Fighting the Vacuum of Meaning

The human mind cannot tolerate a vacuum of meaning. Our minds were built to breathe meaning. If I say "tree" to you, your mind is unthreatened. You know what trees are and you can peacefully await what I am going to say about them.

If, however, I say "schlumf" to you, your mind is jarred, since "schlumf" is meaningless and therefore unwelcome. This hunger for meaning is so great that the mind will gladly accept counterfeit meaning. Better wrong meanings than none at all. Even wrong meanings put the mind at ease. Too much at ease. The task of clear thinking generally (and ethics particularly) is to strip away false meanings and substitute right meanings. That's not easy, since we can fall in love with our false meanings and resist the cure.

As we grow up, society feeds us a lot of true and false meanings. Sorting them out is the work of a lifetime. False meanings, false *whats*, are like junk food; they quiet the appetite but they fail as nourishment. If we are locked into a simplistic false definition, creativity is blocked. Superficiality rather than profundity is our fate as we settle for half-baked understanding.

> **THINKING CRITICALLY**
>
> "Words like 'democratic,' 'reactionary,' 'unscientific,' and a hundred more are amphibious. The danger is that they are used in one part of an argument in a purely expository sense and in another part which involves a pure exposition *plus* an evaluation."
>
> —C. D. Broad,
> *Ethics*

What's in the Name *Marriage*?

An example of this: I will write a word and as soon as you read it, your mind will be at peace since you know full well what that word means. The word will not be *schlumf*. It will be a word that has the comfort of familiarity.

Here goes: the word is *marriage.*

Everybody knows what marriage is, but if I pressed you for a definition—to get to your *what* regarding marriage—you might start out saying: "Marriage is a state of being conjoined, etc., etc." I could stop you right there, insisting that you are already dead wrong. Marriage is not a "state" of anything. That's the wrong *what*. Marriage is a process, not a state. *State* comes from the Latin *stare*, meaning "to stand, to be still," that is, "static," and marriage is not that. It is a process, a dynamic, ever-changing process. That may strike you as donnish quibbling, but it is not. If you define marriage as a state, an either/or thing that you are in or not in, you are saying that you are not in it prior to the wedding and you are out of it if death or divorce do you part. That is simply untrue.

If you concede that marriage is a process, everything changes. A process admits of more or less. Thus, you can be more or less married. If someone asks a married person if they are married and if they reply candidly, they might say, "Oh yes, we are very married . . . very, very married." And that could indeed be true. However, someone else might candidly reply, "We're not really very married. Certainly not as married as we used to be." That, too, could be perfectly accurate. I recall a couple who wanted to divorce but decided to wait until their last child graduated from high school. The very afternoon that happened, they visited a divorce lawyer. How "married" were they when they walked into the lawyer's office? The marital process had stopped long ago and they were now just going to make it legal and public. The reality of marriage was no more, and they would now make that fact official.

Let's take this further. Is it not possible for a couple to be more married before the wedding than they are at some point after the wedding? After all, if marriage is a process, the process of conjoining does not start on the day of the wedding, unless, of course, it is an arranged marriage and the two parties have never met before. Might you—and this shows how reality challenges our language skills—be more married before you are married than you are after you are married? The answer is yes, that is possible. (This is not to say that the wedding is immaterial. It puts a public stamp upon a private decision and has social and legal implications. In "common-law marriage," prolonged cohabitation puts the union into the public realm.)

Still showing the importance of getting the *what* straight, take this definition of marriage: *Marriage is the unique and special form of committed friendship between sexually attracted persons.* Many people could accept that until you point out that there is nothing in this definition that requires that the bonding couple be heterosexually attracted. The issue of same-sex unions, which is being rabidly argued today, is a battle between different *whats*, different definitions. Those who define marriage as imaginable only between a man and a woman exclude a significant percentage of the human race from this rewarding kind of relationship. Such is the power of definition.

What's in the Name *Terrorism*?

Playwright and actor Peter Ustinov entered a naming battle when he said that "terrorism is the war of the poor; war is the terrorism of the rich." The word *terrorism* runs through international discourse today like a greased pig that cannot be pinned down. It became the target of choice for American militarism after communism ceased to be a threat with the collapse of the Soviet Union and with China entering the business world. It is a word used by occupying powers to describe resistance to occupation. Resisters to the Russian occupation of Chechnya, the Palestinian resisters of

Israeli occupation, and the Iraqi and Afghanistani resisters against the United States are branded "terrorists." The word begs for definition.

The broadly accepted definition is this: *Terrorism is the direct and deliberate targeting of innocent people for the purpose of achieving some perceived good, usually from the government of the people killed.*

There are two forms of terrorism: individual (or small group) terrorism and state terrorism. The deadliest by far is state terrorism, given the arsenals of nations. Individuals with bombs strapped to them cannot rival American, Russian, and Israeli air forces. The textbook example of terrorism is the American atomic bombing of Hiroshima and Nagasaki. As political philosopher Michael Walzer says of the Hiroshima holocaust: "The bombing of Hiroshima was an act of terrorism; its purpose was political not military. The goal was to kill enough civilians to shake the Japanese government and force it to surrender. And this is the goal of every terrorist campaign."[7]

Of course, by the time of the atomic bombings, terrorism had become standard operating procedure in the twentieth century. Italy had bombed city populations in Ethiopia; Italy and Germany did the same in the Spanish Civil War. At the start of World War II, the Germans inflicted "saturation bombing" on Rotterdam in Holland, Coventry in England, and elsewhere. Roosevelt at first condemned these German bombings as "inhuman barbarism that has profoundly shocked the conscience of humanity," but his scruples were not long lasting. In January 1943 the Allies meeting at Casablanca agreed on saturation bombing to undermine "the morale of the German people." With that, thousand-plane raids on Cologne, Essen, Frankfurt, and Hamburg followed. One hundred thousand people died in the fire storm we inflicted on Dresden, eighty thousand in Tokyo. Hiroshima and Nagasaki were the logical sequel for this pattern of terrorism. General George Marshall urged that the United States issue a warning to the people of Hiroshima and Nagasaki before those bombings, but he was ignored. Killing civilians to send a message to their governments—in other words, terrorism—was now official Allied policy.[8]

Walzer writes: "The civilian death toll from Allied terrorism in World War II must have exceeded half a million men, women, and children."[9] It is a revealing irony that the main nations decrying terrorism today are paradigmatic practitioners of it.

Atomic and nuclear weaponry is by definition terrorist weaponry since it allows no discrimination between military and civilian targets. This led the Roman Catholic bishops in the Second Vatican Council to declare: "Any act of war aimed indiscriminately at the destruction of entire cities or of extensive areas along with their population is a crime against God and humanity. It merits unequivocal and unhesitating condemnation."[10]

War: How to Define a Mutant

War is a mutant. Its nature changes; science is the principal change agent. No nation wants to fight today's war with yesterday's weapons. The result is that modern war can no longer honor the "principle of discrimination, that was a hallmark of the 'Just war theory.'"[11] South African archbishop Desmond Tutu speaks the widely known and widely unattended facts: "Some two million children have died in dozens of wars during the past decade. . . . This is more than three times the number of battlefield deaths of American solders in all their wars since 1776. . . . Today, civilians account for more than 90 percent of war casualties."[12]

This means that war as practiced with modern weaponry is terrorism, since by its nature it kills innocent people, including children, to achieve a political goal. Does this mean that all state-sponsored violence (the definition of war) is evil? The United Nations faced up to this question at its founding. International studies professor Richard Falk sums up its solution:

World War II ended with the historic understanding that recourse to war between states could no longer be treated as a matter of national discretion, but must be regulated to the extent possible through rules administered by international institutions. The basic legal framework was embodied in the U.N. Charter, a multilateral treaty largely crafted by American diplomats and legal advisers. Its essential feature was to entrust the Security Council with administering a prohibition of recourse to force (Article 2, Section 4) by member states except in circumstances of self-defense which itself was restricted to responses to a prior "armed attack" (Article 51), and only then until the Security Council had the chance to review the claim.[13]

Articles 43 and 45 of the UN Charter provide for collective response to problems of nations where governments are committing crimes against humanity, as in Darfur and Zimbabwe at this writing. The international will to exercise such a response has been weak due to the long-tenured respect for national sovereignty. Ethically speaking, however, just as parents can lose the right to keep their children when they are abusive, so nations that engage in genocide of their citizens have no legitimate claim to sovereignty. Sovereignty, morally understood, is a trust, and such sovereignty is lost when that trust is violated.

The UN Charter pioneered a new definition of a moral "war." It introduced what has come to be called in ethics the **policing paradigm**. A police force may have to use violence *in extremis,* but it does so in a communitarian context under restrictions of law with follow-up scrutiny when violence is used. Similarly, in the revolutionary UN model, state-sponsored violence (war) would only be used in concert with other nations within the rules of the United Nations. If adhered to, this would be a major disincentive to any nation planning to attack another, realizing that a collectivity of nations would respond.

This changes the *what* of war. No vigilante, preemptive wars can be fought by a single nation. Here is a case where ethics ran ahead of policy. The long momentum of warring hangs like a weight around the neck of humanity. Scholars note that humans have been at peace for only 8 percent of the past 3,400 years of recorded history.[14] Since 1945 there have been 135 wars, most of them in the poor world (often misnamed "developing"), and these killed more than twenty-two million people, "the equivalent of a World War III."[15] The addiction has deep historical roots.

Embarrassment and the Need for Heresy

The human penchant for not knowing *what* we are talking about sometimes is lethal in its effects; sometimes it makes you blush. In an article in the *Journal of Mental Science* entitled "Masturbatory Insanity: The History of an Idea," E. H. Hare points out that only a hundred years ago it was the established belief in the medical profession that masturbation is a frequent cause of mental disorder. In explaining what masturbation is, these medical experts said it is an activity that causes an increased flow of blood to the brain and thus is enervating in its effects. As the first textbook on psychiatry published in the United States put it, masturbation, excessive or not, "produces seminal weakness, impotence, dysury, tabes dorsalis, pulmonary consumption, dyspepsia, dimness of sight, vertigo, epilepsy, hypochondriasis, loss of memory, manalgia, fatuity and death."[16] Other experts deemed this listing incomplete and added that masturbation causes senility, stupidity, melancholy, homosexuality, suicide, hysteria, mania, religious delusions, auditory hallucinations, conceit, defective offspring, and eventually racial decay. The masturbator, according to one expert, is incapable "of any generous impulse or act of loyalty; he is dead to the call of his family, his country, or of humanity."

In the year 1710, a Puritan physician in London wrote a scathing book on masturbation, "the loathsome sin of self-pollution." He reveals here that in his day this vice was widespread among both men and women. He lists some of its disastrous consequences: "disturbance of the stomach and digestion, loss of appetite or ravenous hunger, vomiting, nausea, weakening of the organs of breathing, coughing, hoarseness, paralyses, . . . impotence, lack of libido, . . . back pain, disorders of the eye and ear, . . . paleness, thinness, pimples on the face, decline in intellectual powers, loss of memory, attacks of rage, madness, idiocy, epilepsy, stiffness, fever, and finally suicide."[17] The book was translated into many languages and went into nineteen editions.

In 1758, a Calvinist doctor from Lausanne named Simon-Andre Tissot also published a book on masturbation. Tissot reported that his research indicated that masturbation dries out the brain so that one can hear it rattling around in the cranium. The last edition of this book, a book that spread mass hysteria, appeared in 1905. While detailing the horrors of masturbation, Dr. Tissot offered no remedies, saying he preferred to treat "honorable" diseases.[18]

This was obviously enough to strike terror into the heart of any masturbator. Drastic conclusions followed from this misdefinition. At the medical level, in order to discourage masturbators from indulging their catastrophic penchant, there were recommendations for clitoridectomy, the insertion of a silver ring through the prepuce of the penis, castration, ovariotomy, and severing of the pudendal nerves. Moralists, buying into this, responded with a crescendo of condemnation. Masturbation was seen as a heinous moral crime. With such chaotic perceptual errors as to *what* masturbation is and thus as to what effects it could have, rational moral discourse on the subject was not possible.[19]

The *What* and Moral Meaning

A significant fact about the long-tenured masturbatory hypothesis is that the data to refute it had always been available. As Hare says: "Its fall was not brought about by fresh discoveries or new techniques . . . the evidence had always been there for the taking."[20] What happened was that the misconception became orthodoxy. Even the most astute observers were timid about criticizing the established view. Thus, the error reigned from the early eighteenth century into the twentieth. There were various elements that culturally supported the long stand of this view, but its firm survival in the face of contradictory facts illustrates our capacity to accept error as truth when the error enjoys prestigious auspices. And so on we go, full of confidence, while not knowing *what* we are talking about.

It would be comfortable, but not convincing, to say that this error was freakish and unique, the product of an almost unrepeatable confluence of circumstances, a lonely exception to the standard ability of observant persons to see exactly what is. Rather, this history illustrates the ability of the mind to turn from evidence in preference of socially blessed and widely esteemed misconceptions. The beginning of wisdom would be to see that this seemingly peculiar incident represents a stubborn, native inclination to sidestep the prima facie facts and succumb to prevalent social forces. A major task of good ethics is to be on the lookout for other cases where the evidence is, in Hare's words, "there for the taking," but no one is ready to challenge the false orthodoxy. Enlightened "heresy" is a task of ethics. There is a need for an alert distrust of "the conventional wisdom" and "the accepted view of things." Inventors and heretics are as helpful in ethics as they are in art and in science.

What Is Sex?

Sex is a constant and insistent presence in human life. Humans have had major problems in deciding *what* sex is. In Edinburgh, Scotland, in 1811, Miss Marianne Woods and Miss Jane Pirie, two schoolteachers, were discovered having sex with one another. Though the facts of the case were flagrantly clear, the two women sued their accuser for libel. Over eight years of legal and theological debate, the case worked its way up to the House of Lords, where it was decided in 1819 that the women could not have been having sex since they lacked an instrument of penetration.[21] President Bill Clinton, asserting he did not have sex "with that woman," seems to have concurred with the 1819 House of Lords.

Bernadette Brooten, a scholar of early Judaism and Christianity, observes that "across the centuries men share a fundamental assumption about female sexuality, namely that female pleasure requires a penis."[22] Religion and science, a formidable coupling, conspired in misdefining the *what* of sex. One example from Albertus Magnus, a teacher of Thomas Aquinas, serves as an illustration of the theological input on *what* sex is. Theology's conclusion? Sex is awful. Too much intercourse causes premature aging, baldness, and death, Albert assured us. It also causes you to be followed around by dogs since it causes cadaverous smells. Albert recounts the tragic tale of a monk who realized his "ravenous" passion for a beautiful woman and spent a full night of lust with her. This prodigious monk had sex with her that night "sixty-six times." Not surprisingly, he died the next day. "Because he was a nobleman, his body was opened up. And it was found that his brain had been quite drained out, so that what was left was only the size of a pomegranate, and the eyes were as good as destroyed."[23] For a long period of time in Christianity, sex was justified only when used for procreation, thus stripping most of its *what* away.

Power and the "Superpower" Illusion

The "obvious" is often the least understood. Illusions of obviousness bedraggle the human mind. When a term gets used enough, it is assumed that we have its meaning in secure and peaceful possession. As the twentieth century moved to a close, the United States was anointed in international parlance as "the last remaining superpower." (Some preferred "hyperpower.") The chastening facts of history have begun to pull the piling out from under this entitling. American superpower failed to have its way in Vietnam, Iraq, or Afghanistan. Little Davids with slingshots have been humbling this Goliath. On September 11, 2001, a handful of men with nothing more than box cutters and penknives as weapons managed to destroy the Twin Towers and damage the Pentagon, symbols of American economic and military strength. As Karen Armstrong says, "It was an attack against the United States, but it was a warning to all of us in the First World," since it revealed "a new nakedness and a raw [and new] vulnerability."[24] As technology has grown, so, too, has vulnerability. A digitalized society is brittle. A 1998 study by "information warfare" specialists at the Pentagon estimates that "a properly prepared and well-coordinated attack by fewer than thirty computer virtuosos, strategically located around the world, with a budget of less than ten million dollars could bring the United States to its knees, shutting down everything from electric power grids to air traffic control centers."[25] By 2009, this danger had become a priority for the Obama administration, and given the virtuosity of hackers, it remains a central concern.

Guerillas with the unmatchable trinity of advantages—*invisibility*, *versatility*, and *patience*—have been taunting and tripping the tech-heavy American juggernaut. With this shift in power, the weak are confounding the strong. What is happening is that we are redefining the *what* of power. When Mao Tse-Tung said all power comes from the barrel of a gun, he was wrong. When Lyndon Johnson lamented that he had more power than any person in history but he couldn't use it, he was narrowing power to nuclear explosions. A very shrunken view indeed.

Redefining the *What* of Power

The following diagram, while not pretending to exhaust all the modes of social power, shows fourteen forms of political power. Mao and Johnson were fixated on only one of them, kill-power. The chart has three zones, Violent Power, Nonviolent Power, and Switch, that is, forms of power that can be either violent or nonviolent.

Violent Power

The chart lists three forms of power that are always violent: war, empire and occupation, and propaganda. Propaganda is the deliberate use of misinformation to control the citizenry. Empire

generically is the exploitative control of the weak by the strong, usually in the form of one nation occupying and controlling weaker nations. There are many species of the genus *empire*. Racism, sexism, and heterosexism are all violent control mechanisms employed by dominant groups. They are also forms of the violent imperial instinct.

Nonviolent Power

Nonviolent power has also three categories: (1) First is *Diplomacy and Dialogue,* where mutual respect and reconciliation of competing interests are the guiding principles. State actors whose hands are blunted by militarism and bludgeoning are poor candidates for the needlepoint of diplomacy. The lack of diplomatic skills represents a loss of power, a significant fact in recent United States history. (2) Mahatma Gandhi called the second nonviolent form of power *Satyagraha,* literally truth-power, but referring to modes of *nonviolent resistance.* Gene Sharp, in his classic study of nonviolence resistance successes, notes the efficiency of Gandhi's approach. Britain's Indian colony of three hundred million people was liberated nonviolently at a cost of about eight thousand lives, whereas France's

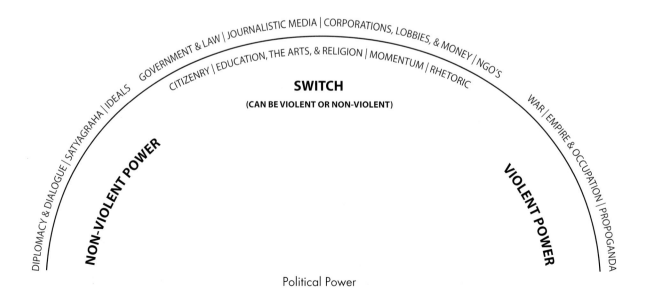

Political Power

Algerian colony of about ten million was liberated by violence, but it cost almost one million lives.[26] (3) *Ideals*. Ideals can emerge and be shared. An ideal is the imagining of a possible good, and ideals have the power to move mountains. Early American ideals of self-governance affected the growth of democracy in the world and gave the United States at that time more influence and esteem than it has with its current military muscle, the largest accumulation of kill-power in history.[27] It was the ideals of communism that gave it its early attraction, and its power faded as its armaments peaked and its ideals abated.

Switch

Most forms of political power are in the Switch category. This starts with government, the agency that has the most carrot and the most stick at its disposal. When government functions as it should, as the prime protector of the common good and the last best refuge for the powerless, it stands at the peak of nonviolent power. Government at its best is the noblest of callings, but it is never the only force, as we saw in our discussion of distributive **justice**. Vying for influence are the powerful forces of the journalistic media as well as corporations and their money-fueled lobbies. Citizen groups and nongovernmental organizations have enormous power. The term *private citizen* is an oxymoron. A citizen (*civis*) is organically and definitionally tied to the *civitatem*, the community. John Dewey saw citizens as offi-

cers of the public good. As Howard Zinn points out in his monumental work *A People's History of the United States*, most social reforms in American history occurred because citizens united, fought, even broke the law to make them happen. Reform rarely comes from on high. Citizen power drives it. Otherwise elites control. A body politic with an uninformed and inactive citizenry is like a human body without a leg.[28]

Education is another power closer to the nonviolent side of the spectrum, but it, too, can be violent when it privileges some classes or takes sides with one gender or perpetuates privilege-based, class-based myths. Momentum is also prominent in social power. Ideas and institutions, even good ideas and institutions, can linger on beyond their usefulness. Change can be disturbing, and so momentum reigns. Needed reforms get ignored as we go with the tide. Thus, the eighteenth-century ideas that shaped the United States get biblical status, and reforms needed by twenty-first-century problems are resisted. The same is true for the United Nations, where allocations of power reflective of post–World War II conditions are set in concrete, limiting the effectiveness of this indispensable world forum.

Finally in this "switch" listing is the bruised word *rhetoric*. The word comes from the Greek *retor*, referring to someone who excelled in the esteemed art of eloquence. That is how Aristotle used it, and that is how it came into the Latin of Cicero. For both thinkers,

THINKING CRITICALLY

Law professor Charles Lawrence writes on the violent power of naming: "In recent years, American campuses have seen a resurgence of racial violence and a corresponding rise in the incidence of verbal and symbolic assault and harassment to which blacks and other traditionally subjugated groups are subjected. There is a heated debate in the civil liberties community concerning the proper response to incidents of racist speech on campus. Some believe . . . that racist speech . . . should be regulated by the university of some public body and [others] believe that racist expression should be protected from all public regulation."

—In William H. Shaw, ed., *Social and Personal Ethics*

7.3

such a person is an important civil servant who wields useful power. The study of rhetoric was for a long time a distinguished part of philosophy. The term has sadly become pejorative and is usually coupled with adjectives like *empty*. Eloquence can cut either way: there were some eloquent spokespersons in Nazi Germany, but as a positive, rhetoric is a neglected part of the art of leadership that can wake citizens from their lethargy and stir their response to societal needs.

Once again, the misdefined *what* diminishes reality contact on the basic category of *power*.

The *What* of Abortion

The question of abortion has been a roiling debate plagued by lack of definition. It has extended into discussions of embryonic stem-cell research. In the extreme position, a little cluster of embryonic cells, about the size of the period that ends this sentence, has been described as a "person," with the same moral standing enjoyed by children and adults. Once again, misdefinition gets embarrassing. Truth well grasped is refreshing. It doesn't embarrass. If embryonic stem cells constitute personhood, remarkable conclusions would follow. The population of the United States would swell by more than ten million. More "persons" could be claimed as dependents for Internal Revenue purposes. If the conception occurred during a vacation in Umbria, this "person" is an Italian, since that would be its "place of origin." The truly convinced might insist on search warrants of the menstrual flow of sexually active women to see if, perchance, there is a citizen in there. And for theists, God would become the principal abortion provider, since most fertilized eggs do not make it to implantation. All of that is unnecessary mental roughness resulting from a wrong *what*.

Better the wisdom cited by authors Daniel Dombrowski and Robert Deltete in their book *A Brief, Liberal, Catholic Defense of Abortion*, where they show the grounds for the position that the early **fetus**, while it is human tissue, does not have the moral standing of a person. This position has deep roots even in the Christian tradition, and indeed in the traditions of all major religions. Sometimes referred to as "delayed ensoulment," this view holds "that the fetus becomes morally considerable between twenty-four and thirty-two weeks when sentiency, and then the cerebral cortex, starts to function." Dombrowski and Deltete add, "Like Saints Augustine and Thomas Aquinas we see sentiency as a necessary if not sufficient condition for personhood."[29] It is significant and illustrative of the "state of the question" that these are two Catholic authors, professors at a Catholic Jesuit university.

When Naming Is Knowing and Misnaming Is Not

The terms *date rape* and *marital rape* only entered the popular lexicon in the last generation. Prior to these acts getting named, victims were hard pressed to describe what had happened to them. Unnamed evils have greater leeway. Their anonymity lends immunity. The unnamed is as dangerous as the misnamed.

When top officers of major corporations are paid a million dollars a week, their boards of directors defend the practice and name it as "incentive pay." The falsity lies in the claim that without forty-thousand-dollar-an-hour wages these executives would not find the motivation to do their job. Common sense could counter that if it takes you a million dollars a week to have incentive to do your job, you should find work you are more interested in doing. A proper naming would be to call this greed. Another accurate name would be theft. When such exorbitant pay is given to some persons in a corporation, there is less left in the money pie for research, for on-the-floor workers, for stockholders, and for contributions to the supportive neighborhoods of their plants. *Incentive* is a grand word, and it serves well to cover what is really going on: greed and the misallocation of funds.

The corporate world can teach us lessons on the power of naming. *Welfare* in American parlance is pejorative, used to demean the poor who need and get government help. Ronald Reagan spoke famously of "welfare queens." However, when the savings-and-loan scandal broke in the 1980s and when Fannie Mae and Freddie Mac sank in 2008, the dip into the public treasury was described as a "rescue." The CEOs were not called welfare kings.

Something similar was done with disastrous effect when the accurately called Department of War had a name change to the Department of Defense.

More misnaming is found in the terms *developed* and *developing* nations. These misnomers are enthroned in economics and in world institutions like the United Nations, the World Bank, and the International Monetary Fund. The deception lies in their normative connotations. "Developed" is what ought to be: "developing" is on its way to the promised land of "developed." Meanwhile, back in reality, those nations called developed are the prime ecological culprits on the planet. Further, the promise that those not yet at this pinnacle of consumption can get there is mendacious. There is enough on this planet, as Gandhi said, for our need but not for our greed. The well-off are pillaging the poor. For example, the population of the Netherlands

> consumes the output equivalent of fourteen times as much productive land as is contained within its own borders. The deficits are made up from other nations. . . . If sharing and use were to be equalized on the planet (an impossibility to be sure) a Dutch person would be able each day to travel 15.5 miles by car, 31 miles by bus, 40 miles by train or 6.2 miles by plane

and to take a flight from Amsterdam to Rio de Janeiro only once every twenty years.[30]

Ecologist David Pimentel and his colleagues argue that only one to two billion people could live on this planet with a level of consumption roughly equivalent to the current per capita standard for Europe and the United States.[31] Talk of endless development with hyperconsumers inviting the deprived to a feast without food underlies the popular misnomers *developed* and *developing*. Since false meanings tend to bundle, there are other untruths in these terms. They imply that to truly "develop," an economy must be maintained by manufacturing and using up limited natural resources as though they were unlimited. This leaves out the possibility of a social economy that meets earth and human needs in a massive, job-providing, organized effort.

More fallacy is wrapped in the term *sustainable development*. It implies that endless growth is possible. *Sustainable community* would be a realistic ideal.

Overloading the *What?*

Significant as this first of the ethical questions is, it can be misused to close the door on subsequent discussion. However morally suggestive the first-stage answers are, the true moral meaning will only emerge when all the questions are asked and all the circumstances are accounted for as far as that is possible. It is never completely possible. It is humbling to think that we will never know exhaustively and comprehensively what we are talking about. Human knowing is a quest that never fully captures the quarry. Modesty, even when we have done our best, is always in order.

Thus, the *what* question should not be answered as though it were the last. One moralist, for example, defines sexual intimacy as "the marital act."

Having done that, he could, with no further questioning, label all nonmarital sex evil. That is too swift by far. His argument:

> Since sexual intercourse and its proximate antecedents represent *total personal* exchange, they can be separated from total personal relationship (marriage) only by undermining their truly human, their expressive character—in short their significance. . . . Regardless of the emotional concomitants, the high purpose, the repeated protestations of love, this cannot be an act of love toward that person, but must remain objectively even if not consciously, an act of manipulation.[32]

That is a pure example of overloading the definition of sex. The result is a reduction of one of the most complex realities of human life into a limpid but unreal simplicity. To say that all sex outside a formal marriage is immoral and manipulative, without any other circumstances considered, is taboo thinking. It stops the inquiry with the *what* question, with all the human meaning awaiting in the answers to the other questions (in the hub of the wheel model) untapped.

At the opposite extreme of oversimplification would be someone defining sex as just one of the cool things two people can do, on a par with chatting, taking a walk, or sharing a beer. This would bypass all the psychological, physical, and possibly medical implications involved in "having sex." Both positions are examples of short-circuited ethics. Both positions are foolish.

With that said, we move on to the other essential, eye-opening questions.

Summary of Key Themes

- Never underestimate the power of naming.
- Propaganda excels in the perverse art of misnaming.
- Terms like *capitalism*, *social*, *terrorism*, and even *war* are used with minimal or no clear definition.
- Power has many forms ranging from violent to nonviolent.
- Taboos are often based on misdefinition.

Key Terms

Fetus
Is/ought
Just war theory
Justice
Policing paradigm
Socialism/socialist
War

Questions for Discussion

1. Would there be a different moral evaluation of abortion at one month, three months, or six months?
2. When a nation is described as "developed" the term usually refers to industrial development. What would be the marks of a morally "developed" nation?

Suggestions for Further Reading

Hedges, Chris. *What Every Person Should Know about War.* New York: Free Press, 2003.

Lakoff, George. *Don't Think of an Elephant: Know Your Values and Frame the Debate.* White River Junction, Vt.: Chelsea Green, 2004.

Singer, Peter. "The Place of Nonhumans in Environmental Issues." In William H. Shaw, ed., *Social and Personal Ethics.* Belmont, Calif.: Wadsworth, 1993.

Deepening the Probe

Why? How? Who? When? Where?

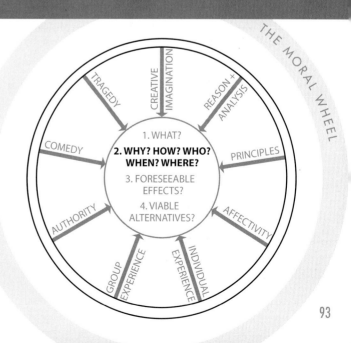

THERE IS NOTHING LIKE a case to concentrate the mind. Here is a real-life story told to me by the parents involved that shows the need to ask *all* of the questions in the hub of the wheel model.

A little baby girl was born and the parents rejoiced. She seemed fine. Pictures were taken and the proud father went off to his work as a mechanic in a garage. There he distributed cigars and shared the happy news. Halfway through the day he received a phone call at work from the obstetrician. "We just examined your daughter, and she has a syndrome that causes severe retardation." The man stood stunned with the phone in his hand; he later told me he never forgot the precise spot on the floor where he had been standing when he heard that news.

At first blush, and asking only the *what* question, the doctor's action may seem unimpeachable. Here was the doctor sharing essential information with the parent. In fact, the doctor's action was immoral when all the other questions complete the picture. *How* he delivered the news was wrong. It was the wrong *where* and the wrong *when* and one *who* was missing. The father received the news alone with no support around him. The mother was not yet informed, raising the *why* question. The shock *effects* of this insensitivity would linger forever. And what were the *alternatives*?

Suppose the doctor, upon discovering the tragic news, went to the mother and found that the father would be back at the hospital around 6:00 P.M. when he got off work. Suppose then the doctor said, "I'll be here then and will stop back to see you." Then, in this supposition of an alternative approach, the doctor called the parents of a child with a similar disorder and asked if they could be available at the hospital when he broke the news, in case these parents would be helped by speaking to parents who had had the same experience and had lived with it. Suppose the doctor knew that the parents were very closely attached to their minister and so he called her and let her know that her support might be needed.

Suppose, in a word, the doctor had asked all the questions—questions that are not "merely academic" in dealing with life—and done it all differently. The tragedy would still be there, but the immorality and insensitivity would not. The doctor would have obeyed the first rule of medicine and the first rule of ethics: *primum non nocere*—your first duty is to do no harm.

Of *Why* and *How* and Ends and Means

Good ethics is characterized by a passion for knowing what one is talking about. Asking the right questions is the way to get there. The hub of the wheel model represents the expository phase of ethics, the phase in which one hopes all of the reality-revealing questions get asked. The enemy here is the unasked question; the goal is the greatest achievable completeness. As simple and obvious as the questions might appear, the annals of human moral discourse indicate that, here again, the obvious is easily missed. All the questions are diagnostic tools, surgical probes to uncover the real meaning of what is going on.

Ethics is a series of lessons on how the human mind knows and how moral knowing is linked to other fields of study such as the social sciences. I will again intersperse this chapter with a variety of examples, thus illustrating the probative power of good questioning.

Motive: Understanding the *Why*

Motive, the *why* (also called intention or end or purpose), is key. Every detective knows that. So, too, do lovers. Until you know *why* something is happening, you don't know what is going on or what is happening. Two men rush into an unoccupied burning home, removing valuables. One is doing it to take things for himself; the other is doing it to rescue things for the owners. The *what* is the same: the *why* makes one a thief and the other a friend. Also, the means you use (the *how* you go about it) are telling. Strangely enough, given how important they are, the *why* and *how* are also the gateway to an enormous amount of confusion regarding ends and means.

For example, it is a prevalent popular error among nations, institutions, and private persons that if your end (**motive**, intention, purpose) is good, the means to that end are thereby blessed and good. Anyone who has experienced the harm done by well-intentioned people should wince at this idea. Still, motivation is so important that it is seductively easy to think that a good end (motive) does sanctifiy whatever means you use to achieve it. In fact, an axiom from moral philosophy seems to say just that: "The end sanctifies the means" (*Finis sanctificat media*). And some have defended the thesis "When the end is licit, the means are licit." The danger in these words is that lofty ends can be a heady wine. Indeed, they have a maniacal potential to cover over many sordid means that are deemed necessary along the road to the glorious end. The widespread, documented stories of torture in a number of nations are all set against a backdrop of unimpeachably noble goals that these nations are allegedly pursuing. Whether one's end is "to remain profitable" or "to make love"—both laudable ends—the means used and the manner of proceeding in the pursuit of those ends are often un-ambiguously outrageous.

Means:
Understanding the *How*
Russian philosopher Nicolas Berdyaev humbles the *why* when he says that the means you choose may even be more important than your alleged motive: "It may actually be said that in a sense 'the means' which a man uses are far more important than 'the ends' which he pursues, for they express more truly what his spirit is. If a man strives for freedom by means of tyranny, for love by means of hatred, for brotherhood by means of dissension, for truth by means of falsity, his lofty aim

is not likely to make our judgment of him more lenient."[1]

In effect, an end conceived as noble and good can blind you to what you are doing. If the end is seen also as having a sacred dimension (as is regularly the case in nationalistic matters or with religious groups), it can be more distortional than a pitcher of martinis. Let's take a closer look at the disasters that happen.

When Means Become Ends

Means have a sneaky way of pulling a *coup d'etat* on ends, usurping their place. A government is a means to promote the common good, but the preservation of that government can easily come to be seen as more important, and the common good will be unhesitatingly sacrificed to it. This, in fact, is a pattern, not an exception, in the behavior of governments, whether socialist or capitalist.

Work, Wealth, and War
Another example: A job is a means to survival and, hopefully, to personal fulfillment. It can become the end of one's existence, so that family, health, creative leisure, simple fun, and the occasional joy of *dolce far' niente* ("the sweetness of doing nothing") can be utterly subordinated. Even life can be sacrificed to the job, as many premature deaths would seem to show. The seductive pull of the means can make you forget your true end, giving the means primary standing. The

---

THINKING CRITICALLY

Archbishop Desmond Tutu was involved in the Truth and Reconciliation Commission in South Africa, where people faced those who had committed crimes against them during apartheid. He sought to harmonize the *how* and the *why,* saying: "We believe in restorative justice. In South Africa, we are trying to find our way toward healing and the restoration of harmony within our communities. If retributive justice is all you seek through the letter of the law, you are history. You will never know stability. You need something beyond reprisal. You need forgiveness."

8.1

popular term *workaholic* describes someone who has become addicted to means-made-end.

Wealth is another means that often becomes an end in itself. Wealth is a means to happiness and well-being, but when it becomes an end, persons under its sway will sacrifice both happiness and well-being and even their lives for wealth. A sure sign of wealth's shift from means to end is the inability to know when enough is enough. If wealth is treated as a means, it is less avidly pursued when the end has been satisfactorily achieved. If the wealth has become an end in itself, then there is no inner logic for ever saying *enough.* Money that we start out owning can come to own us. There is a fundamental irrationality in transmuting means into ends, but humans are at it all the time.

Military budgets are intended to provide security and peace to make the good life possible. The same budget can take on the status of an uncontested end, becoming a consuming demon that threatens security, peace, and the good life. As infrastructure crumbles, excuses are found for useless wars. Czar Nicholas II of Russia, in his proposal for the first Hague Conference in 1898, spotted the fatal flaw in equating arms and safety: "In proportion as the armaments of each power increase, so do they less and less fulfill the objects which the Governments have set before themselves. . . . It appears evident that if this state of things were prolonged, it would inevitably lead to the very cataclysm which it is designed to avert, and the horrors of which make every thinking man shudder in advance."[2]

If armaments debilitate the economy and distract from necessary expenditures for research on energy, water supply, nonharmful waste disposal, the alleviation of poverty and hunger, and so forth, then it is true that "military technology is a Hydra: for each weapon that seems familiar and containable, others rise up threatening to defy containment."[3] If arms breed fear and thus more conflict and then more arms and more fear,

then armaments are means run wild, cut loose from the desired ends. In the words of Nicholas II, "They less and less fulfill the objects" for which they were intended. The *how* supersedes the *why.* By consuming and distracting expenditures, they take away from the overall power of the nation, the *why* of the effort in the first place. Arms races enfeeble nations. By reaching genocidal proportions, weapons cannot even be rationally used, since they could not do more good than harm. The ends are lost; the means go roaring on to ever bigger and senseless budgets. And so indeed, in these United States this has come to pass.

Beyond Dualism

Wisdom is found in the words of Jawaharlal Nehru of India, who said that ideally "perhaps ends and means are not really separable and form together one organic whole."[4] Berdyaev is more precise: "One of the main problems of ethics is to overcome the dualism between means and ends, and make the means more and more conformable to ends."[5] In quotidian life, however, the ends/means split perdures.

Institutions and nations are the main culprits. They simply allege that if their *why* is good, all is well. The Soviets crushed the Hungarian proletariat revolt "to promote the revolution of the proletariat." Oops! Good *why* perhaps; bad everything else. The goal of World War I was to be "the war that ends all wars." A laudable *why* with bloodbath as its *how.* The soldier standing over the ashes of Ben Tre in Vietnam said, "We had to destroy this village in order to save it." The motive of British imperialism was to assume "the white man's burden." French imperialism was *une mission civilatrice* ("a civilizing mission"). American "Shock and Awe" in Iraq was to spread freedom and democracy. A good *why* is a classical alibi.

Dissecting Motives

Motive is as subtle and complex as it is influential. First of all, it is numerically complex. There is never one reason *why* anyone does anything. Nor do any of us know in a conscious way all the motivational forces that move us to act—or not to act. As psychiatry and psychology began in recent times to peek into the subconscious, we came to know better that we are shot through with determinisms and with contradictory motivational elements. Egoistic and primitively instinctive motives can be found operating in tandem with generous and highly idealistic ones. Any notion of "purity of intention" in the older, simplistic sense is passé. The older psychology of freedom felt that freedom was normal, though it might at times be battered and even reduced to nothing by storms of fear or passion. When the storm passes, freedom returns with the fullness that is thought normal. Now we know that a panoply of motivational elements operate in the production of behavior. *Why* we are acting, then, remains in part an unpenetrable mystery.[6]

It's not hopeless, however. We can get a solid sense of motivation if we can avoid the simplism of a mechanical behaviorism that would reduce freedom to nothing, and get away from the old psychology that exaggerates the extent of our psychological freedom. Moral assessment is possible as long as it is chastened by an awareness of the complexity of human motivation. A person who steals, or murders, or the executives engaged in "crime in the suites," may be so controlled by neurotic, unfree factors as to require psychiatric attention. Or they may be discernibly free and responsible to the extent where moral consideration of one's motives is in order. Law has always struggled with whether malefactors need treatment or merit corrective response. Ethics cannot avoid that struggle.

Blossom to Root

The assessment of motive is not just of introspective importance. *Why* something is done is par-

tially but essentially constitutive of what is done.[7] As persons grow and develop in what I have called the foundational moral experience (FME), *community*, something qualitatively better than coexistence, develops. The developing unity and harmony of human life are kneaded through with and knit together by respect, justice, and improving modalities of friendship. Motives that are not grounded in a healthy FME will disrupt community. All human actions either build or disrupt community among persons. Bad motives, however attentively concealed, will seep out and have negative impact. Actions that are externally good but befouled by bad motives, though less disruptive and not without helpful effect, will not humanize persons into communitarian life. The poison will seep out. Defects at the foundational level of caring can be only temporarily concealed and only temporarily constructive.

The link between motive and the foundational moral experience is one of blossom to root. Morally good motivation could only grow from some successful development of that fundamental grounding of moral experience. In this sense, motive is not just numerically, but also qualitatively, complex.

Process, Not Stasis

Furthermore, motive, like the foundational experience, is processual, not static. The motives that move a couple in a young marriage while they are still under the exuberant spell of early romance will not be the same as the motives that may move them in their cherishing in old age. In a true sense it can be said that no couple stays married for the same reason they get married. This need not be interpreted cynically. There may be better reasons (motives) for staying married than there were for getting married. Some of the same things may be done later on in a process but done from motives that tap deeper and better wellsprings of affection. The external sameness is only apparent. Process, of course, can also go in reverse. It is not only true, as Augustine said, that what is begun in fear may come to be perfected in love. It is, conversely, also true that what is begun in love may come to be maintained only by fear.[8] Love's lively beginnings might wither and be atrophied in routine or slowly aborted when one party develops in healthful ways and the other does not. Processes can go forward or backward.

Moral motives can range in their moral quality from the superficial to the heroic. This, too, serves to illustrate the signal importance of motive in determining the moral meaning of behavior. The breadth of moral reality is revealed in responding to the question *Why?*

Volition and Velleity

He who wills the end wills the means necessary
to that end. (*Qui vult finem vult media.*)

The old saw has it that the road to hell is paved with good intentions. Good motives and intentions are often the mask that hypocrisy wears. There is a lot to that. Superficially good motives are like playful flirtations. They lack the strength needed for follow-through. Yet they can serve a devious purpose by making us feel that our heart is in the right place. For example, it is encouraging if someone says he is in favor of racial integration. It is suspicious if he then opposes all the means necessary to that end, such as a certain amount of busing, the use of **affirmative action** where other avenues to fairness are closed, reallocation of funds to address the problem vigorously, and so forth. He who opposes the means necessary to an end opposes the end.[9]

The same applies to the will to have children. If one is not ready for the enormous follow-through, then the desire for children is not real. Likewise, the avowed desire of business management to

be ecologically responsible when there is no readiness to spend what is needed in money and imagination represents a motivational and moral failure. If you do not will the necessary means, you are blowing smoke. All pious protestations about one's commitment to good ends are hollow if there is no corresponding commitment to the means to get there.

In Latin, there is a distinction made between *volitio* and *velleitas* (which can be inelegantly Englished as "volition" and "velleity"). *Volition* comes from *volo*, meaning "I will"; *velleitas* comes from *vellem*, meaning "I would like." **Velleity** moves willing from the forthright indicative to the hedged subjunctive. This means that many apparent volitions are merely velleities. **Volition** refers to what you really will; velleity, to what you would will, were things more to your liking and less taxing. Many apparent volitions, from "I love you" to "Our corporation is committed to improving the environment" or "We will build in a safety net for the poor," are but feeble velleities underneath their fervid exteriors.

Velleities: Epics of Deviousness

It can be argued that the U.S. Medicare and Medicaid systems are examples of velleities. Their goals are excellent, but they fall short on means. They were initiated (over objections that they were socialistic and the beginning of "socialized medicine") because of the problem of poor children and adults lacking health care (Medicaid) and to help the uninsured aged (Medicare). Problem: These programs lack the funding needed to achieve their goals. Close to fifty million children, men, and women are still uninsured. Were these two programs volitions rather than velleities, they would be sufficiently funded to cover all their avowed cohorts. This prompts some to argue for a single-payer system such as exists in Canada and the Scandinavian countries and elsewhere where health care is virtually free, countries where volition rather than a velleity is in place. That these countries actually save money by doing it this way adds to the weight of this argument.

Not only would it be moral to make sure that no child dies for lack of an appendectomy, but it would also be cheaper. Velleities are epics of deviousness, and the facts always embarrass velleities. Harvard University School of Medicine professors David Himmelstein and Steffie Woolhandler write, "Only a single-payer system of national health care can save what we estimate is the $350 billion wasted annually on medical bureaucracy, and redirect those funds to expanded coverage."[10] $350 billion is suctioned out of the American health-care system by lobby-braced insurance companies with exorbitant administrative costs and bloated salaries for top executives. These insurance companies have what the Harvard professors call a "stranglehold on health care" in the United States. This is another case where we could do well by doing good. We could cover all the sick and save money.

A Canadian Comparison. People who do not have insurance neglect their health until they are in an emergency situation. When they arrive at the "tertiary health-care unit," the emergency room, where the most expensive care must be given to them by law, we pay heavily for them. A simple and cheap antibiotic could have cured them two weeks earlier. Alternatives are right at our doorstep. An American woman living in Montreal writes: "Last year my husband and I needed two surgeries, four emergency room visits, radiation and chemotherapy, nuclear medicine cardiology and assorted tests. Our care was timely, compassionate, comparable to care in the United States—and free." She continues: "Our Quebec friends cannot comprehend the notion of 'pre-existing conditions' or 'denial of payment,' and we've come to view the American health care system as backward and discriminatory. . . . The United States provides optimal care for a few, no care at all for

many. Canada provides good care for all its people." That portrait may be too rosy since there are problems in Canada also, but as Nicholas Kristof reports, "America's health care system spends nearly twice as much per person as Canada's . . . yet our infant mortality rate is 40 percent higher than Canada's and American mothers are 57 percent more likely to die in childbirth than Canadian ones."[11]

When the Canadian comparison is made, shrieks of pain are heard about the long lines and long waits for care in Canada. That is true at times since the good system in place is not always adequately funded (as is true in England and elsewhere), but as one Canadian writes, "While Canadians may complain about lines from time to time, and improvement is certainly possible, few would be willing to trade their health care system for the American system."[12]

A writer from Denmark says, "Here in Denmark, taxes are high, but everyone has health coverage (not to mention free university education). Yes, it is 'socialized medicine,' but it works."[13]

Such individual witnesses do not a definitive argument make. There are complaints about efficiency and waits in the Canadian and Danish systems, and in hard economic times governments cut back on their health-care systems, causing delays. Careful and honest ethics does not hide from the objections to one's advocated position and almost always profits from them. The methodological point about velleities is this: if you honestly will the end, you will work to supply and perfect the means to that end. If the Canadian system, for example, lags at times and imposes undue restrictions on care, it slips into the velleity category also.

The grim news is that velleities kill, in the United States or in Canada. The uninsured in the United States die at a higher rate than the insured. Nancy Frazier O'Brien writes that it is "estimated that more than seven Texans of working age and more than eight Californians of working age die each day because they don't have health insurance." The reasons are clear. The "uninsured Americans are less likely to have a regular source of health care outside the emergency room, more likely to go without screenings and preventive care, and often postpone or forgo needed medical care or fail to fill needed prescriptions." And in a biting irony: "The uninsured also pay more for the medical care they do get. Because they cannot negotiate the same discounts on hospital and doctor bills that insurance companies do, uninsured patients often pay 2.5 times more than patients with health insurance."[14] When a national health, care plan in Canada or elsewhere is underfunded, patients also die.

Velleity and Illogic. Good ethics points out logical lapses. A single-payer system—call it a fully financed Medicaid—would cover all poor children and adults, but only if it is adequately funded. That would be a volition. The current American system is a velleity. It costs more and people die. The same is true for Medicare. The illogic built into this particular velleity shows when you realize that we really only have two options regarding the poor: *pay for the poor* or *pay for the poor*. That is, you pay for them in a rational, economical, fully financed governmental system without the insurance company overhead, or you pay for them in the emergency room, which is costlier and kills some of them.

Twenty years ago at this writing, my son Tom developed meningitis. It turned out to be the viral type, and he responded quickly to the usual therapy. In case it was the bacterial form of the disease, however, he was also given penicillin, one of the cheapest antibiotics. When the bill came for the penicillin, the cost was $2,000. This is cost shifting, not fair pricing. Tom enjoyed good insurance. Several children on the same floor probably had none. So Tom's insurance paid for them. Again, you pay for the poor rationally or you pay subversively through cost shifting . . . or you leave the poor uncared for and dying at a higher rate.

Some years ago I lectured at what could be called a socialist hospital. The doctors told me of a case in which a seriously ill patient was being treated by neurosurgeons, cardiologists, endocrinologists, and expert nursing care. The patient had no concerns about paying for the care or receiving a denial-of-care notice. It was, after all, a socialist hospital. The hospital was in Minneapolis, the Veterans Administration Hospital. Unfortunately, as in countries with national health-care systems, the veterans hospitals can fail disastrously, as veterans from the Iraq wars will testify. Both national and private health-care plans can fail from lack of volition and false priorities and lapses. The ideal of healthy follow-through that is the mark of volition easily slips into velleity.

Inconsistencies when exposed can be instructive. It is a peculiar fact that in these United States we do have some rather socialized medicine, but only for certain privileged groups. These are elected politicians, soldiers and veterans, and prisoners in our jails. They enjoy guarantees that the uninsured lack. This could lead to an argument for adding one more group to the privileged politicians, soldiers, and felons: all the children in the United States. So far, we have not done that. The children are not old enough to become politicians, soldiers, or felons. You have to be an adult, a certain kind of adult, to get health care guarantees in the United States. *Illogical* is the gentlest word for that situation. Again, however, even in these three cases of preferential treatment, volition slips into velleity and the preferred groups, except for high-ranking polilticians, get nowhere close to state-of-the-art care.

Velleities and the Law

Sad to tell, velleities abound. To add one more—and again it affects the poor—let's turn to law. When you enter the Supreme Court of the United States, you will see the proud proclamation: *Equal Justice under Law*. Now, the ethical question: Is that statement a volition or a velleity? Supreme Court Justice Lewis Powell was trying to declare it a volition when he said: "Equal justice under law is not merely a caption on the facade of the Supreme Court building, it is perhaps the most inspiring ideal of our society. It is one of the ends for which our entire legal system exists. . . . It is fundamental that justice should be the same, in substance and availability, without regard to economic status."

Now, the facts: In 2005, while the nation was spending more than two billion dollars a week invading Iraq, the Legal Services Corporation, which provides civil legal services to the poor, received $331 million. That starvation budget proves that the Supreme Court proclamation is a vile velleity. Using Wisconsin as an example, John Ebbott, the director of Legal Action of Wisconsin, writes that in 2004, only one of eight impoverished applicants for representation was able to get representation from Legal Action of Wisconsin.[15] For comparison purposes, Mr. Ebbott notes that the repair of a downtown Milwaukee freeway interchange was estimated to cost $810 million.

Added to the list of disgraceful national velleities would be the No Child Left Behind Act and the Clean Air Act and other such initiatives where a need is seen but the response is a half-hearted velleity, to which the ethical term *hypocrisy* applies.

Does the End Justify the Means?

Contrary to popular wisdom, some questions are best answered by saying that they are bad questions. "Does the end justify the means?" is one of them. It is bad because it is misconceived. An end does not justify a means any more than a means justifies an end. Ends and means must be judged in relational tension to one another and to all the other essential circumstances. When we have completed all the questions that are within the

wheel model, we will have shown all the dimensions of any situation that have to be considered to know what that situation means morally. The ends and means will only be two of the many elements that constitute the moral significance of the case to be judged. To ask if the end justifies the means makes no more sense than to ask if the end justifies the effects. Like the detective who achieves insight when he sees how *all* the clues before him relate to one another, so in matters moral, insight is achieved when we see how *all* the circumstances relate to one another. Thus, the answer to the bad question that heads this paragraph is *no.*

That said, what can we say in conclusion about the troubled marriage between ends and means? At the least, we could be attuned to the ethical insight of Augustine when he wrote in a letter to a certain Darius that it was better to maintain peace by peace than to maintain peace by war. This was the same Augustine who had helped to baptize the theory of just war and thus give justified war a respectability in Christendom that it had not previously enjoyed. And yet he sensed the anomaly of justifying such a slaughterous means to so gentle an end as peace.

It is not always possible to have a happy harmony between our ends and our means. We may have to be harsh or, in an extreme situation, violent in defense of justice, integrity, and peace. But the goal is that quoted above from Berdyaev, to "make the means more and more conformable to ends." Disharmony between ends and means is violent and a sign of our moral primitivity. Comfort with it is deadly and inhibits moral development. A simple term for such comfort is *moral decadence.*

If, to return to Augustine's example, we must maintain peace by war, then the situation must be faced in the "mournful mood" Augustine recommended to those going to war, and this tragic necessity must summon us urgently to create the conditions that require less drastic remedies. Treating as "normal" means that are discordant with our ends, treating them as part of the nature of things, the "price of doing business" (as is regularly alleged in politics and in the corporate world), is a surrender to the anomalous and is morally deviate. It also represents an implicit faith that when the chips are down, good ends really do justify any means—a position that is, as we have seen, ethically untenable.

The Moral Status of Style

The *how* question points us not only to means but also to style. A well-intentioned *what* done badly is evil, as in the case of the well-intentioned doctor's inept call to the father about his newborn's disability.

Style might at first seem nonessential, in the category of trimmings, and not something that would make behavior moral or immoral. This is due partly to the fact that concern with style is often associated with superficiality. The superficiality, of course, comes not from the concern with style, but from the concern with little else. This is seen in persons who stress external image and "public relations" to the neglect of substantial performance. The sham of this approach gives style a bad name.

In the terms of our questioning process here, *what* you do may be morally promising. *Why* you are doing it may be heroically noble. But the style may make the action decisively immoral. The Irish story of the man who undertook to inform a woman of her husband's death

provides a blunt illustration. "Are you the widow Murphy?" he asked. "No," she replied. "You are now!" he said and departed. It would be hard to criticize *what* he was doing and *why*, but the *how* was an epic of insensitivity. The way you break news (your style) may, like the way you make love, be of the essence. The way you end a romantic relationship will be morally critical. The way you disagree or correct may make your behavior humanizing (moral) or atrocious. A scolding style of correction is demeaning and less effective, even with children. Style is the soul of diplomacy. A good diplomat is one who knows that being right is not enough, that having military and economic power is not enough, since how you communicate and deal, how much respect you *feel* and show, often gives the definitive tilt to negotiations. Diplomats who do not know that should be fired.

The reason for the importance of style is that it bodies forth the inclinations of the heart. A nation that goes about doing good violently will not be perceived as peaceful in its intent whatever its ideological protestations. Help given arrogantly will produce adverse reactions, however needed the help given may be. Aid that insults will disrupt. This is so because the *how* is intimately related to the *why*. *How* you do something tells much of *why* you are doing it. The *how* can strip away the covers from the avowed motive and show the real motive, because *how* reflects the foundational moral experience and serves as an index of the development of that experience. The insensitive may only see *what* you are doing and only hear your expressed motivation. The sensitive will

> ### THINKING CRITICALLY
>
> *How* we communicate may be the major factor in the moral climate of the twenty-first and following centuries. Internet expert Mark Pesce says, "It is not an overstatement to frame the World Wide Web as an innovation as important as the printing press—it may be as important as the birth of language itself . . . in its ability to completely refigure the structure of civilization."
>
> —Mark Pesce,
> *Proximal and Distal Unity*
>
> 8.2

detect your deepest spirit in the *how* (manner, mode, style, and means) of what you do.

During the Vietnam War, there was a race riot among Marines on base at Camp Lejeune. Afterward, officers were assigned to interview the Marines who participated in this vicious battle. One officer was asked to interview three Marines, all of them African American. He pressed them to try to discover the roots of the bitterness that had exploded. He learned that day the wisdom of Aristotle, who said the insult is the root of all rebellion. Some of the things he heard seemed so trivial, so insignificant that one might consider the response neurotic. One Marine mentioned how when he purchased something in the camp store, the change was put on the counter, not into his hand as was done with the white Marines. Another Marine was decorated for bravery along with four white Marines. He claimed that the general who pinned on the medals seemed to pause longer and be more at ease with the white Marines.[16]

Neurotic? No. Insulting. If your hand is repulsive, you are repulsive. If heroic bravery on the battlefield involving saving the lives of white Marines does not bring you into the comfort zone of the white general, the poison of racism runs deep and scorches the spirit. *How* is more telling than *what* or *why*. Interaction among persons is not merely physical but is, rather, a community-building (or community-disrupting) activity. The sensitivity that specifies our style of acting will easily have greater impact on community than what we do.

On Knowing Who's Who

The fourth morally diagnostic question is *Who?* If it is true, as I have alleged, that we often do not know *what* we are talking about, it is an equally sad truth that we often do not know *who* it is we are dealing with or even, more drastically, *who* we are.

An example: A clinic was built to provide care for the Stoney Aboriginal peoples in Western Canada. So far the *what* and the *why* look good in this venture. The trip-up occurred with the *who*. The clinic had small, well-equipped examining rooms. Too small—made to accommodate two or three people. Religious studies professor Harold Coward reports: "When a young woman or older teenage girl would arrive with gynecological problems, she would be accompanied by her mother, aunts, and grandmother. All would insist on going back to the examining room together. When the doctor was taking the history, often it would be the grandmother who would do the talking, saying when the girl had had her last period, and so forth. Everyone knew everything."[17]

Coward makes the distinction between I-self and We-self cultures. I-self cultures see persons almost atomistically as individual agents with little sense of connectedness to others and to the rest of nature. This is common in much of the Western world. "In traditional Jewish, Islamic, Hindu, Buddhist, Chinese, and Aboriginal societies," the self is seen as part of "a family that may extend out to include caste, tribe, and all humans as well as plants, animals, and the cosmos."[18] Their culture Coward calls a We-self culture. The problem with the clinic in Canada was that it was built from an I-self perspective for We-self peoples. The builders overlooked *who* it was they were dealing with.

The point here is not to say that either I-self, individualistic culture or We-self, communitarian culture is the better. In fact, there are assets and debits in both cultures. I-self cultures have championed individual human rights against the demands of the Leviathan state. That's good, but on the downside, it can also lead us "to seek the maximum benefits for our individual selves here and now over against the good of other persons now, or future generations, or nature itself."[19] The point is that when we do ethics we are operating on hidden and controlling assumptions of what is normal. Persons in We-self cultures find their identity in harmonious interrelationships and have more of a focus on obligations to the rest of society and the world. On the downside, the individual can be absorbed into the collectivity with a diminished sense of individual rights.

Mistakes in ethics are serious and often lethal. Not knowing *who* we are in relationship to the rest of nature is the root of our current ecological disasters. So job one for clear ethical thinking is to know *who* we are and, second, *who* others are. American efforts to try to force the ideals of Jeffersonian democracy onto other cultures (though our own realization of those ideals is hardly exemplary) fail due to our ignorance of *who* these people are and what political and social ideals they see that we do not.

On Becoming a Better *Who*

Being a person is never a *fait accompli*. Personal life, like all of life, is a work in process. *Werde was du bist*—"become what you are"—is an ongoing effort that admits of forward and backward. You can become, in a revealing word, "depersonalized." When a tomato plant grows, it is not any more a tomato plant than it was in its early days. But to grow as a person is to be more of a person. It is growth in essence. What we are precedes what we might become. Personal essence is not a static quality but rather a kind of expanding life potential.

In the Yoruba culture in Africa, "a human being is not fully human by the simple fact of being born from human parents." You have to grow into personhood. A real person is a *Muntu*. This term has a normative quality. It implies a good character, a sense of fairness and compassion. If you do not have these qualities, you are a Kintu, a thing. Yoruba traditional wisdom says: "A man may be very, very handsome; handsome as a fish within the water. But if he has no character, he is no more than a wooden doll." Professor Nkulu-N'Sengha says that Africana cultures also equate moral goodness with beauty: "By using the same word *buya* for 'goodness' and 'beauty,' the Baluba

express an ontological relation between ethics and aesthetics in the sense that good conduct is not understood as a matter of blind obedience to external rules but rather as an expression and celebration of the ontological elegance of the character of a person who lives in harmony with other forces in the universe."[20]

This ancient culture recognizes that persons are at varying levels of moral and psychological development. That has practical implications in ethics and leads to conclusions like these:

- What is right for one person may be wrong for another since no two persons are the same. (For instance, a doctor who has a hard-nosed policy about "laying it on the line" immediately with all patients who have terminal illnesses to make cruel mistakes by neglecting preparation.)
- What is right for a person now may be wrong for the same person at another time. (Having sex before you are emotionally mature enough to deal with all its impact is damaging and therefore wrong.)
- In ethical assessment, some persons are worth more than others. (In a triage crisis situation where there are limited resources, help may be given first to a physician who could give additional assistance to victims, or first to the youngest victims.)
- Persons are social by nature, not by choice. This means that no human rights can be conceived of outside of reference to other human rights. In the triage case, persons are being judged in terms of their sociality, not in an individualistic contest about who is worth more. The assessment is relational since our reality is webbed in relationships.

Making decisions, therefore, about *who* the persons we judge really are is the daily business of ethics. And here the plot thickens. We who are making ethical judgments are not all the same.

Men and women are different in psychological as well as physical ways. Psychologists note that the moral judgments of women often differ from those of men in that they are more closely tied to "feelings of empathy and compassion and are more concerned with the resolution of 'real-life' as opposed to hypothetical dilemmas."[21] Such findings do not give grounds for stereotypes since qualities thought "womanly" are often found in full bloom in men and, conversely, strengths touted as "manly" are not monopolized by men. Still, some male-authored studies of moral maturity, such as that of Laurence Kohlberg, have deemed women's tendency not to shuffle off affective "constraints" as a limit rather than as an intellectual strength. If all moral judgments are grounded in the FME, connection to that affective base of moral wisdom is an asset. It would make women less seducible by poorly grounded abstractions.

Who Are the Poor?

"The poor will always be with you in the land," says the book of Deuteronomy (15:11). Thus, judgments about the poor are a big part of economic ethics. Left and right wrangle over whether poverty is a personal achievement (a difficult position since many of the poor are children) or is a result of social arrangements. In tough feudal times, the poor often had a kind of paternalistic social security. They were part of a unit that shared some essentials out of practical necessity. At the dawn of capitalism, the serfs were cast out to scramble for work. Capitalism had two choices from the start: either fix this problem and help those cast out by the blind mechanisms of the market, or vilify the poor so as not to indict the system. Vilification was the preferred path.

The Statute of Laborers in 1349 in England made it a crime to give alms to the poor. The Poor Law Reform Bill in 1834 said that indiscriminate aid to the poor destroys their desire to work. Right-wing thinking still cherishes this interpretation. Former Mississippi governor Kirk Fordice once told

reporters that all the poor need is a "good alarm clock."[22] This characterization of *who* the poor are has a lucrative payoff: if the poor are undeserving, then there is no need to attend to those outside our gated community.

Of course, the inconvenient truth, as a Brookings Institution study put it, is this:

> Poor people—males and females, blacks and whites, youths and adults—identify their self-esteem with work as strongly as do the non-poor. They express as much willingness to take job training if unable to earn a living. . . . They have, moreover, as high life aspirations as do the non-poor and want the same things, among them a good education and a nice place to live. . . . [There are] no differences between poor and non-poor when it comes to life goals and wanting to work.[23]

Is a Fetus a *Who*?

The question is not whether the fetus is human tissue: it is. The question is whether or when it becomes a person. Interestingly, even though abortion is a consuming issue among many Bible-reading Christians, the Bible itself touches on the subject only once, and then only in the case of an accidental abortion. "When, in the course of a brawl, a man knocks against a pregnant woman so that she has a miscarriage but suffers no further hurt, then the offender must pay whatever fine the woman's husband demands after the assessment" (Exod. 21:22). If, however, the man were to kill the woman, in this case it would be a capital offense and then "you shall give a life for a life" (21:22). As Orthodox Jewish theologian Laurie Zoloth says, in this case the aborted fetus "is not a life in the way that the woman is a human life . . . a crime of some sort has been committed, but it is not a capital crime."[24] The fetus does not have the moral status of a born person. In Judaism this argument was developed in the Mishnah. Abortion was permitted "as a health procedure . . . when necessary, since a fetus is not an ensouled person. Not only are the first 40 days of conception considered 'like water' but also even in the last trimester, the fetus has a lesser moral status."[25]

Such gradualism in moving toward personal status (called "delayed ensoulment" in some religious traditions) is found in other moral/religious traditions. Augustine, who believed in the resurrection of all the dead of history at the end of time, was asked if all the aborted fetuses would also rise at that time and he said they would not. He also opined that not all the sperm of history would rise at that time, which we may assume would be welcome news for the saints rising on that occasion. (The role of the ovum was unknown to him; the sperm was thought to be a little *homunculus* that grew into a fully developed *homo*, that is, a person, as the pregnancy progressed.)

The common sense running through these traditions reflects a distinction between potential personal life and actual personal life. Some who take the position that the fertilized egg from the start is a full-fledged person conflate potential with actual, a fatal error in logic. After all, we are all potentially dead but would not want to be treated that way now. The move of the embryo-fetus toward personal status mimics the process of evolution. Through the long period before *Homo sapiens* appeared, we were potentially here—but not here. The elements that would allow us to develop were present, but we were not. Similarly, the early fetus is potentially, not actually, a person, and abortion cannot be classified as "murder," the term we reserve for the killing of a person. In the terms of this chapter, the early fetus is not a *who*. It has the considerable dignity of life that could become personal, but it is not a person.

Is a Soldier a *Who*?

Conscience is the hallmark of personhood. We are, as Friedrich Nietzsche said, the valuing animal, and our most important valuing is in the area of morality, where we decide on what befits hu-

mans and the rest of living beings in this felicitous corner of our universe. Moral decisions that affect life and death, ecological enhancement or destruction, are among the most important matters for conscience. Thanks to the Quakers in England in the early nineteenth century, conscientious objection to war has become a recognized human right. However, that right is denied those who are in greatest proximity to the realities of war, and hence the best informed experientially—those serving in the military. Military persons who object to war on moral grounds are subject to legal prosecution for their exercise of conscience.

Francesco de Vitoria, a Spanish priest and theologian, was one of the major figures in the history of the law of war, writing in the sixteenth century. His influence is even cited in the UN Universal Declaration of Human Rights. He says that soldiers need not know and, indeed, should not know whether the killing they are doing is moral or immoral. If the prince had to answer such questions from troubled soldiers, "the state would fall into great peril."[26] In this thinking soldiers should have no more conscience regarding what they are doing than do the bullets they fire. The ideal is the solider as automaton. Military "necessity" and obedience to authority trump conscience and morality.

There is a term for such conscience stripping: it is called *depersonalization*.

When? and Where? Questions of Time and Place

The questions *When?* and *Where?* are often irrelevant in ethical analysis. It will probably make no moral difference if you rob someone on a Monday or a Tuesday. Similarly, whether the robbery is on Oak Street or Elm Street will probably not matter morally. Time and place, however, may enter into the substance of moral meaning. Timing could indeed be the most telling of circumstances when it comes to breaking bad news. A psychiatrist who sees early on more than the patient can yet handle may have to use exquisitely sensitive timing to bring the patient slowly to an understanding of his condition. Sometimes denial may serve a purpose until coping power is developed. Psychologist Eugene Kennedy analogizes the timing factor with a story of a man taking an early morning walk on a beach. He looks down and to his delight sees a clam just washing in with the tide. Being a lover of fresh clams, he picks up the closed clam and tries to open it with his fingers, succeeding only in chipping a fingernail. He reaches for his knife and makes another effort, only to have the knife slip and jab his finger. Disgusted, he drops the clam and moves on. Later, as the sun rises and little waves roll over the clam, it slowly opens without stress or violence. Kennedy uses this story to show how we often must wait for the moment of readiness and opportunity.

This is true not just in therapy but also in business negotiations, in diplomacy, and certainly in child rearing. Timing also is key in making love. The Chinese sage Yueh P'u-chia, back in the Ming Dynasty, showed wisdom in urging men to wait for the heavenly moment when women show "a desire to engage as if quite insuppressible."[27] Yueh saw this as part of the necessary kindness needed for good sexual experiences. Good sex is never pressured. The link to kindness explains the importance of the *when.* There are no tidy rules for timing but the gentle are more likely to be aware of people as they are and to be patient in awaiting the heavenly opportune moment in any and all human interactions.

Likewise, many good things done in the wrong place should not be done. Where a corporation decides to locate its plants is a moral decision whose meaning may relate strongly to the *where* question. If the decision is to move to a country where lax laws permit more pollution, the decision is immoral. Governmental and corporate decisions as to where to dump toxic waste are an important *where* issue. Given the privacy that most people in most cultures assign to sexual intimacy, public lovemaking would be the wrong *where.* American Nazis may have a constitutional right to demonstrate their views publicly, but scheduling a demonstration in a predominantly Jewish neighborhood would be the wrong *where.* The choice of that *where* would signal hostile intent and shift the moral meaning of freedom of speech into attack mode. Such is the importance of circumstance.

Summary of Key Themes

- Failure to ask all the relevant ethical questions is morally insensitive.
- The end does not justify the means any more than the means justify the end.
- Sometimes *how* we do something may be more morally important than *why* we do it.
- Nations and corporations tend to justify their policies by touting their motive (end, purpose) while ignoring the other circumstances.
- Obsession with means can defeat the end; the *how* can overwhelm the *why.*
- Many alleged volitions are really velleities.
- Ethics must recognize that no two persons or cultures are identical.

Key Terms

Affirmative action
Motive
Velleity
Volition

Questions for Discussion

1. Pat Anthony, a forty-eight-year-old South African grandmother, served as a surrogate mother for her own daughter's biological infants. Ms. Anthony was implanted with four embryos resulting from ova produced by her daughter and fertilized *in vitro* with her son-in-law's sperm. On October 1, 1987, she gave birth to triplets. Reactions to this story ranged from astonishment to repugnance. Discuss the ethics of this particular surrogacy. Which of the questions discussed in this chapter will be most relevant in this case?

2. There have always been debates about *who* the poor are and *how* they got that way. Some see poverty as self-made. In 1877, John Hay criticized the labor riots, saying: "That you have property is proof of industry and foresight on your part or your father's; that you have nothing is a judgment on your laziness and vices or on your providence. The world is a moral world; which it would note if virtue and vice received the same rewards." Recognizing that most of the poor are children and women, what other causes of poverty could you cite?

Suggestions for Further Reading

Albrecht, Gloria. *Hitting Home: Feminist Ethics, Women's Work, and the Betrayal of Family Values.* New York: Continuum, 2002.

Hobgood, Mary Elizabeth. *Dismantling Privilege: An Ethics of Accountability.* Cleveland: Pilgrim, 2000.

Foreseeable Effects, Viable Alternatives
The Link to the Future

DAVID BEN-GURION OF ISRAEL said there are no experts on the future, and history confirms his point. We can be experts on what has happened but not on what hasn't, because it might not happen. And this is a lesson in humility for ethics. The future is unavoidably involved in moral action. Our choices reverberate out into space and forward into time, with effects sometimes lasting centuries. The future is the product of what was once the present. In subtle ways everything we do

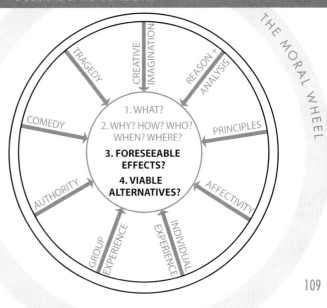

sends flutters out beyond the present, shaping in some ways the contours of the future.

Consequentialism: Gauging the Effects

So if we go back to Aquinas's dictum that human actions are good or bad according to their circumstances, we face the fact that some of those circumstances are in the future tense. Moral responsibility requires that our knowledge follow the impact of our behavior as far as our eyes can see. Effects and consequences are so important in gauging morality that there is a stream of thought in the history of ethics called **consequentialism**. Consequentialism oversteps, however, by trying to make human actions right or wrong solely with regard to their consequences. It overlooks how you could get some good consequences from evil behavior. Nazi medical experiments did produce knowledge, but those effects were achieved through the medium of murder.

Still, what can be said for the consequentialists is that effects are highly important, and moral theory has always recognized that. Two major historical Christian thinkers, Augustine and Thomas Aquinas, justified the legalization of prostitution largely on the basis of foreseeable effects. Augustine's argument, which Aquinas endorsed, was that given the conditions of their times, removing this outlet for aberrant sexual behavior would cause more trouble and thus be a greater evil. Therefore, it would be best to tolerate it. This was a use of the "choose the lesser evil" rule so as to minimize harm.[1]

Their reasoning here is interesting and not without practical applications today. Aquinas's argument is theological. He says that God, who is omnipotent and supremely good, nonetheless permits certain evils lest greater evils ensue. He

then makes the move from God to human government and says that good legislators should imitate God and tolerate things they consider wrong to avoid greater evils and tragedies. Thus, legislators who consider all abortions evil could vote, by this reasoning, to legalize abortions since not doing so would lead to desperate "back alley" abortions resulting in many deaths, especially of poor women. The history before *Roe v. Wade* in the United States gives proof of this likely eventuality. This would not be a radical choice for legislators, nor a betrayal of their integrity, but would, rather, put them in the company of these two saints, Augustine and Thomas, and, according to Thomas, in the company of God, who also uses consequentialist thinking to avoid greater harm.

Legislators could apply similar effects-regarding reasoning to issues such as same-sex marriage. Denying legitimacy to the desires of gay and lesbian persons to be united for life in a faithful, loving, exclusive, publicly recognized union could be damaging to these people who desire this great human good and would benefit from it. So the legislator who thinks such unions wrong and would never enter one could nonetheless vote in favor of legalizing these unions, following the consequentialist reasoning of Aquinas and Augustine. Political decision making is not the same as personal decision making, since it is guided by the complex needs of the common good in a primary way. You may tolerate at the political level actions you would not choose to engage in yourself. The alternative to this is fascism, which would impose the rigid rules of the leader on a subjugated people whatever the consequences.

New Debts to the Future

When we act—or fail to act—we commit our act or our neglect to the future. The big danger comes when choices become a practice for an individual or for a society. The result is a momentum that is potentially immune to reflection and evaluation. Choices that grow into practices can run away with us. That is why ethics must pause for the "reverent stillness" of contemplation. In one way, the effects of our actions are out of our control as soon as we act. We can go after those effects with other actions, but the effects are not subject to recall. Human action, therefore, is an amalgam of power and impotence; the power to touch and shape the future through the consequences of our acts and, simultaneously, the impotence to control those consequences. Hence the centrality of concern for consequences in ethics.

Our sense of the future is undergoing a qualitative change in modern times. In the past, as philosopher Hans Jonas writes, "the good and evil about which action had to care lay close to the act, either in the praxis itself or in its immediate reach, and were not a matter for remote planning. . . . The long run of consequences beyond was left to chance, fate or providence. Ethics accordingly was of the here and now."[2]

Jonas notes that the maxims that came to us from the ethical systems of the past involved others who were "sharers of a common present." We didn't have much of a need to think of the future. "Love thy neighbor as thyself"; "Do unto others as you would wish them to do unto you"; "Treat others as ends, never as means." Throughout previous history, those maxims referred to contemporaries, and future consequences were less a concern. Not anymore. Technology now allows us to invade the future. We can destroy the necessities of future life. Posterity is our new neighbor, and a new ethics bids us to love those future neighbors as we love ourselves. Interpersonal responsibility has swollen to planetary size and reaches billions of years into the future. Never before has moral responsibility for consequences been so keen. Action is interaction; agency is influence, and our influence is, all of a sudden, mammoth. This is the core of the contemporary ethical concern for consequences.

Future Myopia

If we can be dumb about the present, we can be flat-out stupid when it comes to the future. Futurama at the 1939 World's Fair predicted that by 1960 automobiles would sell for two hundred dollars, that Americans would be bored with possessions and be seeking satisfaction in other, less materialistic ways, and that factories would be admirable for their cleanliness.[3] Alas! Adam Smith had remarkable insight into the processes of economics, but he could not foresee the power of monopolies to dominate in the economic practices he recommended. Karl Marx missed the varieties of capitalism. He, too, had no crystal ball. The physical sciences are better at predicting, working as they do within the repetitive and cyclic regularity of much of nature. The developing science of earthquake prediction rests on the traditional hope of science that when all is known, all is predictable. The cultural prominence of the sciences in modern society has set a tone and given us undue hope for successful futurism regarding human behavior.

Arnold Toynbee, with his massive knowledge of surprises in history, enters this corrective: "In the field of human affairs, experience enables us merely to guess. In this field, what has occurred in the past may, of course, recur, but it is not bound to recur and, indeed, it was not bound to occur in the first instance."[4] History—with its lessons—is not useless, as Toynbee well knew. Without a sense of history we are like the amnesiac, unsure of our identity, but humans have some freedom of choice and are haunted by the possible. They can, at times, break precedent; they can create and set events on a new direction. Creativity and surprise make predicting future history the most imprecise of arts.

"A Man Can't Just Sit Around"

Larry Walters may serve as a symbol of our weakness in calculating future effects. He always wanted to be a pilot, but his eyesight was weak. Still, the dream did not die. As he sat in his Los Angeles backyard, watching the planes soaring overhead, desire turned the dream into a scheme. Larry would get some helium balloons, attach them to his deck chair, float some one hundred feet above his neighbors, sip a beer or two, and then pop his balloons with his pellet gun, descending slowly for a celebration with friends.

Talk about nothing failing like success!

On July 2, 1982, Larry took off. When his friends cut the cords that tied his Sears deck chair to the ground, Larry quickly departed this earth and rose to an altitude of sixteen thousand feet. Airplanes zoomed by him, above him, and below him as he floated toward the Long Beach airport. Stunned commercial pilots reported the shocking news to the control tower. "We have spotted a man flying at sixteen thousand feet on a deck chair!!!"

After a forty-five-minute flight, Larry began popping balloons until his dangling cables got caught on power lines, causing a blackout in the Long Beach area. As he disembarked uninjured from his aircraft, the police were his humorless welcoming committee. He was fined $4,000 by the Federal Aviation Administration for operating an aircraft without "an airworthiness certificate." He was also penalized for failing to establish radio contact with nearby control towers.

Even in the face of all this, Larry was not contrite. He told reporters at the scene of his crash landing: "A man can't just sit around."

Larry won top prize that year from the Bonehead Club of Dallas, and that's a shame. He actually was a teacher and, indeed, a symbol for our age. What Larry taught is that technology can take you whither you would not go, and our predictive powers as to where technology is going are not impressive. Scientific genius and prescience are not joined at the hip.

The Model T Ford was an idea welcomed by all. Mr. Ford agreed with Larry that "a man can't just sit around." Speed, convenience, and no more horse droppings on our roads.

Later came the Larry Moment, and we are aloft on an oil economy with no pellet guns to bring us down without injury. Our horseless machines have their own excrement, and it can't be used for fertilizer. Instead, it rises like a noxious miasma, coiling stubbornly around the warming earth.

Larry Walters was a symbol in other ways. Not only was he invited onto major talk shows, but he did a stint as a motivational speaker. His tragic end was even more eerily symbolic. He shot himself to death in the Angeles National Forest in Southern California on October 6, 1993.

Seduction by Projection

The effects on which we base our ethical calculations are to some extent abstract. Their reality is not yet proved, and they may in fact never exist. The danger is this: enamored of what might be, we can ride roughshod over what is. Hoped-for effects can take on the demonic power of romanticized ends. The Communist revolutions in Russia and China sacrificed millions of present-tense people for utopian hopes. The desired effect of military spending and reliance on military power is security, but when this becomes obsessive, present security is undone. Keeping nuclear weapons is justified by the desired effect of security even though the effect is nuclear proliferation and the danger of accidents that make us less secure.[5]

Capital punishment is often defended on consequentialist grounds. An unarmed prisoner guilty of murder is killed allegedly to deter other criminals who are at large, even though there is absolutely no hard evidence that they are deterred by an occasional execution. Professionals might justify the neglect of their family in view of the good things their financial success will someday mean to them. The result could be that the family well-being that is hoped for undermines the family well-being that is.

Corrective: Present-tense realities have a prima facie priority over the future. They may at times have to be sacrificed to make way for future possibilities, but not without due process in the court of conscience. To ensure due process, the other present-tense ethical questions must be asked: What? Why? Who? When? Where? and What are the alternatives? It will also be necessary to use a full ethical method such as I am elaborating in this book. Principles, which are the depositories of wisdom gained by experience in the past, will have to be tested against the facts. Affectivity, imagination, reliable authorities, and all the evaluative resources suggested in the spokes of my wheel model will have to be brought to bear on the case. All of this is necessary to prevent projected glorified effects from getting a mesmerizing grip on our moral-decision-making process.[6]

The Principle of Double Effect

The **principle of double effect** has become a staple in ethics, and it has some limited usefulness as a tool. It deals with the fact of life that the good effect we're going for often entails other effects that we would love to avoid. We remove a cancerous uterus: there are two effects, one good (the cancer is gone) and one bad (the woman who desired children is now infertile). The decision to give a strong painkiller to a patient is another example of mixed effects presenting a moral dilemma; the physician might know that the painkiller will shorten life as it eases the pain. A business that is planning some new system of automation looks ahead to the good effects of improved productivity and better competitive standing, but it may face the undesirable effect of laying off a large number of workers to whom it has here-and-now moral debts. A moral caution: Beware the seductive power of the longed-for good effect; it is a breeding ground for crass rationalization.

For two hundred years, the United States operated with a white-male quota system. Since not all genius is white and male, this was a noxious monopoly. Brilliant women and minority groups were excommunicated and their talents lost. Thomas Jefferson said that the essence of good statecraft is to activate the talent of all in the community. Changing this systemic problem requires the systemic cure of **affirmative action**. It is a case of double effect. Affirmative action enfranchises the previously disenfranchised (good effect) while hurting a number of white males when the previously excluded groups get preference and some white males lose opportunities.

Psychological and Moral Disassociation

The question this double-effect principle faces is this: Are we responsible for the bad effects of our actions and policies? The answer from this much-used and often-abused principle is "No, as long as you really did not want the bad effect and as long as there was proportionality between the effects." The danger in this principle is that we can be so enraptured at the good effect that we want to downplay the disastrous effects that we cause. In times of tension, such as war, this principle gets strangled in rationalization. The desired effect of defeating Nazi Germany and Japan was the good effect intended, and the terrorist killing of a hundred thousand civilians in Dresden, Tokyo, Hiroshima, and Nagasaki was morally downsized before the god of "military necessity." When war begins, moral discernment dims and *nécessité fait loi* ("necessity makes law").[7]

The principle of double effect has been called somewhat cumbersomely but accurately the "principle of psychological and moral disassociation." It is an effort to get morally and psychologically "off the hook" for the tragic effects of our actions. It can be useful as a tool of ethics; it is not a full method of ethics such as the wheel model presented in this book. It can be an escape hatch in the flight from responsibility.

With cold detachment, Henry Davis, S.J., writing four years after the end of World War II, used the principle of double effect to justify starving a whole population by blockade or siege. "Enemy troops may be starved by blockade. If civilians suffered, it is not intended that they should suffer; it is their misfortune, and it is due to the fortune of a **just war** that they happen to be in the same place as their army. Blockade and siege are in principle not different from the bombing of fortified garrison towns."[8] Notice how Father Davis has achieved "psychological and moral disassociation" from the massive slaughter of civilians. More civilians died in the siege of Leningrad than in the infernos of Hamburg, Dresden, Tokyo, Hiroshima, and Nagasaki taken together. Father Davis replies: "It is their misfortune." Alas. They just happened to be in the wrong place at the wrong time. Cold comfort, indeed. It's a clear example of how unduly tidy theory can waft us away from the flesh and blood and earth in which moral value is grounded.

Sadly, Father Davis gets even worse. His detached use of this principle allows him to justify the bombing of "hospital ships with the wounded on board." Bad use of theory can lead ethicists to go where even warriors dare not venture. "The case may be imagined when even a hospital ship will be so valuable to the enemy for future aggression during a war that it may be of vital concern to sink it. Though such a necessity would be deplorable, we think the sinking of it may be justified, for what is attacked is the ship, the deaths of those on board are incidental and not wished."[9] With similarly autistic reasoning he also justified the atomic bombings of the people of Hiroshima and Nagasaki before the ashes were even cooled.

Proper Use of the Principle

This is the pitfall of double-effect usage. It imagines that one could bomb a hospital ship full of the wounded without in any way willing their deaths. The slaughter we are doing is not "willed" or "intended"; it is only "permitted" as a regrettable by-product of the good that we are about. This is hairsplitting at its silliest. Father Davis could have taken instruction from another Jesuit ethicist, John

Ford. In 1944, he broke ranks with the reigning conventional wisdom by publishing an article condemning the "obliteration bombing" that by then was approved Allied policy. He did it by a proper use of "the principle of double effect," noting the impossibility of a bombardier dropping bombs on people while withholding his intention to do what he was doing. He saw the principle being used as a rationalization for terrorism just as Al Qaeda members claimed that civilian deaths were collateral damage in the 9/11 attacks. You can be neither morally nor psychologically disassociated from the effects of what you are doing when you turn a populated city into a cauldron. The bishops of the Second Vatican Council in the 1960s became nuclear pacifists using the principle of double effect, saying that dropping such bombs merited "unequivocal and unhesitating condemnation."[10]

Another example of the proper use of the principle of double effect is affirmative action. Affirmative action is a form of temporary preferential hiring in which the preferred are those who have been cut out of society by a dominant monopoly. The good effect is the liberation of these people and their talents to enrich the common good of the society. The "bad effect" is that in the necessarily enforced systemic readjustment—privileged groups never shed their privileges without pressure—some white males lose opportunities. The gains of this liberation enrich the common good that is the matrix of individual goods and thus satisfy the principle of proportionality. Affirmative action breaks the logjam of monopoly and then allows the free flow of meritocracy. When affirmative action achieves its monopoly-busting end, it stops. An example of its temporary nature can be seen in the case of white women entering schools of law and medicine. Prior to affirmative action, women were largely excluded from these white male bastions. After enforced affirmative action, white women entered and proved their worthiness. Affirmative action for white women's entrance is no longer needed. (Of course, upon completion of their studies, white women still encounter glass ceilings even though they have proved themselves more than competitive with their male colleagues.) Affirmative action for African Americans, the intended primary beneficiaries of the program, is still needed, though some improvements have taken place.[11]

Another example of the usefulness of the double-effect principle is in debt forgiveness for debt-mired poor nations. The good effect is to lift these nations out of crippling poverty, a poverty that not only devastates their people but also unsettles international peace and the ecological health of the planet. The bad effect is that some investors and banks will not get repaid on their loans.

The subprinciple underlying these proportional judgments is this: No rights are orphans. No right is an only child. All our individual claims exist in an intrinsic sociality of interlocking claims and rights and obligations. Life is a shared and sharing reality. Rights conceived atomistically and individualistically are chimeric.

The Tyranny of the Majority: The Utilitarian Temptation

A rigid **utilitarianism**—what is good for the greatest number is good—is another form of overfixation on effects. The effects may indeed be good for the greatest number but disastrous for the rest. It amounts to the tyranny of the majority or sometimes the tyranny of the privileged and powerful few over the less powerful. "What is good for General Motors is good for the country," its CEO famously assured us, as noted earlier. Utilitarianism is not limited to the scholarly devotees of Jeremy Bentham and John Stuart Mill. Utilitarianism has a virulently infectious quality about it to which minds within and without the academe are susceptible. It represents a sneaky escape from

complete moral responsibility. As proponents of utilitarianism are drunk with the glorious prospect of the greatest good of the many, alternatives get ignored and individuals perish. The generic gobbles up the particular.

Utilitarianism asserts that actions are good if they promote the greatest sum of happiness and well-being. That may sound harmless, but it is not. Utilitarianism is an intellectual temptation to be resisted. In utilitarianism, foreseeable effects acquire an unquestioned hegemony. Utilitarianism contains, among other things, the ingredients of totalitarianism. In the natural tension that should exist between the one and the many, between the individual and the common good, utilitarianism comes down on the side of the many and the common good. And that is dangerous because it is abstract. No one ever met the common good or "the greatest sum of satisfaction of the rational desires of individuals," as John Rawls depicts it.[12] That definition is dangerously abstract. That "greatest sum of satisfaction" cannot be touched or hugged. It cannot bleed or cry. The individual can. Any system that becomes obsessed with commonality to the neglect of individuality stands in need of the existentialist insight that a person is more important than justice—meaning that what you mean by justice may be so abstract and detached that it may overlook the good of concrete persons.

This, of course, is not meant to deny all that I have said about the notion of the common good as an indispensable intellectual tool that focuses individuals on the social implications of their humanity. Common-good considerations define social and distributive justice.

A Master of Disguise

Utilitarianism is a master of disguise. It can appear as a revolution of the proletariat where the pursuit of the good of the many can swallow up individual rights and basic liberties. It appears under the flag of "homeland security," with civil liberties its first casualty. It can present itself in the American ideology of freedom, where freedom is identified as the greatest sum of happiness and many things—including justice—may be sacrificed to it. Utilitarian thinking becomes a fervor in wartime. "Victory" becomes the code for "the greatest good," and basic decencies are burned at its shrine. The atomic bombings of Hiroshima and Nagasaki are epics of utilitarian insensitivity. "To save American lives" was the sum of happiness that made us unaware of what we were doing and blind to the alternatives then available and suggested to save lives and end the war. Pope Paul VI, on the twentieth anniversary of the Hiroshima bombing, in uncharacteristically blunt language, called that bombing an "outrage against civilization" and a "butchery of human lives." The weapons we used he saw as "nefarious and dishonorable," the day of their use "disgraceful."[13] Few of the utilitarians who danced in the streets on V-J Day were touched by the signal immorality of what we did without cause to so many men, women, children, animals, topsoil, flowers, and trees.

As Rawls says, "The striking feature of the utilitarian view of justice is that it does not matter, except indirectly, how this sum of satisfactions is distributed among individuals."[14] That's the scary nub of it. It opens the door to exploitation, while stressing, with seeming generosity, the good of the nation or the good of the corporation or the university or the church or the mosque or the goals of the movement. Beware those who are committed to the greatest sum of goodness (in business it is often called the bottom line) until you test their commitment to persons. When the greatest good is defined by an elite—and it usually is in church or state, in politics and in economics—the non-elite on the wayside are the losers.

How to Ponder Proportionality

A final, generally overlooked aspect of utilitarianism is its linkage to the **principle of proportionality**. This principle I have described as a master principle in ethics, since we must always test, proportion-wise, the relationship of value to disvalue in our decisions. But this principle, central as it is, is also abstract, and as such must be washed in an empirical bath. Proportional thinking by its very nature could usher in a mathematical preoccupation with net gain. In mathematics, if the final sum is plus, those minus quantities along the way have no further significance. Ethics has no such right to ignore negative factors affecting persons and the rest of nature and focus just on the final affirmative sum. In ethics the minus quantities will be losses to actual persons and to their natural ecology. Sometimes these losses will be justifiable, but not by the easy utilitarian calculus of being out of debt morally and in the black just because of those happy results on the bottom line.

The principle of proportionality remains a basic intellectual tool. It calls attention to the balancing that must be done to assess the humanizing behavioral possibilities. Awareness of its potential for abuse clears the way for its fruitful use. Ethics is the art of weighing and balancing. It is a pondering activity, and the word *ponder* comes from the Latin *pondus*, meaning "weight." The task is to weigh and balance amid competing values and disvalues. The morally good choice is the one that is the most humanly valuable. The challenge is to balance goods and bads, and when the bads are considerable, we have to judge whether the goods are proportionately greater. If so, they may justify the unwanted elements that are unavoidably entailed in our behavior. A high quota of good effects does not justify any kind of causal action. All of the essential circumstances, not just the effects, are weighed and balanced in a comparative judgment. The alternatives (to which we now turn) are especially important when some considerable disvalue is involved.

Moral Myopia: Missing the Viable Alternatives

Alternative consciousness is the glory of human intelligence and perhaps its least developed talent, a victim of mental sloth. In situations where many alternatives are open to us, it is a mournful fact that our tendency is to see but a few of them and then feel that these few circumscribe reality. Our decision will then be based on that segment of reality that our semi-atrophied imaginations allow us to envision. Many realistic possibilities will be missed, to our moral detriment. A rule-of-thumb estimate would be that in a situation where there are a hundred existing viable alternatives, we normally would perceive about ten of them, and that perhaps only when we are having a good day.

Withered Talents

This claim that our creative talents are withered from disuse might seem an unduly harsh indictment in view of the explosions of technological genius in the past century. However, it is necessary to take a longer view of our history to get a full picture of our inventiveness. Scientist Jared Diamond speaks of "the five-million-year history of the human species."[15] Of course, we didn't start out in our current state. We didn't even stand up, that is, become *Homo erectus*, until 1.7 million years ago. At that point our body size was close to that of today's humans, but the brain was only half its current size. It was fifty thousand years ago that we took what Diamond calls "the great leap forward." First evidence comes from East African sites where more developed tools and even jewelry are found. For a million years, we survived as hunters and gatherers of fruits, nuts, and berries. Life was lived under the constant threat of starvation, and the growth in human numbers was slow and precarious. Nevertheless, through all those eons, necessity was not the mother of invention. Finally, a breakthrough. "It was only within the last 11,000 years that some people turned to what is termed food production: that is domesticating wild animals and plants and eating the resulting livestock and crops."[16] No more sitting around waiting for plants to appear. After a million years, we moved from gatherer to tiller. We probably described ourselves then in some such word as *modern* with the self-satisfaction and boast that such a word implies, little noting the retarded pace that brought us there.

The food crisis did not disappear with this belated leap forward, and indeed, not all humans took the tiller leap. It took another few thousand years for a large-scale, irrigated agriculture to appear. Again, one would think that *Homo sapiens* would have come upon this a bit sooner, just as one would think that it would not have taken us maybe as much as another thousand years to think of harnessing animals to add to our own muscle power! The picture of the animals resting in the shade and watching as *Homo sapiens*

> **THINKING CRITICALLY**
>
> Alterative thinking is easing problems of domestic violence. "The earliest safe spaces for battered women were shelters opened in England and the United States during the late 1970s to respond to the degree of domestic violence. This movement is now worldwide. In Costa Rica, the degree of domestic violence is so high that now not only are there state-supported shelters but also women-run police stations. These stations were established because when battered women went to the traditional police stations to report domestic violence, often they were sexually harassed by the police."
>
> —John Cartwright and Susan Thistlethwaite
>
> 9.1

pulled the plows should give us pause. It was only when it finally struck us that animals could be harnessed to help with the work that the earliest cities emerged. Before then, there was no time for social organization, since we were busy plowing as the animals watched.

Five thousand years ago we thought of harnessing wind power for driving ships. Somewhere around 3000 B.C.E. the Sumerians of Mesopotamia came up with writing. Some two thousand years ago water power was used for driving mills, and only in the last couple of hundred years did we come upon other modes of non-muscular power.[17]

Stay thy boasts, O *Homo sapiens*!

A cynical footnote can be added to this unflattering picture of most of our history. One cannot help but imagine the reactions faced by the first persons who came up with the new ideas. Can you imagine the scorn heaped by the established wisdom upon the first fellow who rolled in what came to be known as the wheel! And probably the first one to think of harnessing an animal to pull the plow was put off by an impressive lecture on the theme "Who ever heard of such a thing?" These are irreverent thoughts, but not unlikely.

THINKING CRITICALLY

Before we overestimate the moral maturity of the human race and underestimate our need for alternative thinking, we should hear Michelle Tooley in her book *Voices of the Voiceless*. This report is from Guatemala, but similar reports come from elsewhere in Latin America, Rwanda, Liberia, Zaire, the Sudan, Burma, Cambodia, Bosnia, Afghanistan, and Iraq.

"During the violence of the early 1980s, many women became widows as their husbands were killed by the military forces of the government. . . . In addition to the death of husbands, sons and fathers disappeared or were forced into military service, never to be seen again. Daughters and mothers were violated by soldiers and members of the civil patrol. . . .

"Women watched powerlessly as soldiers entered their villages, burned houses and fields, kidnapped husbands and children. They watched as soldiers threw babies into fires of boiling water. They watched as half-dead husbands were buried alive. In front of children members of the military raped mothers and daughters."

9.2

Low-Hanging Fruit

In modern times, the same slowness to seize upon a discovery appears. For seventy-five years after the discovery that vaccination could be used to prevent smallpox, no one thought of extending the idea to other diseases until Louis Pasteur did in 1879. In like fashion, Einstein discovered the principle of relativity without the help of any observation that had not been available for at least fifty years. As Arthur Koestler says: "The plum was overripe, yet for half a century nobody came to pluck it."[18] Good ethics should press us to realize that there must be plums galore out there that we have been bumping our heads on, but we haven't had the wit to reach up and pluck them.

This little vignette of history should chasten *Homo technologicus* as she or he stands to sing lauds to human genius. The momentum of technological invention of toys and tools has certainly grown, and one thing has been leading to another at an accelerating pace. Small wonder we are so impressed with ourselves.

In spite of this, wet blankets of suspicion ought to be dropped on the glow of our contentment. If our alternative consciousness were keen, would we be wrecking the planet while benign energy sources surround us, beckoning to us? Would we be reproducing beyond the capacity of the planet to sustain us? Captured by the pull of a sightless momentum, national economies are still absorbed in developing and deploying kill-power. With children and others dying of hunger, we still spend fortunes on catapults and crossbows, acting out the worst in our barbaric past. Swollen military budgets are also a symbol of despair, implying as they do that security ultimately will come from killing people, not from nourishing them.

Remember the wry comment of the Chinese official who chided Americans saying that we invade oil rich countries whereas they simply buy the oil, which is cheaper and avoids violence.

Paralyzed by Insensitivity

Insensitivity to managerial and governmental alternatives paralyzes our imaginations. We have invented some wheels but no steering apparatus. The new world that springs from our inventiveness requires alternate modes of governance. Systems of nation-state sovereignty and independence suited for another time are still ensconced. In many ways, the global community is like a promising new city under the divided governance of a number of old patriarchs in their dotage whose schemes and plans reflect the state of things in an antiquity that is no more. A substantial change has occurred in the social and material conditions of the earth that is not reflected in creative managerial and governmental response. A "Declaration of Interdependence" has yet to be effectively uttered by the world community on its shrinking planet. In spite of noble efforts like the United Nations and treaties galore, anarchy is still the underlying planetary condition, with states playing at independence while corporations become the swaggering new potentates.

As professors Mihajlo Mesarovic and Eduard Pestel put it: "In the past the world community was merely a collection of fundamentally independent parts. Under such conditions each of the parts could grow—for better or worse—as it

pleased. In the new conditions, exemplified by the global crises-syndrome, the world community has been transformed into a world system, i.e., a collection of functionally interdependent parts."[19]

The likelihood is strong if not obvious that there are many wheels not yet invented and many animals not yet harnessed. Intoxication with what we have done hampers possibility perception. The resistance to progress that appeared during our first million years is still in evidence. It was Heraclitus who said that it is not possible to step into the same river twice. The waters are always changing. At times they change with a rush, as they have done in our century. And yet those in a position to direct social forces step down into the river and bathe, confident that these are the same old waters and all is essentially as all was.

Whatever our proliferating skills at the level of tools and toys, it is eerily possible that, at the level of morals, we are still gatherers and primitive hunters. Morals, of course, involve more than skill; they involve caring and appreciation. A defect at the level of caring linked to growing technical skill is a monstrous danger. The soul of barbarism is not so much manifested in active cruelty as it is in apathy, in the absence of caring. Moral barbarians inure themselves to the needs of others. Technocracy in such hands is a fright. It underlies current foreboding about the prospects of our planet.

Thinking Alternatively

It has been waggishly said that when you have no alternatives, you have no problem. If only one choice were open to you, that would indeed simplify life. The usual fact is, however, that you got into that "only one alternative" situation by neglecting alternatives all along the way. It is argued that "humanitarian military intervention" (an interesting concept, given the realities of modern **war**) could have prevented the genocide in Rwanda in 1994. The flaw in that argument is exposed by looking at the years preceding the eruption of violence and the dislocations that follow any military action. Consciousness of alternatives prompts the following response from a group of scholars writing about the all-but-ignored art of peacemaking:

> Had there been international determination to make the Arusha peace accord work—had there been an amnesty provision in the agreement; a demobilisation plan; a genuine attempt to deal with the refugee problem; radio broadcasts to challenge the views of extremists; humanitarian coordination; provision of adequate policing; resources such as riot gear, maps, up-to-date information, early warning systems linked to institutions that could initiate preventative nonviolent action; and a culture of accountability and strong international institutions—the genocide could have been prevented. The failure in Rwanda was a failure of politics—the result of a lack of faith in and commitment to the slow and unglamourous work of nonviolent political action. . . . Military options only seem morally compelling because of a host of lost opportunities.[20]

The Sanity Dividend

What is called "the military mind" is in sore need of psychoanalysis. The avowed purpose of military spending is security. That contention merits alternative testing. Let us take the 2009 U.S. military budget as a test case.

Before losing ourselves in the fog-of-war budget trillions, a trip to visit the USS. *Kitty Hawk* will clear the air. The sight of this nuclear-powered aircraft carrier is stunning. It is almost three football fields long and towers as high as a twenty-story building. On board it has almost six thousand crew members and seventy state-of-the-art aircraft. It is never lonely since it is the king of a

"carrier battle force." In its royal entourage there is an Aegis cruiser equipped to knock down incoming missiles. There are several frigates and destroyers, and one or more submarines along with supply vessels. "The United States has thirteen of these carrier battle groups. No other country has even one."[21] A questioning ethics would have to ask: How much more insecure would we be if we had only twelve or eleven or three or even none of these expensive flotillas? Questions are fair, and that is a very fair one. It is even fairer since it is reported in the *New York Times* that China, which is powering ahead in technology research, "is busily funding new efforts to poke holes in American military pre-eminence. These include space weapons, cyberwarfare and technologies to threaten American aircraft carrier groups."[22]

I would argue that this excess is a product of many unasked questions and of TINA (There Is No Alternative) thinking. Let's probe that illusion with an exercise of creative imagination, our supreme moral talent. Doing so opens up bags of unsavory worms. The official U.S. Defense Budget for 2008 is understated by hundreds of billions of dollars according to the Center for Defense Information. It leaves out a long list of military-related items. The real figure is $926.8 billion. As numbers rise, they seem ethereal. Broken down, this means we spend in one year $77,166,666,667 a month, $17,807,692,307 per week, $2,536,986,301 per day, $105,707,762 per hour, $1,761,780 per minute, and $29,363 every second.[23] Meanwhile, with that hemorrhage of funds pouring into the military, a survey of the twenty-one wealthiest nations on "child well-being" found the United States next to last, with only Britain worse.[24]

Ethical Critique

This staggering expenditure can be ethically critiqued at many levels, for instance, by showing the minuscule (by comparison) budgets of all prospective enemies and by conducting studies of waste and duplication. A critique can also be mounted by focusing on alternative uses of that money and what those alternatives would do to increase our real security and well-being. In this imaginative exercise let's look at what just a few million dollars per hour could do if diverted to sane and rational purposes. Applying a cost/benefit analysis to the transfer of military spending to human and ecological investment reveals the immorality of excessive military spending. The military mania is not restricted to the United States. "In a world where billions of people struggle to survive on $1–2 per day, governments spend on average $162 per person on weapons and soldiers."[25] Here I will focus on U.S. spending.

Suppose we could redirect a few million dollars an hour from the $105 million per hour now being spent on kill-power. With the first million per hour, coming to $24 million a day, we could transform American education. The mind is now our main source of wealth; once it was soil, and if you were "dirt poor," you were impoverished. With our first million per hour, we could double the salaries of K–12 teachers, shrink class sizes, and make all students at least bilingual in this intensely interactive world. We could move school aid from inequitable and inconsistent property-tax schemes. We could institute fully paid sabbaticals for K–12 teachers to keep them up with the latest developments in their field, allowing, in some cases, for major retooling.

We could put some of our idle explosives to good use by combining them and many bulldozers to raze every inferior school structure in the nation—putting in their place buildings full of light, beauty, practicality, and hope. (The girl who writes the best essay could be selected to push down the dynamite trigger plunger that brings the old school down.) Prematurely retired people who have forgotten that financial security without fulfillment can lead to death by boredom could be lured back into part-time teaching and rejuvenated. The genius now present in our overworked teachers would be allowed to blossom as

they themselves decide how to improve teaching. Some of the liberated monies would flow to universities, since the need for teachers would at least double. Unlike military spending, which is capital intensive, domestic spending is labor intensive. Looking at our real needs, there really is enough work for all. As more people are employed, more people are paying taxes, and taxes could really be lowered.

At the current time in militarily rich, educationally poor America, the lower economic classes are being priced out of college education. Without liberated monies we could heed Adolph Reed's suggestion of "a GI bill for everybody." Under that bill, Second World War veterans usually received full tuition support and generous stipends (up to $12,000 in 1994 dollars). A 1988 report by a congressional subcommittee on education and health estimated that 40 percent of those who attended college would not otherwise have done so. The report also found that each dollar spent educating that 40 percent produced a $6.90 return due to increased national output and increased federal tax revenues resulting from the more educated citizenry. For less than the cost of six months of fighting the second Gulf War, all public college and university tuition would be free for all qualified students.[26] Tuitions for private universities could be halved.

Calculating Benefits

The economic and security gains from all of this? A highly skilled workforce. There would be alternatives to despair in the ghettos and barrios and slums. We could anticipate technological advances from better-educated researchers, especially regarding the ongoing ecocide. As unemployment goes down, crime goes down, domestic abuse goes down, and hope goes up. We could have all of that, or more and more bombs and bombers.

With a second hourly million freed from the voracious military budget, we could address the ongoing ecological disaster by ending the petroleum dependency. This is the ultimate security problem and one that militarization only makes worse. As Harvard economist Martin Weitzman says, there is about a 5 percent chance that world temperatures will eventually rise by more than 18 degrees Fahrenheit. As Weitzman points out, that is enough to "effectively destroy planet Earth as we know it."[27] Other prognosticators are even more pessimistic. Author James Lovelock, who developed the Electron Capture Detector, which traces poisons in the atmosphere and revealed the CFCs puncturing of the ozone layer, says it is already too late. The planet cannot support more than a billion people, he says, meaning we now have "80 percent more people than the world can carry." He predicts desertification spreading through southern Europe to the point where there will be almost no food grown in Europe.[28]

If Lovelock is anywhere close to right, security needs could not be made of sterner stuff. A sane budget would have this, not more military buildup, as its prime goal. We could begin to catch up in the search for new forms of energy. In April 1988 a Soviet passenger plane, the TU 155 (comparable in size to the Boeing 727), took off from a Moscow airport on a test flight under hydrogen power. We did not respond to this as we did to Sputnik; the TU 155 had little military importance, and we are more responsive to fear than to hopeful prospects.

Another million dollars per hour could be directed to transportation. American trains are among the least developed in the world. The press reminds us they are frequently off the tracks, and when on the tracks they go nowhere very quickly. French steel wheel trains cruise at speeds of 199 miles per hour. Magnetic levitation trains were tested in Japan in 2003 at the speed of 361 mph.[29] These alternatives are live and tested and neglected. The United States has spent 170 times as much on space travel in recent years as on terrestrial transit. The results are painfully visible in cluttered airports and abandoned rail tracks, with 40 percent of our bridges and 60 percent of our roads in serious disrepair since the beginning of the 1990s.

Continuing with this exercise in moral imagination, we could eliminate the category of the "uninsured patient" from our health-care lexicon, making government the insurer of last resort, as is done in other industrial nations of the West. We could make all medical schools tuition-free, with admission based on talent and commitment alone. In return, new doctors would be required to serve for two or three years in medically deprived areas—something that would give them clinical experience they would not get elsewhere. We could supply the number of drug treatment centers that are actually needed—while not forgetting that the best drug treatment is a job-filled economy.

Scientists redirected from war to peace could help plan for and better predict future major earthquakes. Poisoned lakes and groundwaters could be redeemed, topsoil restored, fish sources replenished, and forests saved. The technology is already available to turn deserts into gardens, as illustrated by projects in Israel and elsewhere. The deserts can rejoice, as the biblical poets imagined.

Like a malignant Don Quixote, we mount our military horse to go tilting at windmills around the world. Meanwhile, "our nation's infrastructure is deteriorating, dying of old age and neglect." The U.S. Department of Transportation reported in 2008 that "nearly 25 percent of bridges in the U.S.—over 152,000 bridges—are 'structurally deficient or functionally obsolete.' Heavier vehicles like school buses and delivery trucks, are forced to take lengthy detours for safer bridges. Nearly one in four miles of urban interstate is in 'poor' or 'mediocre' condition." The American Society of Civil Engineers found "more than 150 levees to be at high risk of failing due to poor maintenance."[30]

In an age when borders are melting, we could look beyond our borders toward the poor world. "The poverty of the poor is their ruin," says the biblical book of Proverbs, and increasingly their poverty is our ruin too. Poverty, like capital, is globalized in its effects. The poor denude their land out of desperation and the results come home to us in the air, the water, the beef, the strawberries, and the microbes seeking new habitats and finding us. It's not the tigers coming out of the forest that we now fear. It's the microbes, and these microbes are world travelers. As Nobel laureate Joshua Lederberg says: "The bacteria and viruses know nothing of national sovereignties. . . . The microbe that felled one child in a distant continent yesterday can reach yours today and seed a global pandemic tomorrow."[31] Self-interest, if not nobility, should open our eyes to alternatives.

As noted in chapter 4 (p. 46), Nobel laureate James Tobin's simple but brilliant suggestion has lain fallow: a 0.5 percent tax on all transactions in foreign exchange. The Tobin tax would help dampen speculative international financial movements but would be too small to deter commodity trade or serious international investments, as previously explained. The money could be used to retire unwieldy debts to poor countries and could finance the efforts of the United Nations and other agencies and nongovernmental organizations to bring education, soil conservation, water purification, microloans for cottage industries, family planning, fight of AIDS, and improved education and communication throughout the world. If the United States took the lead on this, we would have nothing to fear from terrorism. As historian Howard Zinn reminds us, generous and modest nations have nothing to fear from terrorism. The prophets of Israel railed against alternative-blindness: "Have you eyes and cannot see? Have you ears and cannot hear?" (Jer. 5:21).

Lessons for Ethics

There are lessons for ethics in this debility of the species. It is not just a case of not seeing alter-

natives, alternatives that are needed and on the ready. There is a caring deficit that not even self-interest can cure. In 2006, three years into the invasion and occupation of Iraq, *New York Times* columnist Nicholas Kristof reminded Americans that for each additional second we stay in Iraq, taxpayers will pay $380,000 a minute that could alternatively be spent on job-creating school and road projects and the provision of health care to all Americans.[32] This warning was met by hearing but not by caring. What has become "The Trillion-Dollar War," drenched in Iraqi and American blood, has lumbered on.[33]

Our comfort with easily remedied anomalies is acute. Examples abound. Take the Electoral College anachronism that stubbornly persists. This leads to situations such as this: "California, with a population of 36 million, elects 2 percent of the Senate, while twenty-one states with the same total population elect 42 percent. It's surely not 'one person, one vote' when people living in the smallest states have twenty times the say as people in the largest."[34] The caring needed to correct this problem was and is lacking. The blinding power of social momentum will be examined in chapter 16 of this book on the hazards of moral discourse.

> ### THINKING CRITICALLY
>
> "Humankind collectively is notoriously less imaginative than the individual."
> —Reinhold Niebuhr
>
> 9.3

The Effects–Alternatives Link

Stretching to see effects and checking alternatives are both horizon experiences. They represent depth and breadth perception and they run counter to the desire of the mind for a quick cognitive fix. Patience is an intellectual virtue, since the rush to judgment trips the mind. We are easy prey to the facile answer. Sloth prompts us to mistake the familiar for the good, and so the door is barred to the possibilities and broader ramifications of any given situation. In the manner of an addict, the mind's craving to know can become captured by illusory, short-lived satisfactions. Good ethical analysis works against this.

Also, effects and alternatives are dynamically related because a pattern of thinking within the arbitrary limits of short-term effects slackens our need to think of alternatives. Similarly, blindness to alternatives works against the perception of effects. When we become aware of other viable alternatives, a process of comparison must begin that will inevitably involve a study of foreseeable short- and long-term effects. If we are blinded to alternate energy sources, we are less likely to be aware of the effects of the currently dominant forms of energy. If we exclude the possible, the actual takes on a certain inevitability and is thus likely to evade critical judgment. Therefore, in the knowing act, foreseeable effects and existent alternatives are linked even though effects refer to the future and alternatives refer mainly to the possibilities of the present.

Back to the Wheel

This linkage illustrates the relationship of all the reality-revealing questions in the hub of the wheel model. All the questions are diagnostic tools unearthing aspects of reality. Moral insight occurs when we see, compositely, how all of the factors will intersect and relate, just as all clues come together and link in a detective's case solving. The case is solved when the mind can relate all of the clues meaningfully. The same is true in ethical judgment.

With this said, the center of the wheel model is completed. Abstractly speaking, we have thus far been gathering, not evaluating. Actually, we have been doing a lot of evaluating as we have moved through the various cases. In the face of a moral issue, the mind instinctively begins to evaluate.

The wheel model, therefore, like any model, is imperfect and abstract, implying as it does that we could unfold reality with our questions and then, as if by signal, commence evaluation.

The problem is that the initial evaluative reaction to a moral situation will be impulsive, partial, and impatient. By insisting on all of the reality-revealing questions, ethics attacks our reliance on figments and surface impressions. The spokes-of-the-wheel model to which we turn next shows the modes of our pluriform intelligence, the multiple ways we know, that is, make conscious contact with reality. If we ignore some of those ways, we condemn ourselves to incompleteness. We are more likely to make top-of-the-head or top-of-the-culture judgments. We can never know all the ways we make cognitive contact with reality, but trying to know how we know is the beginning of wisdom.

Decisions of the Conscience

In presenting this model and method of doing ethics, I do not imply that people (myself included), when faced with a sudden moral decision, will withdraw, sketch out the wheel model of ethics, and plod from point to point. Such immediate decisions are made by conscience, that is, by the morally sensitive self that is attuned to values as they emerge in the concrete situations of life. The reaction of conscience is often "on the spot" when there may be virtually no time for reflection. (Conscience can also look back, with regret or satisfaction.) The nature of conscience will be discussed later in this book; here it is mentioned to note its distinction from detached ethical reflection. Reflection always requires leisure as its matrix, whereas conscience must normally respond to the urgency of action. Ethics, as we shall see, is the tutor of conscience. It tries to keep conscience from impulsively going astray.

Summary of Key Themes

- Even though there are no experts on the future, ethics must try to calculate the future effects of our actions and policies.
- Few actions have only good effects; hence, there is a need for the principle of proportionality.
- Utilitarianism allows for the tyranny of the majority.
- Ethics requires a search for alternatives.
- History shows that we are more responsive to fear than to hopeful prospects and possible alternatives.

Key Terms

Affirmative action
Consequentialism
Double effect, principle of
Just war theory
Proportionality, principle of
Utilitarianism
War

Questions for Discussion

1. If our military budget were cut in half, thus freeing up over four hundred billion dollars a year, what five alternative uses of that money would you prioritize?
2. Discuss the effects of legalizing same-sex marriage and permitting same-sex couples to adopt children.
3. The U.S. Department of Defense used to be called the "Department of War." Write a brief charter for a Department of Peace.

Suggestions for Further Readings

Blackmon, Douglas A. *Slavery by Another Name: The Re-Enslavement of Black Americans from the Civil War to World War II.* New York: Doubleday, 2008.

MacKinnon, Barbara. *Ethics: Theory and Contemporary Issues.* 6th ed. Belmont, Calif.: Wadsworth, 2009.

McCollough, Thomas E. *Moral Imagination and Public Life: Raising the Ethical Question.* Chatham, N.J.: Chatham House, 1991.

PART FOUR

The Moral Mind in Action

Trusting Our Feelings and Emotions

Great truths are felt before they are expressed.
—Teilhard de Chardin, *The Vision of the Past*

Like great works, deep feelings always mean more than they are conscious of saying.
—Albert Camus, *The Myth of Sisyphus*

We know truth, not only by reason, but also by the heart.
—Blaise Pascal, *Pensées*

ALL MORAL KNOWLEDGE IS grounded in **affectivity**, in the foundational moral experience of what persons and this earth of ours are worth. In John Dewey's words: "Affection, from intense love to mild favor, is an ingredient in all operative knowledge, all full apprehension of the good."[1] In this chapter, however, I am not just speaking of the grounding of ethics in affectivity. Good ethics requires a kind of tactical use of our feelings. Our affections and feelings are cognitive, replete with moral awareness. Knowledge is awareness,

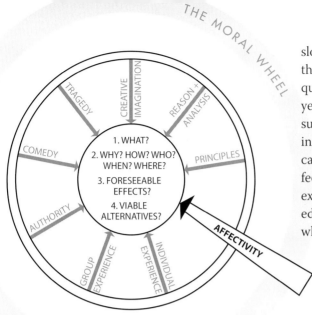

THE MORAL WHEEL

TRAGEDY · CREATIVE IMAGINATION · REASON + ANALYSIS

COMEDY · PRINCIPLES

1. WHAT?
2. WHY? HOW? WHO? WHEN? WHERE?
3. FORESEEABLE EFFECTS?
4. VIABLE ALTERNATIVES?

AUTHORITY

GROUP EXPERIENCE · INDIVIDUAL EXPERIENCE

AFFECTIVITY

slow down long enough to hear it. The awareness that comes through feeling is spontaneous and quite integral to the knowledge of morality. And yet sassy, intellectualized minds that are too cocksure of themselves might refuse to listen. They are, in Shakespeare's words, "sicklied o'er with the pale cast of thought." Certain cultural milieus repress feeling, but even there feelings can never be fully expunged. They are always active, tugging at the edges, tapping on the windows of the room from which they have been barred.

The Power of Evaluative Affectivity

In every religion a rigid orthodoxy on some moral issue can stop ethics in its tracks. The result is a taboo, well ensconced with strong affective moorings. Sometimes the only way to break the grip of the taboo and allow discernment to commence is by way of contrary affectivity. Working on the principle that a story is worth a thousand pictures, I offer an example that illustrates the power of antidotal evaluative affectivity. It involves Roman Catholicism's long-held taboo against remarriage after a divorce. The lessons of the story go well beyond Catholicism.

I began teaching at the Catholic University of America in Washington, D.C., in the summer of 1966. I had a large class of some sixty students, including a number of priests and nuns. Catholic ethics was just awakening from its long slumber, roused by the Second Vatican Council and by breezes from the windows that Pope John XXIII had thrown open. The atmosphere was one of excitement mixed with anxiety as some old absolutes were melting in the light of a new day. My class was nervously receptive as I offered reflections on long-tenured taboos. Among the issues that stirred concern was the topic of remarriage

and much of our awareness is affective, emotive. German ethicists call it **Gemut**. Our *Gemut* feels more than we can verbalize. Ethics must take a systematic account of our affective value-awareness—even though feelings always remain to a degree ineffable.

Much influential thinking in all fields has been impaled on the fallacious dichotomy that divorces feeling from intelligence and affectivity from knowledge. Feeling is a knowing experience, and extreme mischief has been wrought by the failure to recognize this. This is true for ethics and also for the sciences, both social and hard. No thinking in any field is ever disembodied or disaffected. And feelings do not arise as neutral outbursts, but as informed, evaluative reactions. Feelings may be mixed and contradictory—and often dead wrong—just as abstract and intellectualized reasonings may be. Nevertheless, those feelings are a cognitive reaction, not a sideline eruption that takes place off the field of knowing. Uneasiness is often the penumbra of insight. In assessing moral problems, "once again with feeling" is a splendid rule.

We do not have to plan for emotion to happen, nor can we summon the wisdom of the heart, though we may have to discipline ourselves to after divorce. The prevailing teaching was that one could not remarry while one's partner lived. Only death, not divorce, could do them part.

It was clear where I was going as I took up the history of this rigid view. I showed how the Christian Scriptures' condemnation of divorce was related to the devastation visited on divorced women in Jesus' time. It reflected the sensitivity of Jesus' Judaism to the plight of those women. It could not be seen as a universal law binding all ages. I could see that this was a hard saying and not all could receive it. Then to my rescue came this story with all of its emotional power.

Living in Sin?

I'll call them Jim and Sally, though those are not their names. Members of Jim's family called me and told me this story. Jim, they said, was not an icon of generosity or considerateness, but surprising things were happening to him. After their Tuesday night bowling, Jim's family gathered as usual for pizza and beer. Suddenly Jim was insisting that they sit at the table waited on by a young woman named Sally, and the usually tight-fisted Jim was insisting on huge tips for her. Love was in the air, but there was also pain. Sally had been married to a violent man. She had three children. She stayed in this marriage because she was a strict Catholic who had promised to take that man "for better or for worse." She got the "worse" but felt bound by her vow. When the last child was born with problems related to beatings Sally had sustained from her husband, Sally finally took the children and left. Life was difficult. She had to work, get help from friends and family to look after the children, and ward off unfriendly visits from her husband.

During this time she met Jim, and both fell deeply in love. They could not marry in the church and could not consider marrying anywhere else. They would tearfully decide to stop seeing one another, but one or the other would break down shortly thereafter and check in to see how the other was doing. Finally they decided to marry in a civil ceremony. Life immediately got better for the little family. Jim took on these children as though they were his own. He was offered and accepted a job in Los Angeles, and now Sally's ex-husband, left behind in Phoenix, was no longer a problem. A year later Sally became pregnant. They were thrilled that they would have their first child together, but their happiness was clouded by church teaching at the time that said they were "living in sin."

Two months into the pregnancy, doctors told Sally that she had a tumor that required surgery. Sally was in a panic. Her life was in danger and she was "living in sin." It was at this moment that her family contacted me.

At Catholic University we were in our final week of class. I went in the next day and told the story to the class. Applying what I had taught them in theory, I told them what I thought should be done. I said, "Given what I have told you, that first marriage had failed. The second marriage was a success, a great success, one that brought healing and beauty into the lives of Jim and Sally and their three children, who had their first experience of a peaceful home. A priest should go out there and tell Jim and Sally that he could marry them in a private Catholic marriage in their home. This would be strictly forbidden by the church hierarchy, but it is the right and moral thing to do, because of new developments in Catholic theology. The priest should celebrate a private liturgy for them to wrap the moment with all the reassuring symbols of their faith tradition. Then, with their minds at peace, and feeling themselves truly husband and wife, Sally could proceed to surgery."

Exorcising Demons of Habit

When I finished my evaluation, the bell rang, ending class. I wondered how my transfixed class of nuns and priests would react. The answer came quickly. A nun who had been in the convent for some twenty years approached me with a red face.

I expected a rebuke. Instead, she said with impatience: "Don't just tell us about this. Get a priest out there to do it!" I told her I planned to. Next in line, and speaking softly, was a priest who had never spoken a word during the class. He said, "I am a priest in Los Angeles, and I will be going there tomorrow after your exam. I would be glad to do that for Jim and Sally."

This priest could not tell anyone he was going to do this because his archbishop was one of the most rigid of Catholic hierarchs and would reject him from ministry. So the next morning in our last class, before the afternoon test, I announced that a priest from this class was going to go to Los Angeles to take care of Jim and Sally in the way I had suggested. The class rose in a standing ovation for this unknown priest. The priest himself, with his face bright scarlet, rose and clapped, with only he and I knowing he was clapping for himself.

When the class settled down, I completed the theoretical teaching on the right to remarriage after a failed first marriage. I said the ideal of a permanent, faithful marriage cannot always be realized. When such an ideal is realized in a second marriage, that marriage is not to be called unholy. Not a single doubt about that was raised in that class or in the exam that followed.

The story had a happy ending. The operation on Sally's tumor was successful and did not interrupt the pregnancy.

Now to the role of *Gemut* in this incident: Did my theoretical and historical lectures on marriage and divorce do the main teaching? Or did the intense feelings act like an exorcism to drive out the demons of habit in the minds of my hearers? Was affect or reason the main teacher? The answer is not an either/or matter, but more in the realm of reciprocity. The affections played a critical role, but the teachings that had been poured into the minds gave some freedom to the heart. Better yet, both routes to truth, reason and affect, aided and abetted one another. Of such stuff are we knowers made.

Feeling versus Orthodoxy

Orthodoxy is a temptation, as we have seen. Security is the drug of choice for those mentally immobilized in rigid orthodoxy, and it is not just religions that are guilty of this immobilization. This kind of fixation is often immune to reason and argument. Only feeling can liberate. Another true story shows this: A Catholic chaplain with the Marines in Vietnam (disclosure: my brother, Connell) was, in the term of the day, a "hawk" on the war. American orthodoxy said our mission was just. We were there to help and we were doing good, albeit violently. Contrary arguments had not shaken his views. It took a sick little girl to do that.

THINKING CRITICALLY

West Point graduate and Vietnam War veteran Andrew J. Bacevich writes of the American affection for war, an affection that dominates our self-image as a nation: "Today as never before in their history Americans are enthralled with military power. The global military supremacy that the United States presently enjoys—and is bent on perpetuating—has become central to our national identity. More than America's matchless material abundance or even the effusions of its pop culture, the nation's arsenal of high-tech weaponry and the soldiers who employ that arsenal have come to signify who we are and what we stand for."

—Andrew J. Bacevich, *The New American Militarism: How Americans Are Seduced by War*

10.1

He was standing by a road waiting for a long line of American military trucks and equipment to pass by so that he could cross over. Suddenly he was joined by a little eight- or nine-year-old Vietnamese girl standing beside him, also waiting to cross. It was the dry season and the trucks were tossing up clouds of dust. He looked down at the girl and drew back in horror. On her leg was a festering growth. The dust from the road was caking on it. He realized it was bubonic plague. His sense of horror suddenly stretched out to include the millions of dollars of military traffic roaring by. The feeling-thought hit him: What are all those Americans with their expensive equipment doing that is more important than this little girl's leg to which they are paying no heed at all? He could never view the war again the same way. The iron grip of orthodoxy was pried loose by the flood of feelings, piercing feelings of pity and anger that set him free. The Marine chaplain had moved from "hawk" to "dove." No dry syllogism could achieve what those emotions did.

First Response

The nine spokes of the wheel model of ethics show the diverse ways of "knowing." Affectivity, *Gemut*, will be the first responder, especially if we are presented with a new or startling idea. This emotive response gives us an initial position on the topic even before we begin any analysis. This is first-response ethics, although it cannot stand as the final verdict. Our emotive response is evaluative. We have a preliminary, tentative position on whether this proposal is or is not good for people, on whether it really seems to view persons as persons with all of their needs and possibilities. If knowledge is awareness, then in reacting affectively in this matter, I am affectively aware, and probably in a pronounced and heightened way, of the rapport between this proposal and person-

hood as I understand it. Whether the affective response is positive or negative, it means that I am not entirely unknowing about the moral import of this matter. Judgment has feelingly commenced.

It is possible that unlettered persons might not be able to say anything to explain or defend this reaction, yet they would have a definite reaction and would not be neutral on the matter. Upon the necessary follow-up reflection, we might well reverse our first response, or we might eventually decide that this is an idea whose time has come, an idea that only ingrown recalcitrance could resist. The process of knowing is under way, and when we reflect further, using the rest of the wheel model, it would not be a movement from not knowing to knowing, but from knowing to knowing better.

Acts of Knowing Awareness

To shrink from something in a reaction of abhorrence—even if the "shrinking" cannot be articulated by the person except in expletive—is an act of knowing awareness. If one heard an eloquent defense of that reaction later, one would say, "Yes, that was exactly what I *felt*, although I could not explain it in words," and that would be quite accurate.

Example: ***polyamory***. Though the phenomenon in various forms may be as ancient as the species, the word is new, just having arrived in the *Oxford English Dictionary* in 2006. It has even made inroads into religious circles, as seen in the group called Unitarian Universalists for Polyamory Awareness (UUPA).

UUPA defines polyamory as the philosophy and practice of loving or relating intimately to more than one other person at a time with honesty and integrity. UUPA advocates for any form of relationship or family structure—whether monogamous or multipartner—that is characterized by free and responsible choice, mutual consent of all involved, and sincere adherence to personal philosophical values.

Polyamorous families may live together, raise children together, share household expenses, but all of this without sexual exclusivity or monogamous possessiveness in the home. All partners are informed and in agreement on this arrangement of sexual variety. Though the concept of polyamory is new to most cultures, it is not new to Islam. **Polygyny** was considered permissible under all schools of Islamic law.[2] The first marriage of the prophet Muhammad to Khadija was monogamous and is considered the ideal of harmonious partnership. Afterward, the Prophet entered into polygynous marriages. This was not considered the ideal and it could only be justified if there was mutual agreement among all parties. "That the Prophet deterred his son-in-law Ali from marrying more wives while he was married to his daughter Fatima indicates that he considered monogamy the norm and polygyny inadvisable."[3] Contemporary Muslim scholars usually argue that polygyny is *haram*, immoral, since it does not measure up to the demands of mutuality and justice.[4]

Feelings will not be neutral in response to the polyamorous concept, ranging from initial enthusiasm to revulsion. That means ethics has started, but only started. Next come all the questions in the center of the wheel and the other eight spokes. During the analysis, questions will be raised on the prospects of stability in such a plural union. What happens when this mix of multiple weaknesses and personality differences unfolds? Will there be competition and jealousy if sexual partners are viewed with different degrees of ardor? And consider the effects on the children of such polyamorous families, when there are multiple sources of discipline and these not always in agreement. Children are expert at finding the parent most likely to acquiesce. Questions of paternity testing will also arise. Polyamory has not been adequately studied by the social sciences, but when it is, the social sciences and ethics will need answers on all these issues. Still, the emotional response starts the ethical process, and in the end, it might prove

to be accurate when full analysis is completed. *Gemut* may at times arrive at truth first with great ethical accuracy.[5]

Inchoate Judgment

Since examples keep theory honest, here is one more: The science of genetics has pointed out the progressive deterioration of the human gene pool, as it is no longer only the genetically fit who survive. The unfit now not only survive but enjoy prolonged fertility and thus can unleash their unfitness, their "recessive genes," into what becomes the genetic destiny of posterity. Natural selection is not functioning as a screen, and the result is an increasing phenomenon of negative feedback whereby gene-based imperfections are spreading throughout the species. Modern technology causes more and more genetic damage, and that same technology helps genetically damaged people to live longer and to spread their genes by reproducing. Some envision a genetic apocalypse a-building with the human pool eventually so stocked with damaging genes that the whole race will be sick and consumed in medicinal care of itself.[6]

Nobel Prize winner Herman J. Muller suggested one temporary solution: that we obtain and freeze the sperm of superior men, men such as Einstein, Pasteur, Descartes, and Lincoln. (In an earlier edition he included Lenin, but political considerations prompted him later to drop Lenin from the list.) The idea was that no "reasonable" woman could object to being fertilized by such men in service to the health of our species. The sperm would be preserved for as long as twenty years to ensure that the judgment of the donor's moral, psychological, and physical health was not amiss. A panel would then judge after this period which of the men still seemed to be a sterling genetic supplier. Then their sperm could be used in a voluntary program of artificial insemination by couples who were conscious of their own genetic limitations and were generously anxious to strike a blow for genetic improvement within the human species.

This offers to us the picture of a noble and enlightened wife importuning her less enlightened but docile new husband in words something like this: "You know, darling, that you are the joy of my life and the fulfillment of all my dreams of love. Genetically, however, as we both know, you are, relatively speaking, something of a disaster area. Therefore, let us repair to the frozen sperm bank, and select there the choice sperm that will help turn the tide of the deteriorating human gene pool." Science would allow for laparascopic recovery of ova from "superior" women, opening yet another eugenic door.

Thus concretized, with an admitted negative tilt, *Gemut* will rise quickly to inchoate judgment. What we have here is a scientific option that is also a matter for moral judgment. Aside from its scientific feasibility or nonfeasibility, Muller's option is a course of action that befits or does not befit the reality of what persons are; that is, it is either moral or immoral. Before one begins a complete ethical analysis of the suggestion by asking *what* the plan is in its prima facie physical appearance, what effects are imaginable, what alternatives could be found, and so on, someone hearing the suggestion for the first time would not begin the questioning process without a preliminary stance. The very suggestion would evoke some affective response. With most persons, this response would be negative, or at least very hesitant and uneasy. One might even be aghast at the idea. On the other hand, one might also respond with positive fervor.

Full ethical analysis would then follow, treating questions such as these: Would the sperm undergo significant mutations in this frozen state? Could unsuspected recessive traits exist in the sperm of these great men only to surface in their progeny? What psychosocial collisions could result if the intended goals are achieved and a very superior child is born into a very mediocre family environment? Could a genius born to mar-

ginally intelligent parents present developmental problems? What criteria were used to decide on the ideal donor, and how arbitrary—or racially or class biased—were those criteria? And so on.

When these and other questions have been marshaled and tested, one could then accost Muller's idea with a highly informed ethical critique. The final articulated conclusions, however, might not differ from the initial affective response. The work of ethical inquiry may simply be confirmatory. Confirmation, however, is a reinforcement of the known, since, in a sense, what is not confirmed is not known but only suspected—perhaps wisely suspected, but the case is not yet proved.

Affective Knowing

There is an obvious difficulty to be confronted here. I am speaking as though we could have affective response cut off from preliminary intellectualization and conceptualization, as though the wet of emotion and the dry of intellection could have separable existences in a person. This is not the case. Feeling, "emoting," abstracting, and reasoning are all operations of the person, not detachable faculties that can be conveniently taken aside and studied in isolation from the others as one could study the foot while paying no heed to the ear. Knowledge of certain facts or some abstract knowledge may seem virtually free of affectivity, but affection pervades all knowledge. (A mathematician with no "feel" for her subject would be ineffective.) This is especially true for moral knowledge. A complete absence of caring would render all moral categories meaningless. An emotional response to a case such as that of Muller is not severed from previous intellectual and conceptualized experiences. As John Dewey put it: "The results of prior experience, including previous conscious thinking, get taken up into direct habits, and express themselves in direct appraisal of value. Most of our moral judgments are intuitive, but this fact . . . is the result of past experience funded into direct outlook upon the scene of life."[7]

In moral knowledge, there is no purely emotional reaction and no purely conceptualized judgment. Conception and affection are essentially intertwined. Still, the distinction between the two is not a distinction without a difference. Abstract, conceptual knowledge can be distinguished from an affective and emotional response. The problem is that the distinction has been too drastically made and emotion has been considered something precognitive or pretercognitive. Affective knowing should be seen as a genuine though different kind of knowing. It calls for completion, and the mind should move on to other kinds of knowing to find that completion. Otherwise it will not be able adequately to give reasons for its position. Neither will it know, without the intellectual work of comparison, whether its position is the result of bias or of genuine insight.

To quote Dewey again: "As Aristotle remarked in effect a long time ago, the immediate judgments of good and evil of a good man are more to be trusted than many of the elaborately reasoned out estimates of the inexperienced."[8] But Dewey goes on to note pointedly that "there is no such thing as a good man—in an absolute sense. Immediate appreciation is liable to be warped by many considerations which can be detected and uprooted only through inquiry and criticism."[9]

The moral and psychological story of each of us is scarred and twisted. There is no ideal observer of things moral and there is no infallible feel for moral truth in any of us.[10] Affectivity cannot be the only spoke in the wheel model of moral inquiry. D. H. Lawrence's "What our blood feels is always right" must be balanced against Adolf Hitler's "I think with my blood."

Affect Phobia

The animal that describes itself as the *animal rationale*, the animal distinguished by the power of reasoning, has often disparaged the wisdom of the heart. Heart-wisdom is not as tidy as the rationalist would prefer, but in epistemology, tidiness is suspect, and in this case clearly wrong. Still, many of the titans of thought have downplayed affective cognition. Immanuel Kant spoke with little patience of "the alleged special sense, the moral feeling." The appeal to moral feeling, Kant said, "is superficial, since those who cannot think expect help from feeling."[11] Kant summoned ethics into "the court of pure reason," and many are they who hearkened to him. Kant's reaction to the excesses of the "moral sense" ethicians (who slighted reason in favor of a simplistic **intuitionism**) was in turn excessive. But the assault reaches back into history. Plato distinguished between the "philosopher" (the lover of *sophia*, "wisdom") and the "philosoma" (the lover of the *soma*, "the body"). He says this in the *Phaedo*, where Socrates is speaking to Simmias and says, "If you see a man fretting because he is to die, he was not really a philosopher but a philosoma—not a wisdom-lover but a body lover."[12] Actually, he may have simply been a life-lover who hated leaving life, and there is nothing unwise about that.

Let it be said, however, with the redemption brought by inconsistency, that Plato did see that socialization and moral education should be done in such a way that we would delight in and be pained by the things that we ought.[13] Moral education involves the refinement of affect.

Sigmund Freud joined the attack on the affections since he saw that the maladies he analyzed were rooted there.

As he got older, he "became the more convinced of the essential insanity of our desires and of the need to repress the logic of the heart."[14] Karl Marx also sinned here as he saw emotions as the breeding ground for the self-serving distortions of ideology. Christian spirituality, which was enormously influential in shaping Western consciousness, attached negative value to "concupiscence" in a way that stigmatized the emotional and affective side of personal life. Pragmatic concerns arising from the early European invasion of indigenous American peoples and the development of this rich "promised land" ran counter to right-brain sensibility and sentiment. In a symbolic act, these new Americans banished the maypole dancers and with them much of the valid claims of the Dionysian and sentimental forces of our nature. The left-brain Apollo, not the right-brain Dionysus, would be king here.

THINKING CRITICALLY

The events of history have shaped how we feel—and then make moral judgments—about ourselves. It is as though history assigns feelings to us, for instance, the feeling that men are strong and women weak. As Barbara Ehrenreich writes: "By assigning the triumphant predator status to males alone, humans have helped themselves to 'forget' that nightmarish prehistory in which they were all, male and female, prey to larger, stronger animals. Insofar as males have been the human 'norm' and females the deviation, weakness and vulnerability could be seen as something aberrant and incidental to the story of humankind. *Gender, in other words, is an idea that conveniently obliterates our common past as prey, and states that the predator status is innate and 'natural'—at least to men.*"

—Barbara Ehrenreich, *Blood Rites: Orgins and History of the Passions of War*

10.3

volved a stronger sense of transcendence, which included greater tension between that "higher world" and this material one. The duality between them opposed our immaterial spirit to the corruptions of the flesh, denigrating nature, women, and sex—perhaps because they are associated with death? Our animal bodies remind us of our mortality . . . so let's make the soul immortal![15]

Alienation metastasizes when affect is repressed and distorted, just as when you try to push an inner tube under water in one spot, it pops up elsewhere. Repressed affect doesn't go away; it takes negative turns.

Loy alludes to the degradation of women, and indeed, the condemning of the affective does denigrate women. While putting women down, those things that were associated with women—and this included affectivity—were concomitantly slighted. Men were seen as more related to "mind," women to "body." Feminist writers have been struggling to correct this. Feminist theologian Beverly Harrison writes: "If we begin, as feminists must, with 'our bodies, ourselves,' we recognize that all our knowledge, including our moral knowledge, is body-mediated knowledge. All knowledge is rooted in our sensuality. . . . Feeling is the basic bodily ingredient that medizates our connectedness to the world."[16] The an-

Our Bodies, Ourselves, Our World, Our Universe

Buddhist philosopher David Loy writes:

The **Axial Age** that developed in several civilizations during the first millennium B.C.E. incients put it this way: *nil in intellectu nisi prius in sensu*—"nothing is in the intellect that did not start in the senses."

Dangers of Disaffection

The slighting of affect is no slight fault. It is also a flight from woman, from the body, and from the world. It carries a deadly ecological payload. It was this kind of detached and disembodied thinking that could allow the human species to take a generously fecund earth and wreck it. Embodied affective knowing is not just an epistemological ideal: it is the passport to earth-friendly and humanistic ethics.

Manipulative relationships are by definition unloving. A disembodied attitude toward our ecology tilts us toward manipulation. Science allows us to manipulate everything, even our food. We are tempted to see the rest of nature as more manipulable than it is. Autistic speciesism forgets the interconnections of everything. Nature talks back. Monarch caterpillars feed exclusively on milkweed leaves. In 1998, however, it was discovered that milkweed was being contaminated by genetically altered Bt-corn pollen. Genetically engineered potatoes have caused immune system damage to rats. Researchers from the University of California claim that genes from biotech corn have contaminated native maize in the Mexican highlands.[17]

There is also sociological impact in the flight from the heart. It is the tides of affection that move history. Historical changes are moved by valuation, not ratiocination.[18] Reasoning and information can help, but only if they penetrate into our affective awareness. Until they do, they are sterile and peripheral to effective moral and political action. The facts of ecological deterioration have been long present. The ecology movement started only when fueled by feeling. Progress in the field of law is moved by affective forces. A Supreme Court justice who does not grieve over the plight of African Americans will consistently find

ingenious reasons not to support efforts to relieve their pain. Economists and social theorists who are not affectively moved by poverty will offer dazzling rationalizations for the very conditions that foment and sustain poverty. Prize-winning brilliance that is not "grieved at the ruin of Joseph" (Amos 6:6) does not advance civilization or bring relief to "Joseph."

The Sinews of Community

The major religions, shunned by many "sophisticates," are also profound probes into human psychology. The prophets of Israel understood that the affective component of all social reform is key. They knew that any message of reform must get "into the heart" (Isa. 51:7). Unless "our eyes run with tears and our eyelids be wet with weeping," we will come to a "fearful ruin" (Jer. 9:18-19). The "enlightenment" that is the goal of Buddhism is suffused with feelings of harmony and compassion. It is not just "getting smart" in a superficial, rationalistic sense. The many Gods and Goddesses of Hinduism are among the most passionate figures in world literature.

Social cohesion and community are achieved affectively. We become present to one another through our feelings. *Presence* admits of degrees, as does *meeting*. You can be close to someone for years and never truly *meet* them. In a certain sense we meet and are present to those waiting in line with us to board at the airport gate, but only dimly so. We are more present when we take off. But presence and togetherness take a qualitative leap when the pilot announces mechanical trouble and a need to return to the airport. When the plane lands safely after a struggle, there are no strangers aboard. A shared affectivity and felt hope and needs are the sinews of community. Ecological disasters that are planetary in cause and effect are slowly—too slowly?—dissolving the artificial boundaries of nations. The affective tilt is toward the long-denied fact of human oneness.

That the body has its own wisdom needs reasserting, and the affections do just that. It is body consciousness that saves us from our abstractness. It is too easy to forget that we are our bodies. He who wounds my hand wounds me. Ethics, then, which is a work sprung from reverence, needs emphatic reverence for our corporality, too. Simply put, the ideal is to avoid heartless head or headless heart. Those ingenious military planners who coolly and ingeniously calculate in terms of megadeaths are an example of the perils of the unfeeling mind. Those who would lyrically infer that politics could be done without reference to the gritty realities of power would be an example of headless heart.

A Caution:
Beyond Romanticizing Nature

What is not needed, of course, is an overstress on the biological to the point where the biological becomes ethically normative. The Stoics were among those who sinned grievously in this way, blurring the lines between the biological and the ethical. This kind of thinking led, for example, to the conclusion that contraception, since biologically "frustrating," was therefore ethically wrong. Making the case that there is nothing so powerful as a bad idea, this Stoic biologism seeped into the Christian churches, which for centuries condemned contraception, forgetting that they got this from the Stoa, not from God. Such a biologistic caricature should serve as a warning, but not as a block to a strong ethical respect for bodiliness. Those working in bioethics should take special heed here, since the controlling mind, drunk with its new powers that are seemingly boundless in their promise, could deafen us to the gentle claims that the body legitimately presses upon our consciences.

Concern for the legitimate claims of nature and of our bodies should not stop us from cultivating

a benign manipulation of nature. The need to control our fertility on a finite planet is an obvious example. Bioethicist and Jewish scholar Laurie Zoloth notes the need for a middle way between touch-not-nature ecologists and ecocide. The command "given early in Genesis, 'leshev et ha/ aretz,' 'to settle the land,' . . . is precisely the insight that allows for a middle way between the intensely debated arguments for productive development *and* for preservation that marks so much of the literature, scholarly and popular, on ecology."[19]

Nature need not be romanticized to be respected and appreciated. The salmon intent on spawning but that instead becomes a bear's dinner will testify that nature has inbuilt violence. Like the bear, we, too, kill to eat. So nature is a mixed bag. Along with sunsets and flowers and babies' first smiles, nature includes Ebola virus, childhood cancer, and inevitable death—death for ourselves and eventually death for our planet when the sun runs down and we and our planet return to stardust. In the meantime, our lives would still be short and brutish if we allowed unbridled nature to have its way.

The other extreme to romanticizing nature has long been dominant in economics. "Undeveloped" land is nothing until human investment and labor intervene to "make something of it." Before entrepreneurs get hold of natural resources, "every plant is a weed and every mineral is just another rock."[20] As Larry Rasmussen says in critique of this imperial view: "Until humans acquire and transform it, land is thus devoid of value. Five thousand species may live in this unoccupied earthpatch, and its life-support capacity may be very full indeed. But modern economics does not see this and does not understand in either theory or practice that land is embodied energy with its own complex life, its own complex actions and needs, and its own economy."[21] When it comes to nature, developers and economists do not excel in reciprocity thinking.

Show Me Your Delights and I Will Tell You What You Are

Philosophers often get lost up blind alleys, but nevertheless, their preoccupations will often reflect the concerns of their times. Our times neglect—of all things—our capacity to delight, and so, too, does most of modern ethics. In the phenomenon of delight (and its opposite, the **sense of profanation**) we have the most perceptible manifestation of the cognitive power of affectivity. Our neglect of delight reflects our rationalistic unease with feeling. In the moral philosophy of Aristotle, Plato, and Thomas Aquinas, in contrast, delight is given thoughtful prominence. Aristotle, for example, saw delight as a signal of where the heart or the **character** of a person is. He said that we must take as a "sign of states of character the pleasure or pain that ensues on acts." If we delight in doing the acts that pertain to a certain moral value, then this is a sign that this value has woven its way into our character. If we do these things but do them grudgingly and find them a burden, we have not incorporated the value into our moral fiber.[22] Delight arises from unimpeded and congruent activity.[23] In the same vein, Thomas Aquinas says that when our activity is connatural to us, it is delightful.[24]

Delights are the indices of character. Aristotle goes so far as to say in his *Ethics* that just as "truth is that which seems to the good man to be true," so, too, the delights of the good man can be taken as true and properly rooted.[25] The "good man's" delights can therefore serve as a criterion of moral truth. (Aristotle was not as keen on the delights of the good woman.)

Notice that Aristotle's "good man" need not be learned or capable of impressive argument to be reliable. The reliance here is on his affective orientation in the face of a moral question. That which is good vibrates and resonates delightfully—that is, it produces emotions of delight and pleasure—

in someone who is good. The sound that comes from a Stradivarius is good because the Stradivarius is good. There is an affective response to a particular value option that is experienced as congenial, suitable, "connatural," quite in accord with one's moral orientation, and hence delightful. In the good person, this means that it is also good.

These emotional reactions of delight amount to an endorsement of that which is perceived. But endorsement proceeds from evaluative awareness, that is, some kind of knowledge. Endorsement divorced from knowledge is just noise. Delights are not just noise.

Delights as Mind-Stretching

Thomas Aquinas is guilty of taking some liberties with etymology. He had a wise interest in knowing where words come from, but when he had no solid information on that, he often freestyled and just made it up. His transgression is pardonable, however, when he makes valid points.

Thomas suggests that *delight* (*delectatio*) comes from the word for "broadening" (*dilatatio*). It actually comes from *dilectio*, meaning "love." He then goes to do good things with his happy error. Delight is a reaction to that which is congenial and pleasant. In delighting, we are stretched and enlarged as we somehow strain to make room for and contain that which comes to us as a new good. The stretching and broadening effect of delight is part of the urgency of delight through which we attempt to take that which is delightful into ourselves so as to envelop it and enjoy it more fully. Delight has a "can't get enough of it" quality as we stretch for more and more.[26]

The Many Faces of Delight

Permit a digression here to an unlikely locus to reinforce Thomas's point. When I first visited St. Peter's Cathedral in the Vatican City, the guide led me to the high altar. Towering over it is the gilded bronze *baldachino* with its crown and four supporting columns. The four columns rest on white marble blocks with small faces carved by Bernini. The first face is that of a woman in obvious pain. As one proceeds clockwise around the bases of the columns, the woman's face changes on each marble block to a variety of expressions. On the next-to-last block, the grimace of pain returns. The final carving is of a baby's face. According to the guide, the first grimace is the grimace of orgasm; the last is the grimace of childbirth. Both faces are the same, the one expressing ecstasy, the other severe pain. (If this interpretation holds, there is something delightful about an orgasm pictured at the base of the papal high altar.)

Thomas was onto something here. Delight is the bloom of pleasant experience, and yet it does have in it elements of straining and stretching, even to the point of pain. Ecstasy is often described in terms of pain. When the news is too good, we cry. The grimace that manifests extreme pain resembles the "grimace" of exquisite pleasure. Extreme delight, like extreme sorrow, produces tears.

Many of the mystics who write of the supreme joy of their highest mystical moments turn to images of pain such as "piercing" and "burning" to describe their experience. Delight has an inner impatience and insatiability in it that seems to reach for an unattainable more. A heightened need for union with the object of delight seems to characterize delight at its most poignant pitch. Hence the bittersweet or agony-ecstasy tension of intense delight. The dynamic here seems to be toward union and absorption. Delight seeks to take in that which delights and to be identified with it. To some degree we achieve this, and so it is that we become our delights. Delight weaves its stimulus into our being.

The Nether Side of Delight

The sense of profanation, of which I have spoken above, is the nether side of delight. This is the sense of shock, aversion, and withdrawal that we experience in the face of that which offends the value of persons and their environment. If persons and nature are the prime sacraments of delight, their violation in any way evokes the feeling of profanation. Sometimes that which is valuable is taken for granted. *Consueta vilescunt*—"things we are accustomed to become less prized." We become blasé to the delightful reality that is so familiar to us. Only after the sense of profanation that follows upon violation or destruction might we become sensitive to the delight that we in our apathy had missed. The emerging ecological awareness of this time is a discovery of lost delights. If this is more than an ephemeral, epidermal romance, a salvific capacity to delight in the richness of the good earth might be born of the shock of eco-catastrophe.

Character as Moral Architecture

The term *character* in ethics refers to the awesome fact that morally we come to be what we do. The word *do* there refers not only to actions but to omissions that are often more reflective of and determinative of character. In his crisp way, Aristotle sums it up: "By doing the acts that we do in our transactions with other people we become just or unjust, and by doing the acts that we do in the presence of danger, and being habituated to feel fear or confidence, we become brave or cowardly. . . . Thus, in one word, states of character arise out of like activities."[27]

Character is the embodiment of a person's moral orientation. It is the timbre of a person's ingrained moral quality. It is the moral thrust of the personality that is given its direction from the decisions of our moral history. Character is only somewhat genetically inherited. Cultural osmosis also explains some of it. Being born into wealth or into poverty will surely affect our responses to life, although it does not efface our ability to break cultural shackles. But, mainly, character results from what we have done and from the options embraced within our moral environment. The person is not a mindless piece of cork helplessly adrift. We exercise some directioning power so that we can be termed in some decisive sense free and in some decisive sense the architects of our character.

Character, slowly shaped and ingrained, has, therefore, a kind of stability. Atypical behavior contrary to the direction of the character is suspect. It is seen as "uncharacteristic." Sudden and major shifts in character are not to be looked for. A ruthless political operative, for example, who suddenly becomes morally transformed and religiously fervid is duly suspect for a time. Character is a long-haul achievement. As such, it has considerable momentum and cannot go immediately into reverse. The arc of moral conversion is broad, not narrow.

Recognizing Character

Obviously, there is no one who has a purely good or bad character. We are all amalgams of values and disvalues. Certain overall moral traits are discernible in persons, however, and we are instinctively alert to these in "sizing people up." We do not perceive persons as a page filled with unconnected dots. We find connections and patterns, enough to make some judgment on "the kind of person" they are and the kind of thing they are likely to do. What we glimpse is called character.

Thomas Aquinas, often misunderstood as a rigorous rationalist, insists that correct moral judgments can come about in two ways: through a perfect use of reason, or through what he calls a kind of affective "connaturality" with the matters being judged, which come *per amorem*, "through love." Persons who have not studied ethics might judge correctly about it because they have embodied that value in their habitual disposition, that is, their character. Thomas distinguishes between "learning" (*discens*) moral truth and "suffering" or "experiencing" (*patiens*) that truth. In the latter kind of

knowing, love so blends the value into the reality of the person that it becomes "connatural" (second nature) to her. She can judge correctly about that value because she is so personally attuned to it.[28]

Character, then, is a derivative of all the choices driven by our delights and loves. Ethics must take account of it, since the tides of what we know move under the gravity of what we love and will and what we delight in. It is, in Thomas Aquinas's related phrase, "the disposition or form by which the knower knows."[29] Character is the sound chamber in which new moral experiences resonate: its construction affects what we hear. It is a critical source of *perspective* in judging. A person whose character has been shaped by a passion for justice will not be "a person of narrow sympathy."[30]

Love is a unitive and a lively force. Things loved become "second nature to us now, like breathing in and breathing out." The unjust man might be a whiz at ethical theories of justice. His intelligence of justice, however, is flawed by his lack of full experience of what it is that justice means. He sees but does not taste. His knowledge of justice is limited to one kind of knowing. He is weak at the foundational moral experience and thus does not have at his command what Henri Bergson calls "the genius of the will." The reasons of the heart, to which Pascal referred, will escape him. The foundational moral experience is the parent of character and moral wisdom. Weakness in the FME is a cognitive weakness.

Beyond Sociopathy and Stupidity

Important qualifications must be added to this consideration. Just as there is no such thing as an absolutely good person, there is no such thing as an absolutely bad one. The Confucian philosopher Mencius believed that there is some core of indestructible good at the center of every human personality. He proposed the image of a child sitting on the edge of a well. Imagine that the child is losing its balance and is about to fall into the well. It was unthinkable to Mencius that any human being passing close by would not reach out to help the child. This he saw as a "natural" response, illustrating that in each of us is "the mind that cannot bear the sufferings of others."[31] Allowing for the possibility of the disease of sociopathology, Mencius has a point. A total liquidation of sympathy cannot be imagined in any reasonably healthy person any more than one can imagine perfection in a human being. The perfect person, like the "ideal observer," does not exist. There's hope in that.

Also, take note: nobody is totally stupid. The "good person" might have narrow experience and could profit from the "bad person" who may have garnered amid his iniquities a shrewd sense of relationship and predictability that would be valuable in assessing complicated moral matters. Thus, it is not necessary simply to make a choice between the judgment of a good person or that of an expert who is not so virtuous. One would be well advised to hear from both.[32] Sometimes, in doing ethics, when we look for the witness of the heart, we will hear contradictory answers. The heart, like the intellect, does not specialize in unequivocal conclusions. Here, as in all situations of disagreement, sound ethics wants to hear both sides to find the part of truth that each may be presumed to contain. Our affective orientation is not infallible. Bigots, after all, are full of affect. And so, just as a lawyer wants to know the vested interest of his client in legal dealings, so do we have to be aware of where our feelings are pulling us and why.

the meaning of universalizability, the history of principles, and so forth, with a reassuring feeling that this is indeed workable turf. In addressing particular cases, a number of principles of potential relevance have been formulated and may be summoned to test their applicability. In doing this, one can have a good sense of knowing what one is about. But how, in attempting to analyze the moral import of a situation, does one summon affectivity? Should we repair to a meditation room and allow our feelings to play upon the cases at hand and then bring back a report on this to the table where the hard ethical analysis is going on?

These questions, of course, are misconceived. In setting up the wheel model of ethical method, I am not implying that all of the **evaluational processes** and resources signified by the spokes can be similarly employed in ethical inquiry. For example, one of the spokes yet to be discussed is humor and comedy. Obviously, one could not do ethics by reasoning and analyzing for a while, applying principles for a while, and then go looking for the comic side of the matter. What I am stressing in my method is that the unfolding of moral consciousness is multifaceted. Sensitivity to the moral dimension of existence is achieved not only through reasoning or the application of principle or even through the exercise of creative imagination. An ethics that stresses only one or some of these is sinning by partiality. Such partiality is a common failing in ethics.

Yes, but How?

One of the very practical reasons modern ethics has not sufficiently dwelt on affective evaluation is that it is no simple matter to say in a systematic ethical treatment just how one goes about plying one's affectivity. To speak of moral principles, for example, is a more manageable task. There is a lot that one can get a grip on. One can discuss the relationship of the general to the exceptional,

Relief from the Tyranny of Experts

Expertise is the modern cure for vertigo in a world of expanding complexity. Experts, like ordained clergy, are often presumed to be the bearers of privileged knowledge. How can we question them when they have done work we have not done? Our pious docility would seem their due.

Gemut to the rescue. When the "military-industrial complex," against which President Dwight Eisenhower warned us, tells us we have to neglect our infrastructure and our natural ecology to spend almost two million dollars a minute on kill-power, it doesn't take advanced degrees in military science and economics to smell nonsense. Encyclopedic knowledge is not required to sense that "a country that feels secure only if it has the power to kill its enemies one hundred times over has problems that additional missiles will not cure," or that "overkill" is oxymoronic and moronic.[33] Affective wisdom—often called common sense, or horse sense, or intuition—is too often disdained.

Summary of Key Themes

- Reason is never emotion-free.
- Heartless heads or headless hearts are fatal for ethics.
- There are times when the heart is wiser than the head.
- Our feelings can be the first line of resistance to a false, regnant orthodoxy or to tyrannical experts.
- The term *character* refers to the affective orientation of a person.

Key Terms

Affectivity
Axial Age
Character
Evaluational phase of ethics
Gemut
Intuitionism
Polyamory
Polygyny
Profanation, sense of
Proportionality, principle of

Questions for Discussion

1. Since morality is grounded in our affections, what is the role of pictorial and dramatic art in shaping a society's collective conscience for good or for ill?

2. Since our political and economic judgments are not without emotional roots, what are the moral passions and emotions (such as fear, hope, cautiousness, etc.) that characterize "right wing" versus "left wing," "conservative" versus "liberal" thinking? Stress the positive values in both right and left wing thinking.

3. Discuss how disparagement of affectivity and expressiveness of feelings are often involved in sexism, heterosexism, and racism.

4. Discuss the pros and cons of this proposition: It is impossible to discuss political or religious differences unemotionally.

Suggestions for Further Reading

Bellah, Robert N., Richard Madsen, William M. Sullivan, Ann Swidler, and Steven M. Tipton. *Habits of the Heart: Individualism and Commitment in American Life.* Berkeley: University of California Press, 1985.

Girvetz, Harry K. *Beyond Right and Wrong: A Study in Moral Theory.* New York: Free Press, 1973.

Tennov, Dorothy. *Love and Limerence: The Experience of Being in Love.* Chelsea, Mich.: Scarborough House, 1999.

Creativity and Surprise

That which is cannot be true.
—Herbert Marcuse

One has no right to be as small as one's past.
—Clyde Holbrook

What we shall be has not yet appeared.
—John the Evangelist

Fortune favors the prepared mind.
—Louis Pasteur

WE'RE A PROUD SPECIES. Small wonder. We've gone from candlelight, to moon walking, to chess-playing computers, and we did it all in a couple of generations. Truly, we stand above nature as the one and only *animal creativum*. Other animals, fish, and insects keep doing the same old thing with changes coming only from eons-long chance mutation and selection. They can't rethink their lot. For us, the horizon is more impressive than the terrain. Our brilliance will not let us simply pasture

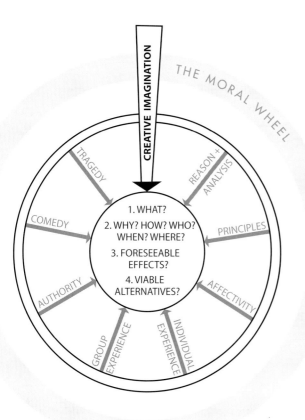

THE MORAL WHEEL

CREATIVE IMAGINATION

TRAGEDY

COMEDY

AUTHORITY

GROUP EXPERIENCE

INDIVIDUAL EXPERIENCE

AFFECTIVITY

PRINCIPLES

REASON + ANALYSIS

1. WHAT?
2. WHY? HOW? WHO? WHEN? WHERE?
3. FORESEEABLE EFFECTS?
4. VIABLE ALTERNATIVES?

on the fields of the given: we are the *eureka* people who thrive on newness. And surprise.

Retreating from Creativity

But wait! How developed is this undeniable creative talent of our big-brained species? What is its track record? We saw in chapter 9 how long it took us to think of planting seeds rather than waiting for them to blow around and plant themselves. Discoverers and explorers are resisted. It was only on his fifth try that Columbus succeeded in persuading one of Europe's hundreds of princes to sponsor him. Inventions often meet suspicion and resistance. As Jared Diamond notes, electric lighting, printing, "and innumerable other innovations" were "at first neglected or opposed in some parts of Europe."[1] There is a timid streak in us, of-

ten called "conservativism," which feels that nothing should be done for the first time, and people of that persuasion often end up in positions of authority. What we discover, we can also lose or forget. Ancient China was afire with imagination. Among its technological firsts were cast iron, the compass, gunpowder, paper, and printing. It led the world in navigation and control of the seas. Hundreds of its ships, some of them four hundred feet long, traveled as far as the east coast of Africa. As inventive as the early Chinese were, they often went in full reverse, retreating from their own achievements. The Chinese court withdrew from overseas navigation. "It abandoned development of an elaborate water-driven spinning machine, stepped back from the verge of an industrial revolution in the fourteenth century, demolished or virtually abolished mechanical clocks after leading the world in clock construction, and retreated from mechanical devices and technology in general after the late fifteenth century."[2]

Some of our retreats from creative advances are truly humbling. During the eighteenth century, the French Academy of Science rejected all the evidence for the fall of meteorites, even though many scientists saw the evidence as clear. Given the prestige of the French Academy, many museums in Europe threw away what precious fragments they had of these meteorites. F. A. Mesmer was treated as an imposter when he brought forth evidence of hypnosis, and all reports of his work were stricken from the minutes of the meetings of the Royal Medical and Chirurgical Society.[3] Habit tends to triumph over originality.

Most civilizations did not invent writing; they borrowed it.[4] Diamond notes that "today almost all Japanese and Scandinavians are literate but most Iraqis are not." This is so in spite of the fact that writing arose "nearly four thousand years earlier in Iraq."[5] We are a species that can lose its own creations. We also fear our creativity. Just as fear drives invention, fear also impedes it. Alfred North Whitehead said the major advances in civilization are processes that all but wreck the societies in which they occur. Leonard Shlain wrote a long book to show the often ignored downside of the marvelous invention of literacy.[6] Sophocles warned, "Nothing vast enters the life of mortals without a curse."[7] The shock of the new makes us afraid of the innovators among us—especially moral innovators. We burn them at the stake, poison them with hemlock, and crucify them. We shoot Gandhi and Martin Luther King.

Our technological genius, impressive as it has been recently, was a late bloomer with a troubled past and many lessons for moderns who study creativity. We are too prone to say *nihil sub sole novi*—"there is nothing new under the sun." When we do invent, we are too quick to say the heavens are closed; let us look back on our golden age. The nineteenth century was productive in technological genius. By the end of the century, a government official seriously suggested we close the U.S. Patent Office because everything had already been invented. In Paris, a panel of art critics claimed the artistic bursts of the nineteenth century "had exhausted the reservoirs of human creativity. The art of the next century, they declared, would simply provide a filigree here and an arabesque there."[8] Military commanders "pored over their contingency plans and fed their horses," not sensing the war technology about to explode in the twentieth century.

The Steep Climb of Morality

Our moral creativity had an even slower ascent. Recall here anthropologist Ralph Linton's reminder that through most of our history moral concern was limited to those near and dear. Members of other tribes were even seen as a legitimate source of meat![9] In ancient Greece, even murder did not strip you of social respectability or take you off guest lists (except, presumably, those of

the family of your murder victim). "Outside the circle of the dead man's kinsmen and friends, there is no indication of any popular sentiment against ordinary homicide."[10] On the principle, "Show me your Gods and I will tell you what you are," the gods of the *Iliad* tell a sorry tale of our not-all-that-distant ancestors. The norm was a cold indifference to the injustice inflicted on others, especially on women.[11] Someone as brilliant as Aristotle could justify slavery, saying some are born masters and others slaves. Women were little more than slaves in his view: "The male is, by nature, superior and the female inferior; and the one rules and the other is ruled; this principle, of necessity, extends to all humankind."[12]

Again, in Teilhard de Chardin's words, if nothing is intelligible outside its history, the lessons of historical ethics hollow out our moral boasts. One story is enough to teach humility and to embarrass *Homo creativum*. It is an epic of dumbness, but it is part of our story. History, like psychoanalysis, reaches back to explain present-tense problems. The past never wholly leaves us.

Rather than being alert to new possibilities— the very definition of a creative spirit—we humans numbly tend to settle into ritualized ways of doing things; the customary is treated as just fine. The collective violence called war has always drawn us like a magnet. That's dumb in itself, but the way we've done it is even more revealing. If we go back to the fourteenth century, we find that the Europeans had a standard operating procedure for warring. Soldiers showed up on a field, dressed in their proper colors so they could tell friend from foe. They wore heavy armor and wielded massive swords and lances. The war began as both sides arrived at the field. They then had at one another until their energies were depleted and the bedraggled survivors returned to their homes to spin the event as best they could. So it had gone for five hundred unimaginative years.

Then came the creative, jarring surprise. The British and French were to engage at Crecy in

1346. The French arrived for battle bedecked in their normal fashion. The British, however, had come upon the longbow, and they discovered they did not need expensively accoutered knights to use it. They could pull peasants from their fields and train them as longbowmen. So they did, and with this new weapon they mowed the French down from a safe distance. One would think that would make an impression on the French military planners. One would think that, but it didn't happen.

Ten years later at Poitiers, "as if in a state of collective psychological denial," as sociologist Barbara Ehrenreich puts it, the French once again rode to their death in a hail of arrows.[13] That surely would drive the point home that something had changed. Not so. In 1415 the French did the same stupid thing at Agincourt. That did it. Light dawned in the military mind and the French realized that the five-hundred-year protocol of charging knights was no longer operative. It was then they turned to a teenage girl, Joan of Arc, to guide these hapless men to more effective modes of warring. (Sad it is that it was in the art of slaughter that this unique girl had to display her heroic talent.)

We may smirkingly dismiss this tragic-comic story as a relic of primitive times past. Yet if we move from Crecy, Poitiers, and Agincourt to Iraq in 2003, we see Americans uniformed and readied for World War II, not realizing war had changed. As with the longbow, guerilla warfare had replaced the old ways, leaving us quagmired because the other side would not play by our rules.[14]

In the Pantheon

Educational psychologist Cyril Burt observes:

> From time immemorial the gift of creativity has been venerated almost as if it were divine. There is more than a grain of truth in the romance of old Euhemerus, which relates how the gods and demigods of the ancient myths were really "men of preeminent accomplishments deified out of flattery or gratitude." Prometheus, the discoverer of fire, Vulcan, the first of the smiths, Hermes, the inventor of writing, Aesculapius, the founder of the most ancient school of medicine—each was welcomed into the classical Pantheon, much as today an outstanding scientist is elected to the Royal Society.[15]

That makes sense. The transcending power of creative breakthrough in technology, art, and ethics has a godly quality. Indeed, creative imagination is the supreme moral faculty. Through it we break the grip of the current state of things. Through it we release the *possible* that is latent in the *actual.* Like the image of God's Spirit in the biblical book of Genesis, creative imagination can find the possibilities of order in the "formless void" and begin the rout of chaos.

Ethical Creativity

Ethics is not just a matter of sitting in state and passing judgment on the passing parade of goods and bads. The moral mind at its best perceives goods that have not as yet existed and brings them into being in the creative act. Ethical creativity enlarges reality and advances moral evolution. As one of the spokes of the wheel model of ethics, creative imagination, obviously, will be most concerned with alternatives in the hub of the wheel model.

Creative advances in morality, such as the denial of "the divine right of kings"; women's suffrage; nonviolent resistance; the discovery that humanity is a shared glory and the dignity of persons is not diminished by race, gender, ethnicity, or sexual orientation; affirmative action to end hostile monopolies—all these ideas are fought tooth and nail. As the Brazilian philosopher Rubem Alves puts it, creativity for the keepers of the status quo "is a forbidden act. The organization of our world is essentially sterile and hates anything that could be the seed of regeneration. . . . Remembering Revelation, 'The dragon stands in front of the woman who is about to give birth, so that when her child is born he may devour it.'[16] Creative jolts upset our timid little arrangements and make the uncourageous cower.

Reflecting this, much ethical theory through the centuries has been content to focus on what *is*, to the neglect of the *more* that might be. Books of ethics did not even treat creativity. Another reason for this is that creativity is hard to get a grip on. Order is more easily analyzed than ecstasy, and creativity is ecstatic. Its sources are in the preconceptual depths of the psyche. Creative insight is a surprise. There is something unpredictable and unchartable in creative intelligence. It is a leap into unsuspected light, and its essential newness presents challenges to the ensconced canons of study.

Creativity as Fusion

History is blessed with multiple moments of creativity. Looking at them, we might be able to say something more about this mysterious, vaulting power we possess, if only inchoately. With a better idea of what creativity is, we can move to see the conditions that encourage creative advance.

Professor Jacob Bronowski, a person in whom science and philosophy were happily wed, turned to the famous incident of young Newton, who saw an apple fall while he was sitting in the garden of his widowed mother. What came to Newton was not the thought that the apple must be drawn to the earth by gravity, since that thought was older than Newton. "What struck him was the conjecture that the same force of gravity, which reaches to the top of the tree, might go on reaching out beyond the earth and its air, endlessly into space. Gravity might reach the moon: this was Newton's new thought; and it might be gravity which holds the moon in her orbit."[17] What Bronowski draws from this is that Newton had discovered a previously hidden likeness; he "seized a likeness be-

tween two unlike appearances; for the apple in the summer garden and the grave moon overhead are surely as unlike in their movements as two things can be. Newton traced in them two expressions of a single concept, gravitation: and the concept (and the unity) are in that sense his free creation." The general conclusion that Bronowski offers is that "the progress of science is the discovery at each step of a new order which gives unity to what had long seemed unlike." Thus, Faraday saw the link between electricity and magnetism, and Einstein linked time with space and mass with energy. **Creation** is an act of fusion; creative science is a "search for unity in hidden likenesses."[18]

In the creative act, then, according to Bronowski, "the scientist or the artist takes two facts or experiences which are separate; he finds in them a likeness which had not been seen before; and he creates a unity by showing the likeness." Creation can be seen as "a hand reaching straight into experience and arranging it with new meaning."[19]

Bronowski's theory seems correct as far as he goes, but even as given, it is enlightening for ethics. There is an experience of previously missed likenesses and of the achievement of a new unity in moral discovery. Take, for example, the belated discovery that women are not essentially domestic and sexual functionaries, but are persons with an infinity of possible meaning beyond their historical roles. This discovery is taking longer to establish itself than the discovery of relativity, electricity, or nuclear physics for reasons that make moral discovery distinctive. After all, a woman is more like a man than an apple is like the moon. It should have been easier to make connections here than between time and space, or mass and energy. I will return in chapter 17 to the peculiar problems of moral discovery in treating the "hazards of moral discourse," which, to some degree, incapacitate the mind's quest for ethical penetration. In the discovery of the genuine and full-fledged personhood of woman, there is a hand reaching into human experience and arranging it with new meaning. Here is a new realization of the fundamental similarity of persons that is more profound than any historically assigned system of roles or social arrangement. Like the scientist, the feminist is moving beyond an unfruitful separateness and is creating a new and promising unity. Something similar happened in the abolition of slavery and is now happening in the incipient discovery of likeness between persons who are heterosexual and persons who happen to be homosexual in their affectional orientation. In each case creative moral imagination is at work. Obviously, likeness says something, but not all. It remains too pale and incomplete an explanation of what happens in creative moral movements.

Work, Discipline, and Creativity

Arthur Koestler produced an insightful study of the act of creation. Like Bronowski, he stressed the discovery of hidden likenesses, but he then moved on to a number of other aspects of the phenomenon of creativity. On the hidden likeness theory, he writes: "The creative act, by connecting previously unrelated dimensions of experience, enables us to attain to a higher level of mental evolution. It is an

THINKING CRITICALLY

Almost everything changes if you have a particular way of viewing things and that way is found to be skewed. This is called a "paradigm shift," as when feudalism shifted to capitalism, unbridled consumerism shifted to the need for ecological concern. All areas of human thought need paradigm shifts, including economics, as life turns unsuspected corners. "Economics contributed to freeing individuals from hierarchical authority, as well as to providing more abundant goods and services. These have been achievements of such importance that it has seemed wise to most persons of good will to treat the negative effects as secondary, as a necessary price for a crucial advance. . . . But with each passing year, the positive accomplishments of the economy have become less evident and the destructive consequences larger. There is a growing sense that it is time for a change. The change may well take the form of a paradigm shift. The recognition of the importance of paradigm shifts in physics generated by the work of Thomas Kuhn has opened the way for thinking about paradigm shifts in the social sciences as well."

—Herman E. Daly and John B. Cobb Jr., *For the Common Good*

act of liberation—the defeat of habit by originality."[20] He distinguishes various kinds of creative activity, such as humor and art, and says that the creative process is always the same: It consists in the discovery of hidden similarities. Thus, Gutenberg's discovery of the printing press came from watching a wine press crushing the grapes. "At this moment it occurs to him that the same, steady pressure might be applied by a seal or coin—preferably of lead, which is easy to cast—on paper, and that owing to the pressure, the lead would leave a trace on the paper—Eureka!"[21]

Koestler adds that the creative event is not unrelated to work and preparation. Again, in the words of Louis Pasteur: "Fortune favors the prepared mind." There is a link between discipline, work, and creativity. This was certainly the case when Pasteur hit on what should have been an obvious idea—extending the idea of vaccination for smallpox to inoculation for other diseases. This involved blending two elements, and Pasteur was especially prepared to see their possible linkage. First there was the technique of vaccination, and then there was independent research on microorganisms. Ground-laying work gave

Pasteur the prepared mind that fortune favored.

Still, Koestler rejects a behaviorist conception of "ripeness" in which, when the conditions reach a peak of preparedness, the creation happens. If that were so, says Koestler, "the role of genius in history would be reduced from hero to midwife, who assists the inevitable birth; and the act of creation would be merely a consummation of the preordained."[22] Still, as is illustrated by the spate of scientific discoveries in our age, inventions do trigger one another, and genius does depend on genius. One genius plants seeds, another waters, and another reaps, as can be seen in the work of Charles Darwin, who profited from the preceding work of Buffon, Erasmus, and Lamarck. Still, there is a solitariness in the creative moment in spite of debts owed to others. It comes from regions of the mind that are not easily visited with inspection.

Sometimes solutions to problems come during dreams. The right brain is not deactivated by sleep, and much that relates to creativity is rooted in the right brain. Art can be born in dreams, as when Tartini composed the Devil's Trill Sonata while asleep, showing that there is in the unconscious "a breeding ground of novelties."[23] Sometimes the messages from our multilayered brains can only be heard in silence. No matter how hard one labors, the creative moment comes only after a period of incubation, the length of which is not in our control. One must work and then wait, with the waiting as important as the working.

The Good News

Obviously, our use of our creative talent has been sluggish. Otherwise we would not be hurtling toward ecological disaster while wasting our substance on military mayhem—acting, in other words, very unimaginatively. As environmental scientist Vaclav Smil says, "Failure of imagination is our constant companion as we face new political, economic, and strategic realities."[24] That sounds like a failing grade for our species. Still, there is hope in the fact that we are creative at our core. There is a creative fire that burns in the human spirit, a thirsting for the new and the not yet. Scientist John Platt says there is an absolute necessity

> throughout our waking life for a continuous novelty and variety of external stimulation of our eyes, ears, sense organs and all our nervous network. . . . Our brains organize, and exist to organize, a great variety of incoming sensory messages every waking second, and can become not only emotionally upset but seriously deranged if these messages cease or even if they cease to be new. New experience is not merely a childish want; it is something we cannot do without.[25]

Restlessness, Capacity, and Joy

Experiments on the eyes have shown that the unconscious movements of the eyes are a necessary condition for vision. If a subject's eyes are mechanically fixed on a stationary object, the object seems to disintegrate. The experiments appear to show that, at the level of physical vision, we cannot see without exploring. There is a stimulating restlessness also in our minds. As philosopher Nikolas Berdyaev writes: "The soul is afraid of emptiness. When there is no positive, valuable, divine content in it, it is filled with the negative, false, diabolical content."[26] Like water, persons or cultures that are unstirred become stagnant. Sloth is a vice that lowers our expectations and blunts our searching instincts. But the nemesis of sloth is boredom. Boredom is the throbbing pain that comes when we are denied newness. It sends us back on the search. We can dull that pain with superficial newness, but that leaves us still unrequited in the deeper regions of the personality, as when we satisfy hunger by eating only candy.

Our intellectual and volitional hunger is such that even fulfilling experiences have a bitter edge to their sweetness. As Loren Eiseley says of the yearning of our minds, "So restless is the human intellect that were we to penetrate to the secret of the universe tomorrow, the likelihood is that we would grow bored on the day after."[27] This restlessness is the wellspring of creativity. Its radical insatiability is our hope that the power of creativity will not disappear. Indeed, there is a possibility that we are only at the budding state of human creative intelligence. Studies have shown that the human brain has increased in size rapidly since we began using tools and fire, so that it is now three times as large as before. This may have happened in a much shorter space of time than had been long supposed—perhaps in "only a few hundred thousand years."[28]

Also, human brains are marked by their capacity to learn. Insects apparently do not learn. As soon as an insect emerges from its pupa, it knows how to search for its particular kind of food and build its special habitat. That's impressive, but the nervous system here is closed and fixed, and any changes in the natural selection process are subglacial in speed. Our intelligence is open and geared to expand throughout life in response to external stimulation and challenge. We can go beyond the instructions embedded in our genes and go on to play Bach and do nuclear science, responding to opportunities our ancestors never met. Smil writes that the historical "success of our species makes it clear that humans, unlike all other organisms, have evolved not to adapt to specific conditions and tasks but to cope with change. This ability makes us uniquely fit to cope with asserted crises and to transform many events from potentially crippling milestones to resolved challenges."[29] The brain may just be awakening to its potential. The hope is that it is not too late on this overpopulated, overtaxed planet.

Also in our favor is the joy that comes with discovery. It is an ecstatic, excited act, and an explosion of joy. André Marie Ampère, for whom the unit of electrical current is named, describes

a moment of mathematical discovery with the words, "I gave a shout of joy." We see Archimedes running from his bath and shouting, "Eureka!" Creative moments enliven us. There is no thrill in cold-hammering old materials. There is boredom in production-line, repetitive sameness.

More Flickers of Hope

Hope can be found, too, in past experiences that deepened the foundational moral experience. The English Quakers in 1802 won exemption from military service on the grounds of the rights of conscience. The passage of time obscures the splendor of their creative achievement. This had never happened before in history. What they convinced the English state to do was to grant legal status to a moral viewpoint that was deemed wrong by that same state. Previous ethical thinking had taught that the person may have a right to feel this way but the state has a right to coerce. The fact that the state was made to yield to the contradicting conscience of individuals in this instance was a major leap forward and an important taming of the divine pretensions of all states. The Quakers' success here was a creative application of the foundational moral experience. Their discovery that persons merit this autonomy was not simply comparable to the discovery of Newton or Archimedes. The knowledge advanced in this case was more formally affective. No sterile syllogisms or dry analyses yielded this revolutionary conclusion. It was an example of the human mind at its creative best, with affect and reason working in tandem.

Israeli soldiers dubbed "refuseniks" are choosing to go to jail sooner than participate in the prolonged occupation of Palestinian territory and the humiliation and oppression of the Palestinian people. They are asserting in a heroic way that conscientious objection is also the right of soldiers. The idea of the soldier as automaton is the keystone of military culture, and these soldiers are challenging it in a revolutionary way, saying they will no longer participate in the occupation and humiliation of the Palestinian people. Some U.S. soldiers have been doing the same, saying that blind obedience is as immoral as slavery.[30]

As addicted as our species is to war, there are flickerings of hope. When the United States announced its plans to invade Iraq again in 2003, the largest call for peace in human history took place on February 15, 2003. There were demonstrations in eighty nations around the planet, pleading with the American nation not to embark on this terrible venture into killing. In the following two years, sixteen tribunals of conscience met in cities such as Barcelona, Tokyo, Brussels, Seoul, New York, London, Mumbai, and Istanbul to show, in the words of writer Arundhati Roy, "faith in the conscience of millions of people across the world who do not wish to stand by and watch while the people of Iraq are being slaughtered, subjugated and humiliated."[31] There is a critical need for these flickerings to come to full blaze. "With more countries possessing nuclear weapons, it is possible to argue that chances of accidental launching and near-certain retaliation have been increasing steadily: since 1945 an additional nation has acquired nuclear weapons roughly every five years."[32]

The slowly budding ecological consciousness is another sign of hope. We have moved beyond the time when concern for earth wrecking was seen as an idiosyncratic concern of "conservationists, and small groups like the Audubon Society. The only species with the talent to wreck the earth is showing signs of belated and desperately needed insight.

Setting the Stage for Creative Breakthroughs

Creativity cannot be commandeered. We can, however, look at the context that promotes it. What are the conditions from which creative breakthroughs are most likely to appear? Are there lessons in this listing for governments, managers, and also parents? I will list seven, without any pretense that this listing is exhaustive.

1. Enthusiasm, Excitement, Passion

Fortune favors the passionate. Edmund Rostand's play *La Princesse Lointaine* urges that indolence and inertia are the only vice and enthusiasm is the only virtue:

> FRERE TROPHIME: *L'inertie est le seul vice,*
>   *Maitre Erasme: Et la seule vertu est . . .*
> ERASME: *Quoi?*
> FRERE TROPHIME: *L'enthousiasme!*[33]
>   (Inertia is the only vice, Master Erasmus. . . .
>   And the only virtue is . . . enthusiasm!)

Creativity has fiery roots. In morality, only those who are alive with humanizing love and care—who are deep into the FME—will lead us across new thresholds or expand the horizons of moral consciousness. The apathetic are constitutionally disqualified, and even if they are "decent" by the accepted mores, they will never do any more than hunker down and dicker within fixed and morally imprisoning limits. I spoke to a corporate "head hunter" once, whose job was to find the talented persons corporations want to bring into leadership roles. I asked him what was the first thing he looks for in a candidate. "Excitement," he said immediately. "If that's not there, I close the books." Administrators, managers, teachers, and preachers, take heed: if you cannot generate enthusiasm, you will lead no one out of the valley of rote. *Cor ad cor loquitur*—"only heartfelt truth enters other hearts and moves people." Only the excited can excite and lead. I have never met a person of genius in whose eyes I did not see fire.

The Daimonic. It's too bad our word *demonic* has such negative vibes. The **daimon** of the Greeks had richer and broader meaning. For the Greeks, *daimon* included the creativity of the poet and artist as well as that of the ethical and religious leader, and was the contagious power the lover held by. Plato argued that ecstasy, a "divine madness," seizes the creative person. This is an early form of the puzzling and never-solved problem of the intimate relationship between the genius and the madman. "The Daimonic," as psychologist Rollo May explains, "*is any natural function which has the power to take over the whole person.* Sex and eros, anger and rage, and the craving for power are examples."[34]

The daimonic is active in morally creative times as well as in morally creative persons, and the daimonic is excited, enthusiastic, and often unsettling. Morally progressive times and persons are usually disturbing, and the forces of moral conservatism react violently. An incident in Gandhi's life illustrates the clash between daimonic reform and established power. In 1930, as Gandhi was beginning what would be the nonviolent ending of British occupation of India, Winston Churchill huffed that he found it "nauseating and humiliating" to see Gandhi, "formerly a Middle Temple lawyer, now posing as a fakir of a type well-known in the East," and "striding half-naked up the steps of the Viceroy's palace to confer with the representative of the King-Emperor." (As an example of the irony and good humor needed by creative reformers taking on the stuffy "establishment," Gandhi, when he heard the comment, wrote to Churchill: "Dear Prime Minister: You are reported to have the desire to crush the 'naked fakir,' as you are said to have described me. I have been long trying to be a fakir and that naked—a more difficult task. I, therefore, regard the expression as a compliment, though unintended. I approach you, then, as such, and ask you to trust and use me for the sake of your people and mine, and through them those of the world. Your sincere friend, M. K. Gandhi.")[35] Thereupon the "naked fakir" went on to give an epochal lesson to the world on the power of creative nonviolent resistance and to oust the mighty armies of the fully and elegantly clothed Lord High "King-Emperor." And Gandhi's lesson did reach "those of the world" as he had hoped. It flowered in the United States in the 1960s. Martin Luther King Jr. studied and applied the thought of Gandhi.

From any perspective, the 1960s were excited times, the best of times for some, the worst for others. The excitement was not without meaning. The civil rights movement peaked at that time. Its prime focus was on the liberation of African Americans and the ending of American apartheid, but its creative impact was not narrow. In a healthy metastasis, it helped shape the women's movement and the struggle for rights among other minorities. In the exciting charisma of that period, oracles too long unchallenged in church and state were reevaluated and idols were toppled. Dissident resistance to war making as policy acquired a new legitimacy. Long-tenured assumptions about the meaning of success, authority, power, the sacred, and peace were stripped and freshly scrutinized in the melee.

In the enthusiasm of the period, it was thought that more was done than could be done, and the greening of society was naïvely and prematurely announced. Likewise, the awful power of retrenchment was underestimated. Excited reforms draw some people to the left, others to the right. The German priest Joseph Ratzinger was a reformer in the Second Vatican Council and was a worry to many in the Vatican. The chaos of the 1960s disturbed him greatly, and he surprised colleagues as he became an arch-conservative and eventually the anti-reformer Pope Benedict XVI. Nonetheless, the 1960s marked a slight but significant turning of some enormous worms, and effects of that turning endured into the graying period of retrenchment that followed.

Marks of Social Excitement. The tumult of the 1960s illustrates some aspects of the social excitement that marks creative moral shifts. First, the development is to a large degree inarticulate. What is going on is a massive shift of affect. Persons begin caring about different things, or caring in a different way. Much of the rhetoric and much of the theory that arises from the movement is likely to be amiss. There will be an abundance of apocrypha, and the true gospels of the movement, if they emerge, will only come later.

Second, the creative period is likely to be highly romantic, not to say confused, in its manifestation. There will be everything from Haight Ashbury to Woodstock to stirring civil rights legislation hammered into historic words. Creative times are the most jumbled of mixed bags. Right-brain, Dionysian exuberance predominates and the disciplinary pull of the left brain is diminished. Such is the price of enthusiasm.

Third, the creative moment can be easily lost. Excitement is not easily sustained; neither is the creativity it brings easily translated into attitudes and social forms and policies that give it the grace of survival. The high moment can pass because moral creativity clashes with tightly held canons of meaning where the priests of orthodoxy stand guard. As Henri Bergson says:

Most great reforms appeared at first sight impracticable, as in fact they were. They could be carried out only in a society whose state of mind was already such as their realization was bound to bring about; and you had a circle from which there would have been no escape, if one or several privileged beings, having expanded the social ego within themselves, had not broken the circle and drawn the society after them.[36]

Bergson sees artistic breakthroughs as illustrating this: "A work of genius which is at first disconcerting may create, little by little, by the simple fact

THINKING CRITICALLY

John Maynard Keynes said, "Words ought to be a little wild, for they are the assault of thoughts upon the unthinking." Indeed, creative thoughts will always strike the comfortably conventional as wild.

11-2

of its presence, a conception of art and an artistic atmosphere which bring it within our comprehension; it will then become in retrospect a work of genius; otherwise it would have remained what it was at the beginning, merely disconcerting."

Elements of Risk. Obviously, then, there is an element of risk in creativity. Not every artistic masterpiece revolutionizes the aesthetic atmosphere, creating a context receptive to its genius. As English poet Thomas Gray put it: "Full many a flower is born to blush unseen / And waste its sweetness on the desert air." Discoverers are often lonely. Oscar Wilde creates this conversation:

GILBERT: For a dreamer is one who can only find his way by moonlight, and his punishment is that he sees the dawn before the rest of the world.

ERNEST: His punishment?

GILBERT: And his reward![37]

The creator is a heresiarch who leads what French historian and philosopher Michel Foucault calls "an insurrection of subjugated knowledges."[38] The discoverer is not always rushed to the pantheon. When Darwin's theory of evolution was first read to a group of his peers, they yawned. And at the end of that year, the president of the Linnean Society, for which the paper was presented, wrote in his annual report that "the year which has passed . . . has not, indeed, been marked by any of those striking discoveries which at once revolutionize, so to speak, the department of science on which they bear."[39] Darwin persisted and turned their world upside down.[40]

Immediate applause certainly does not greet most pioneers in morality, who know the loneliness of creative minds and bold hearts. "I have trodden the winepress alone; no man, no nation was with me," moaned the Hebrew prophet Isaiah (63:3). Love of the comfort spawned by familiarity is stronger than the love of truth. Insight of the most creative sort is pathetically perishable. Some insights die for lack of leadership. Not every great moral movement produces the "privileged beings" who can draw the whole of society after them.

Excitement, of course, is a product of love, and love is the mother and father of all invention. Only love lifts the eyes beyond the encasing perimeter.

2. Quiet Passivity, Leisure

The move to this second precondition for creativity seems to smack up against the first, but the collision is only apparent. It is merely a move to balance the industrious *yang* with the more receptive *yin*. It may be, as playwright George Bernard Shaw felt, that creation is 90 percent perspiration and 10 percent inspiration, but some artists would quibble about those numbers. No one, however, who thinks about creativity will slight the muse. The sense of receiving is strong, as in Picasso's "I do not seek—I find!" What philosopher Jacques Maritain says of artistic experience meshes well with creativity in general. There is motion in artistic creation, says Maritain, the motion that puts notes on scores or color on canvas, but the experience "is of itself a sort of natural contemplation, obscure and affective, and implies a moment of silence and alert receptivity."[41] In a similar vein is Robert Henri: "The object, which is back of every true work of art, is *the attainment of a state of being,* a state of high functioning, a more than ordinary moment of existence. In such moments activity is inevitable, and whether this activity is with brush, pen, chisel, or tongue, its result is but a byproduct of the state, a trace, the footprint of the state."[42]

Notice that Henri couples passive language, a "state of being," with intense action, "a state of high functioning." Maritain speaks of "alert re-

ceptivity." The stillness of creativity is one of the ecstatic intensities of life. It has nothing in common with the leaden stillness of death. *Otium sine litteris, mors!*—"leisure without letters is death." Whether it is letters or images, the openness that leisure provides is not empty space.

Pragmatic Considerations. As theoretical as all of this sounds, its pragmatic value is known by corporations who create a situation of active leisure in their R&D (Research and Development) sections. In effect, these units formalize dabbling. Dabblers are not inactive, but they are more like children at play than production-line laborers. They are experimenting, seeing what works, looking for one thing and finding another. They are more geared toward quest than quarry. And bottom-line corporations know this works. Healthy leisure allows for the happy surprises of serendipity. You start out looking for one thing and—*voila*—suddenly and surprisingly there is Teflon. The idea of sabbaticals for university professors is based on the same insight into the need for a bit of monastic contemplative time as seed-ground for creative scholarship.

At the practical level it is also to be noted that leisure is often costly in terms of cash. During Europe's Dark Ages, the Arab world was a center of creativity. Money enters the plot. "The Arabs were then one of the world's richest peoples, and their craftsmen routinely worked with the rarest and most advanced materials. Their familiarity with glass-making techniques, for instance, helps explain why it was the Muslim polymath Abbas Ibn Firnas whom some credit with inventing eyeglasses in the ninth century."[43] Greater investment in education in East Asia explains much of their rise in technical inventiveness and the decline of United States predominance.

Losing the Talent for Leisure. The talent for leisure can get lost in the din of technopolis. In the engineering school at the university where I teach, there hangs a large poster of a modern city, bristling with lights and buildings and bridges. Beneath it are the words "Engineering Did This." That could be seen as a boast or a public confession. The eerie thing about the poster is that there is not a tree in sight. Nature has been replaced by manipulation. Nature with all its surprises has been dethroned, replaced by a golden calf.[44] The flight from nature is mind-shrinking.

This creates a psychic ambience that causes a creativity depression. The entirely engineered city becomes an epistemological prison where surprise has been almost programmed out. Everything is controlled; surprise is an alien. Even play becomes controlled: children in freestyle play are replaced by children glued to the television or the computer screen for forty or fifty hours a week, with supervised and planned recreation for fun time. Small wonder the American Academy of Pediatrics urges keeping children under two years of age away from the television set.[45] Otherwise growth in our imaginative powers that starts in childhood is stunted. Toddlerhood is the launch base of a creative adulthood.

In the all-consuming city, potted plants and pets are our last best effort to link to our Mother Nature, but the pet on the leash is just as engineered as the potted plants. These faithful dogs of ours have shrunken brains compared to their feral ancestors, who needed sharp wits to survive in the rough of an umpampered life.[46] Our puppies have a lesson for brains: use it or lose it. Indeed, some say the loss is well begun. As Diamond says: "'Stone age' peoples are on the average probably more intelligent, not less intelligent, than industrialized peoples." His experience with allegedly "primitive" New Guineans is that they impressed him "as being on the average more intelligent, more alert, more expressive, and more interested in things and people around them than the average European or American is." At some tasks "such as the ability to form a mental map of unfamiliar surroundings, they appear considerably more adept than Westerners."[47] Brain devel-

opment thrives on challenge. That is another reason why heretics are necessary, lest we sink into the mush of premature consensus.

Esteeming Contemplation. There is an important counsel here for ethics. Ethics could deafen itself with the noise of its own work. If we think that knowing is something that we *do*, then pragmatic pressure is the route to wisdom. Josef Pieper was one of the critics who attacked the influential Immanuel Kant on precisely this point. For Kant, knowledge is discursive, not intuitive. "The reason cannot intuit anything."[48] This has been seen as "the most momentous dogmatic assumption of Kantian epistemology."[49] Because of this assumption, knowing and philosophizing for Kant are *work.* Knowledge is realized by comparing, examining, relating, distinguishing, abstracting, deducing, and demonstrating—that is, by active intellectual effort. Kant had scorn for those who felt romantically that they need only listen to the oracle within one's breast. For Kant, reason acquires its possessions through work.[50] Thus, he could admire Aristotle, whose philosophy was work. The weight of this view is heavy upon modem ethics. Pieper parts with Kant and looks back to an older wisdom. The Greeks—Aristotle no less than Plato—as well as the great medieval thinkers held that not only physical, sensuous perception, but equally man's spiritual and intellectual knowledge, includes an element of pure, receptive contemplation, or as Heraclitus says, of "listening to the essence of things."[51] Obviously, contemplation (not an overused modern term) takes time, and time is in short supply in the busyness of technopolis.

In medieval philosophy, a distinction was drawn between understanding as **ratio** and understanding as **intellectus**. *Ratio* does the work that Kant admired. It searches, defines, examines, and draws conclusions. All good work, but it is not the whole of *knowing. Intellectus,* as opposed to *ratio,* is intuitive, offering "that simple vision to which truth offers itself like a landscape to the eye."[52] The difference is not oppositional, but complementary, as with the *yin* and *yang*. Though both are needed for attaining truth, it was *intellectus* that was considered divine by the philosophers of antiquity and the Middle Ages, just as divinity was attached to creative power. The insight in this is that for this intuitive-contemplative power to be actualized, there must be some repose from the busy tumult of the worker mind.

Leisure as Achievement. This relates to what Aristotle alludes to in his assertion that the highest forms of knowledge were discovered first in those places where people first began to have leisure. Mathematical arts were developed in Egypt only when the priestly caste was allowed to be at leisure.[53] In what strikes students as more than ironic, this is reflected in the Greek word for leisure—*skole*, from which derives the English word *school*. In Latin, too, the word for leisure was *otium*; and one term for work was *negotium*—the denial of leisure. For Aristotle, it was obvious that leisure is a primary value. It stands above work. Work is not our highest achievement; rather, "we are occupied that we may have leisure."[54] Leisure is an achievement. It can become busier than work as *pragma* (work, exertion) prevails over *skole*. We have inverted the priorities between work and leisure, between *pragma* and *skole.* Aristotle saw work as something that prepares the way for leisure; we see leisure as restorative for work. Leisure is not our forte. The "leisure" we have is often busier than work and just as distracted.

This shows up in much of our academe where cultural values are mirrored. The humanities tend to be on the defensive. The minuscule budget of the National Endowment for the Humanities illustrates that on the federal scene we put our treasure where our heart is, and withhold it where the heart is not. All of this is symbolic of a cultural setting in which the intellectual need for silence, receptivity, and contemplation is not a felt need. It signals a culture of *ratio*, not of *intellectus*. One

would look to such a culture for achievements rather than for wisdom. Moral knowledge is wisdom. It comes within the province of the contemplative arts. Having said that, however, it must be insisted that the next condition for creativity is nothing other than work.

3. Work and Discipline

In psychology, "transactional analysis" in its various forms uses the terms *child*, *parent*, and *adult* as personality markers. This can be adapted for ethics because there is in the moral agent—and there should be—all three of these at once. The child is full of right-brain activity. It is at home in play and spontaneity. The parent puts left-brain, neocortical restraints on the impulses of the child, and the adult gets to work. Each is essential. If the child is killed, the moral agent will display plodding efficiency but no creativity. If the child is spoiled by a lack of parental discipline, its creativity will be scattershot. If the adult does not have a work ethic, the mind will not be "prepared," in Pasteur's term, and fortune will not favor it.

So in this trinity of personality forces, the child with its right-brain exuberance has a kind of priority, but its potential will not flower without discipline and work. If fortune favors the prepared mind, it is work that makes for a richly stored mind. If creativity is a matter of finding hidden likenesses and unsuspected links, the diligent mind will be better at finding connections. Creativity is a power to discern the possible within the actual, and so the more attuned you are to what is, the more readied you are to see what might be.

4. Malleability and Collision

When it comes to creativity, agitation is preferable to inert serenity. A closed, classical culture in which it is thought that the answers are all in is geared to produce only more of the same. A culture healthfully jolted by questions and unsettled by value collisions is a happier hunting ground.

Arnold Toynbee has an intriguing theory that

is relevant here. The religious impulse is irresistible and people are always worshiping something, first the forces of nature, from sun god to wind god to water god. When we formed into the first cohesive societies five thousand years ago, we then began to worship our nation, *Roma dea*, the divine Rome. The religiosity of modern nationalism is the offspring of that. In a couple of thousand years, says Toynbee, we started to get over that, and what he calls "higher religions" began to appear, directing the worshiping impulse toward more abstract conceptions of goodness. This was an intellectual refinement, and Toynbee, like a detective, set out to find how and where and when it happened. He made an interesting discovery. "When we mark down the birthplaces of the higher religions on a map, we find them clustering in and around two relatively small patches of the total land-surface of the Old World—on the one hand the Oxus-Jaxartes Basin and on the other hand Syria."[55]

So the question is, What was there about these two regions that made them so intellectually fruitful? Toynbee's answer: "This prominent common feature of Syria and the Oxus-Jaxartes Basin is the capacity, with which each of them had been endowed by nature, for serving as a 'roundabout' where traffic coming in from any point of the compass could be switched to any other point of the compass in any number of alternative combinations and permutations." These areas were bustling crossroads, where caravans from here and there were arriving. They were places where worldviews collided because of the "exceptionally active intercourse between civilizations in these two areas."[56] Rigid orthodoxies crumbled from the impact of these collisions, and deeper answers could be sought and found. The necessary malleability was the fruit of intellectual and value collisions.

A placid cultural setting where no major questions are outstanding, where agreement on the main values of life have gelled, will stimulate no creative movement in personal or social moral consciousness. The native tendency of the mind to take its ease when ease is offered will be acted out. Only in the presence of serious dissent can we expect to be pressed to break camp and move to higher terrain. If the contemporary shrinking world is ill suited for creative moral thought by reason of the absence of quiet and genuine leisure, it is outstandingly prepared by reason of the presence of radical questioning. The Oxus-Jaxartes valley is our home. What brittle consensus on values we achieved in the past is shattered. The caravans of new ideas are coming at us from every direction. This could lead to a situation in which one could become, in the contemporary idiom, "unglued"; or one might profit from the cultural malleability and be moved to look for the answers that lie just beyond the melee. What the Oxus-Jaxartes mood does is to remove any premature notion of completeness or any sloth-serving impressions that reality is a *fait accompli* rather than an incipient process to be tackled creatively. Serious dissent modifies the "already" with the "not yet." It enables us to believe, with John of Patmos, that "it has not yet appeared what we will be" (1 John 3:12).

5. *Kairos*

The next precipitating stimulus to creativity is what I would call, with hedged apology, **kairos**. The hedging is in order because every departure from the enormous richness of the English language must be on the defensive to show that it is not a failure of imagination, a pedantic flourish, or a sin of obscurantism. I submit that *kairos* is rich enough to be brought in from the Greek intact and naturalized as a linguistic tool in English. *Kairos* can be translated "time," but that is precisely why we need the Greek word. Time for us tends to mean chronological time, for which the Greeks had a special word, *chronos*. *Kairos*, on the contrary, means time in the sense of "now is the time!"—a moment filled with special and opportune content. Obsessed as we moderns are with chronology, having organized life around the clock, it is hard to envision that, for many of the ancients, time was not primarily a matter of succession, but of content. The names for months, for example, often described what happened in those months: the month of ripening ears, the month of flowers, the months of perennial streams, and so forth.

Recognizing Opportunity. It is from a linguistic world like this that *kairos* comes. *Kairos* is the time when the circumstances are such that *opportunity* is presented to us. A sense of *kairos* is a sense of knowing when the time is ripe for the new. Involved, too, is a sense that when the circumstances are not ready, all creative effort is doomed to sterility. It is the sense of *kairos* that we see in Friedrich Engels when he with some overstatement says that "revolutions are not made intentionally and arbitrarily, but . . . they were always and everywhere the necessary result of circumstances entirely independent of the will and guidance of particular parties and whole classes."[57] (That's close to Picasso's saying he doesn't seek; he finds.) Reflecting back on the preparatory role of work for creativity, it might be well to remind Engels that, not always, but at times, the *kairos* can be helped along especially at the corporate and political level of life where decisions have a massive effect for good or ill. Still, the main message of *kairos* is watchful patience and a special alertness when the harbingers of opportunity begin to appear.

Bible scholar Geoffrey Wood compares *kairos* to a logjam in a river. Logs coming from many places suddenly coalesce so tightly you can walk across the river. Eventually the water flow dis-

lodges them and they move on. The *kairos* is gone. An example of this is a too-soon-forgotten story of a modern American university being shut down by a strike over an issue of academic freedom and integrity. The university was the Catholic University of America in Washington, D.C. Professor of theology Charles E. Curran was an early dissenter to Vatican teachings on sexual and reproductive ethics. A highly respected scholar, Curran came up for promotion to associate professor with tenure. The university board of trustees, consisting of many cardinals and archbishops, decided to deny him because of his views on what I dub "the pelvic issues" that so consume the Vatican and the church hierarchy. The axe fell on April 17, 1967. Such firings of liberal theology professors had been commonplace at Catholic University prior to the temporarily liberalizing impact of the Second Vatican Council (1962–1965). This was different. This was 1967. The Vatican Council had opened windows, and fresh air was blowing in.

The entire faculty met in assembly and voted to go on strike until Professor Curran was reinstated and promoted with tenure. It was a *kairos* moment. Many logs were coming together into a jam. First of all, it was the 1960s, when authority was being popularly questioned and "Why not?" questions abounded. An imperious university president had alienated professors in many departments, even persons who were not all that interested in theology. It was spring and the sap was flowing. All of this and other factors conspired to prompt the faculty to shut the university down. The long bronze sign outside the university (long because it contained the full title, "The Catholic University of America") now had a broad white streamer across it saying in

> ## THINKING CRITICALLY
>
> Thomas Jefferson saw the need for creative ruction in civil society lest it sink into unhealthy ruts: "The spirit of resistance to government is so valuable on certain occasions, that I wish it to be always kept alive. I like a little rebellion now and then. It is like a storm in the atmosphere."
>
> —Thomas Jefferson, letter to William S. Smith, Nov. 13, 1787
>
> 11.3

bold black letters: "CLOSED." Students and faculty marched in all-day protests. Professors long since retired returned to join in. In five days the trustees buckled and announced the promotion and tenuring of Professor Curran.

In 1977, Curran, now a full professor, was fired for the same reasons. There was no protest. There was no *kairos*. The logs had moved on down the river. As of this writing, he holds the Elizabeth Scurlock Chair of Human Values at Southern Methodist University, where he can teach Catholic and other ethical theories with freedom.

Languishing on the Vine. Of course, ripeness is not all there is to *kairos*. The opportune fruit may ripen and languish unpicked upon the vine. Or it may wait a long time before someone sees it. At long last, the finder watches the apple and the moon and makes the connection, or sees that the slave, too, is a person, or perceives that the state is not divine and that conscience is not a serf in the fiefdom of government, or that state-sponsored violence is not preferable to intelligent and sensitive diplomacy. The opportunity has long been beckoning, but we have been bumping our heads on the fruit without thinking to pick it.

Even when the fruit is picked, the finder may be snubbed, and that happens both in science and in ethics. Opportunities found and cherished for a time can still be lost. Classical religions begin as moral movements. Even their symbols and dogmas have a moral payload. As religions decay, the dogmas can become elaborate boxes, elegantly bedecked and piously revered, but empty of their primordial moral content. Buddhism, for example, began with refreshing insights, marked by a profound simplicity. It sought to cope with sorrow by taking a middle course between self-indulgence and extreme asceticism so as to lead a well-ordered, interdependent, harmonious life. However, as one student of Buddhism put it: "This very simple doctrine was developed in various rather pedantic forms, most important of which

was the 'Chain of Dependent Origination' . . . commented on again and again by ancient and modern scholars, and probably not fully understood by anybody."[58]

Gilbert Keith Chesterton, commenting on the drab moral quality of most Christians, notes that Christianity has not failed; it simply has never been tried. There is more than an acidic *bon mot* here. Christian speculation on the subsistent relations of the Trinity is far from the straightforward moral thunder of the prophets of Israel and the Sermon on the Mount attributed to Rabbi Jesus. Lip service often greets a creative moral advance. Pomp and circumstance attend it, and yet its demanding vitality is such that it is successfully repressed and not admitted into full communion with the less demanding ideas that rule with jealous hegemony.

With all those cautions noted, there is *kairos*, and the creative rise to it. In *The Structure of Scientific Revolutions*, Thomas Kuhn argues that creative moments occur on the occasion of an impasse; we get creative only when we run into a brick wall. In science, for example, new problems can arise that cannot be solved by the established logic. No matter what the scientist tries, the solutions elude him or her. When this happens, it means that the prevailing scientific paradigm is proved inadequate and must be abandoned. It is the time for rejecting the old models of thought and inventing new ones. This is so, says Kuhn, even beyond science: "Just as scientific revolutions are inaugurated by a growing sense that the existing paradigm has ceased to function adequately, political revolutions are inaugurated by a growing sense that the existing institutions have ceased adequately to meet the problems posed by an environment that they have in part created."[59]

6. At-Home-ness

A story is told about a young man who decided he wanted to become an expert in precious stones, specializing in jade. He went to a jade master who accepted him as a student. They were to meet once a week. At the first meeting the master put a piece of jade into the student's hand and told him to hold it in his closed fist. Then the master asked him what was his favorite form of music. The student protested to no avail, and they spent the hour talking about music. The next week, once again after giving the student the jade to hold, the master insisted they spend the hour talking about literature. The next week it was sports. Never jade. Then, after many weeks, the master put a stone in the student's hand and, without looking at it, the student said, "That's not jade!"

"Now," said the master, "we can begin to talk about jade. You know it by touch. You are at home with it and now can learn about it."

The opposite of at-home-ness is alienation. Alienation is antithetical to creativity, especially in matters moral. Creation is expansive; alienation is occlusive. Creation expands and reaches out; alienation cringes and turns in. Moral creation is a force of integration that connects the previously unconnected in the direction of greater and deeper unity. Alienation constricts the foundational moral experience. To be converted from our alienation from other persons and soil and rocks and waters of earth, to break down the artificial barriers that we build on the basis of nation, race, sex, status, or age, is to be readied for creativity. To feel at home in the universe of which we are a part breaks the shell of speciesism and egoism. It prepares you to know what only those who are and feel at home can know. A stranger is unlikely to know *what is*, much less *what could be* in a home.

The Christian ethicist H. Richard Niebuhr poetically expresses the experience of moral at-home-ness in a way that would, interestingly, win plaudits from the nontheistic devotees of Buddhism and Taoism: "We were blind in our distrust of being, now we begin to see; we were aliens and alienated in a strange, empty world, now we begin sometimes to feel at home; we were in love with ourselves and all our little cities, now we are falling in love, we think with being itself."[60] This leads, says Niebuhr, to "an ethics of universal responsibility . . . it is the ethos of citizenship in a universal society, in which no being that exists and no action that takes place is interpretable outside the universal context."[61]

7. The Courage of the Heretic

The world is full of naked emperors: only children and heretics will proclaim them nude. Hype rules in most of life, and much is naked that hype calls clothed. Our hunger for cognitive peace is so strong that we are notorious builders of false consensus, a consensus that hangs over us like a blinding miasma. The heretics of yesteryear can become the saints of today. Not long ago "conservationists" were looked on as worrywarts who couldn't sit back, relax, and enjoy a good thing. Today their fears are slowly being mainstreamed into green laws. Their concerns have spread from the Audubon Society to the Environmental Protection Agency. Social consensus, called "groupthink" by some psychologists, is as comfortable as a warm blanket on a cold night. It takes courage to get out from under it and go downstairs to face the elephant in the living room. Disagreement, said the social theorist John Courtney Murray, is a rare achievement. The timid cringe; they do not create.

Every boardroom, White House, Kremlin, Knesset needs its resident heretics. A White House without heretics can allow the belief that the Iraqis really do have "weapons of mass destruction" to become a dogma, and so a massive army sets out like a colossal Don Quixote to tilt at imagined windmills. Without resident heretics, the White House, the Kremlin, and the Knesset in Israel can all come to believe that they can militarily occupy other people's territories and still live peacefully.

A "heretic" is defined as someone who breaks from established orthodoxy. Since orthodoxies are often dead wrong, the service of and need for the heretic are essential. The word **heresy** comes from a Greek word meaning "to choose." The noble heretic is one who chooses not to believe the hype. It takes courage to do that.

Fear dims the optic nerve. What we dare not see, we do not see. Courage (from the French *coeur*—"heart") is a prerequisite for creativity. It takes courage to break from the pack and find new ways.

Creativity Run Amuck

Nothing is so sacred that it cannot be profaned. Creative imagination, seen by the ancients as a divine power housed in us, can be diverted. We can be monstrously as well as morally imaginative. The present world arsenal with its capacity to blot out all life on the planet many times over is a macabre tribute to the misuse of imagination. And with all of this achieved, evil imagination is not still. Far-fetched schemes are theoretically probed about more diversified modes of killing, including such things as guided tidal waves, changes effected in the electrical environment to affect brain performance, laser death rays, and almost unstoppable, computerized robot "tanks" containing a rich repertoire of nuclear and other kill-power.

The extinction of life on our planet is no longer an apocalyptic dream. It has already begun to be acted out. Bronowski asks, "Has science fastened upon our society a monstrous gift of destruction which we can neither undo nor master, and which, like a clockwork automaton in a nightmare, is set to break our necks? Is science an automaton, and has it lamed our sense of values?"[62] Science, of course, cannot be blamed for the perversions of our possibilities. Science is the errand boy of the culture and does the culture's bidding. In that same culture there is the tender but hope-filled power of moral imagination, our primatial talent as moral beings. That exquisite power, if not perverted, is the linchpin of whatever good our future might hold.

Creativity can go both ways: it can kill us or save us.

Summary of Key Themes

- Creative imagination is our supreme moral talent.
- Creativity is insufficiently used: borrowing is more common than inventing.
- Morally creative persons are often resisted and sometimes killed.
- Creativity cannot be forced, but conditions conducive to it can be refined and encouraged.
- Creativity releases what Michel Foucault calls "subjugated knowledge."
- Creativity takes both good and evil forms.
- Creative heresy is a social service in a world of entrenched orthodoxies.

Key Terms

Creation
Daimon/ic
Heresy/heretic
Intellectus
Kairos
Ratio
Yin/yang

Questions for Discussion

1. Persons serving in the military are not allowed "conscientious objection," on the grounds that it would be impossible to

wage war if too many soldiers objected to the war on the basis of conscience. Others would argue that if so many soldiers thought a war unjust, the war should not be fought. Evaluate this argument and devise a law that would permit soldiers conscientious objection.

2. Discuss feminism as a morally creative movement. Since everyone has a mother, why has there often been so much resistance to feminism?

3. Socrates, Gandhi, Jesus, and Martin Luther King Jr. were morally creative people. What fears drove people to murder them?

Suggestions for Further Reading

Houtart, Francois, and Francois Polet. *The Other Davos: Globalization of Resistance to the World Economic System.* London: Zed Books, 2001.

Keane, Philip S. *Christian Ethics and Imagination.* Mahwah, N.J.: Paulist, 1984.

McCollough, Thomas E. *The Moral Imagination and Public Life: Raising the Ethical Question.* Chatham, N.J.: Chatham House, 1991.

Principles and Their Limits

ULTIMATELY, MORAL MEANING IS found in huggable persons and touchable things because morality has its roots in flesh, blood, soil, air, water, and rock. And the world of flesh, blood, soil, air, water, and rock is complicated. That means that ethics, the systematic quest for moral meaning, is done in an ambience of almost boundless diversity.

The human mind, badgered by literally billions of data, is engaged full-time in making sense and keeping confusion at bay. If all these data were unrelated and unalike, the mind, in self-defense, would go mad. Fortunately, it is equipped with a special talent for organizing the mass of images. The mind can "crack the kernel of the particular in order to liberate the universal."[1] It is able to discover those similarities that are the grounding of our marvelous power to generalize.

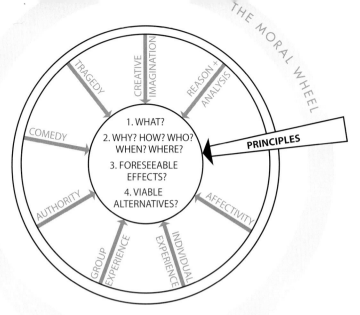

THE MORAL WHEEL

TRAGEDY
CREATIVE IMAGINATION
REASON + ANALYSIS
COMEDY
AUTHORITY
GROUP EXPERIENCE
INDIVIDUAL EXPERIENCE
AFFECTIVITY

1. WHAT?
2. WHY? HOW? WHO? WHEN? WHERE?
3. FORESEEABLE EFFECTS?
4. VIABLE ALTERNATIVES?

PRINCIPLES

The Importance of Generalization

Generalization brings relief from the enormity of mental chaos that would obtain if there existed only atomistically individuated things, persons, and events—unrelated and unalike. We make sense of reality by finding illuminating patterns, constancies, and common denominators. "From one learn all" (*ab uno disce omnes*), said the ancients, and in valid generalization that's exactly what we do.

Beyond this you can also say (which the ancients did not say in so many words), *ab omnibus disce unum*—"from all learn one." You learn about the forest from the tree and about the tree from the forest. The universal that we liberate by cracking the kernel of the particular comes back to illumine the particular. In universalizing, we manage "to leap beyond, yet nearer bring," in Walt Whitman's phrase.[2] By seeing the individual reality in the light of comparison to that which is common, it becomes more understandable. Comparison reveals aspects that could be lost to the isolated

gaze. Experienced attorneys will see more in an individual case than their inexperienced colleagues because their broader base of comparison brings hidden likenesses to light. No amount of study of the individual case can yield the breadth of perspective that "general" knowledge and experience make possible. In fact, without valid generalizations there can be no perspective.

Moral **principles** are intellectual generalizations. They are the repository and the moral memory of a people. They save us from superficial reactions based on prima facie evidence. But again, "human actions are good or bad according to the circumstances." Because of this, there is an element of the unique and the unrepeatable in every person and in every moral case. Not all moral meaning is generalizable. And yet, *and yet*, there *is* valid generalization.

An age that denigrates principles is open to ethical shallowness. "Marry the spirit of the times, and you shall soon be a widow" is an old saying. Principles, by preserving the insights of our forebears, are a hedge against such bereavement. They protect us from ephemeral views that would otherwise be overwhelming in their influence. They relate to George Santayana's truism that those who do not know history are destined to repeat it. Without them we would be like an amnesiac, without history or a true sense of ourselves. Principles do not give us a blueprint that makes our decisions for us, but they do broaden us with a sense of history, thus giving us some depth and making us less vulnerable to fallible projections. As philosopher John Dewey said: "Through intercommunication the experience of the entire human race is to some extent pooled and crystallized in general ideas. These ideas constitute *principles.*"[3]

Moral Principles Are Different

Moral principles are not just empirical generalizations of the sort one finds outside of ethics. In mechanics, for example, one might come up with the principle that a particular engine will operate most efficiently at an incline of three degrees. This would be learned by observation of the performance of the engine at this and other angles of incline. Likewise, generalizations about the boiling point of various liquids can be based on simple uninvolved observation. This is not the way moral generalizations are derived.

Moral principles are as unique as moral experience itself. The experiencing and observing that produce them are not of the scientific sort. Moral principles are derivatives of the foundational moral experience and thus have their roots in affectivity and in faith as well as in observation, memory, and imagination. A moral principle expresses an inference drawn from the perceived value of persons and their environment. It is a conclusion about how persons should behave and be treated in view of their perceived value. Because of their value, they should not be killed, exploited, or deceived; and, positively, because of their value, they deserve truth, fidelity, caring, and so forth. Principles are the voiced precepts of the foundational moral experience.[4]

Beyond Divine Revelation

Religious theists often attribute their moral principles to divine revelation. However, principles do not come to us straight from Mount Olympus or Mount Sinai. The Ten Commandments, drawn from the Jewish Scriptures, for example, are presented in that religious literature as of miraculous origin. This was a mythic way of getting folks to take them seriously. Scholarship, however, can show the Commandments' dependence on previous codes such as the Code of Lipit-Ishtar, the Code of Eshnunna, the Code of Hammurabi, and the Hittite Codes. These laws are primitive by contemporary standards and marked by the limits of tribal consciousness. At some moments they edify, as when they urge acceptance of immigrants: "When an alien settles with you in your land, you shall not oppress him. He shall be treated as a native born among you, and you shall love him as a man like yourself, because you were aliens in Egypt. I am the LORD your God" (Lev. 19:33-34). And again: "When you reap the harvest of your land, you shall not reap right into the edges of your field; neither shall you glean the loose ears of your crop; you shall not completely strip your vineyard nor glean the fallen grapes. You shall leave them for the poor and the alien. I am the LORD your God" (Lev. 19:9-10). This was a break from traditional tribalism that limited humane treatment to one's fellow in the tribe.

Yet the same commandments of God ordered capital punishment for adultery (Lev. 20:10) as well as for homosexual activity (Lev. 20:13). What these old moral codes do is show where moral evolution was among the ancient Israelites and surrounding peoples. They also illustrate the

THINKING CRITICALLY

Principles developed in a male-dominated culture will need correction since men and women view morality differently. Psychologist Carol Gilligan "interviewed both male and female subjects about various moral dilemmas and found that the women she interviewed had a different view than the men of what was morally required of them. They used a different moral language to explain themselves, and their reasoning involved a different moral logic. . . . She concluded that males and females had different kinds of ethics."

—Barbara MacKinnon, *Ethics: Theory and Contemporary Issues*

12.1

halting fashion in which we become aware of the moral implications of our reality, and they make us wonder how primitive our present conceptions will appear to future and, hopefully, more sensitive generations. At any rate, they do illustrate the relationship of principles to the empirical order and to history.

Ethics as Dialogue of Principle and Context

The contextual, empirical basis of moral principles can also be illustrated by an example that presents a very specialized situation and the moral principle that developed to meet its human needs. At one time it was a principle among the Eskimos to practice a kind of socially motivated geriatric suicide. To relieve critical population pressures in the face of severely limited food supply, some of the older folks would resignedly go off to die on an ice floe. In the absence of alternatives, this could be judged a tragic but moral practice. It was the best they could do to survive, since all might have died without this release. One could not, however, rip this moral principle out of that specific empirical context in which it was temporarily defensible and say that this would be a good practice for others to whom more benign alternatives are available. Principles derive from circumstances, and circumstances make moral reality distinguishable and specific.

When birthing was more morally perilous and the survival of children precarious, one could generalize that the more you have, the more might survive. Now, with a grossly overpopulated planet, the moral principle is to limit reproduction to make life on earth sustainable.

Still, there are principles that can be articulated

as relevant to any context imaginable. The prohibitions of rape, lying, and violence are among these, as is the positive principle that urges us to revere and nourish life. But these principles, too, were learned in the concrete circumstances of life, and they cannot be applied except in dialogue with the realities of the concrete order. In circumstances of self-defense, the very desire to revere and nourish life may press us to kill when no other alternatives for the protection of the innocent are available. **Ethics** is at root a dialogue. *Ethics can be defined as a dialogue conducted by the moral agent between the moral meaning found in principles and that found in the unique circumstances of the case at hand.*

Deep down in good principles there is contact with the sanctity of life. Principles may be skewed or reflect outmoded data or myths, but we should not part with them without due process. Therefore, if we find in our cultural reservoirs principles urging the counterproductivity of violence, the need for maturity before becoming sexually active, the duty to company with a dying person and not hasten death, or if we find principles that affirm the value of compassion, truth telling, sincerity, and so forth, we should pause at length before the counsel of these principles before leaving them. And there may be exceptions to those principles, but only one who is steeped in principles has the moral maturity to depart from principles safely.

The Courage to Critique Principles

Moral maturity is marked not just by the discovery of principles but by the jettisoning or modification of principles. Law is applied ethics, and it is humbling to acknowledge that American law

> THINKING CRITICALLY
>
> "Scientists tell how the world is, why the world is that way, and how it is likely to be in the future if such-and-such happens or does not happen. In contrast, the primary concern of the ethicist is with how the world *should* be, what will make it *better*, how we *ought* to live."
>
> —Peter Facione,
> *Ethics and Society*
>
> 12.2

once housed principles regarding the buying and selling of slaves. Very often bad principles achieve honored status in church and state. Slavery illustrates that.

The Council of the Indies, after conferring with theologians, jurists, and prelates of the church, was able to assure the king of Spain that

> there cannot be any doubt as to the necessity of those slaves for the support of the kingdom of the Indies . . . ; and [that] with regard to the point of conscience, [the trade may continue] because of the reasons expressed, the authorities cited, and its longlived and general custom in the kingdoms of Castile, America, and Portugal, without any objection on the part of his Holiness or ecclesiastical state, but rather with the tolerance of all of them.[5]

Prestigious groundwork had long been laid for such favor. Saints Ambrose, Isidore of Seville, and Augustine had rationalized slavery as being, like all secular instruments of coercion and government, part of divine retribution for the fall from grace. Martin Luther thought it clear from Scripture that both masters and slaves had to accept their status, since the earthly kingdom could survive only if some were free and some slaves.[6] A number of functioning moral principles flowed from this and found expression and support in the common law of the land. Children of slaves could be separated from parents, and husbands and wives be separated when sold. A North Carolina judge wrote in 1858: "The relation between slaves is essentially different from that of man and wife joined in lawful wedlock . . . for with slaves it may be dissolved at the pleasure of either party, or by the sale of one or both, depending on the caprice or necessity of the owners."[7]

The principles that came to be accepted regarding women should also stir a critical view of principles, since they show how ossified conscience can seek refuge in principle. An editorial of comparatively recent date gives a sample of what is now being widely documented in women's studies. A *New York Herald* editorial of September 12, 1852, said: "How did women first become subject to man, as she now is all over the world? By her nature, her sex, just as the Negro is and always will be to the end of time, inferior to the white race and, therefore doomed to subjection; but she is happier than she would be in any other condition, just because it is the law of her nature."[8]

As George Bernard Shaw observed, the customs of the tribe are often thought to be the laws of nature. Then, since the sacred is the ever-attendant penumbra of the moral, the laws of nature are easily thought also to be the laws of God. In reality, moral principles that attain a high pedigree in society are often, in the Marxist phrase, "a tissue of lies" covering over some basic pattern of exploitative power and aggrandizement. Principles deserve respect and criticism.

The Quest for a Universal Blueprint

Ethical principles are not like the laws of physics. Even though physics, too, is full of both surprises and the corpses of old hypotheses, there is more predictability there. Ethical principles are not judgments of physical qualities like heat or color, but of relationship in process. The web of relationships can never be entirely identical in different cases, since no two subjects and no two sets of circumstances will be identical. Again, *quasi infinitae diversitates*—"a near infinity of variations."

Kant the Transgressor

Human nature is a shared glory possessed by all members of the *Homo sapiens* species, and so it is possible to speak of a **"natural law"** and to find listings of obligations, as in the UN Universal

Declaration of Human Rights. There are, however, limits to universalizing, and some major thinkers like Immanuel Kant transgressed those limits. Kant was a typical eighteenth-century man, unrealistically in love with the powers of abstract reason. "I should never act in such a way that I could not also will that my maxim should be a universal law." "Can I will that my maxim become a universal law? If not, it must be rejected."[9] Such devotion to principles was certainly a hedge against selfish rationalization, but it was not sensitive to the possibility, indeed, of the inevitability of exceptions. Neither did it do justice to the heroic and to what is called the "supererogatory," that which cannot be commanded of all. His universalizing penchant did get Kant in trouble even in his day.

Kant was obviously a man you could trust. It was clear to him that truth telling is such a good that truth must be told whatever the fallout. "Truthfulness in statements which cannot be avoided is the formal duty of an individual to everyone, however great may be the disadvantage accruing to himself or to another."[10] A French writer, H. B. Constand de Rebecque, took Kant to task, referring to him simply as "a German philosopher."

The moral principle, "It is a duty to tell the truth," would make any society impossible if it

were taken singly and unconditionally. We have proof of this in the very direct consequences which a German philosopher has drawn from this principle. This philosopher goes so far as to assert that it would be a crime to lie to a murderer who asked whether our friend who is pursued by him had taken refuge in our house.[11]

Kant acknowledged that he was the German philosopher in question and then stuck manfully to his conclusion. Quite simply, then, Kant would not be the man you would want to stand between you and someone intent on murdering you—at least if Kant knew where you were. (Aristotle or Thomas Aquinas would take better care of you, as we shall see momentarily.) Common sense and good ethics must say with Dietrich Bonhoeffer that Kant has "unintentionally carried this [truth-telling] principle *ad absurdum*," and common sense and good ethics also must stand with Monsieur Constand de Rebecque in his reaction against the "German philosopher."[12]

Offended by sentimental schools of ethics that would make fluctuating affect the ethical navigator, Kant divorced moral reasoning from affect and was a major force in downplaying the affective dimension of moral intelligence. Reason untouched by affect would author its own principles. At any rate, cut off from empirical con-

---

THINKING CRITICALLY

Brilliant minds can collide when deciding which principles are truly good. Plato believed in a sharing of property and of wives; Aristotle disagreed: "Aristotle dislikes communism, whether of property or of wives and children, for precisely the same reason he dislikes the kind of extreme unity that Plato had set up as his ideal. Plato, as we must recall here, has not made communism of property and wives a requisite for his political community as a whole: only for that part of it represented by his cherished guardian class, the philosophers who would rule it. But it is this very concentration of communism that bespeaks Plato's admiration of it and his dislike of both private property and the family—as well as of other forms of autonomous independent association."

—Robert Nisbet, *The Social Philosophers*

12.3

siderations and the affectivity that would help us plumb the moral meaning there, Kant builds a grid into which he would fit reality willy-nilly, and reality is just too diverse and surprising to be so packaged. Hence the embarrassment of this German philosopher.[13]

Autonomy and Immaturity

Ethics should be geared to the subject who has achieved some of the autonomy that goes with psychological maturity. The very young and the morally immature who are arrested at earlier stages of moral maturation are more in need of rigid rules. We tell toddlers that they should not cross the street alone, not that their contextual sensibilities and imaginations should be their guides. "Thou shalt nots" have their place with the immature.

It is a weakness of those religious called "fundamentalist" that they treat their devotees as children, and religious authorities often wield false negative absolutes. That leads to **"abstinence only"** programs in sex education and prohibition as the response to the fear of alcohol abuse. Both forms of prohibitionism crash on the realities of life that demand more nuance. Ethics must work on the assumption that moral maturity is attainable. Persons who have not yet grown to moral maturity will find comfort in authoritarian religions and be quicker to accept authoritarian governments.

When a Principle Becomes a Fetish

The human mind's penchant for lassitude takes another tack. The American unbalanced fascination with liberty and the right to private property exemplifies this. Nourished and fomented by philosophers from John Locke to John Rawls, these values are wrapped in red, white, and blue. They inform pivotal political and economic concepts such as "the national interest," "private enterprise," and "free trade." They also take the brakes off the mighty hungers of greed. Consumptive consumption becomes the religious equivalent of salvation. The more of it, the better. The discipline of economics gives "theological" blessing to it all.

A value-conscious economics would probe deeply into the presuppositions of that philosophy to check the hidden baggage it has been carrying regarding the primacy of liberty, owning, and consuming. Economics (like all the social sciences) floats on a sea of ethical assumptions. As the "heretical" (by U.S. standards) economist E. F. Schumacher writes: "Economists themselves, like most specialists, normally suffer from a kind of metaphysical blindness, assuming that theirs is a science of absolute and invariable truths, without any presuppositions. Some go so far as to claim that economic laws are as free from 'metaphysics' or 'values' as the law of gravitation."[14]

The economists, of course, are up to their necks in moral value judgments, treating some value options as absurd and others as "the law of nature." Again, Schumacher: "The modern economist is used to measuring the 'standard of living' by the amount of annual consumption, assuming all the time that a person who consumes more is 'better off' than a person who consumes less."[15]

Buddhism views our manic consuming as "excessively irrational: since consumption is merely a means to human well-being, the aim should be to obtain the maximum of well-being with the minimum of consumption." The Buddhist economist can point out that in their system "amazingly small means lead to extraordinarily satisfactory results." The Buddhists also look on the use of nonrenewable goods as violent unless the use is indispensable. Not all in the Weast are alien to these sensitivities, nor are all Buddhists exemplary. Tendentially, however, Western thinkers, often seem to feel that human work is the only expenditure that counts, displaying little sense of being part of an ecosystem. And work is something of a necessary evil to be dispensed with entirely by automation if possible.[16] For the Buddhist, work is a creative, socializing enterprise that has a value in itself. The Buddhist, in other words, has different principles.

All systems of economics decide what befits persons as persons. In so doing, economics is always doing ethics, but rarely acknowledging it. There is no "value-free" economics. The notable stress in Buddhist economics is to maximize human satisfactions by the most humanly suitable patterns of consumption. The temptation in all economic systems is to maximize consumption with little sense of the limits of this planet and with little sense that the economy is a wholly owned subsidiary of the natural environment, and this is happening in both East and West, North and South.

How to Fire a Principle

Principles that become dogma in a society are not easily challenged. One moral and political principle that needs reevaluation is the principle of "national sovereignty." Even to say so causes the orthodox to rend their garments and cry heresy. If we accept Teilhard de Chardin's statement that nothing is intelligible outside of its history, the history of national sovereignty shows it as an idea whose time has passed. If we could pinpoint a date for the birth of this idea, it would be 1648 with the Treaty of Westphalia. It was an organizational idea with practical arguments to support it at the time. Many principles are born out of practical need but then overstay their welcome. Society was rent by multiple forces tugging for control. "Church" and "state" had no tidy boundaries. The various "estates" of the realm vied for control. A sovereign lord was needed to calm the melee and impose order.

Coercive Power and Empire

The late-sixteenth-century French political thinker Jean Bodin gave the French kings what they wanted, a theory of absolute sovereignty. Bodin did not think this could be achieved by gentle negotiation. It had to rest on the power of the sword. "In matters of state the master of brute force is the master of men, of the laws, and of the entire commonwealth."[17] He ruled out cooperation since the king seeking cooperation is no longer in charge; he is no longer sovereign. He used God language to shore up his case. God the great sovereign could not make a sovereign like unto Godself.[18] Neither can sovereignty be divided or shared.

This had to be music to royal ears, but ideas, like people, have progeny. This coercion-based notion of sovereignty seeped into the emerging definition of national sovereignty. Sovereign states based on coercive power, with a "don't tread on me" attitude toward other states, became the norm even into our day. Efforts to substitute cooperative power for coercive power are resisted by the mesmeric claims of sovereign independence. The League of Nations was a nonstarter because of those claims, and the needed evolution of the United Nations is still stymied for the same reason. We do not live in Bodin's world. The biggest problems facing our world transcend nations. As Jonathan Schell writes "The need for global political structures to deal with the globalized economy and the swiftly deteriorating global environment is manifest."[19] Manifest, maybe, but not dealt with. The nations of the world still behave like defiant teenagers with a fictive sense of independence. "Sovereignty" is the nation-state's code name for "doing their own thing." In bizarre cases sovereignty is used as a defense for national crime. Slobodan Milosevic invoked it to forestall intervention against his genocidal efforts in Kosovo. Robert Mugabe used it similarly in Zimbabwe, and George W. Bush used it anomalously to support his imperial military venture into other "sovereign" nations like Iraq, Afghanistan, and Pakistan.

Note the word *imperial*. Empire is the grand-child of "the divine right of kings." It is the effort to extend sovereignty transnationally. It seeks control writ large. Like Bodin's kings, it rests ultimately on coercive power, military and economic. Empire seeks order by subduing all contenders. History shows that empires stretch and stretch until they die of overreach, as the American empire is doing in our day.

Consensual Power

And so it is coming to pass that the principle of national sovereignty is eroding. Royalty is fading and democracy, with fits and starts, is taking root. The facts of global economic and political life are interlocking willy-nilly, and so it is that new modes of unitive power are emerging. Federalism, with bonds of cooperative power, is making its way, aided by a variety of stimuli. The forming of the United States with divided powers stirred the aging and aching royals of Europe. Europe itself, in the European Union, based largely on shared economic interests, has banished the separate sovereigns of Europe's yesteryear. "National sovereignty is now in the process of giving way to new forms in the very Europe in which the concept was born."[20] As Germany's Helmut Schmidt commented, regarding the European Union, this "marks the fist time in the history of humankind that nation-states that differ so much from each other nevertheless . . . have voluntarily decided to throw in their lot together."[21]

The Good Friday agreement in Ireland gave the people of the North the right to remove themselves to another country upon a majority vote. (That's a right that the Muslims of Kashmir, the Tamils of Sri Lanka, and the Tibetans in China would love to have, but there, sadly, the violent logic of coercion holds sway.) In the Irish agreement, the Irish Republic explicitly renounced its demand for sovereignty over Northern Ireland, but in the process gained in the Ministerial Council unparalleled influence over policy in the North. The sword has

yielded to the ballot and a new form of power is in play, as it is in the rest of Europe. Consensual power is replacing coercive power and proving more *powerful*. The myth of kill-power as the final and definitive arbiter is being debunked; new principles are being born. Genghis Khan, Julius Caesar, and Napoleon Bonaparte are giving way to Gandhi, Martin Luther King, and Nelson Mandela. Almost bloodlessly, dictators such as Ferdinand Marcos and at least seven Latin American despots have been driven out. Between 1989 and 1990 some fourteen nations underwent nonviolent revolutions.[22] Gene Sharp lists 198 different types of nonviolent actions that are on the historical record but neglected by historians and journalists who prefer to report on the flash of war.[23] Algeria, a colony of ten million, was liberated by violence at a cost of almost one million lives. Britain's Indian colony of three hundred million was liberated nonviolently at a cost of about eight thousand lives. Do the math. From that new math, new moral principles are taking hold.

It would be foolishly premature to say those principles have set sail everywhere on this troubled planet, but there is some shifting of the tide. As Schell notes, "'Covenants without the sword are but words,' [Thomas] Hobbes said in the late seventeenth century. Since then, the world has learned that swords without covenants are but empty bloodshed. . . . In our time, force can win a battle or two, but politics is destiny."[24]

Moral reform in the political order is more cumbersome than an individual's change of heart. New principles and categories must supplant long-tenured ones. This is happening. International law professor Gideon Gottlieb proposes the separation of the two basic ingredients of sovereignty, the nation and the state.[25] Kurds are a people, a distinct population spread out under competing sovereignties in Turkey, Iraq, Iran, and Syria. These are nations. Insistence that these "nations" must be compacted into each "state" is not working. Gottlieb proposes conferring national status upon the Kurds, giving them cultural and other rights and privileges within the structure of the four states. Forced amalgamation doesn't work; federal agreements could. The shotgun marriage that forced the union of Kurds, Sunnis, and Shiites in Iraq cannot be quickly undone, but the covenental wisdom of a federalism with fair sharing agreed on and with recognition of cultural differences could bring peace. What else could?

Ideals and the "Feeble Mind of a Nation"

Some principles house practical norms. Some contain ideals and they are a different species. One could say ideals, are principles with attitude. Better yet, ideals are visionary principles, electrifying peeks into the possible. Ideals and idealists are troublemakers. They spring from discontent and point toward the not yet. They are enemies of the status quo. Adding to this discomfit, they demand self-criticism, a practice from which persons and, even more so, collectivities shy. As Reinhold Niebuhr wrote:

> Even those tendencies toward self-criticism in a nation which do express themselves are usually thwarted by the governing classes and by a certain instinct for unity in society itself. For self-criticism is a kind of inner disunity, which the feeble mind of a nation finds difficulty in distinguishing from dangerous forms of inner conflict. So nations crucify their moral rebels with their criminals upon the same Golgotha, not being able to distinguish between the moral idealism which surpasses, and the anti-social conduct which falls below that moral mediocrity, on the level of which every society unifies its life.[26]

By a fortunate compensation, however, ideals are powerful. There has never been a major turning point in history that was not pregnant with idealism. In spite of all the pragmatic and petty concerns that characterize all of human life, and to which the American Revolution was not immune, that revolution could not be understood outside of the idealism that surfaces persistently in the documents and history of that period. And many students of communism would agree with political scientist Harold Laski when he says that, in its early vigor, "communism has made its way by its idealism and not by its realism, by its spiritual promise, not its materialistic prospects."[27]

What Makes Ideals Special?

Ideals have a trinity of aspects that makes them special: they have a future referent; they are subversive; and they are gradually and never fully realized. They are beckoners pointing to a plausible and alluring beyond. Quotidian principles such as those directing you not to kill, steal, or vandalize are not offering ideals but rather are spelling out the requirements for survival in the right-now world. Ideals are more obsessed with horizons than with the order-needs of the terrain.

As such, they are *subversive*. They challenge the conventional wisdom that hunkers down in the belief that whatever is ought to be. They taunt the comfort-driven urge to settle for less and the rationalistic reductionism that would make all things look neat and normal. The unrealistically tidy concept of national sovereignty just discussed is under assault from the ideal of interdependent internationalism. It is, of course, an utterly subversive notion, implying that states should no longer putter around like unacquainted shoppers at a fair. Doing one's own thing internationally is losing its respectability—and its feasiblity—as our economic and ecological bonds intensify and interweave. The autism of "national interest" thinking is giving way to the more practical ideal of "planetary interest."

Ideals, though ultimately unreachable, have to be reached for. Since the rise of democracy, we idealize equality, but hard-nosed anthropologists caution us that "the need for leadership and the universality of the power drive, no matter how it may be culturally camouflaged, are responsible for the fact that there are no genuinely equalitarian societies."[28] We could add that there are likewise no just societies or free societies, but that does not mean that justice and freedom are chimeric or illusory. They are horizons toward which we must move, stumble as we may en route.

Sustaining the Hope

Ideals do not have the instant success that the forward pass had in football when it was first conceived. Instead, they get smothered in lip service. In the United States, July 4 is celebrated most enthusiastically, for the most part, by political Tories who would never have joined the original revolution. Yet neither would they vote for anyone who did not proclaim the ideals of that revolution. And the hope is that great ideals will keep pressing like glaciers, flattening mountains of resistance.

Success stories help to sustain that hope. Buddhist theories of compassion, respect, and the fight against greed and delusion may seem hopelessly naïve. The Buddhist scholar Hajime Nakamura offers contrary evidence: "The practical results of the development of compassion have been seen in the way that Buddhism has softened the rough warrior races of Tibet and Mongolia, nearly effacing all traces of their original brutality. In Japan, also, ac-

cording to statistical reports, cases of murder or assault are relatively rare in districts where Buddhist influence is strong."[29]

Similarly, from the Magna Charta to the UN Universal Declaration of Human Rights, the story is one of slowly victorious idealism. The advances in feminism, ecology, democracy, and nonviolent power all show that the record of positive idealism does not leave us bereft of hope.

Exceptions and the Limits of Consistency

Principles are great until life talks back, and life does just that. The French politician Pierre-Joseph Proudhon's remark that "the fecundity of the unexpected far exceeds the statesman's prudence" has application well beyond statecraft. Life does not confine itself to the ridges to which we assign it. Aristotle agrees: "The *data* of human behavior simply will not be reduced to uniformity."[30]

Proudhon's passing remark is one that has application to moral principles. Our principles are open to surprise. Reality is fecund and shocks our expectations. Put another way, morality dictates not only rules but exceptions to those rules. There are moments of ultra-obligation and heroism for which there are no rules. There are utterly new and uncharted situations that do not so much go against principles as go beyond them.

In ethics, neither principles nor exceptions can claim

> ### THINKING CRITICALLY
>
> "If we wish to enquire about Aristotle's moral views, it is no use looking for a set of principles. Of course we can find some principles to which he must have subscribed—for instance, that one ought not to commit adultery. But what we find much more prominently is a set of character traits, a list of certain types of persons—the courageous man, the niggardly man, the boaster, the lavish spender, and so on. The basic moral question, for Aristotle, is not, What shall I do? But, What shall I be?"
>
> —Bernard Mayo,
> *Ethics and the Moral Life*
>
> 124

a higher status or a greater legitimacy. Both are responses to the perceived value of persons. Both have sound credentials. Even sainted luminaries of the past had to deal with odd exceptions. Augustine does not condemn as adultery the actions of the wife who submitted herself sexually to her husband's captors at her husband's request to purchase his freedom from captivity and death. As one commentator put it, Augustine "does not dare to define that these spouses sinned . . . since these spouses 'in no way judged that in these circumstances, that act was adultery.'"[31] However these unfortunate spouses wanted to describe it, it was an exception to the hallowed "Thou shalt not commit adultery" principle.

Thomas Aquinas's Exceptions

Thomas Aquinas allowed the possibility of exceptions to very basic principles. In certain circumstances one could morally and licitly take the property of other persons, have sexual relations with someone other than one's wife, and even directly kill one's self or another innocent person. Pretty surprising stuff for a thirteenth-century Dominican monk. Thomas put it clearly: "although there is some necessity in the common principles, the more we descend into particularities, the more frequently do we encounter exceptions."[32]

With regard to the remarkable exceptions Thomas allowed, he did manage to eat his cake and have it too. Thomas ran into these exceptional cases in the Bible or in the lives of saints of the church; Thomas was rising to the defense of these worthies. Samson seems to have violated the no-suicide principle by pulling the building down on himself; Abraham consented to and was ready to kill his son Isaac; Hosea appeared to have been implicated in sexual sin. Dicey situations, to be sure.

Thomas reacted with a classical *deus ex machina*. He said that all those exceptions were done by divine command. He got Hosea off the

hook by saying that "intercourse with any woman ordered by a mandate of God is neither adultery nor fornication."[33] That may have worked for Thomas and Hosea, but it would not get far with a modern spouse whose partner has strayed. Nowadays such mandates from God are hard to come by. "God told me to do this" would not be a successful defense.

Ethical Realism

Thomas stayed honest and faithful to his ethical realism, however. He did not lapse into a crude nominalism or voluntarism here of the sort that would say that something is good because it was commanded by God. In a secular form this would be "Something is good because it is legal." That's juridical **positivism**. **Ethical realism** says the opposite. As an ethical realist, Thomas held that nothing could be commanded unless it was good. As he saw it, even God is bound by the order of justice and "beyond this order, God can do nothing."[34] So if that extramarital sex and that direct suicide were not *in se* moral and good, God could not command them. Here Thomas was inexorably a child of his times. God's role here was to *reveal* that this was a good exception in the circumstances. God was not making it good by mandating it; God was revealing that these were good exceptions. Thomas was not prepared to admit that persons could come up with this insight by themselves. The bottom line is that, despite his God excuse, Thomas had room in his ethical theory for these thorny exceptions.[35]

Thomas did allow for immutable principles regarding morality, but these are highly generic and abstractly removed from the complexities of life. As such, they can afford to be immutable. They are such things as "Do good and avoid evil" and "Give to each his or her own." Fair enough, but figuring out what is good and evil and what is owed to whom gets messy when those principles meet the street. Since ethics is applied love, missing out on good principles *or* good exceptions is unloving, equally so. Principles have limits, and there are times and circumstances when good principles do not apply. At times it would be positively harmful and irrational to insist on the principle. This would occur in cases where greater values than those contained in the principle supervene and prevail.

The "Situation Ethics" Frenzy

Seven hundred years after Aquinas, in the 1960s, a furor erupted over what came to be called **situation ethics**. Joseph Fletcher, an Episcopal minister and ethicist, was the *enfant terrible* of the time. He teased a wide swath of the public with the news that their principles were not as rock solid as they had thought. One case that he popularized got wide attention. This was the "sacrificial adultery" of a German woman named Mrs. Bergmeier. As Fletcher tells the story, as World War II was ending, Mrs. Bergmeier was picked up by a Russian patrol while she was out foraging for food for her children. She was taken to a Russian prison camp. There she learned that she could be released from prison for only two reasons: illness requiring hospital facilities, in which case she would be sent to a Soviet hospital, or pregnancy. In the event of pregnancy, she would be sent back to Germany as a liability. After some consideration, Mrs. Bergmeier prevailed on a friendly camp guard to impregnate her. He obliged. When her pregnancy was verified, she was released and sent back to Berlin, where she was reunited with her husband and family. As Fletcher reports it: "When the child was born, they loved him more than all the rest, on the view that little Dietrich had done more for them than anybody."[36] Fletcher queried whether Mrs. Bergmeier had not indeed done "a good and right thing." The furor ensued.

What Fletcher did was to bring attention to cases where exceptions to supposedly absolute principles seem to make sense. In Mrs. Bergmeier's case, a higher principle of maternal love and caring for her family did indeed seem to take precedence over the principle prohibiting extramarital sexual exchange. Yet the exception was subjected to a heated trial. Why?

Exceptions to moral principles are put on the defensive for a number of reasons, one of which would seem to be worthy. This worthy reason is that exceptions can run away from the value housed in the principle. A good exception moves beyond the principle to a truer realization of value; a bad exception contradicts the principle. In Mrs. Bergmeier's case, one might sense the problems that little Dietrich might someday have, or the possible problems for the guard who fathered a child he would never know, and so on. After considering all of the circumstances, however, one might conclude that, notwithstanding the risks, the Russian prison code contained a remarkably benign loophole and Mrs. Bergmeier was well advised to avail herself of it. The iniquity was upon the heads of those who caused society to be so disordered that persons could be put in such straits. Mrs. Bergmeier's activities come within the realm of the morally defensible. Her case can be seen as a good exception to a good principle that in no way threatens the value the principle contains.

The Domino Theory

Exception making has its perils. It can send you down a **slippery slope**. This is a danger that has many names. It is called the **domino theory**, or the wedge, or the camel's nose under the tent, or the finger out of the dike, or the parade of horrors. The problem envisioned by all of these terms is that of uncontrollably cascading effects once you allow an exception to what has been assumed to be a solid principle. It is this fear that is behind the hesitancy to admit even a reasonable exception to an ironclad principle. If you grant *A*, which seems reasonable, then you will logically have to grant *B* and *C* and *D*, which might not be reasonable at all. The instinctive defense against this is taboo. Sooner than puncture the principle with exception *A* and then collapse into shady exceptions *B*, *C*, and *D*, you'd best not grant *A*. Taboo builds a fence around a principle and allows no exceptions to escape, not even good and necessary exceptions.

The Pendulum Effect

Sociopsychologically, it is possible for a **pendulum effect** to take place in society when that society leaves the contrived security of an absolutized principle and begins to make distinctions and to exercise freedom in a new area. Recent history shows the shift from Victorian prudishness regarding sex to Dionysian, *Hustler*-magazine, obsessive excess. In the rush of the pendulum from left to right, the middle ground of healthy eroticism is missed. Breaking out of all taboos is a heady wine that can send a whole society reeling. This exposes a society to the same peril that a maturing child faces when he or she moves from reliance on parental authority toward some moral autonomy. The danger should not be minimized. We have to face it or opt for an arrested societal adolescence, lamely enforced with pleas to "just say no to sex."

An old Latin axiom contains remedial wisdom. *Abusus non tollit usum*—because something can be *abused* does not mean that it cannot be intelligently *used*. The possibility of abuse does not forestall use. The possibilities of abuse have to be reckoned with: that is the burden of responsible freedom. The tempting and seemingly safer path is to foreclose on freedom for fear of the abuse. Greater abuse is likely from a rigid taboo, since life will move forward without reflection. Conclusion: A critical pause before new exceptions is very much in order, provided it does not lead to a catatonic state of taboo rigidity. Fear of abuse should

instead remand us to the neglected powers of our creative imagination where our debts to freedom are best paid.

At the level of ethical theory, the domino fear of runaway exceptions is weak. One who allows for the morality of exception *A* need not choose to allow for *B*, *C*, and *D* for the excellent reason that *B*, *C*, and *D* are not *A*. Ethics is not done by deductive logic alone. The exception is not related to the principle as the puncture to the balloon. Principles are applied in experiential dialogue with the circumstances. The unique aspects of one situation do not transfer over into the analysis of all similar, but not identical, cases. Making distinctions where there are differences is the hallmark of clear thought. It has been aptly said that ethics, like art, has the task of knowing where to draw lines. And neither ethics nor art can avoid drawing lines. Domino thinking would commit us to universalization wherever difficult cases are involved. It represents a despair over our power of discernment.[37]

On Sticking to Your Principles

There is something that sounds ethically proper and fitting about "sticking to your principles." The problem is deciding which principles to stick to. In many cases contradictory principles call for applications. Ethics is a matter of deciding which principle connects most valuably to a particular situation. In the case mentioned above, Immanuel Kant was embarrassed by missing that point. If a would-be murderer wants information on the whereabouts of his intended victim, two principles collide: *truth telling* and *life saving*. Truth telling does not connect valuably with that situation. Using the following model, truth telling is principle *A*; life saving is principle *B*.

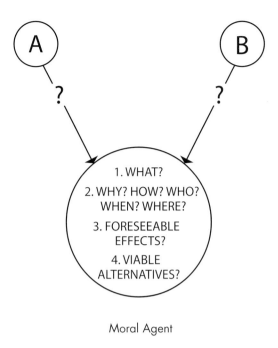

Moral Agent

Weighing of principles is essential to ethics. Even when someone is committed by oath to secrecy, other supervening values may emerge from answering the questions in the center of the wheel and weighing the competing values. Consider the following cases.

When Oath-Breaking Is a Virtue

Take the case of Katharine Gun. Gun was a British intelligence agent bound by her oath and the Official Secrets Act not to reveal any classified information. Secrecy has many advantages in statecraft. In the model, maintaining that sworn secrecy is principle A. As in much of life, that was not the only principle speaking to Ms. Gun's conscience when, in late January 2003, she received a secret memo from the U.S. National Security Agency (NSA) saying that the agency had started a "surge" of spying on diplomats at the United Nations in New York, including illegal wiretaps of home and office telephones, along with interception of all e-mails. The targets were the six countries (Mexico, Chile, Angola, Cameroon, Guinea,

and Pakistan) considered pivotal to getting support for the U.S. and British resolution supporting the planned invasion of Iraq.

Ms. Gun looked at all the circumstances of the situation and saw that the United States and Britain were planning to "blackmail, bribe, or threaten" the six swing nations in order to order a preemptive attack on a nation, something forbidden by the UN Charter. In the model above, she saw a second principle, a life-saving principle that trumped her secrecy obligation. She leaked the memo to the press, where it had broad impact internationally, though tellingly, not in the U.S. media. The government of Prime Minister Tony Blair quickly arrested Ms. Gun, fired her, and charged her with a breach of the Official Secrets Act. She paid a price for seeing that principle B connected most valuably to the context. In her own defense she said, "I have only ever followed my conscience." Her action did not stop the invasion, but her ethics was excellent.

Secrecy and confidentiality can be a value, but no value can be lifted out of competition with other values that may better serve the situation.

Ugly Compromises

A group of public power company executives presented me with this case. To provide needed electrical power for Seattle, a proposal was made to dam a river, which would cause a salmon run to be blocked. The proposal produced outrage and the company was picketed by angry protesters. The executives agonized over the loss of the salmon run, but, as they said, the protesters would go home after the protest and look to see if their protest had been covered on the evening TV news. That would take electricity. If they were hurt in an accident, they would want the hospital to be fully powered to serve them.

This is an interesting case because it presents a "Sophie's Choice" dilemma, where both available choices are tragic. Both principle A, save the salmon, and principle B, provide essential electrical power, house compelling values. One wants to deny neither.

In such a case, all attention should go to line 4 in the center of the wheel model of ethics: *What are the viable alternatives?* The answer, indeed, is blowing in the wind, especially in Seattle. An ugly compromise commands us to expand the alternatives. It points to a principle *C*, find nontoxic, alternative modes of power. The situation signals that bad societal choices had created this dilemma. Previous bad choices make other bad choices necessary, even if only temporarily. Principle *B* could not be justified in the absence of commitment to principle *C*.

This is similar to the situation in Rwanda where military intervention was called for. Once again, ugly alternatives signal a preceding neglect of other alternatives. Remember Rwanda. It was argued that military intervention should have been used to stop the intertribal genocide. That has prima facie verisimilitude. On second look it amounts to saying that if you create a mess, there is no non-messy solution. The issue then is, why did you make the mess in the first place?

Most cases of alleged "humanitarian intervention" point to a lack of commitment to the slow, unglamorous work of patient diplomacy and nonviolent options. Underlying this is the age-old and deeply ingrained conviction that military slaughter is the "final arbiter" in world affairs, when it actually shows only our retardation in the arts of politics. We create situations where bludgeoning is the only apparent solution.

Moral Judgment: Between Wisdom and Principles

Not by principles alone is ethics done. The supreme court is the discerning subject that must evaluate the moral meaning oozing out of the circumstances with the moral wisdom housed in moral principles. Moral judgment is mediation between the two.

Aristotle had enormous respect for universals.[39] Nonetheless, he makes much of the category of **practical wisdom**. The happy yield of practical wisdom is that those who have it "can see what is good for themselves and what is good for people in general." In other words, practical wisdom respects principles. However, it is not "concerned with universals only—it must also recognize the particulars; for it is practical, and practice is concerned with particulars."[40] In a remark that cannot be encouraging for young ethicists, Aristotle says that "it is thought that a young man of practical wisdom cannot be found." Young men, however, need not despair. They are quite capable of becoming mathematicians. While "young men have no convictions" about things related to experience, "the essence of mathematical objects is plain enough to them."[41] They can do fine with Rubik's Cubes, leaving ethics to the more mature.

The Doctor's Dilemma

Now to the doctor's dilemma. A patient arrives in an emergency room. The doctor, after preliminary tests, judges that the patient will pass away possibly within minutes, given the massive damage to his heart. Surprisingly, the patient opens his eyes and asks the doctor, "How am I?"

One winces to think what Immanuel Kant would say were he the physician. If he stuck to his rigid view on truth telling, he would tell the patient he had hours or maybe only minutes to live. Using the above model, two principles hover over the doctor: one is truth telling; the other is life saving. The patient, especially a moribund patient, has a right to know the truth. He may want to use his last moments of consciousness to be reconciled with a loved one, to change his will, and so forth. A lie occurs when you deny the truth to which someone has a right. (Telling the Gestapo you had no idea where the Frank family was even though you were bringing them food on a daily basis was not a lie. It was a justifiable falsehood since the Gestapo had no right to know.)

Back to the patient. If the doctor, heeding the life-saving principle and not wanting to panic the patient, producing instant death, were to say, "You're doing beautifully and you're going to be just fine," the doctor would be a liar. The patient has a right to know the accurate diagnosis. On the other hand, the doctor knows that his is a fallible skill. He has been surprised before, though never in a case like this. Still, he is fallible. He somehow has to give the patient the minimum of peace that might allow the stubborn and surprising healing powers of the body to have a chance. He cannot say, even though he thinks it, "You could die any minute now." This information would be self-fulfilling and would give no chance to the remote, but not negligible, possibility of recovery. Thus, the doctor might well decide to accept something of the truth-telling principle and something of the life-saving principle. He would tell the patient that he has had a serious heart attack but would cushion this news with the assertion that he is in good hands and that it is very important to rest and give the

THINKING CRITICALLY

Some principles, like the principle asserting the moral value of free speech, are selectively honored. Americans have long been known to be very touchy about criticisms of their country. This is particularly true in times of war. After the attack on the United States in September 2001 harsh criticism was visited on anyone who would question US military attacks on Afghanistan and Iraq. It was seen as disloyalty, in some shrill comments, even as treasonous. All nations have this tendency but one sage foreign visitor as far back as the 1830s thought it notably prominent in the United States:

The American, taking part in everything that is done in his country feels a duty to defend anything criticized there, for it is not only his country that is being attacked but himself. . . . Nothing is more annoying to the ordinary intercourse of life than the irritable patriotism of the Americans. A foreigner will gladly agree to praise much in their country, but he would like to be allowed to criticize something, and that he is absolutely denied.

—Alexis de Tocqueville, *Democracy in America*

12.5

heart a chance to heal, even though the doctor thinks rest will not do it. The delicate task of the doctor (and here *how* becomes massively important in the ethical equation) would be not to make the cushion so prominent as to blot out the news of the danger and not to so stress the bad news as to create an immediate panic that could stop the beating of an even healthier heart. He might have to draw from some of the wisdom in each principle (*A* and *B*) while staying alert to all the morally pregnant circumstances and making his moral choice.

Orchestrating Moral Living

The doctor's dilemma illustrates the kind of sensitive orchestration that has to be done in moral living. No problem would exist if ethics could be reduced to the simple application of one relevant principle to the case. Neither life nor the ethics that seeks to meet its complexities is so simple.

A principle, after all, is not a decision, but only the background of a decision. It is the voice of experience past, and, however helpful, it is inevitably limited in the face of the truly new. Moral wisdom requires that our sense of uniqueness not be dulled by the more manageable sense of what is generally true.

Summary of Key Themes

- Moral principles are the storehouses of human moral insights.
- Societies enshrine some of the moral principles as laws.
- There are unique cases that principles do not cover.
- Good principles and good exceptions to principles have equal moral standing.
- There are some principles on which all human beings can agree even though they disagree on their application.
- When principles have no imaginable exception, they are called negative moral absolutes, for instance, principles against rape, torture, or nuclear war.
- There can be exceptions even to the principle of fidelity to vows and oaths.

Key Terms

Abstinence-only sex ethics
Domino theory
Ethical realism
Ethics
Natural law
Pendulum effect
Positivism
Principles
Situation ethics
Slippery slope

Questions for Discussion

1. It is a good principle that patients have a right to know what their condition is. Some doctors hesitate to tell a patient that he or she is terminally ill. Is there ever a legitimate reason to deny a dying patient information on his or her condition?
2. Should there be different principles for the sexual behavior of adolescents and that of adults?
3. A young woman is pregnant as a result of a rape. She opposes all abortions. Would it be moral to gently counsel her that this might well be a good exception to her anti-abortion principle?

Suggestions for Further Reading

Beauchamp, Tom L. *Philosophical Ethics.* New York: McGraw- Hill, 1982.

Nisbet, Robert. *The Social Philosophers: Community and Conflict in Western Thought.* New York: Thomas Crowell, 1973.

Velasquez, Manuel, and Cynthia Rostankkowski. *Ethics: Theory and Practice.* Upper Saddle River, N.J.: Prentice Hall, 1985.

The Role of Authority
and the Work of Reason

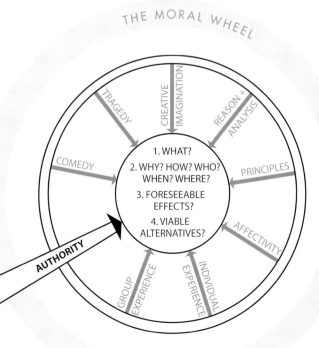

TEACHING IS A TWO-WAY STREET. Parenting proves it. Teach the children we surely do, and by them we are well taught. My son Tom taught me a powerful lesson in epistemology. When he was almost three, it became clear that he had been otherwise occupied and had not taken note of the previous autumnal displays. I found him one September day in the den, looking out the window with his companion, a cloth dog named Patches. I asked him what color the leaves were on the trees in the garden. "Green," he replied. I then broke the news. "Tom," I said, "very soon all those leaves will change. They will become red, yellow, orange, or brown, and all of them will fall down from the tree." He looked up at me earnestly with no sign of belief or disbelief.

The next day I was passing the den. Tom was again at his post and I could hear him talking to Patches. His voice was very serious. He was telling Patches of my prophecy regarding the splendors of fall. "Patches," he said, "all leaves green . . . all leaves turn . . . red, yellow, orange, brown . . . all fall down!" He had memorized the colors and he did not have a doubt in the world that it would all happen.

A sweet parental moment, to be sure, but a poignant lesson. I realized that if I had told Tom that very soon all the trees out back would lift out of the ground, turn upside down, and hang there suspended for the winter, he would have shared this "information" with Patches. My words were in the category of Gospel or Qur'anic truth to which the requisite response is "Amen!" Soon, of course, critical intelligence would develop and he would doubt and question, but in this early stage, he was, as were we all at that age, an unquestioning believer and I was infallible.

Upon reflection I thought of the birthing processes I had witnessed, the first appearance of the little face. What a perplexing moment for the birthling. For nine months this little creature lived in secure comfort, enjoying what you might call womb service, with all needs met including temperature control. Now the aborning child is being pressed through a canal clearly not designed with a baby in mind, and suddenly there is light and cold and metal contact. I thought at the time that if you could put a question into the mouth of the baby as it first emerged, it would have to be "What in the world is going on?" Of course, that question is the beginning of philosophy and theology, which have never really been asking anything else.

Experience and Infallibility

We are born with an inexorable need to know and to make sense of this world into which we are so peremptorily thrust. At the start we have just two sources of information: First, there is sense experience. This is grippingly impressive, almost overwhelming in its immediacy, telling us that enfolding arms are warm, ice is cold, the floor is hard, and the oven is hot. Nothing, it would seem, could be more compelling and convincing. Sense experience is outflanked, however, by our second early source of truth: **authority**. These towering figures on whom we are totally dependent give meaning as well as sustenance. We have no choice but to trust. If the leaves are green and these authorities say they will change colors, we can file that under "reality." Credulousness is our aboriginal tilt.

When intelligence matures and becomes critical (from the Greek *krino*, "to judge"), this infantile pattern of reliance is gradually replaced by questioning, testing, and analysis. However, these early comforts are not forgotten. They linger in the labyrinthian depths of the psyche, making us more credulous than we dare to acknowledge. As Adam Smith put it in his book on ethics, *The Theory of Moral Sentiments*:

> The man scarce lives who is not more credulous than he ought to be, and who does not, upon many occasions, give credit to tales which not only turn out to be perfectly false, but which a very moderate degree of reflection and attention might have taught him could not well be true. The natural disposition is always to believe. It is acquired wisdom and experience only that teach incredulity, and they very seldom teach it enough.[1]

Indeed, there lingers in the strongest minds a hankering for the bliss of early **infallibilism** when parents and others saved us from the disquietude of doubt. Later we will seek to replicate that experience in some infallible guru, which may take the shape of a national government, "conventional wisdom," respected authors, a Bible or a Qur'an, or a pope who is assumed to have the knack of infallibility. In bizarre cases, we may end up feeding poisoned Kool-Aid to ourselves and our children on the word of an authority figure in a place like Jonestown, Guyana. Addiction to cultish controls is not a fringe happening but an enduring temptation in all fields of knowledge. And when the stakes are high—as they are in ethics, where survival is often at issue—we are more credulous still. We are more docile than we suppose. Realistic ethics must take account of that. It is not just religions that are tendentially cults; learned professions and political parties are also. The rush to chimeric security is a permanent lure.

The fact is that when all the praises of reason have been sung, it remains the statistical norm that most of our moral opinions (and thus most of our political and economic theories, which are applications of moral assumptions) are not the result of a reasoning process, but are directly due to the influence of someone we admire or love or to the influence of traditional and accepted wisdom that we have never questioned. Reliance on authority of one kind or another is probably the most common form of moral evaluation, even among those who feel themselves highly independent and "liberated."

Forms of Authority

Having sounded all these warnings, I now move, with only apparent enigma, to presenting authority as one of the spokes in the wheel model of good ethical inquiry. Authority in any field is a resource for understanding. Like all the spokes in the wheel model, it can be abused by over-reliance and mental laziness. To use it well requires the steady slaughter of sacred cows in church and state, and the successful debunking of sacred and secular oracles. It's easy to shy from that. It takes **courage** to use authority well, courage being the precondition of all wisdom.

Since the Enlightenment we have been busy with debunking fake gurus. Could it be that we are now less prone to lean on authorities? No. Using authorities is normal and necessary. Our finitude requires it. We have neither the time nor the talent to think out everything. The illusion of a "universal scholar" who masters all fields is in the past tense. Aristotle may have thought that he could teach not just one subject but them all, but now with complexification and flux as facts of life, there is no one who does not need the authority of experts. Colleagues in some fields cannot understand all that their colleagues in specialized sections of that same field are doing. We are, one and all, expert dependent.

It is healthy to look at this fact of life and visit various forms of authority that affect us all. In the process we can view their ups and downs.

> ### THINKING CRITICALLY
>
> "Obedience, because of its very ubiquitousness, is easily overlooked as a subject of inquiry in social psychology. But without an appreciation of its role in shaping human action, a wide range of significant behavior cannot be understood. For an act carried out under command is, psychologically, of a profoundly different character than action that is spontaneous.
>
> "The person who, with inner conviction, loathes stealing, killing, and assault may find himself performing these acts with relative ease when commanded by authority. Behavior that is unthinkable in an individual who is acting on his own may be executed without hesitation when carried out under orders."
>
> —Stanley Milgram,
> *Obedience to Authority*
>
> 13.1

1. Experts

Even medieval thought in simpler times acknowledged the need for experts, and they offered two tests of reliable expertise: the expert has to be *sciens et verax*—*knowledgeable* and *truthful*. The *verax* test is as important as the *sciens* test. It is perhaps even more important, since expertise breeds arrogance and smarmy arrogance is the enemy of truth. Let us put modern medicine in the dock to illustrate this.

The Oracular Temptation. Doctors have come a long way since 1540 when, by an act of Parliament, they were put into a guild with barbers, the "United Company of Barbers and of Surgeons."[2] They had previously been combined with silk weavers, cap makers, chandlers, and rope makers. For understandable reasons the medical arts were not in the highest repute. All that has changed. Medicine has blossomed and boomed and for good reasons has become the font of great expectations. That is good and we are all the beneficiaries. So where is the danger?

Call it the **oracular temptation**. It comes from the tendency of prominent expertise to sink common sense. As Paul Starr says, writing on the history of American medicine, "When professionals claim to be authoritative about the nature of reality, whether it is the structure of the atom, the ego, or the universe, we generally defer to their judgment."[3] And this is especially true in our attitudes toward medical professionals who seem to hold our lives in their hands. The fallout from this unchallenged authority of doctors is alarming.

In the United States, the most commonly done surgeries are for gynecology (cesarean sections and hysterectomies) and cardiology (stents and bypasses). Conservative estimates are that at least half of all gynecological surgeries should not be done. Despite considerable efforts, the efficacy of newer cardiac surgeries has not been established. Small area analysis and considerations of sham surgery and preventive surgery cast further doubt on the necessity of much surgery.[4]

Back to George Bernard Shaw's contention that every profession is a conspiracy against the laity. Many things in the practice of medicine illustrate that. The use of obscure jargon is not only unfriendly but also a method of control. Prescriptions are still partially written in Latin. Diseases are given terms drawn from Latin and Greek when the native tongue could serve quite well. Thus, one condition is known as hepatosplenomegaly. An impressive term to be sure, and clear enough to one who speaks classical Greek, since *hepatos* means liver and *splenos* means spleen and *megale* means big. The term means no more or no less than an enlarged liver and spleen. Why not say it that way?

Abuse of Authority. I attended a medical meeting where a parent was presenting her daughter who had an undiagnosed syndrome. The mother reported that among her symptoms the girl was "sensitive to light." The presiding doctor said knowingly, "That would be your photophobia." Actually it would be your *sensitivity to light*, which would be more scientifically accurate since the girl did not have a phobia regarding light but was, in the mother's more scientifically precise language, sensitive to it. The condition called *unguis incarnatus* sounds mystical, if not downright religious, and all it means is an ingrown toenail. (There may be conditions best kept in another language out of delicacy, such as *pruritus ani*, an itchiness of the rectum. Otherwise English can serve nicely.)

This calculated obscurantism represents an abuse of authority that is dangerous to one's health. Among other things, it facilitates those unnecessary surgeries. Remedies are arising in the use of second and third opinions. This has begun to relativize the doctor's authority, and many doctors have come to see it as friendly to their work.

It relieves them of the unrealistic demand for omniscience, puts the burden of deciding on the patient or the patient's parents, and lessens fear of malpractice suits.

There are other forms of expert tyranny that plague professional life. Consider the subcommittee that is sent away to study a complicated matter and returns with faulty findings. It takes a special kind of courage to rise up before the authority of those who have done the research on this and who come to us wearing the mantle of expert authority. And then there is the computer, which adds to expertise the attractiveness of apparently unalloyed objectivity. Yet by attributing intelligence to the computer, an attribution that is ambiguous at its very best, we have made the computer the modern oracle. We repair to it with expectations it cannot meet, looking for answers it cannot give. Studies and articles buttressed by masses of computerized data have an immediate prestige, though the mystification often exceeds the yield in truth.[5]

Sacred Tyranny. Authority always operates powerfully in religious and crypto-religious contexts. Wherever the aura of the sacred accrues, there is a tendency for critical judgment to give way to awe. As sociologist Karl Mannheim writes: "In every society there are social groups whose special task it is to provide an interpretation of the world for that society. . . . Thus the magicians, the Brahmins, the medieval clergy are to be regarded as intellectual strata, each of which in its society enjoyed a monopolistic control over the moulding of that society's world-view."[6]

Those who fulfill this priestly role may not always be within a formally religious agency. The allegedly secular is often replete with numenosity; nationalism always is. Recall Toynbee's assertion that 90 percent of the real religion of moderns is nationalism. A nation is no merely pragmatic association of persons but is, rather, a social entity endowed with a unifying sacred mystique that can evoke complete devotion from its citizens even to the point of the "supreme sacrifice" of their lives. National constitutions acquire a biblical quality. Political leaders talk like priests, with the rule seeming to be that the God-talk rises in proportion to the mischief afoot.

Members of the military might be the citizens most abused by sacralized national authority. Modern war requires that soldiers be regimented into a slavish docility and denied the right to conscientious objection. The ideal of the modern soldier is not the swashbuckling knight of yore but the rigid, salute-on-demand automaton.

2. Peer Group Authority

Peer group influence is not always wrong, but it is always imperious. What the peer group does among young and old is to establish an evaluational **orthodoxy**. Sanctions abound. Dissenters against peer-established positions are perceived as a threat by the group, so enforcement is severe with penalties ranging from excommunication to ridicule. This phenomenon is as visible in countercultural groups as it is in monasteries or boardrooms. The devotees of a hippie commune, with all of their avowed commitment to doing one's own thing, are permitted few deviations regarding dress, language, recreational forms, or moral attitudes. Though they have substituted one orthodoxy for another, they have not escaped the dynamics of peer rule.

3. Tradition

Traditions are powerful because familiarity is comforting. Also, that which has stood the test of time merits some confidence. The problem is that error can be as traditional as truth. Also, traditions rooted in another time with other needs can shackle a society that clings to them in new times. The outdated notion of rigid national sovereignty has been noted. Witness, too, the American reluctance to make changes in the eighteenth-century form of government with its elitist and unrepresentative Electoral College and its four-year terms of a president. Voting on Tuesdays, even though it is a busy modern workday (and very inconvenient for many citizens), clings in the way hoary traditions can.

4. Charisma

This term need not be limited to the magnetic qualities of political figures, though it functions mischievously in politics. Hitler had enough **charisma** to convince many Germans they were winning the war as the nation collapsed around them. Crises make people more susceptible to charisma in politics. As the ancients said, *mundus vult decipi*—"people want to be deceived"—and when they are scared, they want deception even more. Charisma, however, is ubiquitous. None of us is so drab that we have none of it.

In any group, charisma will function and will exert a kind of blind influence on the group members. Charisma has many ingredients. The attractiveness of persons, the attitudes and confidence they project, the emotions they engender, and so forth, all give persons more or less influence or charisma. Achievement also lends charisma, as does the mere fact of being famous. Nations can gain charisma because of inspirational achievements (as the United States did in the idealistic Revolution of 1776) or simply because of their technological prowess. The forces that generate charisma might be worthy or quite frivolous. For this reason, a sensitive ethics must alert persons to the presence of charismatic influences in their thought processes. Like moths, we are easily caught by glare.

Charisma is not always negative. Indeed, the neglected art of rhetoric and persuasion relies on the moral credibility of the speaker. As Aristotle said in his *Rhetoric*: "Persuasion is achieved by the speaker's personal character when the speech is so spoken as to make us think him credible. . . . It is not true, as some writers assume in their treatises on rhetoric, that the personal goodness revealed by the speaker contributes nothing to his power of persuasion; on the contrary, his character may almost be called the most effective means of persuasion he possesses."[7]

Thus, authority is not an alien intrusion but rather part of a system of reliance and trust that not only increases our contact with truth but is a normal part of developing moral consciousness. Inability to accept authority influences is a social and psychological problem as well as a problem in ethics.

Some years ago, when speaking at the University of Pennsylvania, the existentialist philosopher Gabriel Marcel was asked how he came to change his attitude toward a personal value question he had discussed. His reply was rather dogmatic for an existentialist. "Personal encounters," he said. "Nothing else ever changes anyone." We need not be as absolute as Marcel to accept the authoritative power that operates through the medium of friendship and trust and to see authority as a natural aid both in the socialization process and in moral discernment.

Reason Hot and Cold

Reason, in the words of the *Oxford English Dictionary*, is "the guiding principle of the human mind in the process of thinking." That is so generic as to be misleading. It would make reason overlap with much that is covered by the other evaluational processes (spokes) in my wheel model of ethics. But reason is more than that, as that same dictionary goes on to show. It gathers facts and makes arguments. Reason is the working mind. It has more to do with perspiration than with inspiration. Reason is not the mind sitting quietly, awaiting the gifting touch of the muse. It is the mind as hunter and gatherer. It is a sibling to analysis, which etymologically means breaking something up to see what it is made of. Reason relates to tough words like *discipline*, *study*, and *homework.* Reason scans the moralscape facing every one of the questions in the center of the wheel model. Among its tasks: to search for the unasked questions; to test the regnant authorities before which minds may be playing dead; to cope with the inevitable partiality of our knowledge; to jog the lazy memory; to fight the allure of too-facile consensus; to break the stranglehold of habituation and "group-think"; to check our myths and other filters; to solve the conflicts between and among principles; and to tend to the reformulation and correction of principles in view of new experience. In a word, reason works to be critical and to fight the superficiality that is the issue of a sluggish mind. As Aquinas said, "To bring order is the function of reason."[8] If reason is not functioning, then disorder is the result.

Early impressions, in ethics or elsewhere, come to us in largely undifferentiated globs. Reason and analysis break them up and sort them out so that we can know what it really is that we are talking about. This is sometimes a mammoth operation. Everyone has some idea of what a multinational corporation (MNC) is. Without a lot of perspiring reason and analysis, however, that idea will remain at the level of an impressionistic mass and no realistic ethics of the MNC will be done. The MNCs have to be judged morally, since they are

THINKING CRITICALLY

Reasoning about moral matters is never cold or unemotional. It is improbable that anyone could hear of the following case without emotive response: In a widely discussed case in 1984, Corinne Parpalaix, a twenty-three-year-old widow, was denied access to her late husband's sperm, which had been deposited at the Center for the Study and Conservation of Sperm. Around the time Alain and Corinne Parpalaix met in 1981, he had testicular cancer and was warned that treatment could cause sterility. It was then that he decided to deposit his sperm. Alain and Corinne were married on December 23, 1983; two days later Alain died. The sperm bank, located near Pris, argued that it was obliged to refuse Mrs. Parpalaix's request because her husband had not stipulated what he wanted done with his sperm in the case of his death. On August 1, 1984, a Paris court ruled in her favor.

13.2

principal agents in the community of persons and have deep effects on the quality of life. Judging MNCs ethically, however, is no simple matter, given the new economic and political complexities that they have foisted upon us. We are only at the first stages of the analysis of these entities. The reason and analysis process will broaden, but it must go on or the MNC will slip beyond the pale of moral consciousness. The moral import of the MNC is too profound to go unordered by moral reason.

Complexity scares the human mind away from ethical analysis, but this should not be indulged when human health and the health of the earth are involved. Another example of this is the annual U.S. federal budget, which arrives in pounds of paper. Few who vote on it read all of it, and yet a national budget is the most moral of entities since it encapsulates all the moral priorities and blind spots of a nation.

Hot Moral Reasoning

In mathematics, reason can reach high levels of abstractness. In science it will combine the theoretical and the practical. In many areas of human thought, reason can be cold and detached. In ethics, reason is hot. **Moral reasoning** is rooted in the affections of the FME, and because of that, discussions on morals are never unemotional. *Recta ratio*, "right reason," was offered by the ancients as the guide to moral truth. Making sure that the *ratio* stays *recta* with all the competing emotions that tug us when we think morally is a challenge. It leads to words like *rationalization*, a term in ethics that means that unworthy emotions are distorting judgment.[9] Given the symbiosis of reason and affectivity, the thrust of the affections can easily be self-serving. This is why ethical method has to be a system of checks and balances, as the various evaluational processes illustrated by the spokes of the wheel model will illustrate. Impulses can present themselves as the inexorable dictates of pure moral reason. A misguided wish is often father to devious conclusions. In value matters we can come to see what we want to see.[10]

Of course, emotions and affections are involved in other forms of reasoning.[11] The mathematician and the logician are moved by emotion to address and solve their conundrums. Affectivity in those cases prods you to think (acting like an efficient cause), but the affectivity is not integral to the thought process in quite the same way it is when one reasons about what people are worth, that is, about moral values. Then the affectivity is intrinsic, like a formal cause of the reasoning. Were a person in no way immersed in the FME, the situation would be like that of persons born blind who hear about colors. Blind persons could understand what science would explain about the physical perception of various colors and they could make true statements about colors, but they would have no unmediated experiential base from which to know color. It's a case more of knowing about than of knowing. The FME involves affectivity at the deepest mystical level. It also involves faith. All that makes moral reasoning unique in human knowing.

A major function of reason is to remind us that life is in process. If we forget that, we can be put into the predicament of the compulsive bettor who, while watching a football game on television, lost ten dollars on a play and then lost another ten on the instant replay. He mistook the

past for the present, as will anyone who loses the sense of process.

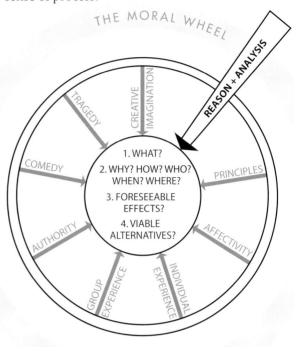

Sociopathic Ethics: When Reason Turns Cold

Since the FME is marked by caring, discussions of human and terrestrial good with a caring gap miss the point. When Garrett Hardin in his "lifeboat ethics" argues that the dispossessed of the world will have to be allowed to perish in their hunger because there is just no space in the lifeboat for everyone, there is the ring of practicality about it, and not a few have pronounced it reasonable. When he further compares the starving poor to cancer cells that cannot be cured by feeding them, he moves further from reality. He reasons about persons as though they are things. He disenfranchises a large number of men, women, and children from full status in humanity. With that done, he can "reason" in a way that many find convincing and commonsensical. These depersonalized beings can be dismissed like diseased cells. This is sociopathic ethics. The pathology in this reasoning is at the level of the caring that is essential to the FME. It brushes aside issues of population management and empowering forms of humanitarian aid.

A similar sociopathy is found in frigid discussions of "collateral damage" in war. This dismissive term refers to all those who are killed who were not prime targets. It evinces a bland "sorry about that" nonchalance as it suppresses moral concern under the blanket of "military necessity." "Acceptable levels of unemployment" can be used by economists in a similar way. "Economic necessity" is the blanket here. I repeat here Alice Rivlin's moral realism when she writes: "It does not seem, from an analytical point of view, that there is any magic number below which we cannot push unemployment. It is a question of the will and of choosing the right mix of policies."[12] Talking about the "right mix" of policies brings justice back into the picture, something that sociopathic ethics definitely leaves out. Economists who list environmental issues as "externalities" thus free themselves from responsibility in ecocide. Social Darwinism, which took the law of the jungle as the law of economic life, dismisses justice claims, making social life a moral vacuum. Reason shorn of caring is lethal.

Moral reason, even when it has not been stripped down to the level of bare technological considerations, may be drawn to painful conclusions amid the complexities and radical imperfections of human life at our early point in moral evolution. Circumstances may arise where killing people in self-defense might be tragically but morally called for. Reason that is not desensitized

would do this in what Augustine called a "mournful mood."

Reasonable or Rationalistic: The Role of Objections and Heresy

Reason has two verbal relatives in **reasonable** and **rationalistic** that are scarcely on speaking terms. The one has felicitous connotations; the other does not. *Reasonable*," the good relative, is not just the adjective that relates to reason. It has a broader meaning and is instructive about the role and nature of reason. To be called reasonable is a compliment. No one would want to be considered anything else. Wrong, maybe, but never unreasonable! *Reasonable* connotes an openness to reality and to being, along with a kind of balance and thoroughness. In a notable way, this sense of reasonableness emerges in the "reasonable person" criterion summoned in law when there are no prior decisions or laws to decide a case. Through usage *reasonable* has picked up a family of happy connotations signifying good contact with reality and fairness.[13]

With its acquired richness of meaning, the word *reasonable* is a kind of shortcut to doing ethics. The truly reasonable is the truly good: the terms are synonymous. This is a freeing thought since many errors can be smoked out that way. The long-held teaching in many of the Christian churches that artificial contraception is

THINKING CRITICALLY

"Practical reasoning is concerned with what our actions can bring about and such things can be brought about in more than one way. Consequently, even though we may be certain about the general premises of a piece of practical reasoning, the more particular the conclusions we try to derive, the more possibilities there are for going wrong."

—Thomas Aquinas, *Summa Theologiae*

13.3

evil was gradually undone by the common sense of good people, sometimes called in the Catholic tradition the *sensus fidelium*. Gradually the good sense seeped up to scholars and church leaders who have begun to realize that the use of condoms is not forbidden but mandatory when it can prevent illness or forestall a pregnancy for which one is not prepared. People trusting their "reasonable" perceptions got there before the theoreticians who were impaled on old and tenured errors. Of course, while *reasonable* is a shortcut to moral judgment, it is not a substitute for a full ethical method with all the checks and balances thereof.

Rationalistic, as signaled by that nasty *-istic* suffix, is an intellectual badness. It tries to put reality into neat little boxes where it just does not fit. It is prone to tidiness even when the truth is sloppy. It is, in an Irish colloquialism, "entirely too smart." It loves schemes that simplify. Returning to sex, the view long favored in Catholic teaching that the primary and unneglectable purpose of sex is reproduction, with all other meanings of sexual exchange given lower status, was rationalistic. Too tidy by far, since in fact sex usually has nothing to do with reproduction except for (one hopes, given today's demographics) one or two times in the sex lives of heterosexual couples. Thus, rather than primary, reproduction is very secondary to all the rich meanings of sexual joy and cherishing.

Yes, But!

Much that we call "medieval" was wise. You see this in the stress on knowing the objections to one's position. This is a helpful remedy for faulty, rationalistic thinking. Facing objections chastens reason and expands its reach. That's why, in books like Thomas Aquinas' magnum opus, the *Summa Theologiae*, Thomas offers no thesis to which he does not first object. If he sets out to say that *x* is right, he begins by marshaling all the reasons he can summon why *x* could not possibly be right. Then he states his case, argues for it, and then returns to answer the objections. (This is still a wholesome intellectual approach. I used it in my book *A New American Justice: Ending the White Male Monopolies.* I began the book by finding every objection to preferential affirmative action in the literature and conjuring others; I followed this with my arguments and finally returned to the objections.[14]) The medieval *disputatio* formalized the idea of debate with opposing views contending as the premier academic exercise.

Indeed, this perceived need for collision as a precondition for the discovery of truth led to the founding of the universities. From the very start at Bologna, Paris, and Oxford the ideal was that truth is best served by many minds competing freely together. When the University of Paris was founded in 1215, the statutes made it clear that the university was to be a haven where scholars and their students could engage in free debate. It was not to be a group of learners clustered around a single teacher or a single school of thought. It was to be a *universitas magistrorum et scholarium*, a community of teachers and students, and to function it needed independence.[15] "Many privileges were bestowed on [the university] making it a body independent of bishops, king, and Parliament."[16] Bishops, kings, and parliament were the most likely inhibitors of free thinking. Targeting them was making this first case for what today is called "academic freedom," the right of many minds to compete and argue together in the service of truth.

The Role of Heresy

However, since many minds competing and arguing together can easily slip into premature consensus, there is a role in reasoning for pesky heretics. *Heresy* is orthodoxy's term for a nonconforming view. Since orthodoxies have a track record of being both right and wrong, heresy can perform an essential service. Imperious orthodoxy with its priesthood of enforcers can stifle reason. In the "roaring" 1920s in the United States, unfettered markets boomed, leading to most wealth going to the top 1 percent of people. Heretics to this unleashing were too few or silenced. In 1929 this top-heavy arrangement toppled. With the arrival of President Franklin D. Roosevelt, regulations on the barons of finance brought stability. Starting in the 1980s with President Ronald Reagan, deregulation became the new orthodoxy. Too few heretics protested, and then came the crash of 2008, followed by calls for regulation. This destructive *to-ing* and *fro-ing* needed the service of vocal heretics. Reason can get stuck in the tight ridges of orthodoxy. Heretics can save us from blind momentum or established caprice by freeing reason for its appointed tasks.

Summary of Key Themes

- We are socialized to be too credulous, and this stunts the growth of the mind.
- Intelligent use of authority is the mark of maturity.
- Ethics has to evaluate the various forms of authority that affect us for good or for ill.
- Reason and analysis are the work tasks of the searching mind.
- Moral reasoning is never without emotional concomitants.
- Heretics are needed to keep orthodoxies honest.

Key Terms

Authority
Charisma
Courage
Heresy
Infallibility/infallibilism
Moral reasoning
Oracular temptation
Orthodoxy
Reasonable versus rationalistic
Tradition

Questions for Discussion

1. Philosopher Raymond Belliotti writes: "Some would argue that the nature of the marriage contract itself entails that any extramarital encounter on the part of either party is immoral (i.e. it involves promise-breaking) since one provision of the marriage contract is sexual exclusivity. But under my analysis the parties to the marriage contract may legitimately amend the contract at any time, and an extramarital sexual encounter need not be immoral as long as both marital partners agree prior to the encounter that it is permissible. If the marriage relationship is construed as a voluntary reciprocal contract the partners are free to amend its provisions insofar as they can agree on the alterations involved" (Velasquez and Rostankowski, *Ethics: Theory and Practice*, New York: Prentice Hall, 1985, 350). Many legal, ethical, and religious authorities would insist that Belliotti is wrong. Is this a case of reasoning run amuck?

2. Civil disobedience is defended as a virtuous response to unlawful authority. On December 4, 2008, a jury in West Palm Beach, Florida, found seven environmental activists guilty of trespass and unlawful assembly. Those convicted had used the "necessity defense," since their actions were to prevent damage to life. They were

told that such a defense could only be used when there is imminent danger to human life, "not trees, not bodies of water, not the environment." Evaluate that judgment.

3. The word *prestige* comes from a Latin root meaning "legerdemain" or "magical trickery." Prestige gives authority to persons or institutions. Discuss the ways in which prestige can be bewitching and a distraction from moral objectivity. Should any red flags go up when the word *prestigious* is used?

Suggestions for Further Reading

Milgram, Stanley. *Obedience to Authority.* New York: Harper Torchbook, 1974.

Shriver, Donald W., Jr. *Honest Patriots: Loving a Country Enough to Remember Its Misdeeds.* New York: Oxford University Press, 2005.

Velasquez, Manuel, and Cynthia Rostankowski. *Ethics: Theory and Practice.* New York: Prentice Hall, 1985.

Group Experience and Individual Experience

"We-Think" and "I-Think"

How will we be remembered one thousand years from now when we are as remote as Charlemagne?

Biologist Edward O. Wilson poses that question in his probing book *The Future of Life*. The answer to this speculation will be controlled by the reigning myths of that future time. In the myths of ancient times, many, like Virgil, Ovid, and Horace, looked back to an *aetas aurea*, a golden age of harmony. They were *laudatores temporis acti*—"praisers of times past." This myth endured into the Middle Ages. Medieval culture "was acutely conscious of its cultural inferiority to previous ages, whose achievements it greatly admired, even if it did not fully understand them."[1] They did not believe that the new was likely to be true; indeed, they thought the opposite and were suspicious of the new. The modern myth (which is no less mythic), fed by the marvels of science and the growth of knowledge, believes that the best lies ahead.

Coming out of this buoyant modern myth is the expectation, as Wilson paints it, that the

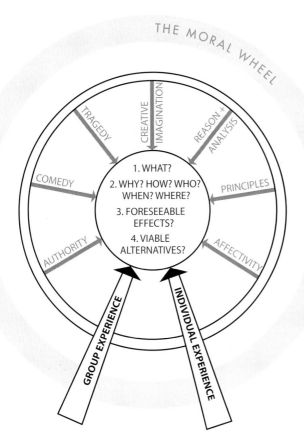

THE MORAL WHEEL

1. WHAT?
2. WHY? HOW? WHO? WHEN? WHERE?
3. FORESEEABLE EFFECTS?
4. VIABLE ALTERNATIVES?

TRAGEDY
CREATIVE IMAGINATION
REASON + ANALYSIS
COMEDY
PRINCIPLES
AUTHORITY
AFFECTIVITY

GROUP EXPERIENCE
INDIVIDUAL EXPERIENCE

The Myth of Moral Maturity

Good ethical decisions stand between us and planetary disaster. Good ethics demands an honest look at our prospects. We should not be beguiled by the word *modern* any more than by the word *developed*. Both words embody self-praise and a sense of "having arrived," of humanity reaching its desired maturity. That is surely questionable. Social scientist Duane Elgin sees us more as a species in adolescence. Our infancy he traces back thirty-five thousand years. Like inventive and promising toddlers, we picked up some simple skills in tool making and cave painting. As we grew a bit more, around ten thousand years ago we settled down in farming villages, still very much children. Five thousand years ago, with the rise of small cities, we moved into late childhood. We learned how to write and make some rules. With the scientific-industrial revolution three hundred years ago, we moved into our adolescence—adolescents with technical skills that have proved both beneficial and lethal. We have swarmed over planet Earth like a tsunami, killing species as we go. Our laggardly moral maturation is more than worrisome. (Wilson calls us the serial killer of the biosphere. Scientists predicted that up to one-fifth of all living species could disappear within several decades as the twenty-first century opened.[5]) Though we are moving close to adulthood, says Elgin, the marks of adolescence are still upon us. Like teenagers we are rebellious—rebelling violently against one another, rebelling against nature for thousands of years, trying to be independent of it. We are reckless, concerned with appearances and status through material possessions, drawn toward instant gratification, and prone to "us versus them" and "in versus out" thinking and behavior.[6] All very adolescent.

The point for ethics is that we are young and unstable prodigies. Our gifted species originated in the savannas and transitional forests of Africa. If you take the two-million-year tenure of our ge-

technoscientific revolution will continue in the next millennium unabated and unstoppable, with "computer capacity approaching that of the human brain; robotic auxiliaries proliferating; cells rebuilt from molecules; space colonized; population growth slackening; the world democratized; international trade accelerated; people better fed and healthier than ever before; life span stretched"; with God in his heaven and all well with the world.[2] It is more likely, says Wilson, that our beleaguered descendants by then will have lost "much of the rest of life, and part of what it means to be a human being."[3] Ouch! In spite of conceding this distinct possibility, Wilson still manages to maintain hope in his book's final words that our species, given its imaginative powers, "will surely find the way to save the integrity of this planet and the magnificent life it harbors." The success or failure, he says, "will come down to ethical decisions."[4]

nus and its immediate ancestors and compress it into a span of seventy years, "humanity occupied the ancestral environment for sixty-nine years and eight months whereupon some of the populations took up agriculture and moved into villages to spend the last 120 days."[7] We're young, but we are already living on an overpopulated planet, armed to the teeth with kill-power and buckling under the maldistribution of wealth—with 82 percent of income going to the top 20 percent and 18 percent left for the rest of humanity. Our prospects look shaky. We have over-stressed Mother Nature. Of this Wilson comments: "After evolving on her own for more than three billion years, she gave birth to us a mere million years ago, an eye blink in evolutionary time. Ancient and vulnerable, she will not tolerate the undisciplined appetite of her gargantuan infant much longer."[8]

Group Experience: The Value of "We-Think"

Pope John Paul II, in a belated papal recognition of this capital problem, got it right when he said that "the ecological crisis is a moral issue." Each of the spokes of the wheel model of ethics represents another way in which we reach for moral wisdom. Group experience is the spoke we now address. The beginning of wisdom is in knowing how we know, so it's the business of ethics to find out. We do not know as independent entities making solitary contact with reality. To know is to be part of a knowing community. We depend on that community not just for language but for attitudes and judgments; the mind develops in a process of social osmosis.

The Illusion of Independence

Strictly speaking, when you say, "I think," you are already wrong. It would be more accurate to say, "I

have been socialized to think." It is not that we are incapable of original ideas. We can at times break from our social cognitive moorings. Otherwise there would be no movement in civilization and every society would be frozen in time. The humbling truth is that truly original thoughts are rare, and even when we are somewhat original, we are standing on the shoulders of those who preceded us. More often than not, we may think ourselves a voice when we are only an echo. Our "original" thoughts proceed out of a fund of cultural traditions. When we break through to a new horizon, we do not take off from nowhere. Creativity is not *ex nihilo*.

This fact of group knowing is important for ethics: it reminds us of how shaped and formed we are by others, how we are more mimics than creators. If you know you are culturally "programmed," you might be able to assess the legacy into which you were born. If we arrive thinking, to repeat the words of George Bernard Shaw, that the laws of our tribe are the laws of nature, we are not going to challenge the folkways of the tribe. If we are unaware of our cultural conditioning, we are stuck in it. Our thirst for meaning is innate, but our minds are absorbent before they can become critical and evaluative.[9] Being critical and evaluative is the whole work of ethics.

The fervent Roman Catholic in Brooklyn or the devout Jew in Jerusalem should know that if they happened to have been born in Indonesia to Muslim parents, they would be Muslims. If they were born in Bombay, they would be Hindus. Our initial religious affiliations, therefore, are an accident of birth, as are our basic worldviews. They are not an unhappy accident. All the world religions are storehouses of good values, so it is not a tragedy to be born in one or the other. It is a tragedy if you think your religion is the law of nature and you'd best start a crusade to make all others adopt it. Since nationalism is religiously toned, the effort of one nation to impose its values on others is a form of religious fanaticism. All empires, from the

Roman to the American, are efforts to impose one set of values on other people.

Add to all this the feeling factor: the cultural values we inherit are emotionally wrapped. We learn best from people we love and admire. Divorce from love-bred notions is bloody and painful. Radical criticism of accepted values—values woven into one's self-image—is not facilely achieved, making moral conversion a steep climb. Knowing how numbed our skulls are can be a jump start on the trek to wisdom.

The Downside of "We-Think"

In manic moments, such as the start of a war, group-think (**we-think**) can be like a demonic possession. The debacle called World War I began in a frenzy, illustrating what the Germans call *Siegestrunkenheit*, a drunken orgy of enthusiasm. "The war is so horribly exciting . . . it is like being drunk all day," wrote a British suffragette.[10] In the emotional melee feminists abandoned their cause and avowed pacifists put aside their creeds to join the war effort. In India, even the gentle Gandhi put aside his scruples and helped recruit his countrymen to join the British army. Amid the social frenzy, Sigmund Freud confessed to losing all perspective, "giving all his libido to Austria-Hungary."[11]

Even aside from crises, when primitive emotions of vengeance mix with permanent, deeply rooted insecurities and fears, society in its calmer days can numb us to encircling evils. Americans managed for almost a century to live with both slavery *and* the Declaration of Independence. Crusaders went on their mission of genocide with the gospel of love in their hands. This would be branded implausible if it were not historically true. The plausibility is found not only in our enduring ability to exploit others for gain with the most improbable rationalizations, but also in the fact that when our moral evaluation is socially blessed, it becomes "natural" to think and act in accord with the social cognitive momentum. A crusader or slaver value-structure is the natural child of a cru-

sading or slaving time. Our consciences tend to bob along like corks on the mythic and emotive tides of the time.

The Role of Class. "**Class**" is a key tool of group-think. The term signifies a social stratum with names like *economic*, *social standing*, and *power* (or *lack of power*). Classes are hierarchical, signaled by such terms as *upper*, *middle*, and *lower*. As biblical professor and ethicist Obery Hendricks writes, "For a society to have classes at all, it must have over-classes and under-classes."[12] The terms *liberal* and *conservative* deal with the inevitable tensions between under- and over-classes. As *The Oxford English Dictionary* says, *conservative* is "characterized by a tendency to preserve or keep intact or unchanged." In modern political usage, "conservatives" are usually identified as those who wish to preserve the privileges of the over-class. Again *The Oxford English Dictionary*: "Conservative and Liberal, as we ordinarily use the terms, are distinctions having reference to a particular practical struggle, the gradual substitution of government by the whole body of the people for government by privileged classes." *Conservative* is not a dirty word in itself; through usage it often refers to "government by privileged classes."

Classes' group-think arises from their perceived interests. This affects ethical judgment in controlling ways. So, for example, in the United States many, not all, conservatives embrace policies based on privilege and not on egalitarian equity. Hendricks delivers a withering critique of conservative Americans:

> Conservative politicians opposed at their inception Social Security, Medicare and Medicaid, unemployment compensation, the right to form labor unions, government guaranteed student loans, child labor laws, the minimum wage, workplace safety regulations, guaranteed bank and savings deposits, oversight to insure the purity of our food and drugs, the environ-

mental protection movement, the Equal Rights Amendment, civil rights legislation, even anti-lynching legislation. Indeed, conservatives have opposed virtually every policy that might narrow the gap between rich and poor, particularly taxation of the wealthy.[13]

Liberals, of course, are not sinless on any one of those issues. Many liberal reforms excel in velleities, not effective volitions. And many liberals do not have the patience to do the taxing analytical work needed to make reforms start and stick.

The Power Differential. The differential between over- and under-class is *power*.[14] The terms *upper class* and *lower class* relate to power. Race and gender also are best analyzed under the power rubric. The terms *upper* and *lower* do not relate to moral values, since the "lower" classes may have higher standards of justice. Those classical justice movements that came to be called Judaism and Christianity emanated from the "lower," poorer classes. The term *democracy*, which represents an ideal, never an established fact, is a movement away from upper-class dominance. Its successes are important but scant. The United States touts itself as the ideal democracy. "Consider that we shall be as a city upon a hill, the eyes of all people upon us," crowed Governor John Winthrop, and generations of Americans after him cried, "Amen!" A lovely ideal, but class has ruled. Michael Zweig gives the actual class-based alignment of this "city upon a hill." What he calls "the working class" has the least power and makes up 62 percent of the American people. The "middle class" makes up 36 percent of the nation and has some modest power, while the "corporate elite class," which makes up 2 percent of the people, has considerably more. He then distinguishes "the ruling class," comprised of the corporate directors who sit on multiple boards and the political elites in the three branches of government, as well as other cultural and educational leaders. This is the smallest class and the one with the most power. Says Zweig, they could all fit into the old Yankee Stadium, capacity 54,000.

This is nothing new. The United States has always been ruled by aristocrats, starting from the founding fathers. The American Revolution was engineered by the colonial ruling class. "George Washington was the richest man in America, John Hancock was a prosperous Boston merchant. Benjamin Franklin was a wealthy printer."[15] "We the People" always made big distinctions between some people and others. Only the propertied could vote, and propertied women could not even do that. From the start, the onerous burdens of the society were placed on the backs of the poor. At the time of the Revolutionary War, "the rich, it turned out, could avoid the draft by paying for substitutes; the poor had to serve." The same was true at the time of the Civil War. "J. P. Morgan had escaped military service in the Civil War by paying $300.00 to a substitute. So did John D. Rockefeller, Andrew Carnegie, Philip Armour, Jay Gould, and James Mellon. Mellon's father had written to him that 'a man may be a patriot without risking his own life or sacrificing his health. There are plenty of lives less valuable.'"[16] Alexander Hamilton so distrusted "the mass of the people" that he thought the upper class, "the rich and well-born," should have a permanent share in the government. He suggested a president and Senate chosen for life.[17] Upperclassism has a long American pedigree.

From Autonomy to Parasitism. The neglect of class analysis in social ethics is not a venial sin. Class-based injustice devastates national and international society. Class makes people poor and keeps them so. And the guilt is widespread since even lower economic classes reap some of the benefits of the poorer classes. Ethicist Mary Hobgood writes: "As we in the upper echelons of the working class feed, clothe, and entertain ourselves, we are intimately connected to the lives of the women, children, and men who are su-perexploited by terrible conditions of overwork, underpayment, deplorable living environments, and sometimes death in order to provide what we consume and what we have been taught to desire. The blood, sweat, tears, and suffering be-hind what we consume are carefully hidden from us."[18] Those who pick our fruit and vegetables work for as little as five to nine thousand dollars a year with no health-care ben-efits.[19] Grim as it sounds, we supposedly autonomous individuals in this individu-alistic society are actually parasites. We mask it with fine names like "free trade."

It is the self-perpetuating power of class that makes it such a gritty problem for ethics. There are multiple ways of disempowering the poor. Religion professor John Raines speaks ironically of his classroom as a "class" room. Schools function as "gate-keepers to a shrinking pool of rewards." Schools mirror the geographic mal-distribution of opportunity. "The function of education becomes not discovering new and deserving talent, but instead assigning desired future place in our society to the already privileged, and getting the losers to blame themselves rather than the injustices of social class." As an example, he tells us that at a high school in an affluent Phila-delphia neighborhood, the chances of getting a college degree are forty times greater than for students in a high school in a poor Philadelphia neighborhood.[20]

THINKING CRITICALLY

Cultures like people can suffer from coronary occlusion, a closing of the heart to others and their values. All societies are weaker because of practicing their own kind of cultural apartheid. W. E. B. DuBois voiced this from the experience of African Americans: "One ever feels his two-ness—an American, a Negro; two souls, two thoughts, two unrecon-ciled strivings. African Americans simply wish to make it possible to be both a Negro and an American, without being cursed and spit upon by their fellows, without having the doors of Opportunity closed roughly in their faces."

—William E. B. DuBois,
The Souls of Black Folk

14.1

Hypocrisy as First Line of Defense. Reinhold Niebuhr observed "that inequalities of social privilege de-velop in every society, and that these inequalities become the basis of class divisions and class soli-darity." A person born into a particular class is heir to a special outlook suited to the perceived needs of that class. The implications of this for ethics are clear. As Niebuhr says, "The moral attitudes of dominant and privileged groups are characterized by universal self-deception and hypocrisy." The moral out-look of members of given classes "is invariably col-ored, if not determined," by the privileges and economic prerogatives of the class.[21] Niebuhr, an ethicist, notes indictingly that this is better noted by economists than by ethicists.

Suburbanism illustrates the apartheid that is inherent in class divisions. Economist Robert Reich has called it "the secession of the success-ful." Suburbanites are camp followers. They are of the city but not in it. The suburban enclaves are there only be-cause the city is there. The etymology of *suburb* implies that. Most would not have been built nor would they survive if they could not feed upon the economic and so-cial resources of the city. The city provides jobs, a workforce, customers, cultural and service fa-cilities, and entertainment. It is a fiction to think of a suburb as an independent social entity. The legalism of separate incorporation gives a kind of Anglo-Saxon gloss to this mode of segregation. There are human problems within the urban-suburban complex that cannot be solved by only one part of that complex. In fact, the cause, and the solution to the city's problems might lie more in the suburbs than in the city. You can't cross an arbitrary line between city and suburb and leave your moral obligations behind. Certain fiscal and integration problems do not abide by the city limits in their causes or potential solutions.

Some years ago a bold state legislator in Wisconsin proposed a metropolitan plan for Milwaukee's city schools. Suburban schools drawing on a higher property tax base have fine buildings and green space for recreation while city schools decay. Drawing from the metropolitan fiscal resources would repair this inequity. The suburbs bridled at the suggestion of fair sharing, and the plan was dead on arrival. Class interest, not justice, prevailed.

The Upside of Group Experience

I have lingered on the debits of group-think because we can be more evil together than we can be alone. Count Cavour of Italy said of himself and his fellow citizens that they would be jailed as scoundrels if they did for themselves the things they do for Italy. But groups are not all bad and not all stupid and self-serving. There are breakthroughs in some nations and cultures that can be instructive for those stuck in old ruts. A good rule for ethics is *circumspice*—look around!

Comparison as Ethical Strategy. The category of "family values" has been prominent in modern American political discourse. An inquisitive, comparative ethics should look at how other societies treat issues involving families.

Sweden is an example of a different kind of group-think. Working on the principle that care of children is in the national interest, Sweden has a policy of state-sponsored parental leave. "Parents are entitled to a total of 480 days paid leave per child, with both mothers and fathers entitled and encouraged to share the leave. The leave can be

taken at any time until the child reaches the age of seven."[22] Parents are encouraged to share this, though it is permissible for the mother to take as many as 420 days of the total leave with the remaining sixty days being taken by the father. Single parents can take all 480 days. In the interest of the child, there is no penalty for not being married.

Beyond this allowance there is another legal right for Swedish citizens. In addition to the paid leave of 480 days per couple per child, parents are entitled to reduce their working time by 25 percent, but this is not compensated. It involves a reduction in salary.

Still more: rather than take full days off, parents can choose to take their paid benefits working half-days or even one-eightieth of a day. It is not permitted for both parents to take leave at the same time, except immediately after childbirth. Parents can also get state compensation when they need to take time off work to look after a sick child. This is valid for children up to twelve years of age and in some circumstances up to sixteen years of age.

Modern life in industrialized nations has brought on the problem of "latchkey children," children who arrive home from school and are unsupervised for long periods of time. In the United States, "families with children in which both parents go off to work constitute a majority (51 percent) of all married-couple families."[23] Leaving young and adolescent children unsupervised is perilous. In Sweden it is not necessary to do so. Parents worried about what their children are doing at home could hardly be working at peak levels of productivity. The plan also brings parents and children closer at a time when basic bonding is occurring and involves both parents in early child care.

Obviously, Swedish society and the group-think of that country reveal different moral priorities when it comes to children and what they need and thus deserve, and those moral priorities are established in national policy. Sweden also has a different mindset regarding national defense in a dangerous world. Their location is not a danger-free zone. They were next to Soviet Russia and Nazi Germany and yet they have not been in a war for over two hundred years. Their weaponry is slight and defensive in nature and thus a threat to no one. This also leaves them financial room for more humanitarian help to the citizens and the children of Sweden. Using group-think in ethics does not imply that you can transplant the experience of one country into another, but group-think contrasts do expand alternative thinking.

Limits of the Private Sector. A healthy economy is marked by a vigorous private sector, effective government oversight, and active citizen participation. The United States is weak on government oversight and on citizen participation, with a blind mythic faith that the market will provide. That means wealth shifts by the gravity of greed to the top. The problem is that when too much income shifts from the bottom to the top, the bottom cannot make purchases or make mortgage payments, as happened in 1929 and in 2008.

Central to the American mythology is the belief that government is inefficient and untrustworthy. Only the private sector can deliver. Again, comparative ethics. In Denmark, the government pays 81 percent of all health-care costs, with 19 percent provided by private insurance policies. The result of this well-run national health-care system is that it only costs 6 percent of the gross domestic product. In the United States, dominated by private sector insurance companies, health care consumes 17 percent of the gross domestic product and still over forty million people are not covered by either public or private insurance. Conclusion: Rather than government being the problem, as Ronald Reagan famously said, *unintelligent, uncaring government* is the problem. Government, after all, is people, and people can do poorly or well. Danish health care has justice lessons for us.

In France, the government provides universal child care for all toilet-trained children. Single mothers receive government payments until their children are over the age of three.[24] Single mothers are not penalized for being unmarried since that would penalize the children. There is a self-serving myth among some in the United States that giving generous benefits to women encourages promiscuity and increased birth rates among the poor. "Empirical studies show no correlation between welfare benefits and pregnancies. European countries generally provide much greater support for single mothers than does the Untied States, yet have much lower birthrates. Higher benefits states within the United States do not have a correspondingly higher rate of unwed births."[25]

American child-care practice is not a moral triumph. "The median wage of childcare center workers in 1997 was $7.03 per hour, three cents less than that of parking lot attendants. Paradoxically, the average childcare worker cannot herself afford the average cost of childcare."[26]

Work or Slavery? The situation of workers in the United States can also benefit from comparative ethical analysis. It is not that American workers are lazy. In fact, they work more than their European counterparts. U.S. workers work almost nine more weeks a year than most European workers. Between 1970 and 1990, American workers on average added a month's worth of work.[27] The Europeans also enjoy four to six weeks of vacation time, and this is protected by legislation.[28] While at work, Americans have fewer rights. The spirit of a nineteenth-century court decision still has resonance: "All may dismiss their employees at will be they many or few, for good cause, for no cause, or even for a cause morally wrong."[29] There are more humane options. "All of our European competitors and Canada have statutes protecting employees against wrongful discharge and establishing tribunals in which claims can be adjudicated. A covenant of the International Labor Organization of the United Nations calls upon all participating nations to adopt such statutes, but the United States—almost alone among industrial democracies—is not party to that covenant."[30] The more employer power is unchecked, the more employment approximates slavery.

The Illusion of Independence. It is difficult to profit from comparing group experiences if a society is constrained by an autistic sense of independence. This is made worse by the American sense of "exceptionalism," which implies that we are paradigmatic for others and may live and think independently of them. Hence the need for an American Declaration of Interdependence. Ecologically and economically we are linked to the global community in ways that early America was not. Going it alone may have worked somewhat for early pioneers, but it engendered a mindset of disconnectedness and an ignorance of the webs of which we are a part. This also leads to close-mindedness and lack of readiness to learn from others. A dose of Buddhist wisdom can be remedial for the American soul. The "enlightenment" sought in Buddhism is a recognition that "the world is a web; nothing has any reality of its own apart from that web, because everything, including us, is dependent on everything else."[31]

The Vietnamese Zen master Thich Nhat Hanh looks at a piece of paper and offers a meditation on connections and on the interrelatedness of everything in the universe.

If you are a poet, you will see clearly that there is a cloud floating in this sheet of paper. Without a cloud, there will be no rain; without rain, the trees cannot grow, and without trees we cannot make paper. The cloud is essential for the paper to exist. . . .

If we look into this sheet of paper even more deeply, we can see the sunshine in it. If the sunshine is not there, the tree cannot grow. In fact, nothing can grow. Even we cannot grow without sunshine. And so we know

that the sunshine is also in this sheet of paper. The paper and the sunshine inter-arc. And if we continue to look, we can see the logger who cut the tree and brought it to the mill to be transformed into paper. And we see the wheat. We know that the logger cannot exist without his daily bread, and therefore the wheat that became his bread is also in this sheet of paper. And the logger's father and mother are in the paper too. . . .

You cannot point out one thing that is not here—time, space, the earth, the rain, the minerals in the soil, the sunshine, the cloud, the river, the heat. . . . As thin as this sheet of paper is, it contains everything in the universe.[32]

A Caution on the Demonic Comparison. Comparison yields perspective, but obsessive comparison to only *one* other experience may paralyze our minds. For example, discussions of the morality of mercy death in extreme situations usually become impaled on the Nazi analogy. The argument is advanced that if we were to allow the morality of even one instance of mercy death, the dominoes would fall one after another and we would find ourselves in the world of Nazism where hundreds of thousands of persons may have perished in "euthanasia centers." With remarkable persistence, this analogy is raised in both popular and scholarly literature to counter the proposition that in certain situations—such as a situation of unmanageable pain in a terminal illness—death might be accelerated by positive means.

Here is a case where the experience of one group is stamped as definitive. Two contentions are implicit: First, if any mercy killing is seen as moral, by some kind of a physical law, a process will thereby be initiated that will carry through to a Nazi-like situation. Second, other group experiences with mercy death are ignored or treated as not relevant. This is a serious misuse of group experience that absolutizes rather than relativizes. The paralyzing absolutism is overcome by seeing the deficiencies of the analogy and by inducing other group references. For the Nazis, "'euthanasia' was only a code name which [they] used as both camouflage and euphemism for a program of murder—killing various categories of persons because they were regarded as racially 'valueless'; deformed, insane, senile, or any combination thereof."[33]

The German experience at this time is limited as analogy in other ways: there the state was normally the deciding agent; the announced concern was utilitarian, the elimination of "useless eaters"; neither individualism nor moral pluralism was a facts of German society in the way that they are facts of American life; and, finally, the question is rising in our day in an entirely different way. The question for us is the value of death in certain circumstances for an individual. The Nazi analogy is valid for any proposal to give to a state, with an avowed and promulgated racist philosophy, totalitarian powers of decision over life and death. It is not an analogy that can be offered as decisive and leading in the contemporary discussion of the morality of mercy death in certain extreme cases. There are contemporary openings to mercy death in the United States and elsewhere that have not and are not deteriorating into a Nazi atrocity.[34] Fixated attention on only one historical human experience is a block to moral discourse.

THINKING CRITICALLY

"Throughout history, under a variety of political systems, people in every part of the world have waged conflict and wielded undeniable power by using a very different technique of struggle—one which does not kill and destroy. That technique is nonviolent action. Although it has been known by a variety of names, its basis has always been the same: the belief that exercise of power depends on the consent of the ruled who, by withdrawing that consent, can control and even destroy the power of their opponent. . . . Although much effort has gone into increasing the efficiency of violent conflict, no comparable efforts have yet gone into making nonviolent action more effective and hence more likely to be substituted for violence."

—Gene Sharp,
The Politics of Nonviolent Action

14.2

Minority Wisdom: The Galileo Effect

Jeff Faux, an economist, says, with deliberate cynicism, that the "conventional wisdom" is always wrong. Consensus can be both tyrannical and addictive. Dissent leaves you open to ridicule and excommunication. Consensus, after all, does carry with it a lot of precious satisfaction: "What everyone thinks must be right"; "Fifty million Frenchmen can't be wrong." Dissent is unsettling and to a degree insulting. The beneficiaries of consensus take poorly to it. Because of all these factors favoring consensus, it is the better part of wisdom to pause at length before the moral-value dissent of even a few. The dissenting minority might be an upstart going nowhere. But it might also be the vanguard pointing to a better way. Moral dissent might be, in tiny bud, a humanizing insight whose time of growth is upon us. The glare of a regnant consensus may dim its light, but that dimness may be the early dark of a new dawn. The minority opinion, after all, has a distinguished past. It may be Galileo.

Among the outcast minority views of the past, we find positions such as the immorality of slavery; the radical inutility of state-sponsored violence (war) and the possibilities of nonviolent power; the nonsacrality of civil government; the immorality of torturing a prisoner to get a confession; the right to conscientious objection; ecological conservationism; and, indeed, democracy itself. Minority views should be deliberately sought out. The outcast might have noble blood.

Individual Experience: The Value of "I-Think"

Leaning is easier than independence. When a baby graduates from crawling to standing and moving upright, she gets around by leaning. Hanging on to chair or couch, she achieves her first upright locomotion. But then comes a day, precious to parents, when the ball rolls out on the floor with no supporting props between it and the neophyte toddler. Desire overcomes prudence and the baby takes her first unsupported steps. But then, very quickly, insight strikes, and the baby drops and returns to crawling, her primal form of leaning. Independence is too scary. More experiments follow and finally we welcome a new *Homo erectus* to our community.

Thinking and valuing follow similar paths. We shy from our own capacity for originality. Henri Bergson was pessimistic about our ability to launch out and trust our own little bit of genius. We belong, he said, both to ourselves and to society, but much of our mental stability is found by clinging to others. Our socialized self is our usual refuge. But there is more to us than that. If we could delve deep down into our uniquely personal consciousness, we could find "an ever more original personality, incommensurable with the others and indeed undefinable in words." Bergson illustrates the situation with a comparison to aquatic plants that interlock with the leaves of other plants at the surface but have deep, almost solitary roots:

In our innermost selves, if we know how to look for it, we may perhaps discover another sort of equilibrium, still more desirable than the one on the surface. Certain aquatic plants as they rise to the surface are ceaselessly jostled by the current: their leaves, meeting above the water, interlace, thus imparting to them stability above. But still more stable are the roots, which, firmly planted in the earth, support them from below.[35]

Bergson was not hopeful about our ability to trust our deeply personal insights. "If possible at all, it is exceptional: and it is on the surface, at the point where it inserts itself into the close-woven tissue of other exteriorised personalities, that our ego generally finds its point of attachment; its solidity lies in this solidarity."[36]

Bergson may have yielded too much to his Gallic pessimism here. To work from the original center of our personalities may truly be exceptional; it is hardly impossible. Those creative geniuses who have turned us inside out with their vision surely exemplify the originality and confidence in the self of which Bergson speaks. Even in less extraordinary and history-turning ways, we are all graced with some persons who exhibit a freshness in their value consciousness that comes from their ability to be something other than faithful mirrors. Still, let us certainly grant the rarity of the original mind. Given our social nature, no mind is purely original. Originality is more a matter of degree. But some minds are almost completely strapped to their social props; others, less so. This is a point that must be of interest to ethics. Good ethics is good reality contact. If persons choke on their own unique perceptive powers and timidly repair to crowd-think, this human community of valuing animals is to some degree crippled. Such huddled thinking must yield something of a blur. In order to hang together, it must rely heavily on stereotypes and generalizations. We have an inner resource: an escape from social hype. Other animals are controlled by instinct; persons shackled to crowd-think are similarly controlled and unfree.

This **"I-think"** spoke obviously overlaps with others in this model of ethical method. In the treatment of creative imagination, affectivity, and authority, for example, the special prerogatives of the individual's knowing capacity have been acknowledged. Still, trust in one's own unique powers of knowing is neglected. Calling attention to that gives "individual experience" a special spot on the ethics model.

Respecting Brainpower

No two persons and no two situations are identical. Even physiologically, the very structure of our brain suggests the unrepeatable uniqueness of every individual member of this species. Evolution is smarter than we are, since we have never invented anything like the human brain. Erich Fromm refers to the "truly fantastic number of interneuronal connections" that distinguish the human brain. As one study of the brain puts it: "If a million cortical nerve cells were connected one with another in groups of only two neurons each in all possible combinations, the number of different patterns of interneuronic connection thus provided would be expressed by $10^{2,783,000}$." In point of fact, the actual intercellular connections "would far exceed the $10^{2,783,000}$ already mentioned as the theoretically possible combinations in groups of two only."[37] For comparative purposes, it is pointed out that the number of atoms in the universe is estimated to be about 10^{66}.[38] That may seem incredible since there would seem to be more atoms than that in a single human body. This ignores the increase of logarithmic expansion.

The very structure of the brain symbolizes the unique veins of experience possible for us. Build on this the fact that no two persons have identical experiences or histories. Nor do any two persons react to the same reality in an identical way. Since affectivity is also one of the ways in which we are aware, another infinitely variable source of uniqueness presents itself. Five artists looking at the same scene will produce five different paintings. Moral insight, like a painting, gives a view of reality refracted through the prism of a unique temperament and cognitive structure.

It is a sad fact of intellectual life that persons may basically know that the emperor is stark naked, but they will join the crowd in discussing his clothes. A lesson that the Buddha gave his followers is forever apropos: "Do not accept a thing merely because it has been handed down by tradition or from generation to generation or from hearsay. . . . You should reject a thing when you know for yourself that a thing is harmful and will bring misery to yourself and to others."[39]

Humans arrived on the planet at an "oops" moment in evolution, "where instinctive determination had reached a minimum and the development of the brain a maximum." We have very little by way of instinctive equipment. As Erich Fromm puts it: "Aside from some elementary reactions, such as those to danger or to sexual stimuli, there is no inherited program that tells us how to decide in most instances in which our life may depend on a correct decision."[40] We are the deciding animal, blessed and pained by responsibility. We shrink from this noble burden when we place excessive reliance on social sources of insight. Ethics always swims in crosscurrents, where new patterns and new problems are forever emerging. For judging that which is new, the established wisdom drawn from past experiences is not enough. The burden again falls on the living intellect of the individual. Human responsibility cannot be deputized. There is an irremediable loneliness to moral knowledge and moral decision.

Religion: Enemy or Friend of "I-Think"?

Religions are tendentially cults, and cults are authoritarian control systems. Religions do not have to go that way, but they often do. From popes to Qur'ans to Bibles, religious authority is prone to overrule and smother the personal insights of the faithful. Happily, no human institution or tradition is consistently loyal to its worst instincts. Religions have also championed in history-changing ways the freedom of individual conscience. Systems of ethics that call themselves "philosophical" and "secular" are often neck-high in debt to ideas that entered culture on religious vehicles. In modern Western culture, religion is thought of as systemized God-talk. In fact, some of the major religions, like Buddhism, Taoism, and Confucianism, do not adopt the God hypothesis; that is, they don't believe in a God. Hinduism uses God-talk with a remarkable fluidity, attributing divinity to a diverse set of Gods and Goddesses. One thing all religions do is search out the meaning of human life. Each of them is a probe into human psychology, and each of them contains the elements of economic and political theory. Their influence spreads and permeates cultures, even cultures that think themselves "secular" and postreligious. Not knowing this face is part of the grand naïveté of modern "secular" culture.

So, on the issue at hand—the prerogatives of personal judgment based on the unique constitution and unique experiential history of individuals—religions are major players. None of them neglects this issue. Each of them struggles with the permanent human struggle between reliance on authority and independent judgment.

Individual Conscience and Ecclesiastical Authority. Let me begin with Roman Catholicism, which is known as a heavily hierarchical and authoritarian expression of Christianity. At the end of the nineteenth century, the First Vatican Council even declared that the pope could make infallible utterances. Given the inherent partiality and lubricity of language, that was no slight claim. And yet there are strong voices in the Catholic tradition supporting the autonomy and supremacy of conscience. Let me start with a cardinal, a pope, and a saint to make the point.

John Henry Cardinal Newman once took the title "Vicar of Christ," usually applied to the pope, and transferred it to his conscience. He said of his

conscience: "I called it the 'Vicar of Christ' in me. I once said that if I had to propose an after-dinner toast, I would drink 'to Conscience first, and to the Pope afterwards'. I must add that conscience can be lazy but at its most genuine it is always a call against pride and towards truth and love." He also said: "An ethical system may supply laws, general rules, guiding principles, a number of examples, suggestions, landmarks, limitations, cautions, distinctions, solutions or critical or anxious difficulties; but who is to apply them to a particular case? Whither can we go, except to the living intellect, our own, or another's?" He drove the point home further by adding: "The authoritative oracle, which is to decide our path . . . is seated in the mind of the individual, who is thus his own law, his own teacher, and his own judge in those special cases of duty which are personal to him."[41]

Similarly, Joseph Cardinal Ratzinger, now Pope Benedict XVI, commenting on the Second Vatican Council, wrote:

> Over the pope as the expression of the binding claim of ecclesiastical authority there still stands one's own conscience, which must be obeyed before all else, *if necessary even against the requirement of ecclesiastical authority.* This emphasis on the individual, whose conscience confronts him with a supreme and ultimate tribunal, and *one which in the last resort is beyond the claim of external social groups, even of the official Church,* also establishes a principle in opposition to increasing totalitarianism.[42]

Thomas Aquinas on Individual Judgment. So there we have a cardinal and a pope asserting the supremacy of individual conscience over ecclesiastical authority. Next I turn to the most revered of Catholic sainted theologians, Thomas Aquinas. Once again, as has been said, conservatives are often the worshipers of dead liberals. Aquinas was in fact one of the most condemned theologians of his day. Bishops condemned him, his books were banned, his lectures boycotted. Later he became the touchstone of orthodoxy. At the sixteenth-century Council of Trent, his writings were placed on the altar alongside the Bible. He had attained biblical status. That is amazing since Trent was out to condemn the Protestant interpretation of freedom from church authority. Thomas was actually more radical in asserting freedom of individual conscience than the Protestants.

In his magnum opus, the *Summa*, Thomas asks what seems an innocent question: whether the moral law for Christians is something written. His answer proved to be dynamite. Everything written, including the Gospels, the whole Bible, and all the statements of popes and theologians, are "secondary" moral law. The primary moral law is the inner spirit of persons where God's Spirit illumines one's conscience. I call this *the Protestant principle plus one.* The Protestant principle is that church officers have no authority over the witness of the Bible. Thomas says even the Bible is "secondary" to the inner lights of the individual.[43] Obviously, this idea could open the door to people saying what they think is the inspiration of God's Spirit when it might have more to do with their second martini. So the primiary authority remained in the individual's conscience, but the collective wisdom written in the tradition should serve as a check. Small wonder Cardinal Avery Dulles could write that it is not clear that Thomas Aquinas, "if he were alive today . . . would be welcome at the Catholic University of America," since Thomas taught that the authority of professors rests "not on formal authority bur rather on the force of reason."[44]

Thomas's defense of individual judgment did not remain at the speculative level. Conservative Christians and church authorities in Thomas's day scorned "pagan" writers like Aristotle, but Thomas did not. Aristotle influenced his treatment of the problem of overpopulation. Given the limits of re-sources, Thomas approved the limiting *by law* of the size of the family. He didn't go into details as to how that would be done, but in the light of current Vatican theology (as distinguished from Catholic theology, which is broader and more liberal), it is a stunning position. Thomas saw that one cannot have a just and stable society if there is infinite growth of the population, and so population should be limited for the common good.[45]

Islam and Authority. Even more than Protestantism, Islam is a religion of the book and that book is authoritative. However, no ancient religious or philosophical system that suppresses all personal judgment and individual conscience can survive. Islam does not do that. It does not simply allege that the Qur'an solves all problems for all time. On the contrary, the prophet Muhammad encouraged what is known as *ijtihad*, "i.e. exerting oneself to solve newly arising problems if no precise guidance was available in the Qur'an and in the Prophet's Sunnah" (*Sunnah* refers to the reported customary practices of Muhammad and his companions). "According to one report, the Prophet appointed Ma'adh bin Jabal as governor of the Yemen and asked Ma'adh how he would govern. 'According to the Qur'an,' Ma'adh replied. And if it is not in the Qur'an? the Prophet asked him. 'According to the Prophet's *sunnah*,' replied Ma'adh. And if he does not find anything of the sort in the Sunnah? the Prophet inquired. 'Then I will exert myself to solve the problem.' The Prophet patted his back in approval."[46] The Prophet even said that if one errs in using *ijtihad*, he will still get merit. According to Asghar Ali Engineer: "The Prophet did this to encourage Muslims to solve problems that were likely to arise in the future. This would be very helpful in treating the status of women today."[47] So even in Islam, with all its stress on faithfulness to the texts, judgment based on personal experience is encouraged. Not to use *ijtihad* would fail to recognize that reality involves both permanence and change: it would "tend to immobilize what is essentially mobile in its nature," in the words of Muhammad Iqbal.[48]

Because of this Islamic right to moral judgment and contextual sensitivity, South African Muslim scholar Sa'diyya Shaikh notes that Muslim legal positions on issues like abortion are varied and "range from unqualified permissibility of an abortion before 120 days into the pregnancy, on the one hand, to categorical prohibition of abortion altogether, on the other. Even with a single legal school the majority position was often accompanied by dissenting minority positions."[49] Since there is no "pope" in Islam claiming the last word on everything, an informed Muslim is not deprived of individual choice and personal judgment.

Those called "fundamentalists" reject the invitation to freedom that is found in the core of even the most authoritarian religions. Beneath all the influences and determinisms, collective and interpersonal, that crush down on our consciences, we remain the supreme court where moral responsibility climaxes. When all is said and done, "the strict specificity of ethical action is perceptible only to the living experience of the person required to decide."[50]

Summary of Key Themes

- The inevitability of progress is a modern myth.
- The culture and class into which we are born largely determine our value system.
- Ethics is the task of critiquing culture and its value regimen.
- The "demonic comparison" can paralyze moral progress.
- "Conventional wisdom" is always in need of serious criticism.
- Individual genius and initiative can get smothered in group-think.
- Religion can be a critique or a captive of culture.
- There is need for a "Declaration of Interdependence" for all nations in an increasingly connected world.

Key Terms

Class
I-think
Technoscientific revolution
We-think

Questions for Discussion

1. Reinhold Niebuhr said in his *Moral Man and Immoral Society*: "The moral attitudes of dominant and privileged groups are characterized by universal self-deception and hypocrisy." Apply this to gender and racial dominance issues.

2. Expand the definition of citizenship beyond the idea of a citizen as someone who has to pay taxes and vote occasionally. What moral duties come with citizenship?

3. Other countries have "wrongful discharge tribunals" where fired employees can seek a day in court. Is this an infringement of

managerial prerogatives or a guarantee of fairness? Is it compatible with a healthy capitalism?

Suggestions for Further Reading

Bradley, Mark Philip, and Patrice Petro. *Truth Claims: Representation and Human Rights.* Piscataway, N.J.: Rutgers University Press, 2002.

Raines, John C. *The Justice Men Owe Women: Positive Resources from World Religions.* Minneapolis: Fortress Press, 2001.

Sharp, Gene. *The Politics of Nonviolent Action.* 3 vols. Boston: Porter Sargent, 1973.

Shriver, Donald W., Jr. *Honest Patriots: Loving a Country Enough to Remember Its Misdeeds.* New York: Oxford University Press, 2005.

The Comic and the Tragic in Ethics

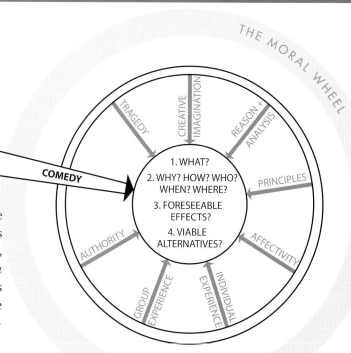

HUMOR AND ETHICS ARE blood relatives. One would hardly sense that looking at staid texts on ethics. The whole quest of ethics is to probe the mystery of the *humanum,* to discover the possibilities of human life fully alive. Humor, like ethics, is also focused on the *humanum* and it is a uniquely *human* talent. Indeed, without humor, no one is fully alive. The ancients spoke of *gratia hilaritatis,* the gift of hilarity. The Greeks called us the "laughing animal" (*zoion gelastikon*), and the Latins called us the only "animal capable of amusement" (*animal risibile*). Only humans laugh, and humans only laugh at themselves. Snoopy in the *Peanuts* cartoons was funny only because he was made into an example of human foibles. It is only human inconsistencies and surprises that stimulate the orgasm of laughter. Inconsistencies and surprises in nature may delight us or threaten us, but they are not funny.

It is not that humor has been ignored by all serious thinkers. The bibliography of J. Y. Greig's *Psychology of Laughter and Comedy* mentions 363 works devoted wholly or partially to the subject of humor. The authors range from Plato and Aristotle to Kant, Bergson, and Freud. Still, with all of this, the interest in humor, has not led to its inclusion as an integral part of ethical method. Grim academics make efforts to dissect humor but the results are more funny than helpful. It has often been said that humor can be dissected as a frog can be, but both frog and humor die in the process. But the fact is that there can be sense in nonsense and wisdom in wit. Often the cartoon is more insightful than the editorial. It was wise for the medievals to consider the jester to be an important civil servant. Laughter, like lightning, clears the air and dissipates fog like the morning sun.

Humor and Knowledge

Knowledge is awareness, and there are many ways in which we become aware. Disciplined reasoning makes us more aware, as do well-applied principles. However, *Homo rationalis* can become too cocksure and lose sight of his or her perspectival bias. Humor reminds us of our limits while allowing us to enjoy them. It dissipates intellectual pomposity. It hints at unsuspected horizons. It is a perspective stretcher and a mind cleanser. It deserves a spoke on the wheel model. The more serious the situation or the subject, the more we need the balancing power of laughter. G. K. Chesterton

put it this way: "Life is serious all the time, but living cannot be. You may have all the solemnity you wish in your neckties, but in anything important (such as sex, death, and religion), you must have mirth or you will have madness."[1]

With a solemn effort not to kill humor on the operating table of analysis, I will argue that the manifestation of intelligence that we call humor involves (1) surprise, (2) a response to incongruity within human life, (3) creative imagination, and (4) **affectivity**.

1. Surprise

Surprising newness is the essence of **humor**. The joke that has to be explained fails. Explanation, however well achieved, takes away the surprise factor and the humor perishes. The repeated joke fails. It may provoke commemorative laughter, but it is of a different sort, whereby we imaginatively relive the pleasant shock of the original amusement. The surprise element in humor is visible all the way from the peekaboo laughter of the baby to stand-up comedy routines and the political satires of Jon Stewart and Steven Colbert. Humor requires a *new* twist. Some illustrative examples:

- If you have a serious disagreement with someone, walk a mile in his shoes. Then he's a mile away and you have his shoes.
- A *New Yorker* cartoon shows two college girls chatting in a dormitory room and holding a sign urging "Abstinence Only" sexual behavior. One says to the other: "The way I see it is that there will be plenty of time for abstinence when I'm married."
- A cartoon depicts a sad-faced Mary and Joseph kneeling beside the manger in which the baby Jesus lay and saying with much disappointment to the shepherds: "We had been hoping for a girl."
- Mark Twain said: "It is by the goodness of God that in our country we have those three unspeakably precious things: free-

dom of speech, freedom of conscience, and the prudence never to practice either of them."

- Kansas will stay dry as long as voters can stagger to the polls.

In each case, the initial seriousness and piety set us up for the unexpected, peekaboo ending. The pleasant surprise of humor has an epistemological function: it shakes the foundations of settled surety. That's good for ethics. A humorous frame of mind is best suited not to miss the surprises that life always entails. Readiness for surprise is a characteristic of mental acuity. Otherwise we will miss many turns in the road as we plod on by a comfortable path leading nowhere. A sense of humor increases the sensitivity of our antennae, and that is good for a realistic ethics in a constantly changing world.

2. Incongruity

Hilarity is a delightful anomaly. By a blessed alchemy, incongruities that could be annoying are converted into pleasure. It is no accident that comics rise from the ranks of peoples who have suffered—witness the glut of African American, Jewish, and Irish comedians. Things that might make us dour instead make us glad. For that reason alone we should treasure our risibility. But there is more. Humor is often the first to unmask the clever disguises of error and fraud. It is an essential tool of ethics.[2] In his celebrated theory of knowledge, Bernard Lonergan notes "the profound significance" of humor and contends that "proofless, purposeless laughter can dissolve honored pretense; it can disrupt conventional humbug; it can disillusion people of their most cherished illusions, for it is in league with the detached, disinterested, unrestricted desire to know."[3] The "unrestricted desire to know" can get restricted in the rationalist. Humor can break up that bondage. Humor grants the superego a leave of absence, and a holiday from pretense is declared.

Humor jolts our bowed head back and makes us look up to discover that the little plot of reality on which we had been gazing with fixed vision is bounded by a universe. Humor bespeaks *more*. In humor we leap beyond the limits of our reasonable conceptions and taste something of the more that is always beckoningly beyond.

Historically, some of our finest thinkers, people with awesome credentials and high station, have said some silly things. They were put on the defensive by the wit of simple and unlettered folk. Take Augustine, the eloquent fifth-century bishop of Hippo in Africa. He had a gifted pen. His Latin was exquisite, and he had a well-cocked eye to his impact on history. He made sure that multiple copies of his writings were made. He succeeded, and some of his worst ideas were the most successful. After enjoying sex for a number of years, he took an antisexual turn and seemed thereafter hell-bent on making sure no one else ever enjoyed it.

Augustine saw sexual passion and sexual pleasure as the conduit for a kind of spiritually stigmatizing original sin that was passed on to all our children. So heinous and infectious was the passionate pleasure of parents which led to conception, that each tiny newborn was spiritually blighted and in need of redemptive baptism to cleanse its little soul.

Augustine said some of the dumbest things ever said in the history of sexual ethics. Had Augustine heard of cloning, he would have had to like it: babies born without the mediation of pleasure would be immaculately conceived. Augustine, along with most of his contemporaries, misunderstood the biblical creation stories of the opening chapters of Genesis as referring to a past paradise that existed, somewhere in the Middle East, until the first humans were expelled for their sins. Actually, those stories are a poetic picturing of what life could be if we rose to our moral and aesthetic potential. It could be a paradise where we and nature live in harmony in a social order knit together with compassion, justice, and beauty.

At any rate, Augustine was asked whether in this paradise lost there was sexual activity. He allowed that there would have been, to allow for reproduction. People then asked if there would have been sexual pleasure in paradise. None at all, said he. He was immediately put on the defensive by witty folks who must have laughed out loud at the image of pleasure-free sex. These practical people raised the question as to how in the world men could get their penises readied for action without sexual pleasure. Augustine's answer: by sheer willpower. After all, he noted, even in our current fallen, post-paradise state, some people can move one ear (and the truly gifted two ears) simply by willing it. Surely men in that golden time of paradise could have elevated their penises with a hefty act of the will. Fortified by wit, and in a tribute to common sense, the doubts perdured.

To ward off the merry and wise dissenters, Augustine, with his back against the wall, was driven to find new examples of feats of willpower. Alas, he turned to flatulence, noting that some people could produce it by mere willpower: "Some can produce at will odorless sounds from their breech, a kind of singing from the other end."[4] His texts remain. The laughter that put him on the defensive we can only imagine, but it was the laughers who best served ethics.

Signaling that it is often the worst of ideas that survive and thrive, Augustine bred generations of anti-sexual-pleasure Christians. Sexual pleasure, even in marriage, was long thought to be sinful. And the rule was, the more pleasure, the more sin. William of Auxerre in the thirteenth century said that a holy man who has sex with his wife and finds it hateful and disgusting commits no sin. He added, with poignant regret (and a bit of insight), that "this, however, seldom happens." At that point a sense of humor could have saved him and he would have smudged out those silly lines in his manuscript.

The twelfth-century Petrus Cantor opined that sex with a beautiful woman is a greater sin since it causes greater delight. His point was debated, however. His contemporary Alain de Lille demurred, saying sex with a beautiful woman is less sinful because the man is "compelled by the sight of her beauty," and "where the compulsion is greater, the sin is slighter." (Taken to its logical extreme, this would justify the rape of overwhelmingly beautiful women.)

These gloomy thoughts are so incongruous, so discordant with human experience, that even the illiterate hearers of these thoughts had a defense against these learned teachers—the liberating ethics of laughter.

3. Creative Imagination

Humor is a work of creativity. That is why it surprises. Humor involves the discovery and sharing of some hidden likenesses brought out in a pleasant and fresh interpretation. It is understandable that part 1 of Arthur Koestler's study *The Act of Creation* is devoted entirely to laughter and amusement, since humor is a signal work of creative wit. The creative mind perceives connections and similarities that are missed in more literal and blunt views of the facts of life. This is the formidable power of the humorist. The humorist has a kind of backdoor entry that skips past tedious analytical discourses. Often enough, the backdoor entry is the only door that is not locked. Indeed, the backdoor entry may be the most effective route to intellectual conversion, as it painlessly pries the mind ajar. A healthy and more enlightened analysis might follow. To bypass humor, because it does not suit our pompous rationalistic conceptions of how proper ethics should be done, is unintelligent.

Moralists should have taken the lead from psychologists who have sensed the importance of humor in a healthy personality. "In a prejudiced personality, humor seems to be the missing ingredient just as it is invariably present in the syndrome of tolerance."[5] Psychologist Harvey Mindess makes the point that healthy humor is not found merely in the capacity to deliver a number of witty one-liners or in the ability to enjoy jokes and contrived comic routines. The sense of humor that is salvific "must constitute a frame of mind, a point of view, a deep-going, far-reaching attitude to life."[6] The cluster of qualities that characterizes this frame of mind shows the relationship of humor to creative imagination, whether in ethics or in science: *flexibility*, a readiness to consider every side of every issue; *spontaneity*, the capacity to leap from one mode of thinking to another; *shrewdness*, a refusal to take anything or anyone, self included, at face value; and *playfulness*, bringing a sense of gaming to life and an openness to enjoy our tragicomic existence with humility. Even those working in the most abstract mathematics need all of the above. Playfulness is central to the inventor's soul. "A man who can shrug off the insufficiency of his ultimate wisdom, the meaninglessness of his profoundest thought, is a man in touch with the very soul of humor."[7] Humor does what postmodernism pompously purports to do. It humbles the mind, making it more docile, removing some of its clutter and presumptiousness. (Much that is labeled postmodern could do with a dose of humor and could be well served by an in-house jester.)

4. Affectivity and Delight

There is some truth in the saying that life is a tragedy for those who feel and a comedy for those who think. There is also some error in it, since tragedy and comedy, as we shall discuss, are no more separable than feeling and thought. What the saying does capture is the link between humor and affectivity. Many of the spokes of the wheel model overlap, while being distinctive enough to merit a separate space. The comedy spoke overlaps with both affectivity and creative imagination. There are many aspects to the joyous effervescence that is humor's delight. Part of what is delightful is at the level of the physical, quasi-orgasmic release of laughter. This is one of the fascinatingly unique things about humor. As Koestler says, humor "is

the only domain of creative activity where a complex pattern of intellectual stimulation elicits a sharply defined response in the nature of physiological reflex."[8] This physical reflex has happy results. "The peculiar breathing in laughter, with its repeated, explosive exhalations, seems designed to 'puff away' surplus tension in a kind of respiratory gymnastics."[9]

The delights, however, are also of a more spiritual sort. Humor has been called the shortest distance between two persons. It is social and socializing, and this in two ways: First, it calls for sharing. Laughing alone, like a meal alone or like sex alone, is an incomplete and abortive experience. Full-hearted laughter calls for company; we must imagine ourselves or actually be in the company of others to indulge fully in humor, and if we do laugh alone, there is a natural desire and urgency to share the moment. As an old Irish saying has it, "Laughter purifies society."

Second, humor helps us face our shared limits. The joke is ultimately on all of us. My folly is everyone's and everyone's folly is mine. Humor plays between the possible and the actual and celebrates the discrepancies between the two. But the common denominator in all of it is our consciously shared human condition. This is a major source of humor's delight. There is, of course, a sour humor that lacks social fullness. This is the experience of those who cannot laugh at themselves, whose humor, therefore, is short-circuited and ultimately hostile. It is turned on others, but it misses the ecstatic joy of celebrating our infirmities together, of recognizing that we're in this together; that is the liberating and socializing delight of genuine humor.

Finally, though not exhaustively on the subject of humor's delight, humor is based on hope, and hope is the fountainhead of all delighting. True humor is not destructive but re-creative. In a sense we tear down in humor, but it is not a tearing down that is unto death. Perverted humor, of course, can represent despair. Its purposes can be vindictive and malicious. The cruel words *derision* and *ridicule* express this. Genuine humor strikes benignly at that which it loves. It prunes that for which it has high hope. That is why nothing is beyond laughter. Even the sacred is within the province of the humorous, and there is no sacrilege in this since the disrespect in humor is only apparent. We need relief from all our imperfect and domineering images, even images that we confect of sacredness and divinity. Hope is vindicated in humor, since there is a strong sense of reality in the humorous perspective, and a depressing sense of unreality in humorlessness. To a degree, reality is hilarious; miss that and you miss a lot. Comedy insists that tragedy does not have the final and only word. Hope perdures. And that is delightful, as well as relevant to ethics.

Institutionalized Humor and the Taming of Power

Societies institutionalize that which they find important. With a stunning unanimity, societies give status and place to the role of **jester**, the *fou du roi*. "The court jester is a universal phenomenon. He crops up in every court worth its salt in medieval and Renaissance Europe, in China, India, Japan, Russia, America, and Africa. A cavalcade of jesters tumble across centuries and continents, and one could circle the globe tracing their footsteps."[10] A man of sufficient skill and talent could acquire a jestership in the court of prince or bishop. In his role he enjoyed an outstanding immunity and could make fun of everything, including his lordly master. The jester was not just a harmless comedian. He performed a further humanizing and serious service. He relativized the pomp and the power of the court and brought redemption to those who might otherwise have choked on their own importance. In many cultures a king was not

a king without a jester who worked at preventing power from losing all sense of human limit. He humbled the strutting absolutes that were everywhere about him. In a word, he was a source of refreshing profanation and a living symbol of the role of humor in moral consciousness.

The Need for Liberative Madness

There is an old Latin saying, "Once a year it is permissible to go mad!" (*Semel in anno licet insanire!*) It seems that cultures instinctively, reacting to deeply felt needs, provide for some liberative madness. From the Dionysian celebrations to the cavortings of Mardi Gras, from the maypole dancers to the somewhat forced revelries of New Year's Eve, some place for madness is allowed. There was method in this culturally ensconced madness. It reached paradigmatic expression in parts of Christian medieval Europe as the "Feast of Fools" (*festum fatuorum, festum stultorum*). Its roots, however, stretch back to antiquity, back to the old *Saturnalia*, the yearly permission (usually in December) to a "brief social revolution, in which power, dignity or impunity is conferred for a few hours upon those ordinarily in a subordinate position."[11]

This was a day when only humor was sacred. All that was customarily sacred was open to mockery and lampooning. Schoolboys and even clerics dressed as prelates and magistrates and made fun of all "the powers that be." Whatever was mighty and great was the natural target of the day. It worked its way even into sacred liturgies. It was tied to the Magnificat of Mary, the one and only speech attributed to the mother of Jesus in Luke's Gospel. One verse, *Deposuit potentes de sede*, "He has cast the mighty down from their thrones," became the banner text. It allowed time for a bit of mockery of those better placed in the hierarchy of the time. It was even also called the *Deposuit* Feast. Lower clergy, the subdeacons, specialized in this so much that the feast was sometimes called the Feast of the Subdeacons. (Another variant was the Feast of the Boy Bishop.)

At any rate, it was so effective as to merit resounding condemnation from unamused hierarchs and academics. The Council of Basle in 1435 imposed severe penalties on participants, and the theological faculty of the University of Paris in 1444 huffed and puffed about this alarming buffoonery, demonstrating only their need for more of the same. Power needs pricking to prevent its overinflation. The jester, the clown, and the Feast of Fools remind power of its human station. They tell power that it is a means validated only by its service to human ends. Jesters are badly needed in the White House, the Kremlin, the boardroom, and in religious power centers like the Vatican. Power without laughter is dangerous.

Puffed-up experts in any field need the cleansing, exorcizing *gratia hilaritatis* whenever they gain too much hegemony. Pedagogical power tends to arrogate to itself the badge of self-evidence. Nineteenth-century Catholicism decided that popes could be not just smart but infallible when they set their minds to it, and every field of human endeavor has its popes. Dynastic clubs develop in every discipline that would banish unsanctioned novelty and rule upon what can be considered truth. In few fields of thought are such clubs not in evidence. Jesters and fools are ubiquitously needed.[12]

The Sacred and the Silly

No classical literature lacks foolery and clowning. Some telling points can only be made that way. Even sacred literature like the Bible has its comedy, and sometimes at key moments in its narratives. The announced arrival of Isaac, the mythical child of promise, is framed in laughter: "God has given me good reason to laugh, and everybody who hears will laugh with me" (Gen. 21:6). Sarah found pregnancy so ridiculous at her age that she called the baby "Laughter," which is the meaning of *Isaac*. The psalms portray God as laughing at the power-ful, swaggering nations of the world: "Why are the nations in turmoil? Why do the people hatch their futile plots. . . ? The LORD who sits enthroned in heaven laughs them to scorn" (Ps. 2:1, 4). The books of Ruth, Jonah, and Ecclesiastes are seen as comic literature.[13] Ruth and Jonah poke fun at the stupidity of narrow nationalism and ethnic pride. Ecclesiastes gives a jolt to pompous intellectuals as it mocks the pseudo-wisdom of the "learned": "They are all emptiness and chasing the wind" (Eccles. 1:14). A banner saying that could be hung over many an academic conference.

Even Jesus is shown spoofing in a Michael Moore fashion. A key moment in his mission is marked with comedy. His ludicrous entrance into Jerusalem—riding an unsaddled little donkey that he borrowed with his little band of followers throwing their garments and palms on the path before him—was laughable spooffery. When Caesar entered a town, it was on regally noble mounts, with elegant pomp and circumstance, with subject people throwing palms on the path before his entourage. Jesus acted in the spirit of the prophets of Israel, who excelled in pointed mockery. In taunting parody, as Jesus was mounted on an ass, his people belittled the military power of the Roman Empire. The story of the event is framed in the Gospel with the words of Zechariah: "Rejoice, rejoice, daughter of Zion. Shout aloud, daughter of Jerusalem; for see, your king is coming to you, his cause won, his victory gained, humble and mounted on an ass, on a foal, the young of a she-ass. He shall banish chariots from Ephraim and war-horses from Jerusalem; the warrior's bow shall be banished. He shall speak peaceable to every nation and his rule shall extend from sea to sea" (Zechariah 9:9-10; Matthew 21:1-9). Imagine—this comic "king" will destroy the most advanced weapons of the day. His impoverished followers threw palms in his path, singing a new song of joyful peace. Today we would call it a peace demonstration in a spirit of meaningful fun.

When Humor Goes Awry

As an ancient saying has it, "The corruption of that which is best, is the worst." (*Corruptio optimi pessima.*) Humor is among the best of the graces. The ways in which it can go awry must not be missed. For one thing, strained humor might be a work of despair—a collapse before oppression. The slave may play at the clown in self-defense, when tears and anger would be more in place. Such laughter is a weak retreat. It trivializes that which should be resisted.

Laughter can also take the terrible form of ridicule and derision. Ridicule is a force for social conformism. It is not funny: it is closer to hostility than humor. It is relevant to ethics, since many of our skewed valuations are driven into us by way of ridicule and derision. Racism, sexism, heterosexism, militarism, and "tree-hugging" jibes at ecologists rely on self-defensive ridicule. Derision and the fear of derision are a major part of society's teaching power. Laughter's service is not always holy.

From comedy we turn next to tragedy. In what must be the oddest of relationships, the tragic and the comic are cousins. The tearless will also be the laughless, and vice versa. Those who cannot take reality as it is with its inexorable tragedy will not have the depth or breadth for a comic vision.

Tragedy: Pain as Moral Pedagogue

Sad to tell, the ninth and last spoke on the wheel model is sometimes the only one that works. At times, only pain can pierce moral obtuseness. The mad crusade of the United States in Vietnam may have begun to unravel because of a simple photograph of pain and violation. An American napalm bomb hit a school. Some of this gel, derived from gasoline, splashed onto the back of a little girl named Kim. As her flesh burned, she pulled off all her clothing and ran out of the building screaming. By the felicity of chance, a photographer was there and caught this horror in a prize-winning picture that was seen around the world. It appeared repeatedly in the press and contributed mightily to the growing disenchantment with the war. The contorted lies supporting that lethal misadventure withered in the heat of this concretized and focused atrocity.

Because of her celebrity, Kim received immediate care. She was able to survive after multiple surgeries. As an adult she came to the United States and spoke to a group of military veterans of that war. She told them she did not blame them for her suffering. She told them they were as much victims as she in the circumstances of that war. Supposedly hardened Marine veterans stood there with tears running down their cheeks. Grief has demythologizing power. Nothing dissolves propaganda more effectively than tears. Logic is impotent compared to honest grief with its power to dissipate the haze of spin.

There was wisdom in the old Catholic liturgy that begged for the *donum lachrimarum*, "the gift of tears." The prayer begged for a healing flood of tears that would break through the *duritiam*, the hardness of the unseeing and unfeeling heart. The prayer recognized that tears do not mean that we are falling apart as macho culture would have it. They signal that we may be coming together.

Tragedy as Road to Moral Truth

The African American comedian Dick Gregory was best known for his gift of comedy, but there were strong elements of poignancy and pathos in his repertoire. I saw him addressing a white audience. He spoke about his grandmother's memories of slavery. She used to speak of a slave woman who had to give up her children for immediate sale. A healthy slave baby who could be trained from infancy could get a good price. Only if the child was deformed could she keep her baby. After having two children taken from her like this, she then prayed that when she became pregnant again, her child would be "deformed." When I heard Gregory tell this story, he paused at this point, and that distinctive silence that attends the hearing of some horror gripped the entire auditorium. He broke the silence to say that if whites would understand blacks, they should think long about that woman's prayer for a deformed baby. His story, however, was not yet finished. The woman's child was born, and it was seriously "deformed." The mother received it lovingly into her arms, saw its deformity, and said with tears of joy, "Thank God!" The silence in the hall deepened as Gregory urged his pain-stunned audience again to "think about *that* prayer."

Gregory was here the tragedian, who was able to get into the consciousness of his almost entirely white audience in a way that a thousand well-formed syllogisms could never achieve. There are many roads to moral truth. Tragedy is one of them. Like its fair sister, comedy, it ruptures cold complacency and offers our moral consciousness a chance for healing. How persons and societies cope with tragedy affects all the other spokes of the wheel model of ethics. Tragedy can blunt our perceptive powers; in other ways it can hone them and be an antidote to superficiality.

Suffering as Moral Teacher

At a conference on behavior control through the use of drugs, Dr. L. Jolyon West made the following comment:

> Let us assume the development of a "happiness" drug which is relatively safe. It would make it possible for a human being to go from birth to death without having encountered suffering, tragedy, and anxiety. Trauma could be swiftly counteracted with drugs. What kind of people are those going to be, those who grow up without having suffered, without undergo-

ing the trauma of "normal life"—as *we* know it? To what extent are our ideas of maturity, nobility, sympathy, and so on, dependent on the experience of suffering? That, after all, is the point of Huxley's *Brave New World*: that the non-sufferer is somehow inhuman.[14]

It may seem impossible to speak in praise of suffering without lapsing into sadism or masochism. Perhaps this is why ethicists have done little thinking about this subject. However, it is possible to admit that suffering is intrinsic to living and also that it is the crucible from which significant influences on our moral consciousness emerge. Concede that and still work to eliminate suffering whenever we can. Medical science, for example, has eliminated many tragedies from life by limiting infant and maternal death and by controlling many diseases. This is an obvious good. Wherever tragedy can be contained, it is a moral duty to contain it. Suffering has no value per se. Whether tragedy and suffering contribute positively to our growth depends entirely on our response to them.

What is special about persons is their ability to transcend suffering and to transform it into something positive. Other animals do not have this capacity to any discernible degree. A horse, for example, that was born deaf and blind would be best put to death. Helen Keller, however, was born with these terrible disabilities, and yet she was a person and as such was able to transcend those debits marvelously and bring much fulfillment to her own life and much hope to the lives of others. Suffering thus borne is a moral teacher. It draws our consciousness more deeply into the foundational moral experience of the marvels of personhood. It sharpens our appreciation of our human capacities and deflates the word *impossible.* Helen Keller's own consciousness had to take on heroic dimensions to rise up and meet the prodigious limits that afflicted her. Her greatness related to her tragedy. The value was in the sufferer, not the suffering.

Suffering and Character

Suffering and how we bear it deeply affect the moral timbre of our consciousness usually referred to as "character." The Belgian philosopher Jacques Leclercq goes so far as to say: "We can take it as a general rule that when we meet a person in whom we discern some profundity of character, that is to say a strong personality, we almost always find when we come to know them well that they have been scarred by suffering."[15] H. Richard Niebuhr also comments that "everyone with any experience of life is aware of the extent to which the characters of people he has known have been given their particular forms by the sufferings through which they have passed." Niebuhr insists, rightly, that it is not what has happened to people that changes them so much as how they responded to what happened to them. With this understood, he asserts that "it is in the response to suffering that many and perhaps all people, individually and in their groups, define themselves, take on character, develop their ethos."[16]

It would seem indeed to be within the experience of all of us that deep suffering can bring greater depth and sensitivity to persons who were, before that, overly self-assured and superficial. (It is also true, of course, that suffering can break a person, and this, too, is revealed by even a little of life's experience.)

Niebuhr's point is also not to be missed when he says that suffering affects the development of an ethos for individuals and for groups. "It has often been remarked that the great decisions which give a society its specific character are functions of emergency situations in which a community has had to meet a challenge."[17] Thus, the American national character was fashioned not so much by its professed ideals or its system of laws as by the way it met situations it did not want but through which it had to suffer.[18] The Civil War, the Depression, the world wars, the challenge from communism, the depletion of resources, and so forth were the tragic situations that led to growth or decline in moral awareness and sensitivity.

Lessons Unlearned

The economic collapse of 2008 taught lessons to the adolescent economic theory called "**neoliberalism**." The losses involved in four lost wars, in Korea, Vietnam, Iraq, and Afghanistan, taught lessons to American militarists on the limits of kill-power and military flailing in international affairs. Lessons taught, however, are not always learned. The imperial temptation has proved almost irresistible to well-endowed nations. Empire-building nations keep repeating the lesson of history that greedy empires grow until they topple from what historian Paul Kennedy calls "imperial overstretch." Writing in 1987, Kennedy compared American overstretch to that of imperial Spain in 1600 and impe-

---

THINKING CRITICALLY

"Suffering is a subject to which academic ethical theory, even theological ethics, usually pays little attention. Yet everyone with any experience of life is aware of the extent to which the character of people we have known have been given their particular forms by the sufferings through which they have passed. . . . [Suffering] represents the denial of our movement toward pleasure or it is the frustration of our movement toward self-realization or toward the actualization of our potentialities. . . . It is in the response to suffering that many and perhaps all people individually and in their groups, define themselves, take on character, develop their ethos."

—H. Richard Niebuhr,
The Responsible Self

15.1

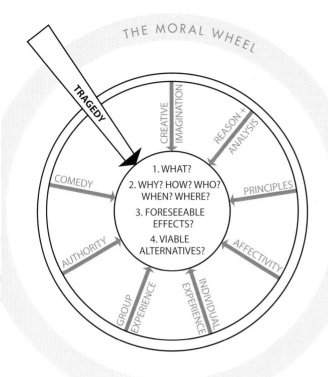

THE MORAL WHEEL

TRAGEDY

CREATIVE IMAGINATION

REASON + ANALYSIS

COMEDY

PRINCIPLES

1. WHAT?
2. WHY? HOW? WHO? WHEN? WHERE?
3. FORESEEABLE EFFECTS?
4. VIABLE ALTERNATIVES?

AUTHORITY

AFFECTIVITY

GROUP EXPERIENCE

INDIVIDUAL EXPERIENCE

rial Britain in 1900. He called on decision makers in Washington to "face the awkward and enduring fact that the sum total of the United States' global interests and obligations is nowadays far larger than the country's power to defend them all simultaneously."[19] Subsequent tragedies validated his judgment.

Tragedy and Cognition

Bernard Lonergan sees a positive role for **tragedy** in the process of human knowing. Persons exist, he says, by developing. Personal consciousness is gripped by a need that "heads us ever towards a known unknown." The human mind is ensouled by "a need to respond to a further reality than meets the eye." To think is to search. We are propelled by intimations of the more that we have not as yet seen. What this amounts to is a kind of "indeterminately directed dynamism." It is not an easily analyzable dynamism. It lacks "the settled assurance and efficacy of form." The creative mind is driven by this driving discontent.

Lonergan is not speaking of some kind of a directed instinct that keeps us sniffing sure-footedly in the direction of truth, our inevitable quarry. The knowing dynamism of human knowing is never so chartable as that. Knowledge deepens sometimes in tranquil, contemplative solitude or "in the shattering upheavals of personal or social disaster."[20] Disaster is obviously something to be avoided, but it is in the unsettlement of disaster, with the beguilements of comfort stripped away, that we might best catch a glimpse of that further reality that lures the eye of the questing human knower. It is often said of those who have experienced great tragedy that "they were never the same after that." Different things are meant by that expression, but here I use it for its epistemological meaning. Tragedy acquaints us with reality in a new way, and that can be positive.

Tragedy works as an antidote to smugness. I speak of smugness in an epistemological sense, as a kind of master myth of omnipotence that can imbue the mind with undue confidence in its assessments of reality. Tragedy attacks the arrogance and superficiality of the intellectually smug. It does this in an obvious way when the tragedy strikes directly at a moral blind spot. For example, the Don Juan who moves from one romantic conquest to another with no feeling for the expectations that he engenders and then leaves cruelly unfulfilled might take instruction only from tragedy and pain of the sort that he has regularly caused. Only when he goes through the sequence of promising intimacy followed by rejection could he possibly learn the value implications of his behavior. The fideistic confidence in military power and unregulated markets, and over-reliance on private sector handling of social needs, can perhaps only be unmasked by pain and failure.

Tragedy can also do the opposite. The tragic effects of an empire in decline can be lethal, as historian Barbara Tuchman presciently notes in her 1987 *New York Times* magazine article "A Nation in Decline?" She recounts the breakdown of mores as American power began to slip after 1945: "It does seem that the knowledge of a difference between right and wrong is absent from our society, as if it has floated away on a shadowy night after the last world war." Inefficiency and incompetence in government were increasingly tolerated without the morally healthy response of anger. Anger is appropriate when the lives of sons and daughters "are sacrificed to official negligence, or when statutes are casually violated by the caretakers of the nation's security."[21]

She wrote two decades before George W. Bush and his vice president lied a nation into war and justified the use of torture, the denial of due process to prisoners, and the unneeded curtailment of citizen privacy without suffering even the threat of impeachment. Impeachment is not removal from office or conviction; it is a move to investigate apparent abuse of office—an option that neither Democrats nor Republicans seriously considered, nor did American somnambulant citizens demand it. The "difference between right and wrong" had floated away; no just anger arose from the body politic.

THINKING CRITICALLY

Sometimes crises are opportunities. Water shortages in the Middle East may precipitate war or may encourage cooperation and peaceful conflict resolution. "Former [UN] Secretary General Boutros-Ghali predicted that 'the next war in the Middle East will be fought over water, not politics. . . .' The Jordan River is shared by Jordan, Syria, Israel, Lebanon, and the West Bank, all of which have vital needs for its water. Jordan's rapidly growing population (3.5 percent per year) will have fully used all known water sources by 2015. Israel's steadily growing population (1.7 percent annually) has exceeded its sustainable annual water yield since the mid-1970's. Water tales are dropping in the West Bank, where one-third of Israel's water originates, and Palestinians have been allocated far less water than Israeli citizens."

—Glenn Stassen,
*Just Peacemaking:
Ten Practices for Abolishing War*

15.2

In conclusion, tragedy can be instructive. Historically, it has even affected the size and functioning of the human brain. Our ancestors' capabilities took a "Great Leap Forward" between about one hundred thousand and fifty thousand years ago.[22] Response to strictures and tragedies played a role in this development. What is true for the physiology of the brain is true also for societies. Tragedy can crush and destroy; creative response to it can also trigger growth.

Summing Up the Wheel Model

With this chapter, I have completed my discussion of the nine spokes of the wheel model of ethical method. The hub of the wheel insists on the need for questioning and empirical thoroughness. The spokes signify ways in which our talented and multifaceted consciousness can evaluate the reality unveiled by the expository, questioning process.

It should be clear that the several spokes are diverse in nature. In assessing a particular problem, it is not possible to sit down and systematically summon these evaluational elements as one might call in a group of witnesses, each in its assigned turn. Some of these spokes may have limited use in certain morally adjudicable cases. There are, for example, heroic situations that call for unique and more intuitive solutions that no principles can adequately prescribe. Sometimes when principles seem to collide irreconcilably, we are cast more upon our affective appreciations. Similarly, there are situations of impasse where old solutions clearly will not do and creative imagination must of necessity strain to find new answers and new questions.

It should also be noted that one's method should not be explicit in all cases of ethical analysis. Method is not technique or tactic. But the spelling out of a method is a way of disciplining the search for moral truth. Following the method suggested here does not mean that when studying some moral problem, one need always have bobbing at the surface every one of the explicitated elements of this method. Nevertheless, if the method has validity, as I submit it does, it should be detectably implicit in all of one's particular analyses of normative issues. One should always "do ethics" with alertness to the various ways in which moral truth is attained. One need not stop and say, "See, I have not forgotten spoke number four in my discussion of this corporate merger." But when the discussion is completed, it should not show neglect of what that spoke symbolized of our knowing potential.

With this said, it is now timely to admit that nowhere in this model of ethical method is there place for the obviously important fact of conscience. One would think that any model would find a place for conscience. Why it does not appear is a matter to which I will now attend.

Summary of Key Themes

- Moral insights are often found in comedic form. The cartoon is often more insightful than the editorial.
- Humor is epistemologically healthy.
- Humor is part of socialization and is a defense against tyranny and delusion.
- Negative humor can support prejudice by way of ridicule.
- Tragedy may be the teacher of last resort.
- Persons at times have a capacity to transcend suffering and profit from it.
- Response to suffering is often the principal shaper of individuals and societies.

Key Terms

Affectivity
Humor
Jester
Neoliberalism
Tragedy

Questions for Discussion

1. What positive lessons were taught by the tragic depression of 1929? Did forgetfulness of those lessons lead to the economic crisis of 2008?
2. Some argue that the United States has lost four wars in a row—Korea, Vietnam, Iraq, and Afghanistan. Can these tragedies be instructive, and could any of those wars have been prevented by the newly emerging art of peacemaking-by-way-of-anticipating-crises?
3. Discuss the ways in which ridicule impedes moral maturity and foments prejudice and protects unjust claims to special status.

Suggestions for Further Reading

Corrigan, Robert W., ed. *Comedy: Meaning and Form.* San Francisco: Chandler, 1965.

Cox, Harvey. *The Feast of Fools: A Theological Essay on Festivity and Fantasy.* Cambridge: Harvard University Press, 1969.

Gioseffi, Daniela. *On Prejudice: A Global Perspective.* Garden City, N.Y.: Doubleday, 1993.

Conscience and Guilt

The Agenbite of Inwit

THE WHEEL MODEL OF ETHICS presented in this book is offered as "a complete method for moral choice." And yet it is a model without "conscience." That would seem a glaring lacuna. The reason is that the wheel is a model of ethics and *ethics is a critique of conscience.* A healthy conscience reflects every aspect of the model, as will be shown.

Everyone seems to know what conscience means, but efforts to define it run riot. The *Oxford English Dictionary* says of it: "Opinions as to the nature, function, and authority of conscience are widely divergent, varying from the conception of the mere exercise of the ordinary judgment on moral questions, to that of an infallible guide of conduct, a sort of deity within us." Origen saw it as a *spiritus corrector*, an "inner corrective force." The poet John Milton saw it as an "umpire." Thomas Aquinas saw it as an inner prodding and chastening pedagogue of the soul; John Locke thought it is simply our own opinion in moral matters; and Lord Byron, the poet, called it "the oracle of God." Some reduce **conscience** to the Freudian "superego," or see it as a precipitate of our psychosexual history, or maybe a mere echo of the social mores. Such a jumbled melange cries out for a bit of clarity.

Clarity is important, since conscience carries a prodigious weight and authority in modern parlance. "Freedom of conscience" is a kind of sacred shibboleth in our culture. Doing something "for the sake of conscience" (a very old phrase in our language) is almost self-justifying. Something done "in good conscience" has a prima facie case going for it, whereas something done "in bad conscience" is the very stuff of corruption.

Our Consciences, Our Selves

Conscience is the conscious self as attuned to moral values and disvalues in the concrete. Conscience is not just one phase of an ethical method; rather, it is the person in his or her actual state of sensitivity or insensitivity to the worth of persons and their environment. It is the embodiment of the **foundational moral experience (FME)** in a person. It is never a perfect embodiment, since no one is morally perfect, that is, fully responsive to the value of persons and this generous earth.

Saying that conscience is the "conscious" self does not diminish its roots in the subconscious. Moral knowledge, as with knowledge generally, springs from the limbic system as well as the neocortex, from the workings of the right and left hemispheres of the brain.

It is as complex as we are. To say "I know" in any context is to say more than we can ever fully understand. Knowledge is always partial, as is our knowledge of how we know.

Is conscience simply **intuition**? Intuitionist philosophers who should have done more living before writing would have us think so. One of them, H. A. Prichard, wrote in an epic of simplism: "The sense of obligation to do an action of a particular kind, or the sense of its rightness, is absolutely underivative, or immediate.... This apprehension is immediate, in precisely the sense in which a mathematical apprehension is immediate, e.g., the apprehension that a three-sided figure, in virtue of its being three-sided, must have three angles." All that is needed, according to Prichard, is not "any process of general thinking," but rather "getting face to face" with the situation and then "directly appreciating" the moral value involved.[1] If only life were that simple!

No two persons get "face to face" with any situation the same way, with the same passions, myths, and perspectives. So conscience is not a judgment proceeding from self-evidence, since very little in the complex world of interpersonal and political morality is self-evident.

Conscience is formed amid the always somewhat chaotic vicissitudes of life. No self, no person, and no society or culture is unscarred by its historical journey. In the course of our development, we will introject unworthy attitudes, identify with persons whose moral vision is in significant ways skewed. We will at times be punished for good things and rewarded for bad, and our natural proclivity for imitation will establish unfortunate habits of thought and conduct. All forms of life bear witness to the struggles that are the price of survival. This is why Berdyaev's call for "a critique of pure conscience" points us to a task that will never be complete. Conscience will never be pure.

Conscience is related to character. Both terms bespeak the moral orientation and timbre of the person. Both signify the kind of person you are;

thus, both describe the qualities of the moral self. Conscience, however, is a broader notion, since it implies the application to real-life situations of one's characterological orientation.[2] Like character, however, conscience has all the complexity and ingrained stability that derive from the innumerable variables of a long history. Thus, one can say that conscience is educable, but instantaneous conversions are not to be anticipated. The critique of conscience must be an eternal fact in human existence.

Nature or Nurture?

Is conscience innate? To some degree it is, but mostly it is not. Augustine was not amiss when he said that we are born with "the seeds of virtue." Conscience is not purely superadded like a graft on the psyche: it is not an extraneous imposition on our subjectivity. We arrive in life, in other words, with impulses to the good. The early English term for conscience, the *agenbite of inwit*, signals this. The key word there is *bite*. It is cousin to *remorse*, which comes from the Latin *mordere*, "to bite" (whence the English word *morsel*). The bite and the remorse come when our actions collide with our being, when being and doing are in discord. That causes the pang and pain of **guilt**.[3] There is, of course, such a thing as neurotic guilt where we feel guilty even when we have done the right thing. That can be helped by therapy. But there is also healthy guilt where we have acted against our very being. The polygraph witnesses to that. Countering our thrust to truth is jarring, and a machine can pick it up. It affects our blood pressure and pulse. The impulse to truth telling is not irresistible, and persons can become so habituated to falsity that it becomes second nature to them. Hence the limits of the polygraph.

The socializing impulses toward play and joy and trust in infants are all part of the conscience thrust with which we are born. We are also naturally tilted toward fellow-feeling and even compassion, as Mencius noted with regard to seeing a child about to fall into a well. It is in the heart of every human being, he thought, to reach out to save the child. From the dawning of literacy, a deep-seated human hunger for peace and harmony appears in the symbolism of Dilmun, the Sumerians' paradise. As in the paradise of Genesis, this was not a history of what was but an imagining of what could be, the paradise we humans could make of life on this fruitful earth. In the Sumerian paradise there was no war or conflict, the fields flourished, and women and men held relatively equal power.[4] Paradise in the Hebrew Bible shows similar longings and envisionings of our pacific moral potential. "Virgil, Ovid, and Horace were among other writers who described a golden past, Happy Isles or other places in which, in their native state, human beings 'kept faith and did the right.'"[5] This imagining of a golden past, an *aetas aurea*, was at root an inborn desire and need for a world where people "keep faith and [do] the right." With all of the bellicosity of our blood-soaked history, there is recurrent witness to the primordial urgings in our natural conscience toward beauty, delight, compassion, and harmony. There is growing evidence emerging from war experience that we are not natural killers. Post-traumatic stress disorder (PTSD) is seen as affecting one-third or more of persons pressed into the violence of war. Indeed, as long-term effects of exposure to state-sponsored violence are studied, the figure of one-third appears to be on the low side. None of these seemingly innate impulses toward moral good reaches the level of compelling instinct found in other animals. And in sociopathic individuals they can be wholly lacking.

Not all of our impulses are benign. Egoism and greed are among our strongest penchants, and they are the notorious parents of iniquity. Impulse-wise, we are a mixed bag.

But whatever our natural leanings toward a healthy moral sense, nurture has the power to trump nature. The cultural and moral variation among different peoples prove its power. Little uniformity is found among the conscientious orientation of peoples of different times and climes. As we look at the shocking mores of other times and climes, it is a reliable and humbling certainty that had we been born there, we would be like them. Such is the force of nurture.

Chastening Conscience

Good conscience is good ethics incarnate in a person. Since there are conscientious orientations in nations and societies, we can also say good national conscience is good ethics embodied in a people. To exemplify this, I return to the method I have been proposing in the pages of this book. If the method has validity and completeness, then the ideal conscience would reflect its various elements.

Smart Love and Communal Conscience

If the FME is truly foundational, as I allege, conscience will show it to be so. The FME is grounded in affect—deep, mystical, affective appreciation for the value of people and the nature of which we are the thinking part. Conscience shows this rootedness in feeling, in *Gemut*. A healthy conscience is alive with emotions, all of them linked to love. Love renders our perceptive powers subtle and keen. The loving eye sees far. It is alert to all that befits and enhances what is loved. The classical doctrine of "prudence," which did not have any of the undertones of timid cautiousness such as characterize modern "prudence," was equivalent in many ways to the discussion of conscience. Thus, it is significant to see Augustine referring to prudence as "love discerning well" (*amor bene discernens*). Good conscience is smart love. It is imbued with the *votum* of the heart. Indeed, this gives meaning to Augustine's often abused phrase:

"Love, and do what you will." Genuine love has its own inherent divining instincts for the good, and a love-informed conscience will have the special sharpness that corresponds to these powers. It will be filled with the practical wisdom of the heart. In this sense it can be said, "Have a good conscience, and do what you will."

Though conscience is primarily a term of personal moral consciousness, one may speak of the conscience of a society. This adaptive use of the term would refer to those distinguishable traits in a society or a culture that mark it with notable sensitivities or insensitivities. (In a similarly extended fashion, one could speak of the character of a people.) Certain values are more highly prized in some societies than others. Freedom, for example, enjoys extraordinary esteem in American society. It is a slippery shibboleth, however, since freedom is not an intrinsically moral term; even criminals value freedom. Freedom often hides a wicked agenda, as in many cases of "free trade" and "free love." In socialist nations, the equitable distribution of goods will command superior commitment. As referred to earlier, some cultures are marked by an "I-self" (individualistic) consciousness; some by a "we-self" outlook. Communal consciences mutate, as do communal moods. The United States in its history has moved from a detached isolationism to a militaristic messianism in the course of a century. Puritanical ideas perdure in the dominant American culture, as is seen in the greater concern over a president's illicit sex than over a president's violation of the Constitution or lying. Looking at group conscience is a bit of a mirror experience, since individual conscience will, to a great extent, reflect the strengths and weaknesses of the group. We might see our cognitional moral debits better when we see them in their communal context.

Affective Evaluation Processes

The affective evaluational process involves the whole panoply of emotions. A good conscience is not tearless; it weeps when faced with desecration. Tears clear the eyes. The virtue of anger resides in conscience, since anger, as Aquinas says, looks to the good of justice; in the face of injustice, the absence of anger would show too little love. Hope and fear also animate a lively conscience, hope for what can be and fear of what deters it. Good conscience also hungers for beauty as our lungs hunger for oxygen and our eyes for color and form.

Conscience also relates to the reality-revealing questions that give form to the expository phase of ethics (the hub of the wheel). The specific nature or quality of a person will be marked by greater or lesser empirical sensitivity. If a person has had considerable experience and has acquired a habit of inquisitiveness in the face of moral decisions, it means that this aspect of moral evaluation has become ingrained. It enters into the dynamism of the moral self; it becomes an aspect of conscience. Many decisions of conscience are nearly instantaneous; they are evaluative reactions within the swirl of life's processes. They do not allow for the leisure to sit down and begin to ask, *What? Why? How?* and so forth, and to inquire after the foreseeable consequences and alternatives. Someone who has made a habit of pursuing the right questions will have a *skill*, and a sharp

THINKING CRITICALLY

Literature and journalistic media are major forces in the formation of national and international consciousness of moral issues. Uruguayan journalist Eduardo Galeano writes of the challenge this presents, especially in Latin America, given the hold that "the possessors of power" have over the popular mind and over cultural conscience. "One writes out of a need to communicate and to commune with others, to denounce that which gives pain and to share that which gives happiness. . . . To awaken consciousness, to reveal identity—can literature claim a better function in these times . . . in these lands . . . ? It seems obvious that literature, as an effort to communicate fully, will continue to be blocked as long as the possessors of power continue to carry on with impunity their policy of collective imbecilization through the mass media."

—Eduardo Galeano, *Open Veins of Latin America: Five Centuries of the Pillage of a Continent*

16.1

conscience can in fact be called a kind of skill, an ability to react without elaborate preparation.[6] Comparison can be made again to an able lawyer who, even before he has had a chance to study a case in depth, has a certain feel for and insight into the main thrust of a case upon its first presentation. Similarly, an inept conscience is comparable to the "skill" of an inept lawyer who might well miss the main point right from the beginning. Poor consciences, like poor lawyers, are educable. The education, of course, may not be easy, since poor consciences, even more than poor lawyers, tend to be possessed of a stubborn and unwarranted self-confidence.

All of the evaluational spokes of the wheel model are reflected in a conscience. A good conscience is creative. It does not just sit like a judge passing verdicts of licit or illicit on situations as they arise. It includes also an "instinct" for the possible, a kind of nostalgia for the good. If human consciousness is distinguished by its capacity for perceiving the possible that is latent within the actual, the conscious moral self (conscience) should exemplify this. A conscience animated by a creative spirit will discern alternatives in moral situations where the less imaginative would be blind. This aspect of conscience is neglected by many ethicists. The reason for the neglect is clear. When one treats conscience, one's method shows through, and many rationalistic ethicists bypass the signal position of creative imagination in cognitive moral experience. Thus, it will not be in evidence in their telltale treatment of conscience.

Principles, Reason, and Analysis. Conscience will also reflect one's established knowledge of the meaning of *principles* and one's habits of *reasoning and analysis.* Principles do not serve moral consciousness merely as a kind of reserve intellectual knowledge. All moral knowledge has an affective dimension. And the affections draw what is known into the interior of the personality. The values contained in principles with which we have sufficiently identified enter into our cognitive framework and into conscience. They are at our service not merely when we view them in propositional form, but they become enfleshed in conscience. Just as we are aware of the rules of grammar when we speak but do not have to keep formulating those rules mentally as we go along, so, too, moral principles that condition the climate of the moral self also condition the reaction of conscience, even if we do not think of them explicitly.

Likewise, patterns of reason and analysis leave their mark on conscience and are influential even in decisions that are made with little or no time for the reflective processes of reasoning. A habit of thorough reasoning endows conscience with what the ancients called *solertia*, a quality of the mind implying a certain nimbleness and adroitness in reaction to new situations. Again, the skillfulness of the seasoned lawyer is an apt comparison.

Reliance. A developed conscience practices the art of intelligent *reliance.* The perception of truth is a social event. Given the limits of the mind and the infinity of the knowable, we are compelled to rely on authorities to fill out our knowledge. Discriminating docility is a virtue. It is not the docility of the weak-minded, but rather the open-mindedness of the intellectually realistic. It has been well said that "a closed mind and know-it-allness are fundamentally forms of resistance to the truth of real things."[7]

Individual and Group Experience. Individual experience and *group experience* also should show through in the living conscience. Understandably, individual experience has special relevance to conscience. The healthy moral self is in touch with its own depths. It reaches for the relief of originality; it tries to move as far as possible from the conditioning influences that would engulf and dominate; and it attempts to express its own unique contact with reality. We have a certain "will to originality," as Berdyaev called it. Beleaguered as we are by entrenched falsity, we have a kind of longing for liberation. It is a respect for self and one's own contact with reality.

Persons communicate at many levels. The contact may be at the level of business, social service, or almost purely physical sex. But when person relates to person *qua* person, the meeting is at the level of conscience. When valuing animals meet, their most intimate contact is at the point of conscience. Conscience touches and speaks to conscience in genuine personal encounter. Although it sounds terribly unromantic, when you really fall in love, you fall in love with the beloved's conscience. There is much along the way that can draw persons together, but in the heart of true love and true friendship, consciences embrace. There are many levels of *meeting.* Not to commune at this valuing core is not to commune. True meeting occurs here.

Group experience and authority are teachers who can also be tyrants. Good conscience has good antennae and is regularly alerted to the signals available to it from our counterparts in the community of persons. But group experience can also suffocate individual genius. Personal conscience can stand against political and religious despotism. *The one* can stake claims against the powers of *the many.* Here is the permanent bastion against the spirit of totalitarianism. Were it not for this lonely center of moral identity and awareness, social conscience would be all. Society would be a herd. Conscience, in a word, gives relief from the abstract strictures of "positive law" and dominant custom. It endows us with the power to dissent from fleshless law and social controllers.

Whatever its grip, we are never fully enveloped by society. As Martin Buber says, "The more or less hidden criteria that the conscience employs in its acceptances and rejections only rarely fully coincide with a standard received from the society or community."[8] There is more to us than our society. We can resist the quicksand absorbency of social-think. That is the mystery of the individual and the badge of his/her worth.

Comedy and Tragedy. The evaluative contributions of *comedy* and *tragedy* are also felt in the stable center of moral awareness that is conscience. As I said above, comedy is important for ethics not so much for individual instances of applied humor, but more for the relativizing effects of the comic perspective of life. The self that has this perspective will have a conscience that is all the better for it. The conscience that is naturally amenable to the comic view will not be easy prey for the absolutizing penchants that we encounter within and without. A sense of tragedy can also add delicacy and sensitivity to conscience. Tragedy adds to conscience a telling sense of limit and fallibility. It leaves the moral self less naïve about the actual malleability of the real, and more readied and equipped for surprise. It brings the peculiar strength of scar tissue to the perduring human task of moral inquiry.

Should You Always Follow Your Conscience?

Should you always follow your conscience? That question deserves a resounding *yes* as well as a resounding *no.* In a sense the question is a bad question, since it is misleading. Obviously, it can be said in a general way that one must act in accord with one's conscience. If conscience is the conscious moral self, contradicting it in behavior would violate one's own identity and integrity. If we are conscientiously convinced that something is wrong, we should avoid it or we would be assaulting our own convictions. This would create that painful fissure within the personality that goes by the name of guilt. From this point of view, then, the answer must be that it is always right to follow one's conscience.

The Fallibility of Conscience

There are misleading implications, however, in the notion of always following one's own conscience. The autonomy of conscience is not absolute. It would be inhuman if it were. Also, conscience is fallible. Ethics is fallible; persons and whole societies are fallible; and so, obviously, conscience is fallible. This should prompt some reservations about conscience's leadership. Conscience should not be conceived of as an independent supreme court that can be judged by no one and that merits naïve loyalty from the individual and uncritical respect from everyone else.

Take the case of the alleged right of pharmacists to withhold contraceptive medicine "on conscience grounds" if the pharmacist feels all contraception is immoral. This would amount to a dictatorship of conscience. It ignores other consciences. It also implies a radical, atomistic individualism that dismisses the social dimension of human life. Pharmacists, other healthcare workers, and professionals generally serve a community, a morally pluralistic community. Conscience claims do not absolve you from the duty to respect differences in legitimate debates. Conscience does not give a dispensation from community. The pharmacists who cannot dispense contraceptives could only function in a cult of similarly minded persons; they are unsuited for public life in a pluralistic democracy. Like a bartender who cannot abide drink, they should find other work.

Similarly, OB/GYN physicians who cannot provide abortions where abortions are legal and approved widely in the community are denying an approved form of health care. Since all physicians are to some degree subsidized in their training by public monies they are refusing to do what they have accepted monies, to learn how to do. They should have claimed a conscientious objection to accepting those monies. By accepting that money and by accepting a position in a public hospital system, they have bound themselves to the legal and standard requirements of that profession. Their situation is not different from a teacher paid by public funds who will not teach evolution and instead teaches creationism as though it were science.

The Principle of Respectable Debate

The underlying political issue here is the tension between fascism and democracy. Fascism is monistic; democracy is pluralistic. In a democracy nothing should be outlawed that is respectably debatable. What are the criteria of a "respectable debate"? This speaks to issues such as prohibition, the outlawing of marijuana and other drugs, and legal prohibition of abortion and same-sex marriage. All of those are debated. The principle of respectable debate concerns what should or should not be outlawed in a pluralistic democracy.

I propose three criteria: if those three criteria are met, the issue in question should not be outlawed. The criteria are these: (1) there are *good reasons* for choosing this option; (2) those good reasons *appeal to a broad spectrum of people*; (3) the option has the support of *mainstream humanitarian institutions*. Take the American experiment with the prohibition of alcoholic beverages. It was a failed experiment because the legalization of alcohol meets all three criteria for respectable debate. There are *good reasons*, including health

benefits, for moderate indulgence in alcohol. A truly *broad spectrum of people* accept those reasons as persuasive. And *mainstream humanitarian institutions* endorse, or at least allow for, alcohol consumption. The Catholic Mass, for example, could not be celebrated without it. The experiment was destined for failure.

To prevent serious harm, the law will and should overrule personal conscience. Some fundamentalist Christians read in the Gospel of Mark that "if they handle snakes . . . they will come to no harm" (Mark 16:18). Relying on this text, some Christians will import snakes into their churches so that people can test their faith. Since churches are not professional snake handlers, and snakes are not good neighbors, the practice may be outlawed. It fails on all three of the criteria. Similarly, persons who believe literacy threatens their faith can be precluded from keeping their children illiterate. A judge may deny parental rights of parents who on religious grounds deem all blood transfusions immoral if they try to deny a needed transfusion to their child. The adults would be permitted to refuse a transfusion for themselves but not to impose their personal choice on children.

There are also political implications regarding the absolutizing of personal conscience. Legislators may have reasons to legalize activities that offend their own personal consciences. Thus, as noted earlier, Saints Augustine and Thomas Aquinas both believed that prostitution is wrong. Nevertheless, they taught that it could be legalized to prevent greater harm.[9]

Thus, by this sound reasoning, a modern legislator who believes all intentional abortions to be evil could nevertheless vote to legalize abortion recognizing that if it were banned, it would go underground and cost the lives of many women, especially poor women. When abortion is criminalized, the rate of abortions does not decline, but maternal mortality increases. To avoid these greater evils, the legislator or judge could legalize what they think is evil in itself. In Aquinas's thinking, they would be imitating God. Legislating for a broad community is qualitatively different from making personal decisions that have an impact only on one's self. Legislators and judges who would impose as law their minority sectarian moral view on a pluralistic democracy are fascistic in spirit and not fit for office. Similarly, legalizing same-sex marriage or medical marijuana fifty years ago would have clashed with community standards and caused chaos. Good laws can move society forward, as in civil rights laws, by extending the application of already accepted standards of fairness; this increases but does not diminish the common good.

Authority and Conscientious Dissent

Since morality is literally deadly serious, both civil societies and religions are prone to assume an overbearing parental control over the consciences of their subjects. Conscience is the proper refuge from this "benign" dictatorship. It is encouraging to see that even in the most authoritarian regimes, conscience will not be ground down and dissent is championed. In Roman Catholicism, a heavily authoritarian tradition, conscience defended itself. It was done mainly through a system developed in the sixteenth and seventeenth centuries called *probabilism*. This system faced situations where church authority maintained a rigorous and conservative view on a moral issue. Probabilism, which was defended by luminaries in the Dominican and Jesuit orders and was even used by church hierarchy at times, justified dissent in moral matters that are truly debatable.

Insight, Not Permission

Probabilism was based on the twin insights that (1) where there is doubt, there is freedom (*ubi dubium, ibi libertas*) and (2) a doubtful law cannot oblige as if it were certain (*lex dubia non obligat*). It taught that even in the face of a formidable consensus of authorities, individual conscience can dissent. Dissent could be vindicated in two ways, intrinsically or extrinsically. Intrinsic warranty for dissent could be achieved by an individual alone with no authority figure in agreement. It was based on insight, not on permission. If persons could find reasons that were carefully stipulated as "cogent but not necessarily conclusive," the sort of reasons that would appeal to a reasonable person, reasons that were not obviously self-serving or frivolous, the person could feel free to act on that view. Insight was their authority and they needed none other.

The "not necessarily conclusive" clause was particularly liberating. It did not set a high bar. One did not have to be so certain about one's dissent that the more authoritative view appeared absurd. Indeed, one might admit that there is a lot to be said for that rigorous view and still be free to dissent from it. All it took was reasonable grounds to hold the liberal view on an issue that is truly debatable.

The extrinsic basis for dissent referred to finding five or six authorities who held the liberal view, even though all the popes and theologians disagreed, and that was enough. The five or six dissenting experts had to be known for their learning and prudence (*doctrina et prudentia*). They had to be seen as reliable authorities. Their minority view constituted a "solidly probable opinion," and one was free to espouse it and act on it. Priest counselors were required to advise people of this option, even if they held the more conservative majority view.[10]

Thus, in the current Vatican theology, artificial contraception is immoral. The vast majority of laity and theologians disagree—and not just five or six theologians—and therefore, according to this hallowed traditional teaching, persons can freely dissent from the Vatican view. The same use of probabilism applies to same-sex marriages and other issues.

Islam also puts great stress on authority and moral orthodoxy. But again, here the role of individual conscience and reliance on reason finds a place. The concept of *ijtihad* allows for personal judgment and dissent. Islamic theologian Ibn Hazm (994–1063) criticized the tendency to imitate blindly the behavior of authorities. "No one is allowed," he wrote, "to imitate someone else, living or dead, but each must perform to the best of his/her ability, an interpretative effort (*ijtihad*)." It is also wrong to follow blindly the example of even the prophet's companions and the founders of the main schools of Islamic jurisprudence. If anyone does that, Ibn Hazm said, "all of the above people wash their hands of him, in this world as well as in the other world." As Islamic scholar Anouar Majid says in his suggestively entitled book *A Call for Heresy: Why Dissent Is Vital to Islam and America*, Ibn Hazm and others "relied on reason and evidence."[11]

The Place of Enthusiasm

Summarily, conscience can be a source of pain, but it can also react with joy and exuberance when our behavior realizes the rich potentials of personhood. And it can do this in any tense—that is, in reacting to past, present, or prospective behavior. Again, the relationship to the foundational moral experience is clear. Behavior that enhances this radical appreciation of what is truly good has its own exhilaration. It complements our ultimately indestructible basal kinship with the true and the good. Morality has been so distorted by preachers, so abstractly and unattractively explained, that it is hard for us to see that morality has its special beauty. Its aesthetic side has been slighted by dons and deans and common folk. We do not expect it to sing. Neither do we normally realize that morality—and with it conscience—is the natural ally of that master virtue: enthusiasm. Again, conscience is the telltale. If one's view of morality is dry and cool, this would be reflected in one's view of the critical category *conscience*.

From Sin to Guilt

We call good that which enhances our humanity and our earthly home. Looking at the "butcher's bench" (Lenin) of history and ongoing wrecking of the earth, we are obviously not very good at doing good. On the other hand, there has been some moral advance: the "good old days" were often awful. Not surprisingly, the comments of thoughtful observers of human behavior have run a broad gamut. Hamlet went effusively overboard: "What a piece of work is a man! How noble in reason! How infinite in faculty! In form and moving how express and admirable! In action how like an angel! In apprehension how like a god! The beauty of the world! The paragon of animals!"[12] The Hebrew Bible is less flattering: "The LORD looks down from heaven on all humankind to see if any act wisely. . . . But all are disloyal, all are rotten to the

> **THINKING CRITICALLY**
>
> Philosophical ethics can become disembodied and adrift in abstraction. "Attention to the novelists can be a welcome correction to a tendency of philosophical ethics of the last generation or two to lose contact with the ordinary life of people which is just what the novelists are concerned with. . . . They are all concerned— Jane Austen, for instance, entirely and absolutely—with the moral qualities or defects of their heroes and heroines and other characters."
>
> —Bernard Mayo, *Ethics and the Moral Life*
>
> 16.2

core; not one does anything good, no, not even one" (Ps. 14:2-3). Ouch! At times, any moral improvement is seen as hopeless: "Can the Nubian change his skin, or the leopard its spots? And you, can you do good, you who are schooled in evil?" (Jer. 13:23).

Blaise Pascal tried for a more balanced view: "What a chimera then is man! What a novelty! What a monster, what a chaos, what a contradiction, what a prodigy! Judge of all things, imbecile worm of the earth; depository of truth, a sink of uncertainty and error; the pride and refuse of the universe!"[13] And after writing us off as hopelessly degenerate, the Bible foresees a day when nothing less than perfect peace and the end of militarism can be hoped for: "All the boots of trampling soldiers and the garments fouled with blood shall become a burning mass, fuel for fire" (Isa. 9:5); "The song of the military will be silenced" (Isa. 25:5). Ecological sanity will obtain and "parched deserts" will "flower with fields of asphodel [and] rejoice and shout for joy" (Isa. 35:2).

So there we are: "rotten to the core" but with angelic potential for peacemaking and love of the earth, at one and the same time "the pride and refuse of the universe."

All of this requires a look at our prodigious downside potential.

The Viability of Sin-Talk

Moralcentric religions have expended lots of energy condemning "sins," so much so that the word *sin* is battered and not terribly useful in modern discourse. Connotations smacking of Calvin's Geneva, an angry God, or prohibitions of things like hanging out laundry on Sunday, spitting, or swearing in the presence of the mayor have been religiously pushed and even enshrined in law. Sin-talk is laced with threats of punishment in an afterlife. It often bypasses ethics, making ethics a kind of positive law decreed by a deity, not discovered through our powers of discernment. In much fundamentalist vocabulary, sin has primary

reference to deviations in the use of sex or alcohol. To many the term denotes very little of matters such as social neglect, racism, sexism, ecocide, or other violations of justice. These *don'ts* are often in the genre of **taboo**—absolutistic and unnuanced.

Connotations have a way of becoming denotations. When a word is brutalized with so many inappropriate understandings, the reality it would describe can easily be overlooked. When you marry a word, you get all the connotative relatives in the bargain. When too many fallacies attach to the word, the word needs either careful and explicit redefinition or retirement as a linguistic tool. My preference is to retire *sin* when possible in favor of *guilt*, a word that has been jostled somewhat by usage but is still serviceable. It, too, has juridical connotations and strong psychological meaning, but as a word it is considerably less encumbered with debits.

A Dangerous Species

Whatever term is used, the fact is that we are supremely capable of wrongful, earth-destroying behavior, and our technical power makes us the most dangerous species in the history of the planet. Again, it is possible that we are a failed species destined for a short tenure, in cosmic terms, on this fair corner of the universe. Political economist Robert Heilbroner notes that the dangers that threaten the human habitat "do not descend, as it were, from the heavens, menacing humanity with the implacable fate that would be the consequence of the sudden arrival of a new Ice Age or the announcement of the impending extinction of the sun. On the contrary . . . all the dangers we have examined—population growth, war, environmental damage, scientific technology—are *social* problems, originating in human behavior and capable of amelioration by the alteration of that behavior."[14]

Three Understandings of Guilt

Wrongful behavior is too obvious to ignore, and so every system of ethics and every culture takes a stand on it. There are at least three ways in which guilt is understood; it may be used in a *taboo* sense, in an *egoistic* sense, or in what I will argue is the *realistic* sense. Each of these ways also reflects a different conception of ethics and conscience, since one's view of guilt will also reflect the presuppositions of one's ethics.

1. Taboo Guilt

Guilt at the taboo level is primitive even though moderns and, yes, postmoderns still indulge in it. There are three markers for the taboo mentality: (1) forbiddenness with implied sanctions; (2) no consideration of harm; (3) no deference to reason. Let us go to earlier times for examples.

Earlier Taboos. The Ark of the Covenant (also called the Ark of God) was precious and revered in ancient Israel. A story was developed to show how seriously God took that ark. It was taboo even to touch it. King David ordered the ark to be brought to a proper place so that all Israel could celebrate its sacramental presence. It was brought on an ox-pulled cart guided by the servants Uzzah and Ahio. One of the oxen stumbled and Uzzah did the sensible thing. He reached out his hand to steady the ark and keep it from crashing. He broke the taboo. Result? God struck him dead (1 Chron. 13:5-14).

There we see all three elements of taboo. Touching the ark was forbidden (to show its sacredness). The avoidance of harm, the crashing down of the ark, did not matter. Reason or reasonableness had no part in the story. Forget harm analysis; forget reason. Forbiddenness is all. Something similar is found in taboos that forbid one to see the person who has been chosen as one's future spouse, visiting sanctions upon anyone who peeks. Once again there is a purpose to the taboo, since the wedding might not proceed as planned if the designated couple got to inspect one another. (Remnants of this remain in the traditions of veiling the bride and instructing the groom not to see the bride in her gown before the wedding.) There was purpose to the ark story also. It emphasized the importance of the covenant and its moral laws. The taboo approach to these goals was not good ethics.

Some taboos made a lot of sense. Taboos on certain foods or activities were literally lifesaving and the fruit of long and dire experience. The incest taboo arose from a recognition of the biologically and socially disruptive force of intrafamilial sexual relationships. So there are elements of a realistic ethics in taboo, but the problem is that taboo is undiscriminating. Once this taboo is in place, the door is closed to important distinctions. Distinctions are not made where there are differences.

Modern Taboos. Taboos are prompted by fear. In areas where we sense danger, the taboo instinct is to build a no-no fence around that activity and preclude further discussion. Sex is scary and taboo laden.[15]

Sexual taboos reign in modern society on masturbation, contraception, abortion, homosexuality, and remarriage after divorce. Although most Catholic scholars have rejected the idea, the Vatican still holds that one may not use a condom even if one's spouse is HIV-positive. Arguments are given that contraception poisons marital love, an argument that overlooks the certain fact that AIDS kills not just love but the lovers. Taboo—pure, simple, and lethal.[16]

A full analysis of issues such as sexism, racism, the moral rights of patients or of students, and the ideologies of nationalism and classism would uncover a host of unsuspected taboos. Discussions about the evil of "flag burning" are about taboos. Professions, too, are heavy with taboos in areas of etiquette and protocol, not all of which make sense.

2. Egoistic Guilt

This is guilt at the level of antisepticity. It is a step above taboo since it does involve concern for harm and it is, within limits, rational. However, it is centered on concern for one's own image and moral purity. It eschews the harm that damaging behavior would do to one's self: "Decent persons don't do that sort of thing . . ."; "I will not punch you in the mouth because I am not that kind of person." That's fine as far as it goes, but it shows little concern for the other person or his or her mouth. Egoistic guilt is not useless and will keep you out of jail, but it is mired in selfishness. Guilt is here perceived as disfigurement.

In sophisticated dress it appears in Ayn Rand's ethics of selfishness. Lacking a theory of genuine altruism, Rand could not see guilt with altruistic components. Guilt comes from a default in one's enlightened pursuit of self-interest.[17] This is a weak base for any consideration of friendship, much less heroism. Heroes have no more nobility than moths caught by glare. All cases of supreme sacrifice would be shrunken to a sick masochism. That Rand has been popular among practitioners of business is not surprising. Egoistic business ethics would involve a desire to do what one must do to avoid getting hurt. It is an effort, in effect, to stay within the law in such wise that one's practices generate no actionable claims. This myopic ethic ignores the creative possibilities that conscientious businesses have to serve the common good while still thriving. It is one step above barbarism, and, clearly, even its low standards are not met by many business practitioners. The notion of guilt that would obtain in such a climate would be no subtler or more profound than the image of a bad investment. Ironically, those who philosophically believe that government should do less and business more, often seem the least likely to be ready to transcend the shriveled confines of ethical egoism. Refuge is sought in faith that an "invisible hand" will bring good things out of the untrammeled and unrestrained impulses of greed in the marketplace. The crashes of 1929 and 2008 illustrate where such superficial theories lead.

Egoistic guilt has many masks. An ethics based on happiness (eudaemonism) could have a decent regard for others but can also be a disguise for hedonism. **Utilitarianism** that sets out to seek the greatest happiness for the greatest number can house not only hedonism but a tribal restriction on whose happiness counts. And nationalized utilitarianism, called patriotism, is often the refuge of selfish scoundrels.[18] All of which presses us to find a definition of realistic guilt.

3. Realistic Guilt

Finally, there is an understanding of guilt that I would call realistic. Guilty behavior is *conscious and free behavior (active or passive) that does real, unnecessary harm to persons and/or their environment.* In speaking of conscious and free behavior, I acknowledge the number of subconscious and unconscious determinisms that are a fact of our psychic life. We are free only to a point. "Conscious and free" simply refers to the fact that behavior that cannot be linked to any conscious control or any freedom does not merit moral evaluation. Sleepwalkers and persons suffering from psychotic illness are not free. Harm done while drunk is morally adjudicable since you are free not to get drunk.

Omission or Commission. Free behavior can be active or passive—it may take the form of omission or commission. Omission can be quite voluntary and influential. It is an interesting insight of the Christian Gospels that it is our omissions that most reveal our moral spirit. In the parable of the good Samaritan, it is not the mugger who is most condemned but those who saw the victim and simply passed by (Luke 10:29-37). Judging guilt when no action has been taken taxes the minds of moralists and jurists. Yet there is a key difference between doing nothing about something that is beyond our influence and failing to respond to what we could effectively correct. The husband who wants out of his marriage and is deliberately slow to be available for his wife in a crisis is not inactive or innocent. Such an omission may also represent heightened and intense personal decision. What the husband has done is an act of refusal that is free and highly significant. This refusal might in fact be the most voluntary action of his life. His behavior is *passive* in the sense that it is not active as it would be if he were to shoot his wife, but it is *active* in the sense that it is free and effective volition. Deliberate omission is not outside the circle of moral responsibility.

What we omit out of **invincible ignorance** is not culpable. The idea of **vincible ignorance**, however, is subtler and more significant. There is a way in which we can have what moralists of the past called a *conscientia larvata*—"a masked conscience." Ignorance can be contrived and self-servingly sustained. It is then not so much ignorance as avoidance. It represents a choice. The morally demanding reality is dimly perceived and then instinctively commended to the shadows of the mind. This may be illustrated by many of the Germans who claimed to know nothing of the Nazi genocidal programs. Affluent Americans who claim to be unaware of the deep poverty existing in various places in this country are another example. Whites who dismiss the unique problems faced by blacks in a racist country, heterosexuals who ignore the deprivations of gays, those who practice what economist Robert Reich has called "the secession of the successful" in gated communities or suburbs could easily learn the sufferings from which they hide. Our active unawareness of hunger in the world and the impact of our national priorities on that hunger is easily corrected and therefore morally indictable.

Sexuality with its rich payload of urgent pleasure can be rife with contrived ignorance. In what I call "the surprised virgin syndrome," girls who, when suddenly and inconveniently pregnant, protest that they had no idea of how it happened are not invincibly ignorant. The onset of sexual ardor and where it leads is noticeable. Similarly, in the "hostile inseminator syndrome," the man who omits prevention is rarely unaware of where babies come from.[19] I would even submit that most harm that comes to the world of persons derives from what is undone. The question of collective guilt, to which we shall return, inevitably entails considerations of responsibility for omissions.

Unnecessary Harm. According to the definition, there is no real guilt unless there is *real, unnecessary harm. Harm* is the critical term here. If we do no real harm, we incur no guilt. In speaking of taboo, I noted that taboo often has realistic origins. It often represents an aversive reaction to perceived harm, even though it finds expression in an absolutized way that allows for no discriminating judgment. Thus, some modern taboo has put all gambling, all drinking, or all divorce under the same negative judgment—even though, in certain instances, these activities do no *real, unnecessary harm.* This is the central failing of taboo, or of any kind of ethics that preter-circumstantially condemns all behavior of a certain class.

The prolonged conviction that all contraceptive intercourse is immoral, which derives largely from Stoic ethics, is a classical example of this. As one ancient writer imbued with Stoic doctrine put it: "It is particularly well established that we have intercourse not for pleasure but for the purpose of procreation. . . . The sexual organs are given man not for pleasure, but for the maintenance of the species."[20] What happened here was that an abstract definition of the intrinsic finality of sex was taken as fully exhaustive of what the sexual encounter means to persons. Such abstraction involves a decision to consider only one aspect of sex—in this case the procreative aspect—as real. Thus, all nonprocreative sex was deemed immoral—not because it would be judged as harmful, but simply because it would offend the chosen conceptualization of what sex means. This kind of abstracting happens in many areas. The stress on harm brings relief from this kind of thinking, because it draws us back to the empirical order where the wrongfulness will be manifested if it is real. It spares us the nominalism present in most cultural codes of ethics that label as evil that which is harmless and potentially good.

The point here is not that you cannot theorize about guilty action. To do just that is a prime task of ethics. The problem arises when the theory has no empirical base. Then that which is called wrong might be harmful only to our theory. Hence the need to insist on *real harm* in the definition of guilty behavior.

The term *unnecessary* has to qualify *harm* in the definition of guilty behavior because it is sometimes moral and necessary to cause harm. Killing in self-defense when there are no less drastic alternatives is obviously harmful to the deceased. It may, however, be judged *necessary* harm. Affirmative action that seeks to correct the white male monopolies that reigned in the United States from its founding does real, *necessary* harm to those qualified white males who are not chosen so that the classes of excluded qualified talent can enter the mainstream of life. When the government takes a third or more of your income in taxation, you could argue that there is harm there, but it is arguably necessary harm for the common good of all. When eminent domain is invoked causing property loss to some, this may be justifiable depending on the reasons.

The Environmental Factor. That wrongful behavior is so because it is harmful to *persons* is obvious. More neglected is the "and/or their environment" part of our definition. This environment includes the animals, vegetables, and minerals that make up our terrestrial context. Like a man who strikes it rich and arrogantly abandons his kith and kin, *Homo sapiens*, having evolved into a conscious and somewhat free animal, treated the earth as though it were a stage that had no intrinsic con-nection with the drama played upon it. We forgot that we grew up out of the material of that stage and that the earth is truly flesh of our flesh and blood of our blood. We are of the earth and of the universe. Our bodies are reconfigured stardust, and unto stardust they shall return.

From this definition of guilty behavior, therefore, it should be obvious how dangerous and intellectually vacuous it is to treat guilt as though it were neurotic. Rather, as J. Glenn Gray writes: "If guilt is not experienced deeply enough to cut into us, our future may well be lost."[21]

Collective Guilt: If Everybody Is Guilty, Is Anybody Guilty?

The week of October 3, 2001, has been called "the week of shame."[22] During that week, befogged by the recent 9/11 attack on the Trade Towers in New York and the Pentagon in Washington, both houses of Congress abandoned their constitutionally assigned right to declare war and gave that right to the president to use at his own discretion. The debacle of the second Iraq war ensued, a war that failed to meet any of the six criteria for a "just war."[23] The question is, how far does the blame spread? Can it be limited to the president and the delinquent Congress? The finger of blame extends far beyond these actors. Indeed, the government found it necessary to convince the people with elaborate propaganda about the imminence of "mushroom clouds" over our major cities. The leaders knew that a resistant populace would make the enormous efforts of war unfeasible. The people had to be hoodwinked because government is powerless without a base of consent. The gullibility and indifference of the citizenry were the indispensable background of the "Shock and Awe" that followed. Flag-waving citizens were complicit in this treason and share the shame. In a true sense, most blame goes to the citizenry because their consent, however flaccid, emboldens the active practitioners of state-sponsored violence.

This is increasingly so since the modern birthing of democracy. As Jonathan Schell says: "In 1793, when the French Revolutionary Convention ordered the mass recruitment of citizens known to history as the *levee en masse*, its decree was the definitive announcement of society's unprecedented militarization."[24] In 1835, Alexis de Tocqueville wrote of the major democratic revolution that was changing modern society. In 1932, the Spanish philosopher Ortega y Gasset asserted that "one fact of the utmost importance in the public life in Europe" is "the accession of the masses to complete social power." Where there is power, there is moral responsibility, and history shows that many people would rather be unfree than responsible. George Orwell considered it possible that producing a breed of people who do not want their human freedom may be as easy as producing a breed of hornless cows. Freedom may be divested, but moral responsibility inheres in our moral bones.

The Limits of Collective Guilt

Still, collective guilt is a dicey matter. Can guilt be inherited? Do we bear the guilt of our fathers who, in centuries of dishonor, drove the Indians from their homelands and slaughtered many of them? Do we owe reparation to women and blacks because we all have been in some way responsible for damaging discrimination that has been visited upon them? Serious scholars have warned of the pitfalls when we start assigning guilt broadly. The "war guilt" clause of the Versailles Treaty undergirded excessive reparations for Germany, which set the stage for a Hitler. The so-called guilt of the Jewish people for the death of Jesus precipitated pogroms and holocausts. Following the Pearl Harbor attacks, loyal Japanese Americans were "relocated," that is, imprisoned for being Japanese. In the past, the loose use of collective guilt, in the case of Japanese Americans and in other cases, provoked the following bill of indictments from ethicist Theodore Weber:

— It linked people to deeds with which they had no proximate and/or volitional connection.
— It brought innocent people and moral monsters under a common judgment.
— It dissolved the necessary distinctions between minor transgressions and major crimes.
— It reduced the complexity of intergroup claims and counterclaims to simple and unarguable moral judgments and demands.
— It erased the faces and histories of unique individuals.
— It ignored the historic diversity and social plurality of designated collectivities.
— It predisposed groups to unrelenting, indiscriminate, unlimited warfare.
— It placed a summary judgment on human beings at conception and left them vulnerable to the execution of sentence at the option of the "offended party" and at a time and in circumstances of the latter's choosing.[25]

Collective guilt can be something for people to wallow in, comforted by the conviction that there is nothing much that can be done about it since responsibility is such a morass. Collective guilt can be a species of self-serving rationalization. In spite of all of this, a proper conception of collective guilt is feasible.

The Ontology of Collective Guilt

Collective guilt is best analyzed in terms of justice theory as presented in chapter 5. Persons have a private, personal dimension as well as a social dimension, and collective guilt can be explained in terms of our sociality. Just as we cannot be understood merely individualistically, neither can our guilt potential be so reduced. A grossly individualistic view of personhood would allow only for commutative justice and a purely individual notion of guilt.

Justice Theory as Key. In reality, the three forms of justice are three forms of indebtedness, and guilt, correspondingly, could occur at any level, since we can violate justice at any level. Collective guilt refers mainly to our failures in social and distributive justice.

First of all, collective guilt arises from what is undone. Albrecht Haushofer, a determined opponent of Hitler who was imprisoned and executed near the end of the war, wrote a sonnet entitled "Guilt." He admits that he is guilty but not at all in the way that the Nazi court judged his case. He did resist the government, but that was not his moral crime.

> Yet I am guilty otherwise than you think
> I should have known my duty earlier
> And called evil by its name more sharply—
> My judgment I kept flexible too long . . .
> In my heart I accuse myself of this:
> I deceived my conscience long
> I lied to myself and others—
> Early I knew the whole course of this misery—
> I warned—but not hard enough or clearly!
> Today I know of what I am guilty. . . . [26]

Here was the sensitive voice of a man who risked all and paid in full for his courage. Yet he was painfully aware of his early compromising hesitations, his "prudent" flexibility, his circumvention by way of contrived obscurity, his protestations about how complicated it all was—all the stratagems that make up the tangled defenses of the cold conscience. Certainly, all of us who were alive and mature before the civil rights movement—and in their own way, those who are younger—can make their own the sentiments of Haushofer. We all take

part even now in segregation. Racism is not just a matter of real estate. There is wide disinterest and inactivity regarding the "unnecessary headwinds" that confront African American children facing life in the United States. We have our own mode of apartheid. Anyone who would claim to be without sin here is surely a liar. Who could say that they cared enough, warned enough, or called evil and the unholy by its name with a clear voice (In Haushofer's words, *hart genug und klar*)?

Social justice refers to our debts to the common good. Aside from the social justice obligations that nations make into law—taxes, obedience to law, and so forth—we owe society an ongoing contribution to equity and fairness and to an atmosphere free of tolerated insult. A true sense of social justice would not ask, "Am I better off than I was four years ago?" It would ask, "Are the poor better off than they were four years ago?" For poverty is not an accident, nor is it unrelated to the social arrangements that we passively or actively endorse. Social justice would require that we pass the "care and dare" rule regarding social problems afflicting the powerless citizens.

Distributive justice is not just the concern of government officials or of social and corporate entities. Recall that Thomas Aquinas sees this as a virtue that resides also in the citizenry. He says that this kind of justice is primarily in the prince who distributes the common goods of the society. But, he says, distributive justice is practiced by citizens if "they are pleased [*sunt contenti*] by a just distribution."[27] The guilt of distributive injustice accrues to citizens if they are *contenti*, pleased and satisfied with unjust systems of distribution that advantage them at the cost of the nation's and the world's poor. In modern language, the passivity of citizens legitimates the priorities of the main power brokers in a society.

Entrenched Egoism. A final point on collective guilt relates to the ugliness of entrenched egoism. In Arthur Miller's play *Incident at Vichy*, the Jew

Leduc, who is awaiting interment in a Nazi camp and probable death, is trying to explain to the decent Von Berg that he, Von Berg, in spite of his decency, is complicit in the hatred that is about to condemn Leduc. Says Leduc: "I have never analyzed a gentile who did not have, somewhere hidden in his mind, a dislike if not a hatred for the Jews." Von Berg protests: "That is impossible, it is not true of me!" Then Leduc addresses Von Berg with special earnestness, with, in the playwright's directive, "a wild pity in his voice":

> Until you know it is true of you, you will destroy whatever truth can come of this atrocity. Part of knowing who we are is knowing we are not someone else. And Jew is only the name we give to that stranger, that agony we cannot feel, that death we look at like a cold abstraction. Each man has his Jew; the black, the yellow, the white, it is the other. And the Jews have their Jews. And now, now above all, you must see that you have yours—the man whose death leaves you relieved that you are not him, despite your decency. And that is why there is nothing and will be nothing—until you face your own complicity with this . . . your own humanity.[28]

Leduc's cynicism may be excessive, as even the play suggests, since after this conversation, Von Berg gives his pass to Leduc, allowing him to escape while Von Berg remains to face the consequences. Still, there is the scent of some truth in Leduc's outburst. Egoism is still so strong in the species that we can bear the ills of others with "a cold abstraction." As Leduc says pointedly, another man's death "leaves you relieved that you are not him, despite your decency." Egoism also encourages particularized hostilities. "Each man has his Jew. . . . And the Jews have their Jews." In-

secure in our sense of our own worth, we almost seem to need to downgrade others. We need the barbarians, or the Jews, or the communists, or the blacks as alien others whose imputed inferiority or malice sets our value in a more favorable light. Subterranean, boiling hatred undermines society. The distinguished law professor Derrick Bell writes: "The burden of racism has scarred us all, and there are few whites who at some level of their being do not believe that whites are superior, and even fewer blacks who do not recognize that feeling and resent it."[29] There is nothing new about this. In India, centuries ago, we can see the rise of groups of people who were known as untouchables or outcasts. As A. L. Basham writes, the practice of social ostracism appeared even among the outcasts: "The outcasts themselves had developed a caste hierarchy, and had their own outcasts. In later India every untouchable group imagined that some other group was lower than itself."[30]

It would seem that the enthusiastic malevolence of the lynch mob appears in subtle disguise in human society more often than we would care to admit. This grim side of our psychic history is something that must be included in an estimate of collective guilt. We have an instinct not just for grouping, but for grouping *against*. The group gives strength to our baser proclivities. In a face-to-face encounter with all of its chastening immediacy, we feel ourselves on the spot. Our reactions are likely to be more benign. But group experience dilutes individual conscience. Egoism finds freer rein. Blurring abstractions develop, which give a sense of cohesiveness and comfort to the group. From such a base it is easier to do *real, unnecessary harm* in multiple ways to persons. To speak only of individual guilt is to miss the greater part of our guilt.

Summary of Key Themes

- Conscience is the conscious self as attuned to moral values in the concrete.
- Ethics is a critique of conscience.
- Guilt involves a collision between *being* and *doing*.
- One may speak of the conscience or character of a society.
- The autonomy of conscience is not absolute.
- "Conscience claims" and "conscience clauses" do not permit the imposition of a personal or sectarian religious view on a morally pluralistic society.
- Issues that are "respectably debated" should not be outlawed in a democratic society.
- The concept of "collective guilt" requires analytical critique.

Key Terms

Conscience
Foundational moral experience (FME)
Guilt
Ignorance (Vincible/Invincible)
Intuition
Probabilism
Taboo
Utilitarianism

Questions for Discussion

1. Pharmacists who disapprove of contraception will sometimes invoke their rights of conscience to refuse to fill prescriptions for contraceptive medicine. Can their refusal be justified on grounds of the sacredness of conscience?
2. Some citizens will refuse to pay taxes because of their disapproval of some of the uses the government makes of tax revenues. Can a person who is aware of some objectionable use of tax revenues still pay taxes in good conscience? Why or why not?
3. In our therapeutic cultures, "guilt" is often spoken of as neurotic, an illness needing to be cured. What are the ethical grounds for speaking of healthy guilt that requires reform, not therapy?

Suggestions for Further Reading

Beauchamp, Tom L. *Philosophical Ethics: An Introduction to Moral Philosophy.* New York: McGraw-Hill, 1982.

Galeano, Eduardo. *Open Veins of Latin America: Five Centuries of the Pillage of a Continent.* New York: Monthly Review Press, 1997.

Harrison, Beverly Wildung. *Our Right to Choose: Toward a New Ethic of Abortion.* Boston: Beacon, 1983.

PART FIVE

Hazards of Moral, Political, and Economic Discourse

The Power of Myth

The great enemy of the truth is very often not the lie—deliberate, contrived and dishonest—but the myth, persistent, persuasive and unrealistic. Too often we hold fast to the clichés of our forebears. We subject all facts to a prefabricated set of interpretations.
—John Fitzgerald Kennedy

We have created a myth. This myth is a faith, a noble enthusiasm. It does not have to be a reality, it is an impulse and a hope, belief, and courage.

Our myth is the nation, the great nation which we wish to make into a concrete reality.
—Benito Mussolini

IF THE IDEALS ARE GOOD, then the myths that manifest them can be very positive. As Mussolini himself illustrates, however, the bad myth can be blinding, and all the thinking that is done under its sway will be impaired. My concern here is with myth in its pejorative sense—with myth as a warping and limiting force in cognition.

Negative Myths:
Interpretation and Ideology

Reality is not transparent. The human mind is not a docile camera or a mirror that obediently and accurately reflects things back to us as they are. The human knower is both a taker and a giver. Human knowing is interpretive. The word *interpretation* comes from the Latin *interpres*, which means "a broker, a negotiator, an agent who arranges a bargain between two parties." This is in fact what goes on in the interpretive act of knowing. A kind of bargain is struck between the knower and the known. The consuming need for meaning drives the mind as it bargains with reality. Meaning is the oxygen of the mind. The mind cannot stand a vacuum of meaning. It must make sense of things, that is, make the new data coming at us meaningful.

The new known must be related to the already known because knowledge is relational; we know by relating. Things known are not stored up like photographs in a drawer that do not relate to other photographs kept there. To be known is to be related, to be set in a meaning-giving web, a reassuring, familiar context. The new gets meaning only when we see that it somehow relates to the already known. Otherwise the new candidate for knowledge is like the proverbial man from Mars, meaningless and disturbing. He does not fit into the established interpretive scheme and so he appears as a threat to the mind. He triggers a rejection mechanism. It is even possible that we will not see him at all. We can actually be blind to the presence of that which seems unrelatable to the already known and accepted. In a word, we value meaning above knowledge. We would rather not know that which appears meaningless. We shy from anything that shakes up our established universe of meaning. We notice this in others more than in ourselves. We wonder how they can be so blind! And others who have different filters and interpretive structures have similar wonderings about us.

Myth is the first of the silent but busy filters that drop between the mind and reality. Since the word *myth* is polyvalent, definition to the rescue. In my usage, *myth is a complex of feelings, attitudes, symbols, memories, and experienced relationships through which reality is refracted, filtered, and interpreted.* By that definition, knowledge is always to some degree mythic. Interpretation will always be affected by the complex of our feelings, attitudes, and so forth. Sometimes this will be gainful. Buoyed by a creative myth, persons may rise to heights to which they never would have aspired in the absence of the myth. The confidence-inspiring myth of "American know-how" has historically served to keep our technologists working to the point of success when those working without the myth would have given up at an earlier, more "reasonable" point. The myths surrounding parenthood sometimes bring forth generosity and imagination from the most unlikely subjects. But our attention is on negative myths.[1]

The notion of myth as I am using it obviously relates to ideology. **Ideology** has a broader meaning than myth, which implies that ideology represents more systematized thought than does myth. Ideologies contain myths and, to some degree, marshal them into the work of understanding and organizing collective movements. But more than myth, ideology imparts a rational and organizing element. It also carries its own historically derived pejorative connotations. After its first popularization in the beginning of the nineteenth century, it came quickly to be associated with highly abstract thinking. Napoleon said that all the misfortunes of France were due to ideology, and for Marx it was a pathology of human knowledge that would be eliminated in a classless society. It was the "tissue of lies" that societies drape over their actual purposes. Given the linguistic facts of life, however, one must be judged on how he or she chooses to use these verbal vagabonds.

Seeing Myth in Action

Examples show the dominating power of myth. Vietnamese communists worked out of a myth derived from the Russian revolution. According to that myth, the czarists and related nobility had to be eliminated to make way for the revolution of the proletariat. As the Vietnamese communists arrived in very egalitarian villages, they found no czarists, so they simply designated certain impressive persons as the ignoble nobles, killed them, and started their reforms. Nothing looks sillier than behavior derived from myths we do not share.

Myth and Foreign Policy

Minds, even brilliant minds, caught in a distorting myth achieve a quasi-psychotic detachment from reality. Nations are thick with myth. Political scientists laud "fact-based," "hard-nosed" analysis. Not bad as an ideal, but if a myth interposes between policy makers and the world, facts dissolve and fantasies abound. The master myth that dominated American foreign policy in the past and is only now falling victim to power shifts on the world scene is the myth of American exceptionalism and moral supremacy. The myth is messianic in nature and rooted in America's historical civil religion.[2] Let's listen to a chorus of American theocratic preachers.

Sacral Hues

"And we Americans are the peculiar, chosen people—the Israel of our time; we bear the ark of the liberties of the world. . . . Long enough have we been skeptics with regard to ourselves, and doubted whether, indeed, the political Messiah had come. But he has come in us, if we would but give utterance to his promptings." These are the words of Herman Melville, writing in 1850.[3]

"Almighty God . . . has marked the American people as the chosen nation to finally lead in the regeneration of the world. This is the divine mission of America. . . . We the trustees of the world's progress, guardians of the righteous peace." Thus spake Albert J. Beveridge, Pulitzer Prize–winning historian and U.S. senator. He braced his comments with a quote from the Gospel of Matthew: "Ye have been faithful over a few things; I will make you ruler over many things."[4] The senator was celebrating the Spanish-American War.

President Woodrow Wilson exulting in victory in World War I: "America had the infinite privilege of fulfilling her destiny and saving the world."[5]

American patriotism has always been limned with sacral hues. The American Revolution was creedal in nature, consisting of events "under God." Many early documents of the nation articulated this idea. The Puritan experience imbued America with notions of the promised people in the promised land. Early America was not just founding a nation but fulfilling a destiny. This land would be a saving sign to the aching monarchies of Europe of the freedom and democracy that were God's will for all men. The new Zion was in this nation, and energetic preachers drove home the idea that God was initiating a new era in the new world. The nation said "Amen" when Yale University chaplain Nathaniel W. Taylor preached with confidence that this nation was the one "on which the Sun of Righteousness sheds his clearest brightest day."[6] George W. Bush, during the disastrous war in Iraq, could still give voice to the faith of Nathaniel Taylor that God's will and the American calling are at one: "The ideal of America is the hope of all mankind. That hope still lights the way and the light shines in the darkness. And the darkness will not overcome it."[7]

Even the gore of the Civil War did not dispel this sanctimonious predestination complex. The war was seen as an expiatory event that further demonstrated our divine calling. Evidence of divine blessing in Union victories was traced out by

George S. Phillips of Ohio in his literally incredible book, *The American Republic and Human Liberty Foreshadowed in Scripture*. Phillips averred that God's Old Testament promise to found a nation fully obedient to him was fulfilled when he established the United States. Phillips found our story in the pages of sacred Scripture. The Bible apparently was written to foretell our coming. According to him, Isaiah and Daniel clearly foresaw the day and the hour of the Declaration of Independence; Isaiah predicted the Boston Tea Party and even the coming of Chinese immigrants to California. Phillips roared on to this conclusion: "The United States is to fill the earth . . . so to occupy the place of government in the world, as to leave room for no other government."[8] George W. Bush, proclaiming all who did not join in the American "crusade" in Iraq as "irrelevant," was at one with George Phillips. If Phillips were an outrider in the American tradition, he could be studied as a curiosity. In fact, as religious studies professor William A. Clebsch says of his work: "The patent unoriginality of Phillips' book signifies its representing a major body of religious and nationalistic sentiment in the north."[9]

Nations drape their origins in unrealistic myth. Ethical historians, like Howard Zinn, use truth and facts as solvents of those myths: "Arawak men and women, naked, tawny, and full of wonder, emerged from their villages onto the island's beaches and swam out to gt a closer look at the strange big boat. When Columbus and his sailors came ashore, carrying swords, speaking oddly, the Arawaks ran to greet them, brought them food, water, gifts. He later wrote of this in his log: 'They brought us parrots and balls of cotton and spears and many other things, which they exchanged for the glass beads and hawks' bells. They were willing to trade everything they owned. . . . They were well-built, with good bodies and handsome features. They do not bear arms, and do not know them, for I showed them sword, they took it by the edge and cut themselves out of ignorance. They have no iron. They would make fine servants. With fifty men we could subjugate them all and make them do whatever we want. I took some of the natives by force in order that they might learn and might give me information of whatever there is in these parts.'"

—Howard Zinn, *A People's History of the United States*

The American mythology, with all of its religious underpinnings, can be seen in vigorous bloom in the words of President McKinley when he explained his decision to hold the Philippine Islands after our war with Spain. We had not wanted these islands, he avowed, but "they came to us, as a gift from the gods." He said that he sought help from Republicans and Democrats as to what to do with them, "but got little help." Then, he said, "I went down on my knees and prayed Almighty God for light and guidance more than one night." God apparently was not unresponsive. Late one night the answer came, according to McKinley. The islands could not be returned to Spain, for "that would be cowardly and dishonorable." Neither could we turn them over to our commercial rivals, France or Germany, for "that would be bad business and discreditable." (One wonders whether God is still speaking at this point, and if so, one must credit God with a keen sense of business—at least for American business.) Our duty, as McKinley saw it, was to "uplift and civilize and Christianize" the people of the Philippines and "by God's grace do the very best we could for them as our fellowmen for whom Christ also died."[10] He failed to notice that they were already Catholics.

Later, Warren G. Harding, while still a U.S. senator, would look back on our work in the Philippines and dub it "the most magnificent contribution of a nation's unselfishness ever recorded in the history of the world." Comparing our heady new imperialism to no less a personage than Jesus Christ, Harding professed that "we ought to go on with the same thought that impelled Him who brought a plan of salvation to the earth. Rather than confine it to the Holy Land alone, He gathered his disciples about him and said, 'Go ye and preach the gospel to all nations of the earth.'"[11] These words were uttered in the Senate and addressed to "Mr. President and Senators." This pious writ for imperialism was, we can assume, not decried. Jonathan Edwards felt that through the United States "divine providence is preparing the way for the future glorious times of the church, where Satan's kingdom shall be overthrown throughout the whole habitable globe."[12] Empire theory dressed in the robes of religious mythology.

The Imperial Urge

Close to the surface of this myth-heavy hypocrisy was a very down-to-earth imperial urge. When Spain was ready for peace, President McKinley had instructed the Secretary of the Navy to investigate "the desirability of the several islands; the character of their population, coal and other mineral deposits; their harbor and commercial advantages; and in a naval and commercial sense, which of the islands would be the most advantageous."[13] The myths of "manifest destiny" and "benevolent assimilation" were controlling.

In foreign affairs, myth provides the "tissue of lies" needed to justify our real acquisitive aims. In a way that presaged Lyndon Johnson's deceptions leading to the Tonkin Bay Resolution and George W. Bush's claims of Iraq's "weapons of mass destruction," George Kennan illumines the mythic

elements in our decision to enter the Spanish-American War. The causes regularly cited for this war are the extreme harshness of Spain's Cuban policy, the leaked and published letter of the Spanish minister in Washington that insulted President McKinley, and the sinking of the USS *Maine*. These causes, however, do not explain the consequent military outburst. A new government had just come to power in Spain that seemed more moderate in its attitudes toward Cuba; the imprudent minister was immediately removed with proper apologies; and, as Kennan says of the *Maine*:

> There has never been any evidence that the Spanish government had anything to do with the sinking of the vessel. . . . Spanish authorities, as well as our own consul-general in Havana, had begged us not to send the vessel there at that time for the very reason that they were afraid this might lead to trouble. The Spanish government did everything in its power to mitigate the effects of the catastrophe, welcomed investigation, and eventually offered to submit the whole question of responsibility to international arbitration—an offer we never accepted.[14]

Possibilities of fruitful negotiations with Spain were ignored. Alternatives to war were bypassed. Something other than a direct perception of the reality of the situation was operating. The same thing would later be present in our entrance into wars in Vietnam, Afghanistan, and Iraq. Myth dislocates our fact-finding talents and also desensitizes our gentler feelings. After the 9/11 bombings on the Twin Towers in New York and the Pentagon in 2001, myth-spawning rage abounded. Columnist Ann Coulter, writing for the *National Review*, unleashed the following comment: "This is no time to be precise about locating the exact individuals directly involved in this particular terrorist attack. . . . We should invade their countries, kill their leaders and convert them to Christianity. We weren't punctilious about locating and punishing only Hitler and his top officers. We carpet-bombed German cities; we killed civilians. That's war. This is war."[15]

But it was not just a writer speaking from the frenetic right fringe of society who vented the need for unrestrained massacre. U.S. Senator John McCain, on October 26, 2001, said we should "shed a tear" (not multiple tears) for the innocents to be killed in the forthcoming invasion of Iraq. But he urged that, having briefly indulged this minimal debt to decency, we should then "get on with the business of killing our enemies as quickly as we can, and as ruthlessly as we must. We did not cause this war. Our enemies did, and they are to blame for the deprivations and difficulties it occasions. They are to blame for the loss of innocent life. They are to blame for the geopolitical problems confronting our friends and us. We can help repair the damage of war. But to do so, we must destroy the people who started it."[16]

Washed away in this mythic, rage-fueled surge were all humane reservations about **noncombatant immunity** and the moral duty in "just war theory" to avoid "collateral damage." McCain's comments reveal "a cold willingness to kill innocents on the other side of the world—and then assign the blame to others."[17] Myths allow persons and nations to behave like sociopaths and to call their condition patriotism.

Myths as Mutants

Myths that grip a society can change with such rapidity and to such contradictory positions that

THINKING CRITICALLY

Voices from those outside our mythic vision seem to come from another world, as in this poem published in an African American newspaper in January 1943. It was entitled "The Draftee's Prayer."

Dear Lord, today
I go to war.
To fight, to die
Tell me what for?

Dear Lord, I'll fight
I do not fear.
Germans or Japs
My fears are here
America!

17.2

an individual who did the same would be recommended for psychiatric care. For example, our attitude toward the Germans in the beginning of this century was quite benign. They were perceived as industrious and clever folk. They helped the Wright brothers build the first airplane. Then came the war. The *Lusitania* was sunk, and even though it became known later that it was carrying munitions, this disaster became an unambiguous symbol of German perfidy.[18] Suddenly, all the symbols changed. The Germans were Huns. Killing them was redemption for the earth. Even the German language became taboo in many parts of this country and sauerkraut had to be called "liberty cabbage." Then the war ended, and with the imposition of unrealistic reparations on the Germans, our crusading spirit was sated; the Huns left and the Germans returned—even the sauerkraut came back. We were slow to react to the demonic qualities of Hitler, but when we did the Germans became Huns again. Today they are once again revered international partners.

In studies done in 1942 and again in 1966, respondents in the United States were asked to choose from a list of adjectives those that best described the people of Russia, Germany, and Japan. In 1942, the Germans and the Japanese, who were then enemies, were seen as "warlike," "treacherous," and "cruel." None of these adjectives was chosen for the Russians, who were then allies. By 1966 the Germans and Japanese were no longer treacherous or warlike or cruel. These adjectives now described the Russians.[19] Saddam Hussein went from being an ally against Iran and a beneficiary of American aid to being the devil incarnate and a cause for war. Pity the psychiatrist who would take a nation as a patient.

The Mythologized Woman

Often historical circumstances lay the foundations for myth. The myth of "woman," which is belatedly coming under searing social critique, shows that. Because a man does not get pregnant and cannot nurse a baby, in most societies he was the more natural candidate to leave the cave and go forth to meet the challenges of the hunt or of self-defense. Growing out of this, there emerged in history the myth that a woman is essentially a creature of *die Küche und die Kinder*; "cooking and children" are the realities that define her, and when she is engaged in these contexts, her true being is accurately reflected. Domesticity, then, became woman's identifying essence in the view that this deep-rooted myth communicates.

The belatedly obsolescent word *spinster* shows the force of the myth, especially when compared to *bachelor*. The bachelor, provided he is not prissy and effeminate (another myth-laden concept), may be admired for the very absence of marriage. His male friends, married or not, are less likely to be anxious to "find somebody for him." He is not a truncated person because of his single state. Although this is changing slowly, the unmarried woman cut off from the child-filled kitchen is considered a creature exiled from her natural habitat. She lacks the reality that symbolizes her meaning. As the first epistle to Timothy puts it, "She will be saved through motherhood" (1 Tim. 2:15).[20]

Even in classic Catholic spirituality, where virginity is in high esteem, nuptial imagery is often employed to explain the nun's dignity—she is "the spouse of Christ."[21]

When deep myths die, civilizations tremble. This is seen today in the heated resistance to women's reproductive rights. When women insist, *pace* 1 Timothy, that they can be saved by more than motherhood, patriarchies are threatened. Old patriarchal enemies are bonding as friends against this new threat of free women defined as persons and not as brood mares. For instance, at the United Nations the Vatican and conservative Muslim nations, after fourteen centuries of murderous battling, have conspired against any liberalization regarding family planning. I submit that the perceived threat of liberated woman is at the root of this new unholy and surprising alliance.[22]

The Myth of Development

Contemporary orthodoxy has divided the world up neatly into "developed" or "developing." Both terms are epics of mendacity. Both are laden with favorable value judgments: it is good to be developing, and it is better yet to be developed. Both falsely assume the infinity of earth's resources. Though improvement of the human condition is an ancient dream, "development" in modern usage is traced by some to Harry Truman's inaugural address as president in 1949. There, with fascism defeated, the world's chance for prosperity had arrived. With malice toward none, Truman spoke of the "improvement and growth of underdeveloped areas." This birthed the dichotomy of "developed" and "developing." At first the terms were defined in terms of "production" through modern scientific means.[23] The limits of planet Earth were ignored in this adolescent outburst of postwar euphoria. No one talked "sustainable development." That came later and was enshrined at the World Summit of 1992. This was a bit of maturing progress, though "sustainable" was not always shorn of the illusions of infinity or of the "growth is good" conviction.

Reality cares to differ. As Edward O. Wilson says, "The key elements of natural capital, Earth's arable land, ground water, forests, marine fisheries, and petroleum, are ultimately finite . . . for the rest of the world to reach United States levels of consumption with existing technology would require four more planet Earths."[24] The World Bank and the International Monetary Fund consider Thailand a showpiece of "development." Bangkok is filled with the hardware of "development," including cars. As a result of this mindless process, the average speed of vehicles in Bangkok is six miles per hour. "In Bangkok, the average worker loses the equivalent of forty-four working days a year sitting in traffic."[25] Cornell University professor David Pimentel and his colleagues argue that no more than two billion people could enjoy a standard of living comparable to that of central Europe or the United States.[26] "The people of the Netherlands consume the output equivalent of fourteen times as much productive land as is contained within its own borders."[27] It makes up the difference by extracting from other parts of the world.

Therein is the lie of the word *developing*: when Zimbabwe "develops," where will it find the equivalent of fourteen Zimbabwes to draw upon to supplement its own production potential? *In development mythology, growth is divinized while sharing is downsized.* Ultimately, the mythology of

development is reducible to the exploitation of the weak by the powerful. "Lawrence Summers in his capacity as chief economist of the World Bank argued that it is economically most efficient for the rich countries to dispose of their toxic wastes in poor countries, because poor people have both shorter life spans and less earning potential than wealthy people."[28] (After massive criticism, Summers claimed he meant it as an ironic counterpoint rather than an actual proposal. Perhaps his comments on women's scientific ineptitude while he was president of Harvard were another playful bit of irony. Perhaps.)

At any rate, the thought was not a new one. Cecil Rhodes (of Rhodesia) said: "We must find new lands from which we can easily obtain raw materials and at the same time exploit the cheap slave labor that is available from the natives of the colonies. The colonies would also provide a dumping round for the surplus goods produced in our factories."[29]

At their moral core, *developed* and *developing* are the new strategic euphemisms for rich and poor.

Myth and Historiography

Myth relates to the epistemological fact that new information is not written on a *tabula rasa*. It is

---

THINKING CRITICALLY

"Classical Western cultural traditions, which were codified between 500 B.C.E. and 800 C.E, and of which Christianity is a major expression, have justified and sacralized relationships of domination. In particular, the way these cultures have construed the idea of the male monotheistic God, and the relation of this God to the cosmos as its Creator, have reinforced symbolically the relations of domination of men over women, masters over slaves, and male ruling class humans over animals, and over the earth. Domination of women has provided a key link, both socially and symbolically, to the domination of earth, hence the tendency in patriarchal cultures to link women with earth, matter, and nature, while identifying males with sky, intellect, and transcendent spirit."

—Rosemary Radford Ruether, *Gaia and God*

17.3

poured into mental molds, into well-dug-in channels of knowing and cataloging. Memory is not a pure mirroring of what was but a fitting of the past into patterns we inherit. One of the most striking examples of this centers on the person and the work of one Joachim of Flora.

Joachim's Trinitarian Symbolism

Though Joachim is not a household name today, Eric Voegelin argues that "Joachim created the aggregate of symbols which govern the self-interpretation of modern political society to this day."[30] Joachim broke with other conceptions of the course of **history** and applied the symbol of the Trinity as a master rubric. He speculated that the history of humankind had three periods corresponding to the three persons of the Trinity. The first period in history was the period of the Father. The second period, beginning with Christ, was the age of the Son; and the final period will be the age of the Spirit. The three ages will be characterized by improvement; things keep getting better. (This is at the antipodes of the ancient myth that the golden age has passed and we are in dismal decline.)

Joachim's trinitarian symbolism took off in a way he never could have imagined in his most egotistical moment. In effect, he gave birth to a myth in which history would be best understood as a sequence of three ages in which the last would be the ultimate in fulfillment. Voegelin mentions some of the applications of Joachim's master rubric that have extended into our own time.

As variations of this symbol are recognizable the humanistic and encyclopedist periodization of history into ancient, medieval, and modern history; Turgot's and Comte's theory of a sequence of theological, metaphysical, and scientific phases; Hegel's dialectic of the three states of freedom and self-reflective spiritual fulfillment; the Marxian dialectic of the three stages of primitive communism, class society,

and final communism; and finally, the National Socialist symbol of the Third Realm.[31]

Voegelin sees further reflections of Joachim's vision in the Franciscan revival, which saw St. Francis of Assisi as the leader of the final spiritual age. It also shows through in Dante's speculation on the leader of the new spiritual age, in Machiavelli's Prince, and in the secularized supermen of social theorists like the Marquis de Condorcet, Auguste Comte, and Karl Marx. Joachim's final age would be marked by the withering away of the church and the development of men into a community of the spiritually perfect who can live together without dependence on institutional structuring. Voegelin finds traces of this in medieval and Renaissance sects, in the Puritan churches of the saints, and, in secular dress, in the "Marxian mysticism of the realm of freedom and the withering-away of the state."[32] It is also a discernible component of the contemporary faith in democracy and in the myth of American messianic destiny that sends America storming around the globe, forcibly imposing its fulfilling dream of what the final days must look like.

The Myth of Modernity

Joachim also had a role to play in shaping the modern myth of modernity. *Modern* is a weighted word. Etymologically, it comes from *hodiernus, hodie*—that is, it refers to today, to that which is now existing. It was originally a term to distinguish present realities from the past, as in the expression "our most gracious queen modern," where it did not signify that the queen was "up to date" but that she was the queen at this time. Gradually, however, the term picked up normative connotations. Not to be modern is to be imperfect. The related word is *passé*, which carries strong impressions of turning up one's nose at that which is so described. Direct lineage to Joachim could not easily be established in this linguistic development, but it can at least be said that the contemporary usage of *modernity* is filled with Joachimite presuppositions.

Modern does not just mean that which is most recent; it means, further, that which is in some way definitive in its excellence. It certainly imports a denial of our relative primitivity. Morally speaking, judging from the chaotic and inequitable distribution patterns that exist among the human species, it could be said that the word *primitive* describes us well. Geologically speaking, we are, on a scale, in the early beginnings of a twenty-four-hour day. Temporally, the earth has some twelve billion years to go before it is swallowed up in the solar apocalypse—that is, if we behave and do not induce premature planetary calamity. The sense of qualitative or temporal ultimacy, therefore, implied in the word *modern* is certainly mythic. We are only modern in the sense that the term is used in geology and zoology—that is, as belonging to a comparatively recent period in the life history of the world.

The danger in this myth comes from believing that we have reached the definitive phase of human development, the "third realm." So why not rest a bit and wait for its blessing to unfold? Moral imagination and sensitivity could only atrophy in the false peace of such a myth.

Myth-Busting and the Fog of Communication

Myths that serve our interests are like the proverbial "sugar daddy." They keep purveying comfort and we cling to them. Since myths are fact aversive, facts would seem to be the natural antidote. Getting to facts is the problem. In society, facts get to us through many intermediaries. Philosopher Jacques Ellul worried to the point of despair about getting to the facts in the modern "psychopolitical universe." In simpler times, he said, the facts that people knew were of immediate interest and were directly ascertainable. So a case of local bankruptcy, or famine, or a succession crisis in the local lord's family could be observed directly by everyone interested and affected. There was no global or national solidarity, and local events were only remotely connected with national political affairs. At that level a political elite operated, and their doings were normally far removed from the little burgher who heard little about them and that largely from ballads and troubadours.[33]

Now, one might think, global communication has removed that distance and we are the best-informed people in history, linked instantaneously—with live pictures—to all world events. But these new ballad singers and troubadours, like their less technical medieval predecessors, import their own distortions and blind spots, and even the data they bring have to penetrate our thick mental filters and the blocks set up by self-interest. As the prophets of ancient Israel noted, we have eyes that do not see and ears that do not hear—especially when seeing or hearing would inconvenience us. Ellul notes that Admiral Karl Doenitz's diary indicates with some plausibility that he did not know what went on in the Nazi concentration camps even as late as 1945. Many would say that Doenitz was guilty of a contrived naïveté. Not so fast, says Ellul. Many disagreeable facts do not register in the political world of indirect knowledge. Indeed, many agreeable facts do not register in the public mind. Public opinion "obeys mysterious rules, secret motives and forms and deforms itself irrationally."[34]

Facts register when ensconced myths do not filter them out. Stereotypes and propaganda have the greatest success in the modern psychopolitical universe. Symbols replace experience. Facts that jeopardize the reigning symbol system simply dissolve. Every society has, in equivalency, its concentration camp secrets, secrets that will not be evidenced in the diaries of the people. In the United States in the mid-1990s, 22 percent of children lived below the poverty level. In Sweden that figure was 3 percent; in the Czech Republic, 6 percent. In sub-Saharan Africa, the infant mortality rate for children under five is 175 per 1,000; in the industrialized countries it is around six.[35] These deadly facts are as close as one's computer, closer than the concentration camps were to Doenitz, but they do not register in the psychopolitical universe of citizens or affect their lives, religious practices, or voting patterns.

This does not mean that myths are to be viewed as inexorably overwhelming. What is required first of all by sound ethics is consciousness of the mythic bent of our knowing. Acknowledgment is the beginning of criticism. The very forces that enhance the creation of myths can demythologize. The shrinkage of the planet through communication and mobility thrusts us against competing cultures and worldviews. The kind of soporific enclosure that nourishes and preserves myths is now hard to come by, but the desire to avoid unwelcome information functions apace even in this mass communications age. Although myths in collision are less secure, they retain their stubborn fiber in any context. A chastening walk through history is sometimes the best way to puncture myths. An example drawn from the past is a parable of the pain to be experienced by those who blow whistles on beloved myths.

Mundus vult decipi: People Want to Be Deceived

On March 13, 1842, the Reverend Sylvester Judd delivered a discourse to the people of his Unitarian church in Augusta, Maine. Judd's words were published under the copious title *A Moral Review of the Revolutionary War or Some of the Evils of That Event Considered.* As the title can suggest, Judd was accosting a heavily mythologized event.

In his address he criticized the motives of the colonists for going to war, suggested that the goals of the war could have been peacefully achieved, deplored the barbaric behavior of the American freedom fighters, and excoriated our genocidal treatment of the Indians. When he gave the address, Judd was the chaplain of the House of Representatives and the Senate of the state of Maine. One day later, he received the following communication:

> State of Maine,
> House of Representatives, March 14, 1842
> Ordered, That Rev. Mr. Judd be dismissed as chaplain of this House.
> Read and Passed. Attest: Wm. T. Johnson, Clerk.[36]

When Facts Are Not Facts

Judd adds that "a note of similar import was received from the Senate."[37] Judd was charged with libeling the patriots of the revolution. In the published introduction of his discourse, he says in his own defense (writing in the third person): "In the conduct of the discourse, he has confined himself chiefly to facts; facts which are a matter of historical record, facts which in the copiousness of the references are open to every one's revisions. If there be any sentiments in the discourse, they are the sentiments of facts . . . if any libel it is the libel of facts. He took the facts as he found them, too stubborn things to be winked out of sight, and he presented them as he found them, hoping that the facts, and the facts alone, would have weight with his hearers."[38] Judd would discover, in the language of a later day, that the facts would not be perceived as facts in the psychopolitical universe of his time.

It is illuminating to rehearse just a few of the things that Judd recounted in his heavily footnoted discourse. He first of all pointed out that the British contracted huge debts as a result of the Seven Years' War with France. The taxes that so aggrieved some of the colonists were, he argues, within reasonable limits in view of the great expanses of rich land that the colonists got after the French defeat. He speaks of the "dictatorship of Washington" and the absolute despotism that reigned in this country for the space of six months.[39] During this period and beyond it, the army was empowered to take what it wanted from people and to arrest and confine anyone who would appear to be "disaffected to the American cause."[40] He quoted accounts of the torture of soldiers and civilians by the revolutionary army, the popular weaknesses of support for the revolution, and the corruption of the officers and political leaders.

Judd was particularly emphatic about the abuse of the Indians. "They did not tax the Indians, without representation, but exterminated them and planted themselves in their territories."[41] He describes the treatment of the Six Nations of Indians who lived in New York. These Indians were "in the way of the western lands that had been promised to such Americans as would join the war." It was determined in the language of the times to "chastize these savages." General Washington ordered some troops under General Sullivan on this expedition. Judd relates the story:

> "The Six Nations," says De Witt Clinton, "were a peculiar and extraordinary people, contradistinguished from the mass of the Indian nations, by great attainments in polity, in negotiation, in eloquence and in war." They inhabited the beautiful and fertile valley of the Genesee River. They had several towns, and many large villages, laid out with considerable regularity. They had framed houses, some of them well finished, having chimneys and painted. They had broad and productive fields, orchards of apple, pear and peach trees. . . . Churches to the true God had been erected in their villages. Some of them were attached, as well as they could be, to the Americans. Sullivan, as I have said, started against them with peremptory instructions from General Washington not to listen to propositions of peace until he should have "very thoroughly completed the destruction of their settlements." The American army approached the valley of the Genesee, which, says the historian, they beheld with astonishment and delight. "The town of Genesee contained one hundred and twenty-eight houses, mostly large and quite elegant. It was beautifully situated, almost encircled with a clear flat, extending miles around, over which extensive fields of corn were waving, together with every kind of vegetable that could be conceived. But the entire army was soon engaged in destroying it, and the axe and the torch soon transformed the whole of that beautiful region from the character of a garden to a scene of drear and sickening desolation. Forty Indian towns . . . were destroyed . . . the Indians were hunted like wild beasts till neither house, nor fruit tree, nor field of corn, nor inhabitant remained in the whole country. . . . I would add that General Washington after this received among the Indians the name of town destroyer, and in their bitter complaints against him they say, when "your name is heard, our women look behind them and turn pale, and our children cling close to the necks of their mothers."[42]

The Fate of Revisionist History

Judd's revisionist history fell with drastic suddenness upon the beautiful people of Augusta. His facts might, as he admitted, be contested by some on certain points. This, however, would imply a rational debate—something that obviously did not take place between the delivery of the address on March 13 and the reaction of the legislators on March 14. Judd was attacking the sacral myths of the people. He was also speaking to persons who were beneficiaries of the Indian repression. The actual historic facts had become irrelevant. Thus, he could be dismissed with an expeditiousness that is hardly typical of the performance of any legislative body.

I have said that these myths were sacral. This compounded Judd's problems because of the peculiar power that accrues to the sacred and the religious. Religion, even in its perverted manifestations, has phenomenal power. As Huston Smith says, "wherever religion comes to life it displays a startling quality; it takes over. All else, while not silenced, becomes subdued and thrown without contest into a supporting role."[43]

Some whistle blowers have more success in unseating myths. The Flemish physician Vesalius turned the study of anatomy around in 1543 with his book *The Structure of the Human Body.* Be-

fore this time, in what is a sorry lesson on human epistemology, "anatomists had generally held that the writings of Galen, dating from the second century A.D., contained an authoritative description of all human muscles and tissues. They had indeed dissected cadavers, but had dismissed those not conforming to Galen's description as somehow abnormal or not typical."[44] Galen's views had functioned as a myth functions by becoming a data-resistant interpretive screen. Vesalius broke through to reality and thus became the symbol of the myth breaker, as Galen was the symbol of myth. Sound ethics should presume that there are upon our minds the effective ghosts of more than one Galen, blocking discoveries and preventing the growth of moral consciousness.

Summary of Key Themes

- Myth analysis is a prime task of ethics.
- Myth has the power to control the consciousness and the policies of a society.
- Ideologies marshal myths to impose a systematic interpretation of political life.
- Religion is often enlisted to brace myths.
- Empires require effective myths to achieve extended control and to mask their true intentions.
- Myths mutate, turning former enemies into allies and vice versa.
- We tend to remythologize as we demythologize.
- The myth of "woman" is paradigmatic of the oppressive use of myth.
- Myth operates also in economics on issues such as the meaning of "development."
- Facts and myths compete in historiography, or the study of history

Key Terms

Historiography / history
Ideology
Myth

Questions for Discussion

1. How do you define feminism? Can a man really be a feminist?
2. Do myth-based prejudices interlock and interconnect? Is there a link between sexism, heterosexism, and speciesism?
3. Karl Marx said that the powerful in any society protect their privileges with dominating myths and ideas. "The ruling ideas of an era are always the ideas of its ruling class." Ethicist John Raines says, "Ideas have the power to rule and they do so with more subtlety, and therefore with more effectiveness, than guns." Identify some of the common myths and ideas that protect upperclass privilege today.

Suggestions for Further Reading

Oelschlaeger, Max, ed. *Postmodern Environmental Ethics.* Albany: State University of New York Press, 1995.

Ruether, Rosemary Radford. *Gaia and God: An Eco-Feminist Theology of Earth Healing.* New York: HarperCollins, 1992.

Zinn, Howard. *A People's History of the United States: 1492 to Present.* New York: Harper Perennial, 1995.

Obstacles to Right Thinking

Forbidden Memories

In 1882, in a speech at the Sorbonne, Ernest Renan observed that "forgetting" is "a crucial factor in the creation of a nation."[1] In creating a national unifying narrative, certain difficult memories of unseemly events have to be erased. As Renan said, these include the wholesale slaughter of certain ethnic and religious groups within the claimed national borders.[2] These must be whitewashed off the screen of public consciousness. There are many tricks on the way to calculated oblivion. Nations specialize in those tricks regarding state-sponsored violence, with the inevitable mayhem that war entails. State-inflicted slaughter fits no national narrative, since every nation spins its own self-serving *Aeneid*. Neither the government nor the people can face with candor the horrors of war. And so we forget with a vengeance.

Marilyn Young, in her essay "Remembering to Forget," looks at an appalling American atrocity from the Korean War, called by historians "the forgotten war,"[3] and shows how it was immediately repressed with forced strategic forgetfulness. When this story would not go away, resurfacing in all its repugnance and offending the established American myth that the My Lai massacre in Vietnam was the only atrocity in recent wars, rationalization took over. The massacre at No Gun Ri in Korea, however, did happen. Korean refugees, driven from their homes by American bombs that had leveled their cities and towns, were herded onto a railroad track, where U.S. planes then began strafing them. "Running for their lives, dragging their children, abandoning the dead and dying, people took shelter in a culvert beneath the tracks. American soldiers then opened direct fire on the people in the culvert. One Korean survivor, Chung Koo Hun, told a *Washington Post* reporter that American soldiers then walked among the wounded, 'checking every wounded person and shooting them if they moved.'"[4]

Marilyn Young dissects a revisionist essay written for the *Wall Street Journal* by James Webb, once Secretary of the Navy and now a U.S. senator. By the time he finished his rewrite, the facts had been so smudged that guilt was everywhere but where it belonged. He brushed it off with a blithe *c'est la guerre* (or "that's war"). Webb regretted that the incident had been dredged up again and he blamed rapacious lawyers "trying to squeeze millions out of a long-ago tragedy of the sort that seems always to accompany battles fought where other people live." As Young comments, "Some readers might pause to wonder what Americans were doing fighting their battles in someone else's country."[5]

President George W. Bush forbade pictures of the flag-draped coffins of soldiers coming home from Iraq, which successfully pushed the war off the front pages. General Tommy Franks, when asked about civilian Iraqi casualties, said we do not do body counts. Statistics are more forgettable than photographs. President Barack Obama has reversed this policy, allowing photographs if permitted by the next of kin.

Nations are more prone to selective amnesia than individuals. The United States and Israel can serve as examples of this. Both of them suffer from suppressed memories about their origins. At their founding, both engaged in ethnic cleansing, the removal of long-tenured populations to make room for the new nations. Native Americans were treated genocidally and their survivors were quarantined in reservations. Similarly, Israel's founding in 1948, some 700,000 Palestinians were forcibly removed from their homes in the territory now claimed by the still-expanding Jewish state. That event, called *Al Nakba* (the catastrophe) by the Palestinians, is as painful for them as the memory of the Holocaust is to Jews. As long as forgetfulness of these events is socially enforced, ethical evaluation is stymied.

In the United States, as we saw in chapter 17, when the Reverend Sylvester Judd in 1842 tried to recall the crimes against the Indians, he was promptly dismissed. The United States was still firmly in a state of history-denial. Eventually critical ethical thinking supported by good scholarship broke through and the veil was largely lifted from early American atrocities against the native peoples. Ethical memory was allowed to begin its crucial work, and this is making its way into popular culture, where films no longer pit white "cowboys" against "Indians," with the cowboys being the good guys and the savage Indians being the bad guys.

Though it has not had as much time in Israel, ethical critique of Israeli imperialism is emerging, though still as a minority effort. The expansion into Palestinian territory continues in the form of "settlements." The United States and Israel have a uniquely close relationship. Ironically, ethical criticism of Israeli policies toward the Palestinians is sharper, freer, and more abundant in the Israeli press than in the United States, and it is democratically pushed by activist groups in Israel like *Gush Shalom.* Criticism of Israeli policies is still subdued in America, but there too the veil is lifting.

One incident illustrates how effectively forgetfulness can be enforced and the work of ethics blocked. On June 8, 1967, during Israel's six-day war with its neighbors, Israeli planes flew over the USS *Liberty*, a surveillance ship off the coast of Egypt, and identified the ship as American. Later, Israeli planes returned and attacked and torpedoed the ship, killing thirty-four American sailors and seriously wounding 171 other members of the crew. At first President Johnson protested, but then, taken up with his own failing war in Vietnam, the incident was buried and remains the only such incident never investigated by Congress. Calls to finally investigate it while some of the survivors of the USS *Liberty* are still alive go unheeded. The work of ethics, however, is commencing. In books like *The Attack on the Liberty: The Untold Story of Israel's Deadly 1967 Assault on a U.S. Spy Ship* (New York: Simon & Schuster, 2009), James Scott joins others who are using newly declassified materials to tell the long-suppressed story.

Also, scholars like Marc Ellis, founder and director of the Center for Jewish Studies at Baylor University, joins others, like former president Jimmy Carter, in arguing that the embargo on criticism of Israeli policies and actions is not in the interest of either Israel or the United States. It is surely not in the interest of the Palestinians. It illustrates how the work of ethics can be effectively obstructed by memories deemed inconvenient.[6]

Falling in Love with Mastodons

When anomalies become habitual, they transmogrify into norms. The habitual comforts and breeds addiction. We end up worshiping things that should have been allowed to go extinct and stay that way.

The Mastodon of War

Take that **mastodon**, the idea of war as "the final arbiter," the ace in the hole on which we could always fall back when less effective means had failed. That is a grand fallacy that has had a long reign. The state, indeed, was defined by historian A. J. P. Taylor as "an organization for power . . . i.e. for war."[7] Max Weber said the state can be defined as "the rule of men over men based on the means of legitimate, that is allegedly legitimate, violence."[8] This made the state a confederation of fear.

In fact, war has not been the "final arbiter," even though written history makes it look that way. William the Conqueror did not conquer. He simply walked in, and "combat played no role in the Glorious Revolution," though historians wrote it up as though it had.[9] The withdrawal of popular consent, not bloodshed, explains the collapse of the Soviet Union as well as the English, American, French, German, and Indian revolutions. As John Adams said of the American Revolution: "The revolution was in the minds of the people and in the union of the colonies, both of which were accomplished before hostilities commenced."[10] Both democracy and dictatorship depend on the consent of the governed. Ultimately a successful democracy is cooperation writ large. One can risk charges of lyricism by saying that democracy is friendship writ large. And friendship involves sharing and cooperative, not coercive, power.

This is the lesson missed by empires. Their fatal flaw is their trust in coercive power exercised militarily, economically, and culturally. But coerced consent is brittle at its core. The prescient John Adams looked at the empires of France, Spain, England, and Holland and said: "They may depend upon it, their present systems of colonization cannot endure. Colonies universally, ardently breathe for independence. No man who has a soul will ever live in a colony under the present establishments one moment longer than necessity compels him."[11]

Still, the idea of "society as military" lingers and grips the popular imagination. War is the pinnacle of patriotic commitment, that which best serves the common good. Imagine a conversation between two old friends who meet after a long time apart. One asks the other: "Your two children, where are they now?" The other replies: "They're both off serving the country." "Oh, are they in Iraq or in Afghanistan?" "No, they are not in the military. John is teaching fourth grade in Richmond, and Mary is a nurse in Seattle." "Service" has been commandeered to mean only killing and getting killed for one's country. There are no parades for teachers and healers, and all too few statues immortalize their service.

> **THINKING CRITICALLY**
>
> The Reverend Bob Edgar, General Secretary of the National Council of Churches, said of right-wing Christians' zeal for war: "What part of 'Blessed are the peace-makers' don't they understand?"
>
> —Bob Edgar, *Middle Church: Reclaiming the Moral Values of the Faithful Majority from the Religious Right*
>
> 18.7

income to go to the top 1 percent: the same occurred by 2008. As John Gray said at the start of the 2008 meltdown, a change has occurred "as far-reaching in its implications as the fall of the Soviet Union, an entire model of government and the economy has collapsed."[13] Past failures were not instructive. Bad ideas can develop momentum, and momentum is blind. Neoliberalism substitutes unfettered freedom for social justice, and it lacks a theory of government. Hence, it has no provider for the common good, the essential function of government and an essential category of ethics. A balance between entrepreneurial freedom and governmental regulation is healthy.[14] Neoliberalism lacks it.

The Neoliberal Mastodon

Neoliberalism is a weird misnomer, since it is neither new or liberating. It is the *idée fixe* of the right wing. As to its longevity, Richard Hofstadter calls it "the ideology . . . of beneficent cupidity upon which Americans have been nourished since the foundation of the Republic."[12] Neoliberalism is more accurately described as right-wing, ultraconservative greed theory that promises that unleashing greed will create a cornucopia whose treasures will spread out (or trickle down) to all in society and everyone will live happily ever after. The "market" has the role of a god, and its dictates must be given free sway. Darwinian competition is the rule of life, and, of course, as in any competition, some win and some lose.

But even the winners lose as money is sucked to the top with the base increasingly starved and unable to pay its mortgages or make purchases. In 1928, this greed theory allowed 25 percent of

Other Mastodons

Other mastodons are clung to. Some are silly and impractical and could be easily jettisoned. The Electoral College can cut the legs out from under the popular vote. It traces its roots back to a time when slaves were counted as three-fifths of a person. The result of this queer device is that three times since the Civil War it has awarded the presidency to the loser of the popular vote. Blind social momentum leaves us with it still. Add to that the anachronism of voting on a single day, and that a Tuesday in the middle of a work week, and the dumbing power of socialized habit is manifest.[15]

Stoic philosophy planted some bizarre ideas in Western culture. It was a broad-based philosophy that served the good-order needs of the Roman Empire. Its spokespersons spanned the society of the time, as illustrated by the fact that one was Marcus Aurelius, an emperor, and another Epictetus, a slave. What it sorely lacked was a respect for feeling and emotion. As a result, they reached the conclusion that sex was primarily for procreation. This led to the eventual banning of contraception and to the heteronormativity that bans homo-erotic love unions. Along the way in history, this picked up the prestige of religious adoption, but this exemplifies the stubborn rootage of a bad *idée fixe* and the rule of ancient mastodons.

Thinking Through Moods

Mood is simple to recognize and hard to define. Children learn early on when is and when is not a good time to ask. They sense moods. Animals, too, can pick up on it. Mood affects how we see, and its influence might at times be controlling. Mood is a conditioner of our subjectivity. It can sharpen our vision or place a veil between us and reality. It can also induce a darkness that sends us back apologizing later when another mood ensues and lends light. The cognitive effect of mood, then, is not always negative. But since it can be negative and since mood is such an omnipresence, it merits consideration among the **hazards of moral discourse**.

Enough and More

A type-A American tourist was in Ireland trying to relax. Since he was also an amateur artist, he set up his easel each day by the little dock in a Donegal town. He observed the doings of a lobster fisherman who arrived around ten each morning to begin his day. His preparations were slow, painfully slow for this tense American observer. He chatted with every passerby, paused to make tea, and smoked his cob pipe. Then, toward eleven, he pushed off. Around three in the afternoon, he returned with his catch. Again there was tea, the pipe, and chatting. At last he took his catch to the square to sell his lobsters. So it went day by day.

The type-A observer could bear it no more. He approached the fisherman with the intensity of a prosecuting attorney, his questions on the ready. His first question focused on supply. "If you went out earlier and came back later, could you catch more lobsters?" With a quizzical look—and slowly, for the man had lots of time—the fisherman replied, "Yes, thanks be to God, there are plenty of the lobsters." The observer turned then to the issue of demand and marketing. "Could you sell more if you caught more?" Tapping his pipe slowly, the man replied, "Ah, yes. They love the lobsters. You can always sell the lobsters." The observer moved in for the kill. "Then why don't you do that?" With a patient smile the man replied, "Enough is enough, you know." Of course, his questioner did not know. What the man was saying was material for the erstwhile House Committee on Un-American Activities based on a culture and a mood where enough is just the beginning.

One senses that if that fisherman had a daughter who was a physician, she might be quicker to say enough is enough in treatment of patients. Mood affects all of life's decisions and one's sense of balance. In the twenty years since that conversation between the harried tourist and the leisurely fisherman, Ireland's economic development may have made for many mood changes.

> ## THINKING CRITICALLY
>
> Alfred North Whitehead said the conversion of the Roman Empire to Christianity led to a "deeper kind of idolatry," an idolatry exceeding that of pagan polytheism. By this he meant "the fashioning of God in the image of the Egyptian, Persian, and Roman imperial rulers. . . . The church gave unto God the attributes that belonged exclusively to Caesar."
>
> —Alfred North Whitehead, *Process and Reality: An Essay in Cosmology*
>
> 18.2

Corresponding changes would follow in ethical judgments elsewhere in the moralscape.

Another story is from a traveler in Morocco.

A dazzling sun falls on the whitewashed dwellings of Tangiers. The sea is turquoise, and behind the dwellings rise high and noble palms. The Mediterranean clime inspires a feeling of timelessness. Tomorrow is just an extension of today; it has no separate, threatening identity. It would be a strange man or woman who could live principally by calculation in Tangiers. These people wait long periods for each other and are patient with nature. They give themselves fully to the present moment. The future does not mortgage them; the past sits naturally upon them and grows within them. In the peace of Morocco, life and the world seem fully embodied in the tangibles that can be felt in the present moment. A line of Camus hangs on my mind: "I am learning that there is no superhuman happiness, no eternity outside the curve of the days." . . . The morning mood on Tangiers' main boulevard has no throb or rush. People move as languidly as in the hours after lunch. The shops open desultorily one by one. . . .[16]

The story is one of mood. Obviously, in the background is an experience of another mood and another place and clime, where the shops do not open desultorily one by one and where impatient achievers, mortgaged to the future, rush through the present almost as though they were in flight from it. The mood of Tangiers is different; it is easier to say that than to say what makes it so. The weather, the degree of cultural homogeneity, the religious faith of the people, hard-learned historical lessons about the futility of spastic activism, a sense of hope, or maybe its opposite. All of the above and more may enter in some part into the mood so sharply felt by the foreign visitor to Morocco. But whatever the causes of the mood, the effects are many and significant. Different things

are prized and different expectations reign over human affairs. Tracing the impact of all of this would not just be a cultural study of ethics, but a study of economics, politics, art, and psychology in Morocco. Mood casts long shadows over all our valuing, whether those values be aesthetic, commercial, or specifically moral.

Defining Mood

Mood is broader than myth (and indeed includes myths, which can spawn moods); it cannot be as neatly defined. In fact, it is description rather than definition that we can bring to this rich term. *Mood is an affective and intellectual mode of attunement to an environment.* It signifies an emotional outlook and a bent of mind; it could be transient and personal or a settled part of culture.

A mood reflects the accents within the psychic air. Certain things are cherished and certain things are ignored. In the mood of the 1950s and 1960s, ecological concerns were seen as idiosyncratic. Bite-backs from nature have changed the mood. The mood of most American blacks before the 1950s was one in which some aspirations were simply excluded by what was seen to be the nature of things. Paolo Freire's work on conscientization opened up the minds of the poor in South America to the fact that their deprivation was not an ontological and immutable datum. For this reason, the forces of oppressive government were instinctively shrewd enough to challenge and ban his work, since he would transform the mood of the passive poor. In the mood of earlier presidents, journalists turned a blind eye to the sexual misdeeds of their leaders. The mood had changed and President Bill Clinton failed to note it, to his undoing.

Sometimes the collection of our deeds creates a consuming mood. Hannah Arendt notes a fundamental change in attitudes resulting from the successes of science. She writes: "The radical change in moral standards occurring in the first century of the modern age was inspired by the needs and ideals of its most important group of people, the new scientists; and the modern cardinal virtues—success, industry, and truthfulness—are at the same time the greatest virtues of modern science."[17] I would dispute that "truthfulness" has cardinal status in modern science or culture. But certainly, the heady discoveries of science in the nineteenth century created a mood filled with airs of infallibility that affected the people of science, state, and church. The spread of the Internet creates a new mood of interconnectedness with an unfolding impact not unlike the discovery of writing.

Those who ignore the emotive-cognitive pull of moods and the accompanying myths are as handicapped as prisoners unless they know of such a force and are disposed to test for its presence.

Belief and Mood

Belief is a normal state of human beings, whether it takes the form of religion or not. As Alexis de Tocqueville declared, "Unbelief is an accident, and faith is the only permanent state of humankind." And belief is not limited to formal religion. Even the philosopher and the scientist are filled with it. Again Tocqueville: "There is no philosopher in the world so great but that he believes a million things on the faith of other people and accepts a great many more truths than he demonstrates."[18] We have neither the time nor the power to demonstrate all that we need to accept to make life feasible and possibly good. And, therefore, we believe. There is nothing irrational in this, as I have argued above (see chapter 4). Belief is an achievement of discerning affectivity. Although it may be utterly misguided and foolish, it may also have access to truth that reason cannot reach.

What we believe and what we then dare hope for set the tone and make the mood in which we know and evaluate. Those who believe little and hope little will see life through dark eyes. Their mood will be chill and self-preservative. Creativity will not be their forte, for creativity proceeds

from mood—not inexorably or without that discontinuity that is the mark of genius—but mood relates to those preconditions that set the stage for the creative leap. In the words of an Irish poet, there are those who are "born of homes that never bred a dream." Moods, too, can be like those sterile dreamless homes.

The Autonomy of Mood

Though it is true that our decisions and commitments can importantly affect our moods, it must be said that mood is never entirely of our making. To some degree it comes upon us for good or for ill. Certainly we cannot reason ourselves into one or out of one. The arrival and the departure of the mood have their own pace. Mood is, after all, affected by other people and even by such unmanageable things as weather and climate. When Montesquieu published his *Spirit of the Laws* in 1748, he reported his conclusion of seventeen years of work: that a large variety of factors have to be considered to understand the laws of any people. One has to look to the economic facts of those people as well as to what could be called their character. Beyond this, Montesquieu said it is necessary to look at their climatic conditions, for, as he saw it, the climate helps to form the character and passions of a people. The British are simply not like the Sicilians, and laws fitted for one would hardly serve the good of the other. Montesquieu did not see the climate factor as utterly determinative of the spirit of their laws and institutions, but as a clear influence. Similarly, I would say that climate and geography are factors that may enter into and shape mood. Climate can influence the tempo of life, as well as our choice of symbols, our closeness to or alienation from the earth, and our dependence on technology. All of these factors have resonance in the thinking and feeling subject.

Mood also relates to the action-reaction pendulum in human values. Although we are always in search of the elusive center that we call balance, human history is marked by broad and eccentric swings. We move from Victorian discomfort with sex to contemporary pornography in all of its frantic forms. We move from global messianism to isolationist nationalism, from comfort with established values to suspicion of all that is socially structured. So the symbol of the pendulum must again be recalled to understand mood. What we are reacting against is often most revealing of why we are for what we are for. What we are reacting against, as we ride the pendulum from one unbalanced view to another, is also a mood setter of which we cannot afford to be unaware.

Finally, it can be said of mood that it may be transient and ephemeral or enduring, just as it may be personal or somewhat settled into a culture. Sometimes mood will be of little relevance to our evaluation and represent a very minor epistemological consideration. At times it can be controlling. Ethics must remind the valuing animal that he or she is not a smoothly meshing reasoning machine but a buffeted beast who is caught in the swirl of myriad enveloping influences. To ignore all of this and not attempt to get some critical assessment of it represents an unacceptable naïveté.

One of the most common human failings is simplistic **epistemology**. Part of the original sin of everyman is to think that reality is there and we see it with mirrorlike immediacy and reliability. The chastening gospel that ethics must preach is that even mirrors can deceive and that, mirrors aside, we tend to see only what we are willing to see. Myths and moods condition our willingness to see. We are substantially limited by the language and symbols available to us in our time and culture. Individually and collectively, we are prone to infatuation. Knowledge is a process full of hazards that are especially damaging to those who think their path is clear. *It is only when we know how we know that we can begin to be free.*

Short-Circuiting by Way of False Analogy

Paradox, rather than clarity, is often the marker of truth. Exemplifying this, note the truth in both of these statements: *history repeats itself* and *history never repeats itself*. If you insist on only the first of these statements, you commit yourself to a cyclical view of history (*nihil novi sub sole*—"there is nothing new under the sun" [Eccles. 1:9]). You have programmed out surprise. Every new situation is marked by different answers to all the questions in the center of the wheel model, that is, the expository phase of ethics. If you insist on only the second statement, you have deprived yourself of all the lessons of history and are more likely to commit again all of its mistakes. Ethical antennae must be set to the old and the new since unfolding reality is a fluid amalgam (another paradox) of both.

Knowing by way of comparison and **analogy** is not a hazard of moral discourse. It's what we do. As we know, we relate the unknown to the known. Our experience gives us a fund of references to which the mind turns for enlightening comparison when something new presents itself. No two persons will have the same fund of experiences. The Trobriander tribesman and the vacationing heiress will not bring the same ensemble of recollects to bear when they see an impression in the sand. We know out of our histories, and since our histories are unique, there is a unique character to the way each of us knows. (Hence the advisability of consulting many minds in complex moral matters—and in any other matters, too.)

The Hazards of Analogical Knowing

The problem arises when our analogical knowing is based on false analogues. When we are coming to know something new, an ensemble of what I have called recollects is instinctively summoned. Not all of our recollects will be called forth—only those that appear to have similarity to that which is now being known. Herein lies the hazard. We can be so impressed with how similar the new candidate for knowledge is that we overlook the differences. If *B* looks very much like *A*, we might turn our backs on *B* and proceed as though we were talking about *A* and *A* only.

When President Lyndon Johnson justified our invasion of Vietnam, he used the analogy of the European nonresistance to Hitler. He ended up speaking more about Hitler and Europe than about Vietnam, which we were about to invade. He was talking about *A* when he should have been addressing *B*.[19] A debacle ensued. The historical analogy he should have used was to the French imperial experience in Vietnam. So the problem is not with using historical analogies; it is deciding which to use. An atomistic notion of national sovereignty suitable to needs in the seventeenth century beclouds contemporary needs for interdependence and cooperation. The reliance on military power when it can no longer deliver what it promises is another fatal fixation on the past. An appeal to history can actually be the last firm bastion of a closed mind.

At a more personal level, parents might easily use their first child as an analogue for their second without realizing the unique dynamism of this second child. Each child has a different tempo and genetic disposition. If the reality of the first child becomes the domineering analogue, the authentic potential of the second child might be stunted and serious psychic wounds may be inflicted. The answer to "Your sister never did that" is "I am not my sister." (Of course, if you are doing something stupid, your sister's example might be helpfully instructive.

Such is the way of analogies.) Similarly, one business venture might be sidetracked by comparison to an earlier one that is similar but, of course, not identical to the present one. Surgeons may attend more to a past case than the present one, missing the absolute uniqueness of every body and every personal history. This partially explains the widespread phenomenon of "unnecessary surgery." Economic considerations also enter in.[20]

False Analogies to Animal Behavior

Discussions of mercy death, a personal decision to accelerate an ongoing dying process when death becomes friendlier than continuing a dying life, have been sidetracked by the analogy to the Nazi practice of killing off "useless eaters" through state action. Historically, Stoic philosophers, and many Christian thinkers depending on the Stoa, taught that intercourse during pregnancy was wrong. A farmer, after all, does not sow seed in a field that is already planted and growing. The ancients were also generally confident in the sexual continence of pregnant animals and applied this analogy to persons. Pliny thought that few pregnant animals copulate, suggesting that this was more natural. Latching onto this, the Christian Origen condemned those women "who, like animals, serve lust without any restraint; indeed I would not compare them to dumb beasts. For beasts when they conceive know not to indulge their mates further with their plenty."[21] The ancients could match us in dumb analogies.

Modern debates on sexual ethics and same-sex marriage are also impaled on false analogies to animal behavior. The fervor that animates homophobia seeks ill-fated support from zoology, hoping to show that nature requires heteronormativity.

Alas, the desired evidence is not there, and contrary evidence abounds. In his extensive study *Biological Exuberance: Animal Homosexuality and Natural Diversity*, biologist Bruce Bagemihl shows that homosexuality is part of our evolutionary heritage as primates. He reports that more than 450 species regularly engage in a wide range of same-sex activities ranging from copulation to long-term bonding. Even the assumed male/female dimorphism is not fixed in nature. Many animals live without two distinct genders, or with multiple genders. Finding evidence that our preferred social arrangements are exemplified in edifying animal conduct is also doomed. The lovely mallards sometimes form "trio-bonds" with one male and two females or one female and two males.[22] Thus, some analogies can prove disedifying as well as wrongheaded.

Our proclivity to draw too much from comparisons is understandable in view of the gains that are temptingly offered by this indulgence. For one thing, the mind's gnawing hunger for making sense of things is quickly satisfied if the new is exactly like the old. Our minds are comfortable with the familiar, and this comfort can give rise to the level of passion in those whom we classify imperfectly as "conservative." "I have never heard of such a thing" will be seen by such persons as a disqualification. Undoubtedly that objection was raised to all major inventions throughout human history. The reply to it is "Now that you have heard of it, can we get on?"

Abstractly Speaking

We can think again of Jean-Paul Sartre's warning that the greatest evil of which we are capable is to treat as abstract that which is concrete. It is illustrated by the comfortable bishop alleged to have commented: "I know poverty. I have been driven through it." The Russian novelist Fyodor Dostoevski coupled the words "abstract and therefore cruel." Still, abstracting power is the glory of humans. We do not graze like cattle reacting instinctually to particulars. Abstractions, like analogies and metaphors, are essential means of thought. To condemn abstract thinking in one sense is impossible and contradictory, since one could not do so without using abstractions. Abstraction is the soul of theory, the "very life of thought."[23] It is also the very life of creativity. If we could not abstract, we would be prisoners of the status quo. If we could not abstract from the grip of the currently given, we could never perceive what might be. We could discover no ideals. We would be unaware of the constancies that exist even in this infinitely variegated universe. We would have no basis for critique.

However, beware abstractions that have lost their contact with flesh and blood, soil, rock, and air. You can't hug abstractions, and they don't bleed. It is this noxious power of abstraction that leads lexicographers to list such things as "impersonal," "removed," "separate," "abstruse," or "insufficiently factual" as possible meanings of this term.

Abstract language has many seductive powers. Ease in the pursuit of meaning is its first and most obvious lure. How pleasant it is to soar above the gritty complexities of the empirical order and impose meaning through detached abstractions from on high. It takes away the onerous duty of knowing what one is talking about. A return to the facts can embarrass errant abstractions, but if the cognitive mood of the time is not all that concerned with the facts, and if the attendant myths add their special luster to the deceptive abstractions, the abstractions may long endure and prosper. What is even more delightful is that the abstract presentation of truth can often sound impressively learned. Is not abstraction the hallmark of intellectuality? Here, then, is a form of reality avoidance that enjoys the sweetness of prestige.

Abstraction and Propaganda

Note, too, that abstractions are the lifeblood of **propaganda**. Nothing hides your real agenda better than a noble-sounding abstraction. Hitler campaigned on "law and order." Law and order are wonderful but had nothing to do with his agenda. The right-wing attraction to "family values" shows the blind spots that abstractions hide, since among those "family values" we do not find a healthy concern for the environment or a commitment to the work of peace or the breakdown of class and gender bias.

"Terrorism" is, at this writing, the *pièce de résistance* of propagandistic abstraction. It justifies killing occupied peoples without indicting the occupiers, as in Palestine and Iraq. In its most common usage—and its usage is loose—it refers to those who challenge the reigning power. It ignores that states, too, are terrorists. Like its immediate predecessor, that *bête noire* "communism," it is applied promiscuously to totally different realities without empirical differentiation.

Words that describe very concrete reality, such as *war* and *jihad*, can get abstracted and thus defanged, their horror hidden in the unfurling of flags and symbols. In times of danger when fear can be manipulated, as after 9/11, abstractions rule the roost. Thucydides, describing the conditions preceding the Peloponnesian War, complained that the meaning of words no longer had the same relation to things. This he saw as a major mark of the unrest of that time. Words are the houses of our thoughts and abstractions, good and bad, and a study of the use of words is an analytical necessity. Understanding is not limited to words. We know, feel, and intuit more than we could ever say. Still, words are the most common tender in the exchange of thought and information.

Falstaff, in Shakespeare's *Henry IV*, has lessons on the misuse of words, especially in time of war. He saw that the good word *honor* was being asked to cover over abstractly some lethal realities that he was not ready to bear. When battle with all of its call to glory and honor was imminent, the unimpressed Falstaff was reminded by the Prince, "Why thou owest God a death." Upon the Prince's exit, Falstaff declares:

'Tis not due yet, I would be loath to pay Him, before his day. What need I be so forward with him that calls not on me? Well, 'tis no matter. Honor pricks me on. Yea, but how if honor prick me off when I come on? How then? Can honor set to a leg? No. Or an arm? No. Or take away the grief of a wound? No. Honor hath no skill in surgery, then? No. What is honor? A word. What is in that word honor? What is that honor? Air. A trim reckoning! Who hath it? He that died o' Wednesday. Doth he feel it? No. Doth he hear it? No. 'Tis insensible, then? Yea, to the dead. But will it not live with the living? No. Why? Detraction will not suffer it. Therefore I'll none of it. Honor is a mere scutcheon. And so ends my catechism.[24]

There should be an Office of Falstaff in the Pentagon, where words flee from reality as a matter of course. Torture of Inquisition caliber becomes "enhanced interrogation techniques." "National interest," like Falstaff's "honor," can cover a multitude of sins, and a pandemonious retreat becomes "a retrograde action." What villains words can be.

"Making love," a very "concrete" activity, can cover exploitation, dishonesty, and even hostility. "Free trade" can be a healthy economic system of exchange or a writ for muscular economic imperialism. Abstract ideas like "national security" and "making the world safe for democracy," when stripped of their mythic robes, can have a sordid tale to tell. The sly move to change the Department of War to the Department of Defense opened an era of more war-making than the Department of War of yesteryear ever could imagine.

The "Ought-to-Is" Fallacy and Stereotypes

The **"ought-to-is" fallacy** shows abstracting power gone awry. In this fallacy, we can see how abstractions relate to the will and enter the service of its errant purposes. From the willful impression that this is the way things "ought to be," we can abstractly leap to the judgment that this is the way things are, or, in an inverse form of this fallacy, we can be so consumed by what we deem ought to be that we reject what is. The wish, then, is father to the abstraction. A young man (or an old one) may leave the concrete reality of his friend's genuine preferences and conclude—quite abstractly—"She ought to want to have sex with me. Therefore, she does." Subsequent pain and embarrassment may illustrate the rueful process of exorcism in which demonic abstractions are routed by forced immersion in concrete reality. At the political level we might similarly suppose that a nation should want a democratic system of government, and therefore it does. With such abstraction in control, it may take a long time to realize that the nation may be no more ready for democracy than the woman of our previous example was ready for sex—however regrettable this may appear to the abstracting minds in either case.[25]

The ought-to-is fallacy is a relative of the *stereotype*. The stereotype generalizes what is not generalizable. In the stereotype, as in all false abstractions, the specific is blurred in the generic. The existence of genuine variety is ignored. For instance, there is the example of the great American stereotype hidden in the symbol of the "melting pot." Now it has been discovered that the various cultural and ethnic branches have not homogenized into some stereotypical "American." Behind the idea of the melting pot was an abstract notion of nation and community that could not brook cultural pluralism and the real diversities that characterize humanity. This misconceived "ought" could never become an "is."

Selective Virtue

We humans have a devilish talent, *rationalization*. It is visible in toddlerhood and grows steadily in sophistication. We absolutely need it, since no one can think of him- or herself as evil. Flight from blame is no minor failing; it could be the fatal flaw that leads our species to extinction. Chemists in Sweden began to warn of global warming late in the nineteenth century. Their warnings were washed away in a tsunami of rationalization and collective avoidance, aided by greedy short-term interests and propaganda from the energy industry. PhDs funded by affected industries threw dust in the air so we could not see the carbon rising. The results portend virtually irreversible damage to this finite planet. In recent years, Arctic waters opened so that you could pilot a ship from the Atlantic to the Pacific without going through the Panama Canal or around the Cape of Good Hope, something never before possible in recorded human history.[26] In the past century, evidence was no match for our power of avoidance and deviously misdirected moral concerns. Meanwhile, our politicians, at our insistence, assure us that we are a good and a kindly people.

The Evasion Gambit

Beyond the earth wrecking, the evasion gambit takes many forms at all levels of life experience. Fleeing inconvenient moral challenges, we rush to less demanding issues to achieve an aura of rectitude. Right-wing piety agonizes over the death of "the unborn" while cutting essential services for the born. Jean Reith Schroedel, in her study of abortion policies across the fifty states, observes that "states [that] make it difficult for women to have abortions . . . do not help these women provide for the children once born."[27] "Six of the states with the strongest antiabortion laws in the country do not make it a crime for a third-party to kill a fetus."[28] The fetus, in other words, is not their top concern. Such states also "spend less money per pupil on kindergarten through twelfth grade education."[29] The "pro-life" banner, then, is not "pro–born children." Similarly, so-called "pro-life" churches also are on record as opposing equal rights for women."[30] Again, the alleged passion for fetal well-being covers a different agenda that is not friendly toward women or children. "Many pro-life [*sic*] conservative churches also have a poor record on the issue of wife beating. . . . The response of conservative churches [on this issue] has been 'a pervasive holy hush.'"[31] Again: if you are up to mischief in zone *A*, become very mock-virtuous in zone *B*.

The noble Englishman who, in the days of the British Empire, was punctiliously careful to curb his dog and mind the queue was also able to participate in the exploitation of colonized peoples, all with an air of propriety. Businessmen who would never break a local ordinance at home by burning their leaves or not shoveling their walks can go to work and make and cover up decisions that will pollute the air we breathe and the water we need without any troubling compunction. Spouses can justify themselves by noting their fidelity to little things even though they are avoiding the great demands made of those who would build a true marital friendship.

What I call the Elvira Syndrome is another example of displaced moral concern. In the year 309 the Christian church, beginning to find favor in the Roman world, called its leaders together in Elvira, Spain. The Christians were about to move from persecution to preferment under Constantine, and the sect set out to redefine itself. Suddenly, sexuality came to define orthodoxy. As upper-class persons gravitated toward this new religion, concern for the poor and social justice waned. Sexual sins were more serious than the beating of a slave. As Samuel Laeuchli says, at this council the Christian elite sought to carve out a clerical image of the church, and sexual control was the tool in that project.[32] It still infects right-wing Christianity and its "family values" ideology.

Bizarre examples serve as instructive caricatures of the selective goodness escape mechanism. The German chaplains who accompanied the armies of the Third Reich in its ruthless invasion of Holland were preaching sermons warning the troops against Dutch prostitutes. A cynic might say blushingly that the world would have been better off if the whole German army had stayed home and fornicated. During the open slave trade, some learned ethicists pondered just how many slaves it would be permissible to carry on a slave ship. And the mafioso who lavishes money on the struggling little downtown church is just another seamy example of the selective virtue hideaway.

Selective Memory

Closely tied to selective virtue is *selective memory*. It is also cousin to forbidden memories treated at the beginning of this chapter. It is part of the tactical manipulation of memory to which ethics must attend. History is organized memory, and we banish a lot of unpleasantness out of written memory. Americans worry about immigration from the South with no record in the standard history books of the rape of Latin America until someone like Eduardo Galeano, in his *Open Veins of Latin America: Five Centuries of the Pillage of a Continent*, reminds us that "human murder by poverty in Latin America is secret; every year without making a sound, three Hiroshima bombs explode over communities that have become accustomed to suffering with clenched teeth."[33] Africa has the same history.

> **THINKING CRITICALLY**
>
> "Consciousness does not determine life, but life determines consciousness."
>
> —Karl Marx
>
> 18.4

The Rule of Role

Role can be as constraining as a straitjacket. Role is related closely to myth, cognitive mood, and stereotype. It refers to the kind of lifestyle associated with a particular function or life situation. The potential problem with role is that a particular code of ethics may come along as an unsuspected stowaway when one embarks on a new role. A role is powerful because it is socially and mythically endorsed. This has great positive potential. Selfish persons may rise to unpredicted heights of altruism when they assume a new role that implies a new way of life.

It is not hard to think of the rather dissolute student who becomes serious and responsible when given a position (and role) that seems to call for this. The psychology is as simple as that used in making the bad boy a patrol leader in the scout troop. However, a new role may contain a poor code of ethics. The role of soldier, for example, dictates the compliance patterns of an automaton with no power of conscientious objection. The role of student may be presented as an empty receptacle waiting to be passively filled rather than an active participant being invited into the search for truth, a search that is never ended or complete.

Society has many role definitions for husbands and wives. There is a terrible one in the Bible's letter to the Ephesians: "Wives, be subject to your husbands as to the Lord; for the man is the head of the woman, just as Christ also is the head of the church . . . just as the church is subject to Christ, so must women be to their husbands in everything" (5:22-24).

The socially assigned role of doctor may require that the doctor appear as infallible, never admitting she or he does not know the answer. This could block the doctor from learning from the patient and from nurses who may know more of the clinical unfolding of the disease. It could also deter the doctor from suggesting a second or third independent opinion. The role of the business-person may make it "natural" to engage in many questionable practices. The role mentality simply prescribes that this is the way things are done. A lawyer may be convinced by his established role that idealism is incompatible with his calling. As a boy begins to play the role of "a man," he may inertly accept the expectations that he will show no fineness or delicacy of taste and that he will, in sorrow, abandon the natural resource of tears. The intellectual may see himself as above manual labor. The father may not pause enough before the ecstasies of his child's infancy. Roles require full inspection and the opening of all their baggage.

The Numbing Death of Awe

Regarding *banalization*, the words of Teilhard de Chardin are instructive: "What too closely envelops us automatically ceases to astonish us."[34] The truth of this is illustrated by the story of two men laying bricks. One was asked what he was doing, and he replied: "Laying bricks!" But when the second man was asked the same question, he exclaimed: "I am building a cathedral!" Banalization is a loss of crucial perspective. It is a blunting of our sense of wonder, our ability to find "eternity in a grain of sand." There is a sad old saying, *Consueta vilescunt*, or "the things that we grow accustomed to, we undervalue." The *awe* of childhood can give way to the *blasé* of adulthood. Banality is the opposite of ecstasy, and the moral understanding is built on the ecstatic discovery of value. Even our routines can sing. Ethics is hampered by those who are deaf to any part of the human and terrestrial song.

In conclusion, regarding these various modes of reality avoidance, I repeat that the list is not exhaustive. There are many ways in which human knowing goes astray. As I have mentioned above, each of the evaluative processes and resources represented by the spokes of my model of ethics can be abused and serve to diminish our contact with reality. Some of these hazards overlap with others and with problem factors treated in the development of my method. I do not apologize for the overlap if it serves, as I intended it, to show an undisclosed side of doing ethics well. The important thing is for ethics to resist the temptation to view its enterprise as transpiring in a chaste vacuum. It transpires in the maelstrom of social and personal history.

Summary of Key Themes

- Nation building involves studied forgetfulness of foundational iniquities and exploitations.
- Old ideas that freeze in place impede the development of creative social ethics.
- Mood exerts major influence in personal and in collective social ethical judgments.
- Abstractions are necessary for thought but can impede empirical sensitivity.
- Analogies illumine but also can lead to a blurring of major differences between those things or events that are compared.
- Selective virtue helps us avoid inconvenient truths.
- Role definition incorporates moral assumptions and value judgments.
- Wonder and awe are the underpinnings of moral evaluation.

Key Terms

Analogy
Belief
Epistemology
Mastodon
Mood
Neoliberal
Obstacles/hazards of moral discourse
"Ought-to-is" fallacy
Propaganda
Stoic (philosophy)

Questions for Discussion

1. Show how cognitive mood can affect moral evaluation of issues such as oil exploration and drilling, capital punishment, and immigration laws.
2. Explain how cognitive mood can refer to the ethical questions *When?* and *Where?* Could a corporation have a certain cognitive mood?
3. Early America was dependent on the slave trade, and early American prosperity depended on it. What arguments, pro and con, can be developed for making reparations to today's African Americans by way of a special tax cut for all African Americans?
4. How many of the hazards treated in this chapter relate to the current zeal to deny women the right to choose an abortion? How many relate to the slow response to the AIDS epidemic?
5. Give examples that confirm Karl Marx's observation that "consciousness does not determine life, but life determines consciousness."

Suggestions for Further Reading

Bloom, Harold. *Where Shall Wisdom Be Found?* New York: Riverhead, 2004.

Johnson, Chalmers. *The Sorrows of Empire: Militarism, Secrecy, and the End of the Republic.* New York: Henry Holt, 2004.

Johnston, Douglas, and Cynthia Sampson. *Religion, the Missing Dimension of Statecraft.* New York: Oxford University Press, 1994.

Steffen, Lloyd. *The Demonic Turn: The Power of Religion to Inspire or Restrain Violence.* Cleveland: Pilgrim, 2003.

Religion, Ethics, and the Social Sciences

Epilogue

KNOWLEDGE IS AMBULATORY. When we *know*, we rarely know or acknowledge the passages our knowledge has taken on the way to our mind. Take, for example, those churning cultural upheavals we call the world religions. These evolving, symbol-powered moral traditions are full of both error and insight. Pseudo-sophisticates who pride themselves on secular purity would blush if they knew the cognitive proceeds of religious traditions that fill their **"secular"** minds, occupy their assumptions, and guide their ethics.[1]

What is well known about **religion** is its veer toward the weird. Religion at root is a poetic response to that which we find most precious and call by our highest compliment "sacred." Nothing stirs the human imagination so much as the tincture of the sacred. The religious poetic response waxes exuberant, often stretching the skin of metaphor. No area of literature produces the fantastical images that religious literature does. From Jupiter to Kali the enigmatic Hindu Goddess to Jesus; from sexy Gods who create with masturbation or intercourse to Gods who create chastely with a simple word; from the extravagant Gods of Sumer to the rambunctiously misbehaving Gods of Olympus to the more disciplined specialized Gods who focus on agriculture, fertility, or war—the *dramatis personarum divinarum* is endless. As the ancient Thales said, everything is full of Gods, and what a remarkable ensemble they are. The Gods of religious imagination are never static; they grow in talent with the human species. With the invention of writing, they turned to script, whether on tablets of stone on Sinai or by sending angels with names like Gabriel and Moroni to write books or uncover hidden tablets filled with script.

On top of that there are divinized planets, mountains, and rivers, as well as angels, virgin births, resurrections from the dead, and the ability to ascend straight into the heavens without ever going into orbit. No other literature can match that of the religionists in imaginative excess.

Those who see religion as the mind gone mad can produce bookfulls of derision. The religions offer plenty of grist for their critiquing mills. A bevy of angry books have appeared by authors whom historian Anthony Gottlieb has dubbed "atheists with attitude." They compete with one another in the art of shrill. The authors are not religion scholars. The best-selling Sam Harris is a graduate student in neuroscience. Christopher Hitchens is a verbally gifted gadfly who stings for a living. And Richard Dawkins is an evolutionary biologist. Many things they write are correct, but their weakness is that they are like amateur oceanographers who look and write from the beach without ever plumbing the depths. Hitchens's subtitle for his best-selling *God Is Not Great* is *How Religion Poisons Everything*. (Sorry, Mr. Hitchens, but no religion is organized enough to do all that.) Harris sees the greatest grotesqueries in Islam and cries out that if Muslim states get nuclear long-range missiles, our only resort may be "a nuclear first strike of our own . . . [which] would kill tens of millions of innocent civilians in a single day."[2] Down, boy!

Of course, these and other critics of religion are joining their voices to an ancient choir. And they really do have something to be angry about. The disasters religions spawn have long been lamented. An ancient Latin poet wondered how "religion could generate so many evils" (*tantum religio potuit suadere malorum*).[3] Lucretius praised Epicurus for saving humankind from the "burden of religion"; religion was seen as a "blind dragon" and an obscuring "cloud."[4] The potting soil from which religions grow has even been called *Urdummheit*, "primal stupidity." Studying the historical derivation of religion, classicist Gilbert Murray says of the *Urdummheit* hypothesis that it "is so typical of similar stages of thought elsewhere that one is tempted to regard it as the normal beginning of all religion, or almost as the normal raw material out of which religion is made."[5] Not very promising.

Facing the Downsides of Religion

Before looking to any positive yield from religion, the downside should be faced. Religion is never a weak player in the development of the social imagination of a people. Referring to its power, the poet Alexander Pope said that the worst of madmen is a saint gone mad. Religion with its poetry and symbols is to a large extent a product of the right hemisphere of the brain. It is charged with the emotive and symbolic energies of "the limbic system" of the brain, and its messages are not easily disciplined by our talents for neocortical analysis and reasoning.[6] Given the motivational energies in religion, it is small wonder that thirty-four renowned scientists led by Carl Sagan and Hans Bethe, in their "Open Letter to the Religious Community," urged religions to attend to the plight of the planet. "Efforts to safeguard and cherish the environment need to be infused with a vision of the sacred. . . . Problems of such magnitude, and solutions demanding so broad a perspective must be recognized from the outset as having a religious as well as a scientific dimension."[7]

Since religions are exercises in ethics that sally for good or for ill into all the moral problems of society, their ubiquity and prodigious clout cannot be ignored in any serious study of ethics and morality. Religious ideas, says historian Daniel Pals, "affect our literature, philosophy, history, politics, art, psychology, and, indeed, almost every realm of modern thought."[8] American foreign policy has been repeatedly skewed and bungled and blinded by ignoring the religious realities of other societies. The well-titled book *Religion, the Missing Dimension of Statecraft* chronicles instances of the mistakes that have come from this disabling bias.[9]

Certainly religion does teeter toward superstition, and superstitious ideas are sticky and not easily peeled away. Almost three-quarters of Americans believe in the reality of the devil and of angels, and the same number believe in the existence of permanent postmortem torture, that is, hell.[10] By reading the poetry of religious writings as though it was prose, by confusing metaphors with facts, fundamentalist religion misses out on

THINKING CRITICALLY

"Ecology matters to religion for a number of reasons. Any dispassionate view of the past indicates that religion is partly responsible for the environmental crisis. Religions have been, at turns, deeply anthropocentric, otherworldly, ignorant of the facts, or blindly supportive of 'progress,' defined as more science, more technology, and much more 'development.' Thankfully, however, this is no longer the case . . . world religion has entered into an 'ecological phase' in which environmental concern takes its place alongside more traditional religious concerns. In order to make this change religions have had to engage in several arduous and problematic tasks to discover their own distinctive ecological vocation."

—Roger S. Gottlieb, "Religion and Ecology: What Is the Connection and Why Does It Matter?," in *The Oxford Handbook of Religion and Ecology*

19.1

the moral positives that are there for the finding in the religious traditions.

It must also be noted that religions, touching as they do on the ultimates, are all tendentially cults. Cults are authoritarian; they impound the judgment and consciences of their devotees. Clergification sets in with its claims of privileged, *ex officio* knowledge. In the nineteenth century, popes decided they could be infallible when they set their minds to it, and similar pretensions are found in imams and gurus and cult leaders. The infallibilist spirit smothers dissent and dialogue. All such parlous influences in a society deserve critical attention from social ethics since they affect civic conscience and public policy.

Noxious religious influences affect all the important issues that are of concern on our embattled earth. Regarding ecology, Lynn White, in his widely anthologized essay in the journal *Science*, says that Christianity with its anthropocentrism "bears a huge burden of guilt" for our eco-crisis. He says that the biblical mandate to "fill the earth and master it" influenced Western society's "ruthlessness toward nature."[11] Belief in an afterlife often translates into neglect of this one.[12] Wars that are given religious motivation are the cruelest. Small wonder theologian Catherine Keller could write that theology "over its complex and conflictual history has legitimated more violence than any other -ology."[13] Similarly, ethicist Jack Nelson-Pallmeyer entitled his 2003 study *Is Religion Killing Us? Violence in the Bible and the Quran*.[14] This book is a harrowing read since it chronicles so many of the truculent and barbaric ideas that found their way into the "sacred writings." The Indian scholar Ignatius Jesudasan has written a powerful little book on the roots of religious violence.[15] Small wonder the founders of the United States insisted on a "Godless constitution."[16] They were not denying the right of religious people to voice their consciences, but they feared the civic disruption that comes from imposing religious tests arbitrarily drawn from the bad side of religions.

Would the Positives Please Come Forward!

With all that conceded—and more could be added—religions are also the repositories of some of the most civilizing values in human history. Underneath their often extravagantly mythological superstructure, the world's religions are classics, classics in the art of cherishing. They are flawed classics, to be sure, filled with flotsam and jetsam and poisons accrued on their journey, but classics all the same. No classic is uniformly classical; not all the writing attributed to Shakespeare achieves classical excellence. The three principal marks of a classic are *excellence*, *universalizability*, and *fecundity.* Classics succeed in touching the deepest predicates of human intelligence and sensibility. As such, they enjoy "perpetual contemporaneity." They melt borders because they are "the voice of a metropolitan whole of which we are but provincial parts."[17] Classics are fructiferous in that they spawn other classics and, through reinterpretation, they are open to reincarnation, to metamorphosis. They are perennials that can rise to new life with each new vernal opportunity.[18]

Amateur critics buoyed by illusions of postreligious secularism and uncontaminated reasonableness miss a lot, including these five points:

1. Religions are doing ethics and shaping culture. Beneath their mythological overlay religions are one and all doing a full court press on exploring what we are, who we are, and what we should be doing about it. That's ethics. What's more, they are often the decisive ethics doer, the major influence on a culture's moral climate, permeating the politics and economics of even supposedly secular nations like the United States. While not being presented as theory, they contain the elements of personal, political, psychological, and economic theory.

2. There is a widespread and parochial assumption in the West that all religions have a God concept. This is false since some of the world's major religions are Godless with no expectation of an afterlife.

3. Amateur critics lack a sophisticated hermeneutics for understanding and critiquing the complex "sacred writings."

4. Religions are mutants. Most scholars and people generally underestimate the radical pluralism and variety within the religious groupings and symbol systems. There is no one Judaism, Christianity, Islam, or Buddhism. Hinduism is best described as a confederation of different religions and spiritualities. Criticism of what *was* may miss the reality of what *is.*

5. Properly understood, the secular is religious. Most of what can be called religion is outside the "organized religions," those traditions that have special names like Hinduism, Buddhism, and so forth. The amateur critics miss that, too.

1. Religions Are Culture Shapers

Culture, as anthropologist Clifford Geertz says, is "an historically transmitted pattern of meaning embodied in symbols; a system of inherited conceptions expressed in symbolic form by means of which people communicate, perpetuate and develop their knowledge about and attitudes toward life."[19] More simply put, cultures are the socialized likes and dislikes, passions and aversions of a people. Religions are major instillers of these social predilections, tilts, and proclivities that allow us to speak of the "ethic" of a people.

Religion's Democratizing Power. The early Hebrews in a historic heist showed the power of religious symbolism when they stole the badge of royal hegemony and democratized it. This illustrates what Orthodox Jewish scholar Pinchas Lapide calls the "theopolitical dynamite" of biblical religion.[20] The "image of God" symbol was claimed by political potentates, arrogating to themselves "the divine right of kings." The king was the living "image of God," a claim that would obviously enshrine his power and demand total obeisance. Early Israel demurred and expropriated the "image of God" symbol. They said that you need not go to the palace to find the "image of God"; see it in your children, in yourself, and in all people.

Culture is a battleground of metaphors, and in this case the battling Hebrews won. The U.S. Bill of Rights is in debt to this happy theft.

As biblical scholar Elaine Pagels says, "The Genesis accounts of creation introduced into Greco-Roman culture many values . . . for example, the intrinsic worth of every human being, made in God's image (Genesis 1:26)."[21] Jews and Christians "forged the basis for what would become, centuries later, the western ideas of freedom and of the infinite value of each human life."[22]

By the time of the Declaration of Independence, the message of this revolutionary religious symbol—that everyone is created equal—was considered self-evident, and it would permeate the laws, ethics, and political institutions of the West. It was not an idea that was empirically provable. Aristotle, among others, would have considered it absurd, since he saw it as empirically provable that some are born to rule and others to be slaves.[23] It is a gift from religion to modern cultures, an idea grafted onto many cultures, an idea that is as at home in philosophical ethics as in religious ethics, and it is assumed by the most secular practitioners of social sciences. Are those using this insight doing philosophical or religious ethics? The question is misbegotten. Alert and open-minded ethics welcomes wisdom. Truth is truth, however generated, and special passports are not required for admission into open minds. Historically, those social movements we call religions have been the conduits of some of the most basic premises of political life. It is an adolescent and haute naïveté that would snub this fact of life.

> ### THINKING CRITICALLY
>
> Ethicist Larry Rasmussen says that religions, in spite of their conservative and preservative tendencies, may be opening up to an epochal reform in the face of current world crises. "The religiously committed are often poorly poised by their traditions to discern the new, the deviant, and the non-normative, much less to judge these with clarity, insight, and foresight. At the same time, it is precisely a deep cultural crisis that initially gives birth to religions and later to their reform. Religions typically come to be and take their distinctive shape in the breakup of worlds. They accompany the long and painful birth of epochs in the making and breaking."
>
> —Larry L. Rasmussen,
> *Eath Community Earth Ethics*
>
> **19.2**

Religion's Subversive Power. Some major critics of religion's deviations, such as Friedrich Engels, did not snub this reality. In his study of class struggles, he is enthusiastic about the political power of early Christianity, a power that drove Diocletian and a number of emperors into harsh, repressive reaction. Engels saw early Christianity as "the party of overthrow." He says it undermined not only the imperial religion but "all the foundations of the state." It was anything but a pious sideshow because it "flatly denied that Caesar's will was the supreme law." It introduced a universalist, post-tribal mode of socialization. It was, in Engels's words, "international" and "without a fatherland." He hailed its powers as effectively "seditious." Only the naïve see religion as an externality in any culture. For good or for ill, religious power is ubiquitous in every polity.

Surprisingly, Engels saw the Christian movement as paradigmatic for socialism. Playing with the words, he wrote, Diocletian "promulgated an anti-socialist—beg pardon, I meant to say anti-Christian—law." The symbolic reenvisioning of political life that Christianity brought contributed to the collapse of Roman imperium. Engels, however, lamented the corruption of Christianity when it became the state religion and thereafter lost all of its subversive force.

That subversive religio-political power would periodically reassert itself, as it has done in the twentieth and twenty-first centuries in Latin America, where it is again pulsing though the social justice reform movements in that region. Historian Garry Wills asserts that most of the revolutionary movements that transformed, shaped, and reshaped the American nation—"abolitionism, women's suffrage, the union movement, the civil rights movement, and such—grow out of religious circles."[24]

American slaveholders were at first reluctant to offer biblical religion to the slaves, bearing unwitting witness perhaps to the unsettling things they feared the slaves might find there. The unlettered slaves found a lot. When they heard of the "image of God" symbol, they saw immediately that it applied to them as well as to the master and his children. They took risks to meet in groups to discuss this and other chain-dissolving images and liberative thoughts they found in this religion being foisted on them. Their apparently harmless spirituals deftly housed the theopolitical dynamite of the Bible and later animated their fight for freedom.

Ingredients for Theory. The classical texts of the world religions do not offer dry theories of economics or politics, but they do house insights and experience that can chasten reigning theories and give bits of ore from which theory can be extracted. All the strutting abstractions of neoliberal theory that sired the economic collapse of 2008 should have gone to school on the insights of Buddhism that *greed*, *delusion*, and *a lost sense of interdependency* are fatal flaws in human personal and collective conduct. Neoliberalism acts out all three basal ethical deficiencies in an unknowing illustration of Buddhist wisdom.

Neoliberal economists could also take instruction from the Taoist appreciation of balance between *yin* and *yang*. The *yin* of private enterprise has its place in a dynamic society, but so, too, does the *yang* of regulation and restraint of greed by government, the prime caretaker of the common good. Too much *yin* and too little *yang* leads to a crash. And so it did.

Peace and Redistribution. There are three texts in the Hebrew Bible that, as a composite, deserve the Nobel Prizes in both peace and economics: Isaiah 32:17; Deuteronomy 15:4; and Proverbs 10:15. Those texts go to the heart of economics and advance the increasingly plausible viewpoint that it is not state-sponsored violence (war) that guarantees security, but rather the elimination of poverty. Isaiah 32:17 says that only when you plant *tsedaqah*, the form of justice that eliminates poverty, can you reap peace. The biblical poets saw that war does not bring peace in a way that could not sound more contemporaneous: "If you go on fighting one another tooth and nail all you can expect is mutual destruction" (Gal. 5:14). You cannot build "Zion in bloodshed," said the ancient prophet Micah, giving a lesson that modern Israel still has not learned. Nor has the rest of the world. "Perhaps as many as 187,000,000 people died as the result of warfare in the twentieth century, the equivalent of one-tenth of the total world population when the century began."[25] Internationally coordinated police action in various "hot spots," as envisioned by the UN Charter, will be necessary for the foreseeable future, but aside from that, war is outmoded.[26] You can no more win a war than you can win a hurricane. "Innovations in physics, biology, chemistry and information technology—and soon, possibly, in nanotechnology and genetic engineering—have had the unforeseen effect of threatening to put in a few hands the destructive power that, in former times, could be exercised only by sizable armies."[27] The biblical suspicion of violence as policy could now be called political realism.

Deuteronomy 15:4 states the goal of Hebrew political life: "There shall be no poor among you." The reason is practical: "Poverty is the undoing of the helpless" (Prov. 10:15). It is the ruin also of the rest of society, since you cannot build a secure society on the crumbling chaos of poverty. In this view the prime role of government is to create peace by eliminating poverty. This insight has worldwide application. The ancient Hebrews were a remarkably creative group with literary talents unusual in that day. They saw the need to build **redistribution** into the political economy. Their chosen metaphor for society was a *household*. According to theologian M. Douglas Meeks, the "first and last question of economics" from the biblical perspective is: "Will everyone in the household get what it takes to live?"[28]

To ensure that everyone would get enough on

which to live, the Hebrews built into their laws specific modes of redistribution. Wealth bore a burden of proof: the assumption was that great wealth was never innocent: "The spoils of the poor are in your houses" (Isa. 3:14). Excessive accumulation of wealth was seen as a form of violence. The prophet Habakkuk looked at the homes of the rich and said that they had "built a town with bloodshed" (Hab. 2:12). Biblical scholar Norman Gottwald says that "the voice of the poor and needy sounds throughout the Bible more persistently than in any other classical literature."[29] Poverty and wealth were seen as correlative. Since wealth is voracious and insatiable it will gobble up everything unless there is systemic redistribution.

The Israelites institutionalized redistribution. Every seventh year (the Sabbath year) and every fiftieth year (the Jubilee year), all debts were to be relaxed with the goal that no one would be destitute. No one should ever harvest all of their crops but should leave some for the poor, the widows and orphans, and foreigners (Deut. 15:12-18; Leviticus 25).[30] You can't live, said Isaiah in a cogent critique of individualism, as though you are "alone in the land." Without systemic sharing patterns, society will collapse and "down go nobility and common people" alike (Isa. 5:8, 14). Subsequent millennia offer proof galore of this brilliant perception.

Dismantling the Royal Pyramid. Religions are also psychological probes, and the ancient Hebrews saw that one of our human penchants is to set up society in pyramidal form, with privileged royalty at the top resting on a large slave base. These early Israelites were so cynical about the moral reliability of royalty that they broke with all neighboring societies and banished it entirely for the first two centuries of their existence. Hosea the prophet said that the whole institution of royalty could be dismantled. Israel could entirely "abandon this setting up of kings and princes" (Hos. 8:10).

Part of the genius in the religious tradition is in uncovering ingrained moral deficiencies and strategies that are present in every age. Royalty seems to be the undefeatable compulsion of humankind. Thus, modern corporations are structured after the manner of the royal pyramid, with privileges, power, and perquisites shifting to the narrow top, with all that is below cast in a supporting role. The International Monetary Fund (IMF) was set up for benign purposes, to bring collective action to international economic crises. The royalty syndrome quickly asserted itself. "Kings and princes" took over. As Nobel Prize winner Joseph Stiglitz writes: "The IMF is a *public* institution established with money provided by taxpayers around the world, . . . [but] it does not report directly to either the citizens who finance it or those whose lives it affects. Rather it reports to the ministries of finance and the central banks of the governments of the world." The central banks who have control are in the countries who were richest at the time of Bretton Woods, where the IMF was conceived. Among these countries, only the United States has effective veto power.[31]

Similarly, the United Nations was founded for the good goal of achieving collective action to achieve political stability, but only the victorious powers of World War II have veto power. The royal impulse is again in full view.

The royal corporate model has also seeped into the modern academe. Presidents and administrators claim high six- and even seven-figure salaries. Tenured faculty are second-level royalty who more and more depend on underpaid and uninsured part-time faculty to do the heavy lifting. Today nearly three out of four new faculty hires are outside the tenure system. Since part-time, "contingent" faculty (adjuncts) do not have security or academic freedom, the very nature of the academe is changing, succumbing to the royal temptation.[32] This "setting up of kings and princes" is an endemic human stratagem spotted early on by the seers and poets of ancient Israel.

Toppling Top-Heaviness. These insights born in the religions of the world are not the dreams of raving idealists. They are epics of practicality drawn from experience of how humans tend to behave socially. There is nothing dreamy about the royalty diagnosis. The hard fact is that you cannot build elite structures on the sand of poverty. The building collapses as it did in 1929 and in 2008 when a quarter of all wealth had moved into the top 1 percent of society. Those below can no longer purchase goods or pay their mortgages. By 1992 this greed-fest had gone global. The UN Development Programme reported that year that the richest one-fifth of the world population were receiving 82.7 percent of world income, leaving the rest for the impoverished base.[33]

The biblical insight is that such top-heaviness topples. That is the down-to-earth payload of Deuteronomy's advice: "There shall be no poor among you." Eliminating poverty is good for everybody—not just for the poor (most of whom, by the way, will be women and children). There is no economic need for poverty. The needs of society for earth healing and care are infinite, and those needs cannot be met robotically. Meeting society's needs is job creating. As economist Jeremy Rifkin says: "Feeding the poor, providing basic health care service, educating the nation's youth, building affordable housing, and preserving the environment" are urgent priorities that will employ many, even as "virtual" workerless factories loom.[34] Only an economics fixated on *making things* could ignore the opportunities and needs awaiting in the social economy. And it is all very doable. Once again the Rivlin challenge: "It does not seem, from an analytical point of view, that there is any magic number below which we cannot push unemployment. It is a question of the will and of choosing the right mix of policies."[35]

2. Godless Religion

The atheists *du jour* assume that all religions, all responses to the experience of the sacred, employ

God-talk. Not so. As Chun-fang Yu says of the Chinese religions, Buddhism, Taoism, and Confucianism: "Unlike most other religions, Chinese religion does not have a creator God. . . . There is no God transcendent and separate from the world and there is no heaven outside of the universe to which human beings would want to go for refuge."[36] And yet, if you define religion as I do as a response to the sacred, these religions are a strong response to the sacredness of life on this privileged earth. They have shaped and transformed cultures. Warlike Tibetans became a peaceful people under the influence of Buddhism. St. Patrick's Christianity also tamed the Irish.

The Indian prince Ashoka had dominated much of India by military force. He converted to Buddhism and he and India changed. For the next thirty-seven years, he pioneered a new mode of governing. He planted orchards and shade trees along roads, encouraged the arts, built rest houses for travelers and water sheds for animals, and devoted major resources to the poor, the aged, and the sick. His soldiers were converted into peacemakers, building goodwill among races, sects, and parties. His kingdom lasted two thousand years until the British Empire arrived with a different, violent, and less long-lasting paradigm.[37]

3. The Missing Hermeneutics

The "sacred writings" of the text-based religions are not orderly anthologies. They are a veritable farrago of mixed grains and contradictory images from different times and places. Some religionists

THINKING CRITICALLY

"In earlier times when more children were an asset to the community as a whole, a woman had an obligation to have children, and on the whole, more rather than fewer of them. All the great traditional religions arose during that period, and their teachings are deeply affected by that social need. Today, however, a different basic attitude is required. Having children now is a privilege rather than a duty. . . . Those who choose not to exercise that privilege deserve the respect and appreciation of all."

—Herman E. Daly and John B. Cobb Jr., *For the Common Good*

19.3

claim divine origin for their texts, but scholars find no such unifying source, instead declaring many of their literary roots untraceable. In the din of history, much that is "God awful" found its way into the religious texts. For that reason, the prime principle of **hermeneutics** is to insist on distinguishing between *descriptive* and *prescriptive*. For example, much that found its way into the Bible of the Jews and Christians is descriptive of the way life was lived in primitive times. That is of historical interest, but it is not edifying. The book is revered because of the *prescriptive*, positive breakthroughs, the creative envisionings of new ways of living and relating justly and compassionately to one another and to our parental earth.

When the Bible says women should be subject to their husbands "in everything" as if those husbands were God (Eph. 5:22-24), that was very *descriptive* of the mores of that time: sexism, impure and simple. The breakthrough, *prescriptive* text is found in Galatians 3:28. This text is one of the earliest expressions of egalitarianism and liberation found in Western literature. It negates the hostile divisions of its time between men and women, slaves and free people, and people of different nations and ethnic groupings. "There is no such thing as Jew and Greek, slave and freeman, male and female: for you are all one person in Christ Jesus." In other words, in the subversive perspective of the Jesus movement, such hostilities should melt away. That is a *prescription* for a new ethic and a new society.

Isaiah 2 says that swords should be hammered into plowshares, while Joel 4 urges hammering the plowshares into swords. Discernment is called for. Jews and Christians no longer go along with the commands in Leviticus to "burn to death" all gays, lesbians, and sex workers. Writers like Harris and Hitchens seem to believe that religionists have devoured their sacred texts and are living with literal fidelity to the ghastly horrors they find there. If so, they would all be in jail. These shallow critics are very uninformed about progressive movements in world religions, particularly regarding Islam, a topic where a writer like Harris has all the depth of a tabloid.[38] Good ethics does not wallow in the blur of stereotypes.

4. Religions as Mutants

Superficial analyses of religions miss out on the undefeatable pluralism and variety within the religious groupings and symbol systems. There is no one Judaism, Christianity, Islam, or Buddhism. Hinduism is best described as a confederation of different religions and spiritualities. Glib critics also miss the fact that religions are mutants that are constantly reinventing themselves. Criticism of what *was* may miss the reality of what *is.* Criticizing the junk that is in the attics and cellars of these religions, they often miss the life in today's living room.

History Chastens. Nothing is intelligible outside of its history, as paleontologist and philosopher Teilhard de Chardin wisely advised us. Religious history gives a chastening lesson in historiography. Devotees of the particular religions prefer to think of their own faith system as a given that floated above the winds and storms of history, arriving unaltered into modern mosques, churches, and synagogues. We see this conviction in Christian history, where it was said that we should cling only to what was always and everywhere believed (*semper et ubique*). That would leave believers with fairly empty hands. There was a lot of "making it up as they went along" in all the religions. History is a rough ride.

Church historian Dennis Nineham takes us on a chastening trip back to tenth-century Europe. If modern Christians were beamed back there, they might find texts of some old creeds and conclude that all was as all now is. Wrong. As Nineham says, it would be a serious mistake to say "that tenth-century Christianity was fundamentally the same religion as ours with only relatively minor and peripheral features separating them."[39] Tenth-century Christianity believed that God had made humans to make up for the defection of angels from heaven and that God had made more humans than there was room for in heaven. Thus, as few as one in a thousand people could avoid the only alternative then imagined, hell with its eternal torment and torture. Some thought the volcano on Mt. Etna to be the mouth of hell. Purgatory and Limbo had not yet appeared in the religious imagination of the time. Only baptism could save you from hell, and unbaptized babies went straight to hell. Obviously, the God who could do all this was viewed as arbitrary and threatening.

Reimagination. The saints were considered to be the necessary intermediaries between a desperate humanity and such an ominous God. "The cult of the saints was at the very heart of popular religion." It was said that "the true religion of the middle ages . . . is the worship of relics."[40] The eighth-century Greek theologian John of Damascus "claimed that the saints were 'genuinely Gods' (*alethos theoi*) and as such proper objects of worship (*proskynetoi*)."[41] The term *polytheism* could aptly be applied to this teaching. The idea of the pope in Rome being in charge of the church was a late bloomer. "It is not til the seventh century that the history of the papacy, in any full sense of the word, can be said to have begun."[42] The papacy, in other words, was not original equipment.

Obviously, Christianity has reimagined itself in crucial ways since then, but a sophisticated appraisal of any religion must look at its mutant character before assigning primacy to any of its historically shifting configurations.

5. The Secular Is Religious

Religion by definition is the response to the **sacred**. The category of the sacred is not limited to institutionalized religions. It is much broader than that. All legal systems, for example, are based on the "sanctity of life," a meaningful concept to both atheists and theists. There is no one who finds nothing sacred, and the things, ideas, and causes that people find sacred are as varied as people. It follows that there are good and bad sacreds. Since *sacred* is the term for that which we find most precious—it is the ultra-superlative of *precious*—it often gets misplaced. Sacralizers are promiscuous. Things are called sacred and treated with religious fervor that do not deserve that encomium. Nationalism, for example, always has sacral hues. Arnold Toynbee concluded that "nationalism is 90 percent of the religion of 90 percent of the people of the Western World and of the rest of the World as well."[43] Political leaders instinctively know that, and hence their ritualistic invocation of divinity, especially when faced with a hard sell. Western wars are just as religiously charged as the jihad of fundamentalist Muslims.

Misplaced Sacreds. There are other misplaced sacreds. Modern militarism is a belief system that is not based on empirical evidence. Its sacred dogma is that violence saves. Jack Nelson-Pallmeyer goes so far as to say that functionally "violence is the *real religion in the world today. . . .* Most people—including believers, atheists, Christians, Muslims, Marxists, Jews, politicians, clergy, revolutionaries, counter revolutionaries, communists, capitalists, anarchists, fundamentalists, government leaders who sanction state-sponsored terror, and terror-

ists who fly airplanes into trade centers—believe that violence saves. If religion and faith are about ultimate allegiance, then it can be said that violence is the world's principal religion."[44] Only religious fervor at a fanatical level could have a nation like the United States spending almost $30,000 a second on military matters. Only a deep faith in salvation through state-sponsored violence could have more confidence in kill-power than in diplomacy, as witnessed by the U.S. State Department's budget being only 8 percent of the military budget.[45] Budgets are moral documents that reveal one's moral commitments and priorities.

Any cause that generates ardent enthusiasm, any cause that people will suffer for and even die for, is suffused with sacrality. That which we value most highly evokes the sense of the religio-sacred. Fervid atheists are thus in this true sense "religious" about their convictions. Therefore, any narrow ethics that limits the category of the religio-sacred to the various religious institutions is missing out on a major force in human psychology and motivation. Economists who *believe* that "maximizing one's utility" is the heart of human motivation and that is what humans ultimately find sacred are short-circuited in their treatment of religion, psychology, and economics. We're simply not that simple.

Money has religious status. As political scientist William Greider writes: "*Moneta*, the Latin root for 'money,' was an epithet applied to the Goddess Juno, in whose temple the first Roman coins were made. . . . Greeks, Babylonians, Egyptians—virtually every early society conferred sacred qualities on its currency."[46] The sacrality of lucre extends into modern times, sometimes with the religiosity not at all concealed. Conservatives once argued that the United States had offended God when it abandoned the gold standard. "Money-theism" may have more devotees than monotheism. In any area of human life and in any academic discipline, finding what folks find sacred is the beginning of wisdom and of hard-nosed analysis.

Beyond Divorce and Excommunication. Ethics and religion are twinned. What enhances life and its parental universe we call moral: its mysterious and awe-filled grandeur we call holy or sacred. Some conclude to one—or, more often, many—divinities at the root of this grandeur. Others say theistic conclusions undercut our sense of wonder and detract from the miracle that is life and its setting in the universe. Whatever the explanations of sacrality—theistic or not—the fact remains that the good and the holy are concentric—or more simply, the sacred is the nucleus of the good. Those values that we find sacred become the basal assumptions of our laws, our politics, our economics, and our ethics.

Divorce between ethics and religion, properly and holistically understood, is infeasible, and the positivistic conceit that it can be done is dumb. All the major religions were "discontent movements," intent on escape from the crimping lockboxes of society's regnant and stagnant orthodoxies. Like poetry, religious literature is at root a quest for alternatives to the myopia of the imperious status quo. In fact, religious imagination is, at its core, poetic. As Matthew Arnold says, "The strongest part of religion is its unconscious poetry."[47] Religions fail when their poetry is read as prose or when their metaphors are taken as facts.

Ethics cannot excommunicate poetry or religion without breaking its ties to the dynamic and unfolding real. The preciousness of life in this universe is, at its depths, ineffable. In religious poetry the mind stretches its arms like the figure of an *orante*, a figure with arms reaching high in prayer, reaching up to mysteries it will never fully see. That stretch and that reaching are essential to the quest that is ethics.

In Fine . . .

Justice Oliver Wendell Holmes used to say that science makes major contributions to minor needs. Ethics addresses major needs. *Homo technologicus modernus* has been little attracted to the work of ethics even though our technological genius has caused exponential increases in the number of questions requiring ethical judgment. The decline of ethics accompanies the rise of science. Science has become a symbol of an age that takes its minor needs more seriously than its major needs. The major needs, however, are being newly felt. Scientist René Dubos declares that people are beginning to doubt "that Galileo, Watt, and Edison have contributed as much and as lastingly to human advancement and happiness as Socrates, Lao-tze, and Francis of Assisi."[48] A renewed interest in the formal investigation of the deepest human needs is a renewed interest in ethics. No professional ethicists who seek to serve this renaissance dare deem themselves "profitable servants." I do not so deem myself. What I have done in these pages is to present the fruit of many years of professional effort to discover how the valuing animal should best do his valuing. I have not sought to solve all the problems I have introduced, but I have attempted to show how those problems can best be addressed.

The ethics that will meet civilization's needs will call Socrates and Galileo, Lao-tse and James Watt, Francis of Assisi and Thomas Edison, Beethoven, Charles Darwin, Rembrandt, Charles Dickens, and the poet Robin Morgan into an ecumenical community of discernment. There is no area of human experience that is not the bearer of moral meaning. The professional task of ethics is to bring method and some completeness to that human conversation on moral values from which no one is dispensed. If it does that even somewhat well, it has served a world that is, thus far, more clever than wise.

Summary of Key Themes

- Religion is ubiquitous and powerful for good or for ill in forming moral attitudes.
- Organized religion is only a part of religion as a social force.
- The "secular" United States is more religious (embracing sacred principles) than most Americans realize.
- Many of the foundational ideas of modern democracy have religious roots often unnoticed by amateur critics.
- The classical texts and rituals of world religions contain seeds of economic, political, and psychological theory.
- Not all religions have a God or afterlife concept.
- Institutionalized religions are mutants involved in constant reimagination.

Key Terms

Culture
Hermeneutics
Religion
Sacred
Secular

Questions for Discussion

1. Iran is admittedly a "theocratic" society. In what ways is the United States theocratic? What politically intense issues are dominated by religious opinions?
2. Why was the term *God* deliberately left out of the U.S. Constitution? Was this an insult to religion or a political statement?
3. How can religions like Buddhism, Taoism, and Confucianism, which are very animated by the "sanctity of life," be called "religions" when they do not believe in a personal God?

Suggestions for Further Reading

Jesudasan, Ignatius. *Roots of Religious Violence: A Critique of Ethnic Metaphors.* Delhi, India: Media House, 2007.

Johnston, Douglas, and Cynthia Sampson, eds. *Religion, the Missing Dimension of Statecraft.* New York: Oxford University Press, 1994.

Maguire, Daniel C. *Whose Church? A Concise Guide to Progressive Catholicism.* New York: New Press, 2008.

Miles, Jack. *God: A Biography.* New York: Knopf, 1995.

Pals, Daniel L. *Seven Theories of Religion.* New York: Oxford University Press, 1996.

NOTES

Preface

1. Adam Smith, *The Basis of Morality*, 2nd ed. (London: George Allen & Unwin, 1915), 500.
2. Arthur Schopenhauer, *The Theory of Moral Sentiments* (New York: Augustus M. Kelley, 1966), 8.

1. Ethics: The Renaissance

1. Quoted in Douglas Sloan, "The Teaching of Ethics in the American Undergraduate Curriculum, 1876–1976," in Daniel Callahan and Sissela Bok, eds., *Ethics Teaching in Higher Education* (New York and London: Plenum, 1980), 9 n. 16.
2. Arthur Schopenhauer, *The Basis of Morality*, 2nd ed. (London: George Allen & Unwin, 1915), 6.
3. Eric Voegelin notes that the terms *value judgment* and *value-free science* became part of philosophical vocabulary only in the second half of the nineteenth century. "This situation was created through the positivistic conceit that only propositions concerning facts of the phenomenal world were 'objective,' while judgments concerning the right order of soul and society were 'subjective.' Only propositions of the first type could be considered 'scientific,' while propositions of the second type expressed personal preferences and decisions, incapable of critical verification and therefore devoid of objective validity." *The New Science of Politics* (Chicago: University of Chicago Press, 1952), 11. Since law is a derivative of ethics (what we find moral or immoral we codify in our laws), this positivist notion would undermine all laws.
4. Clive Ponting, *A Green History of the World: The Environment and the Collapse of Great Civilizations* (New York: Penguin, 1991), 374.
5. David W. Orr, *Earth in Mind: On Education, Environment, and the Human Prospect* (Washington, D.C.: Island, 1994).
6. Duane Elgin, *Promise Ahead: A Vision of Hope and Action for Humanity's Future* (New York: William Morrow, 2000), 26–28.
7. John Tuxill and Chris Bright, "Losing Strands in the Web of Life," in *State of the World 1998* (New York: Norton, 1998), 42.
8. Edward O. Wilson, *The Future of Life* (New York: Knopf, 2002), 121.
9. Leonard Shlain, *The Alphabet versus the Goddess: The Conflict between Word and Image* (New York: Viking,

1998). Shlain may overburden his bold thesis on the downside of literacy, and he concedes that in his epilogue, but he insists that "overlaying these templates upon human history has helped clarify many complex currents and has made certain patterns apparent that otherwise would have remained murky" (431).

10. See, for instance, Arthur Schlesinger Jr., "The Necessary Amorality of Foreign Affairs," *Harpers* 1455 (August 1971), 71; and George F. Kennan, *American Diplomacy: 1900–1950* (New York: New American Library, 1951), esp. 50.

11. Carol Bly, *Bad Government and Silly Literature* (Minneapolis: Milkweed, 1986), 3.

12. David R. Loy, "The Religion of the Market," in Harold Coward and Daniel C. Maguire, eds., *Visions of a New Earth: Religious Perspectives on Population, Consumption, and Ecology* (Albany: State University of New York Press, 2000), 15–16.

13. Ibid.

14. See John Mihevc, *The Market Tells Them So: The World Bank and Economic Fundamentalism in Africa* (London: ZED Books, 1995).

15. Loy, "Religion of the Market," 15–16. There is a spawning literature on this idea of the market as doing ethics for us in the manner of the traditional religions. See Richard Foltz, "The Religions of the Market: Reflections on a Decade of Discussion," *Worldviews* 2, no. 2 (2007): 135–54.

16. Arnold Toynbee, *Change and Habit* (New York: Oxford University Press, 1966), 13.

17. Larry Rasmussen gives an ethical judgment of the reality of "globalization." It is "a loose ensemble of free-trade agreements, planet-spanning information technologies, and the integration of financial markets [that] erases borders and invades communities while uniting the world into a single brutal, lucrative marketplace where all is game and booty." Larry L. Rasmussen, *Earth Community Earth Ethics* (Maryknoll, N.Y.: Orbis, 1996), 329.

18. Quoted in Goran Moller, *Ethics and the Life of Faith: A Christian Moral Perspective* (Leuven, Belgium: Peeters, 1998), 35.

19. Quoted in Elizabeth Kolbert, "Annals of Science: The Climate of Man—III," *The New Yorker*, May 9, 2005, 57.

20. *Mother Jones*, November–December 1997.

21. The phrase of B. Hayes, "Statistics of Deadly Quarrels," *American Scientist* 90 (2002): 15.

22. Chris Hedges, *What Every Person Should Know about War* (New York: Free Press, 2003), 8.

23. Richard Falk, "Why International Law Matters," *The Nation* 276, no. 9 (March 10, 2003): 20.

24. Andrew J. Bacevich, a retired military officer, says that Americans are more addicted to war now than at any time in their history. See his book, *The New American Militarism: How Americans Are Seduced by War* (New York: Oxford University Press, 2005). The Center for Defense Information in Washington, D.C., is staffed by military veterans who decry the self-defeating American addiction to violent solutions.

25. Vaclav Smil, "The Next 50 Years: Unfolding Trends," *Population and Development Review* 31, no. 4 (December 2005): 632.

26. On the occasion of the Liberty Medal Ceremony, Philadelphia, July 4, 1994.

27. Thomas Aquinas, *Summa Theologiae* I II, q. 40, a. 6; q. 45, 3 c.

28. David Korten, "Sustainability and the Global Economy," in Coward and Maguire, *Visions of a New Earth*, 39.

29. Ponting, *Green History of the World*, 254.

30. To see the recognition by the world's religions of the need for contraception with abortion as a backup as needed, see Daniel C. Maguire, ed., *Sacred Rights: The Case for Contraception and Abortion in World Religions* (New York: Oxford University Press, 2003).

31. James B. Martin-Schramm, "Population Growth and Justice," in Azizah al-Hibri, Daniel Maguire, and James B. Martin-Schramm, eds., *Religious and Ethical Perspectives on Population Issues* (Milwaukee: The Religious Consultation on Population, Reproductive Health and Ethics, 1993), 17.

2. Is There Such a Thing as Moral Truth?

1. J. Glenn Gray, *The Warriors: Reflections on Men in Battle* (New York: Harper, 1967), 185–86.

2. As I shall argue shortly, belief is a kind of knowledge, a kind of reality contact, a conative probe that can touch the real in important ways beyond the glare of self-evidence. My point here is that belief does not come near the certainty of direct, immediate knowledge such as we have of our embodied here-and-now existence.

3. May Edel and Abraham Edel, *Anthropology and Ethics* (Springfield, Ill.: Charles C. Thomas, 1959), 19.

4. Ruth Fulton Benedict, "Anthropology and the Abnormal," *Journal of General Psychology* 10 (1934): 73. In the same vein, William Graham Sumner said that something was called "right" if it conformed to

the established folkways of the group. Sumner did, however, use some utilitarian criteria to adjudicate the values of varying folkways, and thus his ethical relativism was tempered to this extent. See his book *Folkways* (Boston: Ginn & Co., 1906).

5. Benedict, "Anthropology and the Abnormal," 79.

6. See Walter Laqueur and Barry Rubin, *The Human Rights Reader*, rev. ed. (New York: New American Library, 1989). Among United Nations publications, see *Human Rights: A Compilation of International Instruments*, vols. 1 and 2 (1994). Human Rights Watch began in 1978 in Helsinki and today includes divisions covering Africa, the Americas, Asia, and the Middle East. It has copious publications and maintains offices in New York, Washington, D.C., Los Angeles, London, Brussels, Moscow, Dushanbe, Rio de Janeiro, and Hong Kong.

7. See Mutombo Nkula-N'Sengha, "*Bumuntu* Paradigm and Gender Justice: Sexist and Antisexist Trends in African Traditional Religions," in John C. Raines and Daniel C. Maguire, eds., *What Men Owe to Women: Men's Voices from World Religions* (Albany: State University of New York Press, 2001), 69–108. This abuse did not originate in any particular religion but has been adopted by various religions.

8. See Daniel C. Maguire, *The Horrors We Bless: Rethinking the Just-War Legacy*, Facets (Minneapolis: Fortress Press, 2007), 3–5.

9. Thomas Aquinas, *Summa Theologiae* I II q. 18, a. 3. *Actiones humanae secundum circumstantias sunt bonae vel malae.*

10. Robert Nelson, *Economics as Religion* (University Park: Penn State University Press, 2001), xv.

11. Ibid., 8–9.

12. Harvey Cox, "The Market as God: Living in the New Dispensation," *Atlantic Monthly*, March 1999, 20. For a critical look at these trends, see Richard Foltz, "The Religion of the Market: Reflections on a Decade of Discussion," *Worldviews* 11 (2007): 135–54. Foltz writes of "Thomas Friedman, a breathless advocate of economic globalization, who concludes his 1999 book *The Lexus and the Olive Tree* by musing over how an ideal world created by a 'visionary geo-architect' (i.e. God) would no doubt closely resemble the American system we have today" (137). This would implicate God in outsourcing, strikebreaking, and the games that the Enrons play. See also Thomas Frank, *One Market under God* (New York: Anchor, 2001).

13. Quoted in Walter L. Owensby, *Economics for Prophets: A Primer on Concepts, Realities, and Values in Our Economic System* (Grand Rapids: Eerdmans, 1988), 77.

14. Larry L. Rasmussen, *Earth Community Earth Ethics* (Maryknoll, N.Y.: Orbis, 1996), 118.

15. Chun-fang Yu, "Chinese Religions on Population, Consumption, and Ecology," in Harold Coward and Daniel C. Maguire, eds., *Visions of a New Earth: Religious Perspectives on Population, Consumption, and Ecology* (Albany: State University of New York Press, 2000), 162.

16. Ayn Rand, *The Virtue of Selfishness: A New Concept of Egoism* (New York: New American Library, 1961), 15, 17, 22. In my 1978 book, *The Moral Choice* (Garden City, N.Y.: Doubleday), I tried to quote Ms. Rand's writings seven times. Since this came to a total of some 320 words in all, the standard request for permission was made. Ms. Rand, through her secretary, denied permission, relaying the word that she resented such excerpting and quotation of her material. In response to her virtuous selfishness, I had to paraphrase Ms. Rand and deny my readers the experience of her thought in its original originality, unless they went out and bought her book like selfishly virtuous people should.

17. Ibid., 24–25.

3. The Roots of Moral Meaning: The Foundational Moral Experience

1. Edward O. Wilson, *The Future of Life* (New York: Knopf, 2002), 132.

2. *Moral* may be used in two ways: as the opposite of immoral or as the opposite of amoral. The amoral is that which cannot be ethically evaluated. Money in itself (or technology) is amoral; the use people make of it puts it in the realm of the morally adjudicable.

3. B. F. Skinner, *Beyond Freedom and Dignity* (New York: Knopf, 1971).

4. Peter Caws, in a piercing review of *Beyond Freedom and Dignity* in *The New Republic*, October 16, 1971, 32–34. See also Daniel C. Maguire, "Pigeon Ethics: The Moral Philosophy of B. F. Skinner," in *Living Light* 9, no. 3 (1972): 26–32.

5. Skinner, *Beyond Freedom and Dignity*, 114.

6. Ibid., 113.

7. Ibid., 110, 116.

8. Ibid., 53, 111.

9. Ayn Rand, *The Virtue of Selfishness: A New Concept of Egoism* (New York: New American Library, 1964), 44–46.

10. Eric Voegelin, *The New Science of Politics* (Chicago: University of Chicago Press, 1952), 11.

11. Albert Camus, *Resistance, Rebellion and Death* (New York: Knopf, 1969), 114.

12. See *Gorgias* (4690) and books 1–2 in *The Republic*.

13. R. L. Bruckberger, *God and Politics* (Chicago: J. Philip O'Hara, 1972), 46.

14. Ibid., 47.

15. *Sutta Nipata* I, 8, quoted in Kenneth W. Morgan, ed., *The Path of the Buddha* (New York: Ronald Press, 1956), 386.

16. A. L. Basham, *The Wonder That Was India* (London: Sidgwick & Jackson, 1954), 339. The quotation is from the maxims of the early *Tirukkural.*

17. See Jakob J. Petuchowski, "The Limits of Self-Sacrifice," in ed. Marvin Fox, ed., *Modern Jewish Ethics* (Columbus: Ohio State University Press, 1975), 103–18. Although Ahad Haam taught that "your own life comes before the life of your brother," and notes that this has strong support in the Jewish tradition, the issue is not as simple as such a strong expression might suggest. As Raphael Loewe observes, *Halacha* (a term for the written and oral laws of Judaism) was "governed by a common-sense appreciation of what may, and what may not, be realistically expected of the average Jewish man and woman and this has preserved it from utopian idealism when framing its requirements, recommendations, or encouragements as to how to meet a given situation" (ibid., 110). Thus, the supreme sacrifice of self could be appreciated as ideal in certain circumstances without becoming enshrined within the regular stipulations of *Halacha.*

18. Aristotle, *Nicomachean Ethics*, bk. 9, chap. 8, 1169a, 2026, in Richard McKeon, ed., *The Basic Works of Aristotle* (New York: Random House, 1941). Aristotle defends this noble option in a eudaemonistic context in which the good man out of proper love of self chooses nobility as "the greater share." One might part from him on his philosophical explanation here and still accept him as a witness to the perceived nobility of self-sacrifice. Indeed, it might be more striking in such a context and give accent to the paradox at the heart of this human experience.

19. Adam Smith, *The Theory of Moral Sentiments* (New York: Augustus M. Kelley, 1966), 489.

20. Abraham H. Maslow, *Religion, Values, and Peak-Experiences* (New York: Viking, 1970), 42; Richard L. Means, *The Ethical Imperative* (Garden City, N.Y.: Doubleday, 1970), 84.

21. Aristotle, *Nicomachean Ethics*, bk. 1, chap. 3, 1904b, in I. A. K. Thomson, *The Ethics of Aristotle* (Baltimore: Penguin, 1955), 25.

4. The Elements of Moral Thinking: Affectivity, Faith, and Process

1. Edward O. Wilson, *The Future of Life* (New York: Knopf, 2002), 132.

2. Ibid.

3. Loren Eiseley, *The Firmament of Time* (New York: Atheneum, 1960), 144–45.

4. Ibid., 145.

5. See Arnold Toynbee, *Change and Habit: The Challenge of Our Time* (New York and London: Oxford University Press, 1966), 22.

6. Max Weber, *The Protestant Ethic and the Spirit of Capitalism* (Chicago: University of Chicago Press, 1981), 180–82.

7. Thomas Berry, "Christianity's Role in the Earth Project," in Dieter T. Hessel and Rosemary Radford Ruether, eds., *Christianity and Ecology: Seeking the Well-Being of Earth and Humans* (Cambridge: Harvard University Press, 2000), 127–34. Rasmussen's comment is in Larry L. Rasmussen, *Earth Community Earth Ethics*, (Maryknoll, N.Y.: Orbis, 1996), 55.

8. Thomas Berry with Thomas Clarke, S.J., *Befriending the Earth* (Mystic, Conn.: Twenty Third, 1991), 97.

9. Rita Nakashima Brock and Rebecca Ann Parker, *Saving Paradise: How Christianity Traded Love of This World for Crucifixion and Empire* (Boston: Beacon, 2008).

10. Abraham Heschel, *Who Is Man?* (Stanford: Stanford University Press, 1965), 83.

11. Rasmussen, *Earth Community Earth Ethics,* 175.

12. Charles Birch and John Cobb, *The Liberation of Life from the Cell to the Community* (Denton, Tex.: Environmental Ethics, 1990), 45.

13. Annie Dillard, *Pilgrim at Tinker Creek: A Mystical Excursion into the Natural World* (New York: Bantam, 1974), 96, quoted in Rasmussen, *Earth Community Earth Ethics*, 263. See Sallie McFague, *The Body of God: An Ecological Theology* (Minneapolis: Fortress Press, 1993), 38.

14. Thomas Aquinas, *Summa Theologiae* II II q. 157, 158; I II m q, 46–48.

15. Josef Pieper, *Fortitude and Temperance* (New York: Pantheon, 1954), 108.

16. Gregory the Great, *Moralia* in Job 4:45. *J.P. MIGNE, Patrologia Latina.*

17. Michael Polanyi, in his *Personal Knowledge: Towards a Post-Critical Philosohy* (Chicago: University of Chicago Press, 1962), insists that faith is operative in all knowledge, even in science and mathematics. "Objec-

tivism has totally falsified our conception of truth, by exalting what we can know and prove, while covering up with ambiguous utterances all that we know and *cannot* prove, even though the latter knowledge underlies, and must ultimately set its seal to, all that we *can* prove. . . . For all truth is but the external pole of belief, and to destroy all belief would be to deny all truth" (286).

18. W. D. Ross, *The Right and the Good* (Oxford: Clarendon, 1930), 20–21.

19. Blaise Pascal, *Pensées*, trans. William F. Finlayson (New York: Washington Square, 1965), nos. 282 and 277.

20. Henri Bergson, *The Two Sources of Morality and Religion*, trans. R. Ashley Audra and Cloudesley Brereton (Garden City, N.Y.: Doubleday, 1956), 58.

21. John Macquarrie, *Principles of Christian Theology* (New York: Scribner, 1958), 88.

22. Thomas A. Harris, *I'm OK—You're OK* (New York: Avon, 1969), 254.

23. Thomas Aquinas, *Commentum in Quatuor Libros Sententiarum Magistri Petri Lombardi*, Dist. 23, q. 2, a. 3. Thomas somewhat confusingly speaks of certitude as "outside the genus of knowledge in the genus of affection" (*Extra genus cognitionis in genere affectionis existens*). Elsewhere he is clear that faith is a kind of knowledge when he says that "the knowledge of faith proceeds from the will" (ibid., Dist. 23, q. 2, a. 1). See also his treatment of "knowledge by way of connaturality through love" in *Summa Theologiae* II, q. 45, a. 2.

24. Immanuel Kant, *Foundations of the Metaphysics of Morals*, trans. Louis White Beck (New York: Liberal Arts, 1959), 27 n. 1; 46.

25. Jonathan Schell, *The Unconquerable World: Power, Nonviolence, and the Will of the People* (New York: Metropolitian, 2003), 207.

26. Martin Buber, *I and Thou*, 2nd ed. (New York: Scribner's, 1958), 8.

27. Thomas Carlyle, "Characteristics," in *Essays*, vol. 3 (Boston: Houghton Mifflin, 1962), 9.

28. Scientist John Rader Platt speaks of the capacity for self-sacrifice as essential for human society. He observes that the self-sacrificial behavior "of the mother for the child or the soldier for his buddy is so instinctive and irresistible in moments of crisis that it proves we have grown up in families and tribes and have survived only by being willing to *dare* for each other" (*The Excitement of Science* [Boston: Houghton Mifflin, 1962], 169, emphasis added). From that statement alone it may appear that Platt is going to practice reductionism on the mystery of self-sacrifice, treating it as a phylogenetic, instinctive, almost mechanical reflex geared to the survival of the species. However, he moves on to speak of it as faith, saying that we are capable of self-sacrifice because "we have faith in the ultimate value of acts of love and mercy even when all the consequences are not foreseeable." He concludes that "science can add nothing to these moralities of faith" (ibid.).

29. Ralph Linton, "The Problem of Universal Values," in Robert F. Spencer, ed., *Method and Perspective in Anthropology: Papers in Honor of Wilson D. Wallis* (Minneapolis: University of Minnesota Press, 1954), 157.

30. United Nations Development Programme, *Human Development Report 1992* (New York: Oxford University Press, 1992).

31. Robert J. Bonner and Gertrude Smith, *The Administration of Justice from Homer to Aristotle* (Chicago: University of Chicago Press, 1930), 16.

32. Adam Smith, *The Theory of Moral Sentiments* (New York: Augustus M. Kelley, 1966), 192–93.

33. Ibid., 193.

34. Ibid.

35. David Korten, *When Corporations Rule the World* (West Hartford, Conn.: Kumarian, 1996)321.

36. Vladimir Solovyev, *The Meaning of Love* (London: Centenary, 1945), 25.

37. Bergson, *Two Sources of Morality and Religion*, 40.

38. Eiseley, *Firmament of Time*, 123–24.

39. Arthur Schopenhauer, *The Basis of Morality*, 2nd ed. (London: George Allen & Unwin, 1915), 163, 166–68.

40. Martin Luther, *Weimar Auflage*, I, 654, 13–26, 6–30, *Ad Dialogum S. Prieratis de Potestate Papae Responsio (1518)*.

41. John Dewey and James H. Tufts, *Ethics*, rev. ed. (New York: Henry Holt, 1932), 302.

42. Schopenhauer, *Basis of Morality*, 163.

43. Ibid., 8.

44. The experience of guilt shows how unloving to the self immoral activity really is. Guilt is a tearing and disintegrating experience. Bernard Haring writes of it: "*C'est la conscience mauvaise, qui ronge. C'est d'abord un sentiment sombre, retrecissant, la douleur non rachetee, provenant du dechirement interieur.*" (A guilty conscience bites and gnaws. It starts as an ominous feeling, a kind of choking, a persistent pain coming from an interior laceration.) *Le Sacre et le Bien* (Paris: Editions Fleurus, 1963), 72. To want to avoid this experience is in a proper sense self-loving.

5. Theories of Justice:
What's So Good about the Common Good?

1. Aristotle, *Politics* I, 2, 1253.
2. Aristotle, *Nicomachean Ethics*, 1132b. Aristotle puts it in more cryptic language, saying that it is by "proportionate requital" that the city holds together. That means that the right kind of sharing and just enough sharing holds the community together. That is the work of justice.
3. Ibid., 1155a.
4. Though *suum cuique* is the quintessential statement of what justice imports, the ancient literature offers broader and richer appreciations of the notion. Cicero, who reflects a whole tradition in this matter, says that "justice is a predilection for giving to each his/her own and for protecting generously and equitably the common good of persons" (*Quae animi affectio suum cuique tribuens atque hanc, quam dico, societatem coniunctionis humanae munifice et aeque tuens justitia dicitur*). *De officiis*, L. I. Cap. 5, #15. This is one of the best expressions of justice in classical literature. It includes reference to the affections, where moral knowledge is rooted, and it signals that justice is incipient love marked by generosity of spirit. Ambrose is similar: "Justice, which renders to each his/her own, does not lay claim to the goods of another and even neglects its own interests in the interest of an equitable common life" (*Justitia, quae suum cuique tribuit, alienum non vindicat, utilitatiem propriam negligit, ut communem aequitatem custodiat*). *De officiis ministrorum*, L. I, Cap. 24, #115. Again, there is no minimalist spirit in this formulation. Ulpian stresses the need for follow-through: Justice requires "a constant and perpetual willingness to give to each his/her own." *Dig.* I. I, 10, pr. Each of these definitions imports the value of every person, the needs of society, the presence of affectivity in the notion of justice, and a concern for the common good.
5. I treat justice theory more fully in *A New American Justice: A Moral Proposal for the Reconciliation of Personal Freedom and Social Justice* (San Francisco and New York: Harper & Row, 1980).
6. The ethics literature contains a befuddling multitude of justice forms. This resulted from efforts to give justice a new definition in every situation to which it applied—and it applies to the whole of life. To mint a new title for justice in every distinct situation of rendering to each his/her own allows for infinite and unhelpful proliferation. Thus, you will find forms of justice called vindictive, judicial, familial, antipeponthotic (yes!), synallagmatic, legal, distributive, retributive, attributive, recognitive, providential, syndical, corporative, reparatory, penal, and cosmopolitical. This rabid multiplication of justice terms bears witness to the breadth of application that justice has as well as to the felt need for meaningful definitions of the term. Justice-talk has further been confused by a long tradition of treating justice as universal virtue, the sum of all goodness. Plato was a mighty force in this direction; see *The Republic*, I. 6, 331 E; I. 7, 332 D; IV. 10 433 A. This remained as a tension in Aristotle and also in Thomas Aquinas. Finally, justice was taken as just one virtue among the many, missing the fact that it is the primary and foundational category of communal existence. See Georgio Del Vecchio, *Justice: An Historical and Philosophical Essay* (Edinburgh: University Press, 1952). For an excellent treatment of the tripartite nature of justice, see Josef Pieper, *Justice* (New York: Pantheon, 1955). This has been published also in Josef Pieper, *The Four Cardinal Virtues* (New York: Harcourt, Brace & World, 1965).
7. Daniel C. Maguire, *The Moral Core of Judaism and Christianity* (Minneapolis: Fortress Press, 1993), 182.
8. Thomas Aquinas, *Summa Theologiae* II, q. 61, a. 1, ad 3. Quoted in ibid., 334.
9. Thomas Jefferson, Letter to M. Correa, November 25, 1817.
10. Andrew J. Bacevich, a West Point graduate and Vietnam veteran, spells out this disaster in his book *The New American Militarism: How Americans Are Seduced by War* (New York: Oxford University Press, 2005).
11. Quoted in Yehoshua Arieli, *Individualism and Nationalism in American Ideology* (Cambridge: Harvard University Press, 1964), 335.
12. Quoted in ibid., 334.
13. Richard Hofstadter, *The American Political Tradition* (New York: Vintage, 1954), vii.
14. Robert Nozick, *Anarchy, State and Utopia* (New York: Basic, 1975), ix, 33, 169.
15. Aristotle, *Politics*, 1265b.
16. David R. Loy, "Pave the Planet or Wear Shoes? A Buddhist Perspective on Greed and Globalization," in Paul F. Knitter and Chandra Muzaffar, eds., *Subverting Greed: Religious Perspectives on the Global Economy* (Maryknoll, N.Y.: Orbis, 2002), 71.
17. Thomas Jefferson, letter to Rev. James Madison, October 28, 1785.
18. See Plutarch, *Banquet of the Seven Wise Men*, chap. 11.

19. See Leonard Goodwin, *Do the Poor Want to Work? A Social-Psychological Study of Work Orientations* (Washington, D.C.: Brookings Institution, 1972), ix, 7–8, 81, 112, 117. See also Barbara Hilkert Andolsen, *The New Job Contract: Economic Justice in an Age of Insecurity* (Cleveland: Pilgrim, 1998); Mary Elizabeth Hobgood, *Dismantling Privilege*: *An Ethics of Accountability* (Cleveland: Pilgrim, 2000); David K. Shipler, *The Working Poor: Invisible in America* (New York: Knopf, 2004); and Knitter and Muzaffar, *Subverting Greed.*

20. Alice Rivlin, U.S. Congress Hearing, Joint Economics Committee, *Thirtieth Anniversary of the Employment Act of 1946—A National Conference on Full Employment* (Washington, D.C.: Government Printing Office, 1976), 276. See also Gar Alperovitz, "Planning for Sustained Community," in *Catholic Social Teaching and the United States Economy*, ed. John W. Houck and Oliver F. Williams (Washington, D.C.: University Press of America, 1984), 331–58.

6. From Awe to Strategy:
The Art and Science of Ethics

1. Rosemary Radford Ruether, "Sexual Illiteracy," *Conscience* 24, no. 2 (Summer 2003): 16.

2. John Dewey and James H. Tufts, *Ethics*, rev. ed. (New York: Henry Holt, 1932), 298.

3. Ibid., 299.

4. Arthur Schopenhauer, *The Basis of Morality*, 2nd ed. (London: George Allen & Unwin, 1915), 8. One may compare ethics to art without adopting the position of John Stuart Mill to the effect that ethics is not a science but an art. Mill saw science as a description of things as they are and ethics as a normative discipline concerned with things as they ought to be. He saw science as moving from the particular to the general and ethics as going from the general to the particular. It is not all that simple, as will be seen in this elaboration of ethical method. See John Stuart Mill, *Utilitarianism* (New York: E. P. Dutton, 1910), 1–2.

5. Thomas Aquinas, *Summa Theologiae* II, q. 49, a. 3. *Prudentia consistit circa particularia operabilia. In quibus cum sint quasi infinitae diversitates, non possunt ab uno homine sufficienter omnia considerari nec per modicum tempus, sed per temporis diuturnitatem.*

6. Eugene Fontinell, "Reflections on Faith and metaphysics," *Cross Currents* 16 (1966), 8.

7. Hannah Arendt, *Between Past and Future* (New York: Meridian, 1963), 48.

8. Paul F. Knitter and Chandra Muzaffar, eds., *Subverting Greed: Religious Perspectives on the Global Economy* (Maryknoll, N.Y.: Orbis, 2002), 5.

9. Daisy Sewid-Smith, "Aboriginal Spirituality, Population, and the Environment., in Harold G. Coward, ed., *Population, Consumption, and the Environment* (Albany: State University of New York Press, 1995), 69.

10. Daniel C. Maguire, *Whose Church? A Concise Guide to Progressive Catholicism* (New York: New Press, 2008), 36–45.

11. The work of Jean Piaget, Lawrence Kohlberg, and Jane Loevinger on the developmental patterns of moral evaluation have been most illuminating. They are especially helpful for work in moral and pastoral counseling as well as for warning ethicists away from the presumption that moral maturity is statistically normal. By calling attention to the way people actually do ethics, these psychologists can help the ethicists in their study of how they *ought* to do ethics. It is a mistake, however, to think of these scientists as ethicists. Theirs is an effort to show psychometrically how persons do and may do moral evaluation. While some normative implications are unavoidable in this, these people are not plying the theoretical-practical and normative discipline of ethics.

12. A final and brief word on my definition of ethics relates to the key category *moral* of which I have already spoken. *Moral* cannot be defined in the sense that it could if it were a species of some more generic reality. Thus, you can define a "chair" by saying it is a piece of furniture, etc. You go from the general to this specific item. Morality is a basic concept and hence can only be described. *Moral* in my definition means human in the *ought* or normative sense. The word *human* can be used normatively (what humanity ought to be) or descriptively (what it is observed to be). Thus, you can say descriptively that *it is human to lie* (meaning that people do), and you can say normatively that *it is not human to lie* (meaning that people should not). It is in this latter, normative sense that I use "human" as the synonym of "moral." When we say that rape is immoral, we are saying that it is inhuman activity, that it is not what humans ought to do in expressing their sexuality. Some cultures will express moral disapproval by saying, "That's acting like a dog or a pig," meaning it is not what humans ought to do (i.e., it is immoral; whether the poor dogs and pigs would act that way is not the point).

13. There are enormous differences in the way morality is assessed for individuals and for collectivities. The model, however, may be accommodated as a methodical framework for evaluation in both kinds of

situations. All the issues studied in hard and social science have an ethical dimension, since they always in some way affect the good or ill of humanity and the rest of nature. This doesn't mean that ethics can, like a detached monarch, judge all issues from the sidelines. Ethics must be in conversation with all the disciplines that affect human good. There is no pope in this dialogue. Ethics cannot ignore the data from the sciences, and the sciences cannot ignore evaluative ethical theory.

Ethics is not just a discipline among other disciplines. I do not say this as a prelude to proclaiming it the queen of all disciplines. Rather, it is less circumscribable than other disciplines since it views the whole of human conscious behavior. Thus, to do its work, it needs dialogical communion with all the other disciplines that study the human phenomenon.

In a university, ethics ideally would be done in what could be called a Center for the Study of Moral Values. This center would relate formally to the other departments of the university so that moral evaluation would proceed in an interdisciplinary way. The ethicists in the center would learn to establish lines of communication with the experts in other areas and so further the multidisciplinary study of moral values. From this contact the ethicists could return to correct and expand their theoretical framework in ethics. Realistically it must be allowed that formidable vested interests in academe stand against the hopes for any such creative restructuring.

14. Thomas Aquinas, *Summa Theologiae* I II, q. 18, a. 3. *Ergo actiones humanae secundum circumstantias sunt bonae vel malae.* There is no insight so clear that some philosopher hasn't denied it or mucked it up. In ethics, the terms *good* and *bad*, *right* and *wrong* are equivalent. Oh no, said H. A. Prichard. *Right* refers to the action aside from motive, and *good* relates solely to the motive. Since motive is essential to moral meaning, we cannot speak of what is right or good while ignoring motive. This pedantic and silly distinction leads to saying that a right action might be bad, because of motive, and a wrong action might be good, also because of motive. Prichard wrote this nonsense in an essay in which he wondered why there was so much dissatisfaction with moral philosophy! "Does Moral Philosophy Rest on a Mistake?" *Mind* 21 (1912); reprinted in W. T. Jones, F. Sontag, M. O. Beckner, and R. J. Fogelin, *Approaches to Ethics*, 2nd ed. (New York: McGraw-Hill, 1969), 469–80.

In the category of unnecessary roughness, some ethicists have gotten bogged down in the terms *teleological* and *deontological*. The terms do not serve the

mind well. Teleological theories tend to hold that actions are right or wrong depending on whether they produce consequences that are good or bad. Teleology asks: "What is the end or good man seeks?" Deontological theories hold that certain kinds of actions are right or wrong regardless of the consequences. These terms are unhelpful. First of all, it may be impossible to find a pure type of either kind of theorist. Kant is seen as a deontologist, and yet, for example, in defending his view of truth telling, he argues by reference to consequences. Furthermore, ethics is by its nature both deontological and teleological, concerned with the *ought* and not merely in consequentialist terms. Ethics does not prescind from consequences, which would be theoretically irresponsible and practically disastrous. For a painful look at the typical uses of deontology and teleology, see C. D. Broad, *Five Types of Ethical Theory* (London: Routledge & Kegan Paul, 1930), 206ff.

15. Thomas and all serious ethicists recognized that certain circumstances do not affect the morality of an action. Thus, it might be immaterial to the morality of an action if the circumstances of time or place were changed. (If you are robbed on a Tuesday or a Wednesday, it would probably make no moral difference.) Such circumstances may be quite incidental and have little or no effect on the moral status of the behavior in question. Not all circumstances, however, are such. In fact, notes Thomas, there are circumstances that constitute the "principal condition" of the conduct to be judged and establish the moral status and species of that conduct. Thus, to the question whether the moral judgment is circumstantial, Thomas's answer is affirmative, and he was dead right.

16. Bernard J. F. Lonergan, S.J., *Insight: A Study of Human Understanding* (New York: Longmans, Philosophical Library, 1957), ix.

17. The term *situation ethics* is almost useless to describe what we are speaking about, since it has been stretched to cover so many things. Any ethics that is not sensitive to the situation it is judging is not ethics at all. Pope Pius XII condemned what he called "situation ethics" in very vigorous terms, but since he did not say whose work he was attacking, it is not easy to say what he attacked. See *Acta Apostolicae Sedis* (*AAS*) 48 (1956): 144–45, for a condemnation of "situation ethics" by the Holy Office, which forbade "this doctrine of 'Situation ethics,' by whatever name it is designated, to be taught or approved in Universities, Academies, Seminaries and Houses of Formation of Religious, or to be propagated and defended in books,

dissertations, assemblies, or, as they are called, conferences, or in any other manner whatsoever." For the pope's statements, see *AAS* 44 (1952): 270–78, and *AAS* 44 (1952): 413–19. Yet we read Louis Monden, S.J., a Jesuit moral theologian, saying the obvious, that "we must clearly affirm with the great classical authors that Catholic morality is, in fact, a *situation ethics*." *Sin, Liberty and Law* (New York: Sheed & Ward, 1965), 104.

18. Jean Piaget, *Six Psychological Studies* (New York: Vintage, 1968), 54–58, 37. See also Piaget's *The Moral Judgment of the Child* (New York: Harcourt-Brace, 1932).

19. Daniel C. Maguire, *Death by Choice* (Garden City, N.Y.: Doubleday, 1974; New York: Schocken Books, 1975), chap. 8.

20. Joseph M. Kitagawa, "The Asian Mind Today," *Worldview* 16 (January 1973): 8–9.

21. Josef Pieper, *Silence of Saint Thomas* (Chicago: Henry Regnery, 1965), 103.

22. *Commentary on Aristotle, De Anima,* I, 1, 15. Pieper comments that "it would be easy to set alongside of it a dozen similar passages (from the *Summa Theologica*, the *Summa Contra Gentiles*, the *De Veritate*, and the other *Quaestiones Disputatae*)." *Silence of Saint Thomas*, 65.

23. *Quaestio Disputata de Spiritualibus Creaturis*, 11, ad 3, and *Quaestiones Disputatae de Veritate*, 4, 1, ad 8. The I II q. 18 of Thomas's *Summa* is a pivotal part of his ethical theory. All the articles of this *Quaestio* are important, even though Thomas does stray from these insights. Thomas says that "everything has as much of good as it has of being. . . . But God alone has the whole fullness of his being in a manner which is one and simple [*secundum aliquid unum et simplex*], whereas every other thing has its proper fullness of being according to diverse things [*secundum diversa*]" (a. 1). Facing the objection that circumstances are mere "accidents" and thus could not determine the moral species of the action, Thomas says that some circumstances are *per se accidentia,* not *accidentia per accidens* (a. 3), which means that some accidents enter into the principal condition of the object in such wise that they determine the moral meaning. *Circumstantia . . . in quantum mutatur in principalem conditionem obiecti, secundum hoc dat speciem* (a. 10). See also *Summa Theologica* I II, q. 64, a. 1, ad 2, where Thomas says that the means of the virtues is established "according to the diverse circumstances." Thomas's imprecision in the use of the term *object* has allowed his theory to be distorted by "Thomists" plying the idea of intrinsically evil actions, a rever-

sion to taboo thinking. Thomas does not clarify the relationship of the object, which includes some circumstances, to other specifying circumstances. For example, in I II, q. 18, a. 2, Thomas says that an action is specified by its object getting its primary goodness therefrom. Thus, using one's own goods is *ex obiecto* good and accepting the goods of someone else is *ex obiecto* bad. It would have helped if Thomas had noted that sometimes receiving or taking the goods of others, e.g., food when one is starving, is good because different circumstances have entered into the "principal condition of the object," to use his words from I II q. 18, a. 10. Also, using one's own goods in a way that damages the environment is bad. Thus, his examples in a. 2 can be misleading, since they imply something like intrinsically good or intrinsically evil, although this is not what his overall theory imports. For an example of the misuse of Thomas in the Catholic manuals of moral theology, see A. Tanquerey, *Theologia Moralis Fundamentalis*, Tomus Secundus (Parisiis, Tornaci, Romae, 1955), 130–37.

24. *Quaestio Disputata de Spiritualibus Creaturis*, 11, ad 3.

25. *Human Rights: A Compilation of International Instruments* (New York and Geneva: United Nations, 1994), vols. 1 and 2.

7. The Subject of Ethics: Defining the Model of the Wheel

1. George Lakoff, *Don't Think of an Elephant: Know Your Values and Frame the Debate* (White River Junction, Vt.: Chelsea Green, 2004), 3.

2. Quoted in Peter Singer, "What Should a Billionaire Give—and What Should You? *New York Times Magazine*, December 17, 2006, 60.

3. Ibid.

4. Paul M. Sweezy, "The American Ruling Class," in *The Present as History* (New York: Monthly Review, 1953), 126; Roger Garaudy, *Marxism in the Twentieth Century* (New York: Scribner, 1970), 13.

5. Robert L. Heilbroner, *An Inquiry into the Human Prospect* (New York: Norton, 1975), 64.

6. Ibid., 65.

7. Michael Walzer, "An Exchange on Hiroshima," *New Republic*, vol. 185 (September 23, 1981): 13-14.

8. Howard Zinn, *A People's History of the United States: 1492 to Present*, rev. ed. (New York: Harper Perennial, 1995), 412–15.

9. Michael Walzer, *Just and Unjust Wars: A Moral Argument with Historical Illustrations* (New York: Basic, 1977), 255.

10. *The Documents of Vatican II* (New York: Herder & Herder/Association Press, 1966), 294. This declaration of the bishops simply endorsed a similar judgment by Pope Pius XII, Pope John XXIII, and Pope Paul VI. See ibid., n. 260.

11. See Daniel C. Maguire, *The Horrors We Bless: Rethinking the Just-War Legacy*, Facets (Minneapolis: Fortress Press, 2007), 42–59.

12. Desmond Tutu, "Stop Killing the Children," *Washington Post*, November 24, 1996, C7.

13. Richard Falk, "Why International Law Matters," *The Nation* 276, no. 9 (March 10, 2003): 20.

14. Chris Hedges, *What Every Person Should Know about War* (New York: Free Press, 2003), 1.

15. "The World at War—January 2002," *Defense Monitor* 31, no. 1 (January 2002), 1–17.

16. Quoted in E. H. Hare, "Masturbatory Insanity: The History of an Idea," 8.

17. Quoted in Uta Ranke-Heinemann, *Eunuchs for the Kingdom of Heaven: Women, Sexuality and the Catholic Church* (New York: Doubleday, 1990), 313.

18. Ibid., 313–14.

19. Hare, "Masturbatory Insanity," 2, 10–11, 15.

20. E. H. Hare, "Masturbatory Insanity: The History of an Idea," *Journal of Mental Science* 108 (January 1962): 1–25.

21. Bernadette J. Brooten, *Love between Women: Early Christian Responses to Female Homoeroticism* (Chicago: University of Chicago Press, 1996), 189.

22. Ibid., 190.

23. Albertus Magnus, *Quaetiones super de animalibus XV, q. 14*, quoted in Ranke-Heinemann, *Eunuchs for the Kingdom of Heaven*, 182.

24. Karen Armstrong, *The Battle for God* (New York: Ballantine, 2001), vi.

25. See the *Future Survey* review "Averting an Electronic Waterloo," CSIS Global Organized Crime Project (Frank Cilluffo, task force director and editor), (Washington, D.C.: Center for Strategic and International Studies, December 1998), quoted in Duane Elgin, *Promise Ahead: A Vision of Hope and Action for Humanity's Future* (New York: William Morrow, 2000), 110.

26. Gene Sharp, *The Politics of Nonviolent Action* (Boston: Porter Sargent, 1973–75) 3:552.

27. Obviously, if the conception of the possible good is off target, the power of ideals would remain but its power would be violent.

28. When citizen commitment to the common good lags, "the rules of the competitive market, not the practices of the town meeting . . . are the real arbiters of living." Commitment to the common good is formed by "those habits of the heart that are the matrix of a moral ecology, the connecting tissue of a body politic." R. Bellah, R. Madsen, W. Sullivan, A. Swidler, and S. Tipton, *Habits of the Heart: Individualism and Commitment in American Life* (Berkeley: University of California Press, 1985), 251.

29. Daniel A. Dombrowski and Robert Deltete, *A Brief, Liberal, Catholic Defense of Abortion* (Urbana and Chicago: University of Illinois Press, 2000), 56. To see the openness of world religions to the moral choice of a direct abortion, see Daniel C. Maguire, ed., *Sacred Rights: The Case for Contraception and Abortion in World Religions* (New York: Oxford University Press, 2003). Also Daniel C. Maguire, *Sacred Choices: The Right to Contraception and Abortion in Ten World Religions* (Minneapolis: Fortress Press, 2001). On the legal standing of the fetus in the United States, see Jean Reith Schroedel, *Is the Fetus a Person? A Comparison of Policies across the Fifty States* (Ithaca, N.Y.: Cornell University Press, 2000).

30. David Korten, *When Corporations Rule the World*, (San Francisco: Berrett-Koehler, 2001), 33, 34.

31. David Pimentel, Rebecca Harman, Matthew Pacenza, Jason Pecarsky, and Marcia Pimentel, "Natural Resources and an Optimal Human Population," *Population and Environment* 15, no. 5 (1994): 352.

32. Richard A. McCormick, "Human Significance and Christian Significance," in Gene H. Outka and Paul Ramsey, eds., *Norm and Context in Christian Ethics* (New York: Scribner's, 1968), 254, 253.

8. Deepening the Probe: Why? How? Who? When? Where?

1. Nicolas Berdyaev, *The Destiny of Man* (New York: Harper & Row, 1960), 80.

2. Quoted in Philip Noel-Baker, "We Have Been Here Before," in Nigel Calder, ed., *Unless Peace Comes* (New York: Viking, 1968), 215.

3. Ibid., 231.

4. Jawaharlal Nehru, *The Discovery of India* (New York: John Day, 1946), excerpted in Paul E. Sigmund Jr., ed., *The Ideologies of the Developing Nations* (New York: Praeger, 1963), 88.

5. Berdyaev, *Destiny of Man*, 164.

6. Studies of pigeons and ants can tell us a lot about us but cannot show that we are pigeons or ants. Sociobiology and evolutionary biology may be seen as ef-

forts to explain human behavior and psychology as purely mechanistic, genetic outpourings, but they need not be. The wise Edward O. Wilson is proof of that. Much of his writing involves appeals to creativity and to better free choices in people who are not preprogrammed into automated response.

7. Here I am speaking of "what" in a generic sense, not in the narrowly defined sense of first-stage cognition.

8. Augustine said, *Pietas timore inchoatur, caritate perficitur.* (Morality begins in fear and is perfected in love.) *De Vera Religione*, cap. XVII. *Pietas* means devotion to duty, doing the right thing. Fear may constrain us to do that; love (*caritas*)—deeper immersion in the FME—will propel us.

9. This does not mean that all will agree on which means are best suited for the job at hand. The absolutizing of one means to address a problem could signal the death of imagination.

10. David U. Himmelstein and Steffie Woolhandler, "I Am Not a Health Reform," *New York Times*, December 15, 2007.

11. Julie Lambert, letter to the editor, *New York Times*, February 17, 2003, A22; Nicholas D. Kristof, "This Time, We Won't Scare," *New York Times*, June 11, 2009, A25.

12. Hart Posen, letter to the editor, *New York Times*, February 17, 2003, A22.

13. Emily Clark, letter to the editor, *New York Times*, November 6, 2007, A24.

14. Nancy Frazier O'Brien, Catholic News Service, "Washington Letter," April 11, 2008.

15. John F. Ebbott, "In truth, equal justice is not available to everyone in Wisconsin," *Milwaukee Journal Sentinel*, August 12, 2005, 19A.

16. Disclosure: The officer who did these interviews was my brother, Connell Joseph Maguire.

17. Harold Coward, "Self as Individual and Collective," in Harold Coward and Daniel C. Maguire, eds., *Visions of a New Earth* (Albany: State University of New York Press, 2000), 46.

18. Ibid., 44–45.

19. Ibid.

20. Mutombo Nkulu-N'Sengha, "*Bumuntu* Paradigm and Gender Justice," in John C. Raines and Daniel C. Maguire, eds., *What Men Owe to Women: Men's Voices from World Religions* (Albany: State University of New York Press, 2001), 82.

21. Carol Gilligan, *Harvard Educational Review* 47 (November 1977): 482.

22. Quoted in Gloria Albrecht, *Hitting Home: Feminist Ethics, Women's Work, and the Betrayal of Family Values* (New York: Continuum, 2002), 79. See Herbert J. Gans, *The War against the Poor: The Underclass and Antipoverty Policy* (New York: Basic, 1995); Walter L. Owensby, *Economics for Prophets: A Primer on Concepts, Values, and Realities in Our Economic System* (Grand Rapids: Eerdmans, 1988); Daniel C. Maguire, *Whose Church? A Concise Guide to Progressive Catholicism* (New York: New Press, 2008), chap. 5, "Upwardly Mobile Poverty"; Mary Elizabeth Hobgood, *Dismantling Privilege: An Ethics of Accountability* (Cleveland: Pilgrim, 2000).

23. Leonard Goodwin, *Do the Poor Want to Work?* (Washington, D.C.: Brookings Institution, 1972), 112.

24. Laurie Zoloth, "Each One an Entire World," in Daniel C. Maguire, ed., *Sacred Rights: The Case for Contraception and Abortion in World Religions* (New York: Oxford University Press, 2003), 38.

25. Ibid., 39.

26. Francesco de Vitoria, *De Indis et De Iure Belli Relationes*, quoted in Michael Walzer, *Just and Unjust Wars* (New York: Basic, 1977), 39.

27. See Ping-Chen Hsiung, "Heavenly Way and Humanly Doings: A Consideration of Chinese Man's Body Management During the Late Imperial Period," in Maguire, *Sacred Rights*, 208.

9. Foreseeable Effects, Viable Alternatives: The Link to the Future

1. Thomas Aquinas, *Summa Theologiae* II, q. 10, a. 11, in corp., quoting Augustine in II *De ordine. Aufer meretrices de rebus humanis turbaveris omnia libidinibus.*

2. Hans Jonas, "Technology and Responsibility: Reflections on the New Talks of Ethics," *Social Research* 40, no. 1 (1973): 35–36.

3. William Manchester, *The Glory and the Dream* (Boston: Little, Brown, 1974), 199.

4. Arnold Toynbee, *Change and Habit* (New York: Oxford University Press, 1966), 199.

5. The basic moral flaw in nuclear weaponry is that its alleged purpose is to deter, but for it to deter, we must be ready to use it and let the designated enemies know we are ready to use it. However, to use it is, by definition, terrorism, since the weapons are undiscriminating in their effects. Thus, keeping these weapons is an announcement of terrorist intent, which, of course, stimulates terrorist responses. The policy itself is immoral because of the readiness to inflict massive slaughter. There is no way that such readiness could proceed from the perception of the value of persons (the FME). The only moral reaction

to the nuclear deterrence policy that we have created as a monstrous prop for "peace" is to move out of it by urgent negotiations and trust building. A piddling, ineffectual approach to disarmament indicates that the moral barbarity of our current posture is not appreciated and that the respectability that accrues to the familiar has sedated the sting of guilt.

6. Intuitionism says that some actions can be seen as self-evidently wrong, regardless of their circumstances. Just as you can see that something is yellow or red, you can, in like manner, see that some things are simply wrong. Thus, framing an innocent man and sending him to his death would be offered as an example of an action that is wrong regardless of its circumstances. In fact, it is wrong precisely *because* of its circumstances.

7. "Une fois la guerre declaree, ne serait-il plus vrai que 'necessite fai loi'?" P. Goreux, "Une Consultation de Theologiens sur le Probleme de la Moralite de la Guerre," *Nouvelle Revue Theologique* no. 10 (December 1932): 59.

8. Henry Davis, S.J., *Moral and Pastoral Theology*, vol. 2, 6th ed. (London: Sheed & Ward, 1949), 150.

9. Ibid. Davis even violates the usual textbook restraints on the use of the principle of double effect, which require that the "bad effect" not precede the "good effect desired" or it would contravene the axiom that you can't do bad things to get good things. What he does show is that when you want something strongly enough, you can justify just about anything.

10. Walter M. Abbott, S.J., gen. ed., *The Documents of Vatican II* (New York: Herder & Herder, 1966), 294.

11. See Daniel C. Maguire, *A New American Justice: Ending the White Male Monopolies* (Garden City, N.Y.: Doubleday, 1980); published in paperback as *A New American Justice: A Moral Proposal for the Reconciliation of Personal Freedom and Social Justice* (San Francisco: Harper & Row, 1981).

12. John Rawls, *A Theory of Justice* (Cambridge: Belknap Press of Harvard University Press, 1971), 14.

13. Pope Paul VI, "Remarks before Recitation of the Angelus, August 8, 1965," in *The Pope Speaks* (1965), 358, 406.

14. Rawls, *Theory of Justice*, 26.

15. Jared Diamond, *Guns, Germs, and Steel: The Fates of Human Societies* (New York: Norton, 1999), 9.

16. Ibid., 86.

17. Ibid., 218. Toynbee, *Change and Habit*, 21.

18. Arthur Koestler, *The Act of Creation* (New York: Dell, 1967), 111.

19. Mihajlo Mesarovic and Eduard Pestel, *The Second Re-*

port of the Club of Rome (New York: New American Library, 1976), 5.

20. Stanley Hauerwas, Linda Hogan, and Enda McDonagh, "The Case for Abolition of War in the Twenty-first Century," *Journal of the Society of Christian Ethics* 25, no. 2 (Fall–Winter 2005): 31. The 1991 Gulf War in Iraq was defended solely on grounds of Saddam's blundering aggression. This ignores what Alan Geyer calls "the United States' lack of meaningful political memory of its past policies and actions that contributed to the hostilities" (*Just Peacemaking: Ten Practices for Abolishing War*, ed. Glenn Stassen [Cleveland: Pilgrim, 1998], 83).

21. Clyde Prestowitz, *Rogue Nation: American Unilateralism and the Failure of Good Intentions* (New York: Basic, 2003), 26.

22. Nicholas D. Kristof, "China's Rise Goes beyond Gold Medals," *New York Times*, August 21, 2008, A23.

23. *Defense Monitor* 37, no. 2 (March–April 2008): 3.

24. David McHugh, Associated Press, "U.S., British Kids Fare Worst in Survey," *Milwaukee Journal Sentinel*, February 15, 2007, 3A.

25. Michael Renner, "Military Spending Near Record High," *World-Watch*, September–October 2005, 7.

26. See Adolph Reed Jr., "A GI Bill for Today," *Dissent*, Fall 2001, http://www.dissentmagazine.org/article/?article=903 (June 1, 2009). See also the prescient work of Seymour Melman, *The Defense Economy: Conversion of Industries and Occupations to Civilian Needs* (New York: Praeger, 1970). In a lifetime of publishing, Melman has scored the American commitment to what he calls military socialism. See also the prescient Alan F. Geyer, *The Idea of Disarmament: Rethinking the Unthinkable* (Elgin, Ill.: Brethren, 1982).

27. Quoted by Paul Krugman, *New York Times*, August 2, 2008, A24.

28. Sarah Sands, "We're all doomed! 40 years from global catastrophe—and there's NOTHING we can do about it, says climate change expert," *Daily Mail*, March 22, 2008, http://www.dailymail.co.uk/pages/live/articles/news/news.html?in_article_id=541748&in_page_id=1770 (June 1, 2009).

29. John Quain, "Fast Track," *Popular Mechanics* 184, no. 12 (December 2007): 89–93. In 1991, a report from the National Academy of Sciences said that "most analysts agree that Federal research grants would be needed to promote the most advanced magnetic levitation, or maglev, technology for the fastest possible trains." Those subsidies were not forthcoming.

30. Eric Lotke, "Collapsing Bridges, Sinking Levees. It's (Past) Time to Invest," Campaign for America's Fu-

ture, July 31, 2008, http://www.ourfuture.org/blog-entry/sinking-levees-collapsing-bridges-it-s-past-time-invest (June 1, 2009).

31. Joshua Lederberg, "Medical Science, Infectious Disease, and the Unity of Humankind," *Journal of the American Medical Association* 260, no. 5 (1988): 684–85.

32. Nicholas D. Kristof, "Iraq and Your Wallet," *New York Times*, October 24, 2006, A26.

33. Linda Bilmes, "The Trillion-Dollar War," *The New York Times*, August 20, 2005, A25.

34. Mark Green, "How to Fix Our Democracy," *The Nation*, March 12, 2007, 20.

10. Trusting Our Feelings and Emotions

1. John Dewey and James H. Tufts, *Ethics*, rev. ed. (New York: Henry Holt, 1932), 296.

2. Ghazala Anwar, "Elements of a Samadiyyah Shariah," in Marvin Ellison and Judith Plaskow, eds., *Heterosexism in Contemporary World Religion: Problem and Prospect* (Cleveland: Pilgrim, 2007), 92.

3. Ibid., 93.

4. Temporary marriage is permitted among the Shi'a but not among the Sunni schools. Ibid., 91.

5. Before polyamory there was "open marriage." In 1973, Nena and George O'Neill published *Open Marriage* (New York: Avon). The book was on the best-seller lists for more than a year. They argued for nonexclusive sexual relationships. Though married, both partners should be free to have satellite sexual relationships with others with openness and candor—no secrecy. They argued that "the idea of sexually exclusive monogamy and possession of another breeds deep-rooted dependencies, infantile and childish emotions, and insecurities. The more insecure you are the more you will be jealous" (237). They cited studies of societies where sexual exclusiveness in marriage was not normative, societies such as the Eskimo, the Marquesans, the Lobi of West Africa, the Siriono of Bolivia, and others. Sexual exclusivity for the married, therefore, "cannot be regarded as 'natural' to man's [sic] behavior" (256). Jealousy, they said, is a learned emotion and it can be unlearned. Jealousy, of course, can be neurotic, or it could signify fear of the loss of something precious, which would not be neurotic. In reacting to this, a study from the Playboy Press (!) by Morton Hunt concluded, regarding open marriage, that "most people continue to disapprove of such behavior because they believe that when it becomes a reality rather than a fantasy, it undermines and endangers the most important human relationship in their lives." He adds in his extensive study that "no more than a tiny minority of Americans have yet attempted such open marriages, and fewer still have made them work." *Sexual Behavior in the 1970s* (Chicago: Playboy, 1974), 236, 256. More recently, ethicist Mary Elizabeth Hobgood has argued that monogamy is "neither natural nor universal." It is dominant because it serves "male-dominant, class stratified, racist interest." *Dismantling Privilege: An Ethics of Accountability* (Cleveland: Pilgrim, 2000), 124–25.

6. See Herman J. Muller, *Studies in Genetics: The Selected Papers of H. J. Muller* (Bloomington: Indiana University Press, 1962); Theodosius Dobzhansky, *Mankind Evolving* (New Haven, Conn.: Yale University Press, 1962); Gordon Wolstemhomme, ed., *Man and His Future* (Boston: Little, Brown, 1963).

7. Dewey and Tufts, *Ethics*, 293.

8. Ibid.

9. Ibid., 299.

10. In the nineteenth century, impressed as we were by our burgeoning cleverness, there were airs of infallibility in many disciplines. The Catholic Church, in the spirit of this, declared its hierarchical teachers, especially the pope, to be infallible in their utterances on "faith and morals." This betrayed the deeper insight in the Catholic moral tradition that aside from hierarchs and learned intellectuals, there was another source of truth, the *sensus fidelium*, the lived and living experience of ordinary folk that could serve (and often did and does) as a corrective to aberrant leadership.

11. Immanuel Kant, *Foundations of the Metaphysics of Morals*, trans. Lewis White Beck (New York: Liberal Arts Press, 1959), 61. Kant did allow that feeling had some closeness to morality, since he allowed for an unselfish admiration of moral beauty.

12. Plato, *Phaedo*, 67 B.

13. Plato, *Laws* 653 Aff.; *Republic*, 401 E, 402 A.

14. Rubem A. Alves, *Tomorrow's Child* (New York: Harper & Row, 1972), 46.

15. David R. Loy, *Money, Sex, War, Karma: Notes for a Buddhist Revolution* (Boston: Wisdom, 2008), 71.

16. Beverly Wildung Harrison, *Making Connection: Essays in Feminist Social Ethics* (Boston: Beacon, 1985), 13.

17. Loy, *Money, Sex, War, Karma*, 123–24.

18. The discovery of affective shifts is a major need for successful social ethics. Robert Nisbet, in *The Sociological Tradition*, says that to know a society you need to study what he sees as the five essential unit-ideas of sociology: *community, authority, status, the sacred, and alienation*. These ideas he sees as "timeless and

universal," though their presence will ebb and flow in history. He sees them as underlying categories in Plato and Aristotle, in the Roman philosophers of the first century B.C.E., and in the work of the early Christian philosophers. These categories are chock-full of moral values in which we are, quite inevitably, affectively implicated. As Nisbet says, "Major ideas in the social sciences invariably have roots in moral aspiration." Applied to the five unit-ideas on which he bases his study, Nisbet says, "The moral texture of these ideas is never wholly lost." As the social sciences were birthed, they were first seen as subsections of ethics. They then succumbed to the "value-free" illusion, which allowed them to hide their moral assumptions and the affective preferences that are always working on the human mind. There is truth in Nisbet's statement that "the great sociologists never ceased to be moral philosophers." They simply stopped admitting it. *The Sociological Tradition* (New York: Basic, 1966), 7, 18.

19. Laurie Zoloth, *Visions of a New Earth*, ed. Harold Coward and Daniel C. Maguire (Albany: State University of New York Press, 2000), 100.

20. Peter Drucker, "The Age of Social Transformation," *Atlantic Monthly*, November 1994, 30.

21. Larry L. Rasmussen, *Earth Community Earth Ethics* (New York: Orbis, 1996), 119–20.

22. Aristotle, *Nicomachean Ethics,* bk. 2, chap. 3, 1104b.

23. Ibid., bk. 7, chap. 12, 1154a.

24. Thomas Aquinas, *Summa Theologiae* I II, q. 31, a. 1, ad 1: *Quando constituitur res in propria operatione connaturali et non empedita, sequitur delectatio* ("Doing what comes naturally, i.e. congruent activity, delights.")

25. Aristotle, *Nicomachean Ethics*, bk. 10, chap. 5, 1176a.

26. Thomas Aquinas, *Summa Theologiae* I II, q. 33, a. 1, ad 1, ad 3. Thomas adds a host of stretch words to make his point. *Magnificari, dilatari, ad . . . interius capiendum, ampliatur, ut capacius reddatur.* The *interius capiendum* is particularly striking. We want to get the source of delight more and more inside of us.

27. Quoted in Reinhold Niebuhr, *Moral Man and Immoral Society* (New York: Charles Scribner's Sons, 1932–1960), 163.

28. Ibid., II II, q. 45, a. 2.

29. Ibid., I, q. 87, a. 2 ad 3. Thomas, of course, did not have the word *character* with its current significance in his vocabulary any more than Aristotle did. What he was talking about in this text is *habitus*. See ibid., I II, q. 49, a. 1; II, q. 171, a. 2, in corp; I II, q. 49, a. 2 ad 3.

30. This is John Dewey's term. See Dewey and Tufts, *Ethics*, 297.

31. Mencius 2A: 6. See Paul F. Knitter and Chandra Muzaffar, eds., *Subverting Greed: Religious Perspectives on the Global Economy* (Maryknoll, N.Y.: Orbis, 2002), 1–2.

32. Thomas's dichotomy between a "perfect use of reason" and knowledge by way of connaturality is a bit too neat. Reason is never shorn of affective influence.

Some of Thomas's classical commentators are even clearer on the idea that affectivity is insightful. The seventeenth-century writer John of St. Thomas is certainly the strongest in the Thomistic line in this respect. He develops an explicit notion of "affective knowledge," which also ties in with the idea of character. John follows Thomas in distinguishing (again, a bit too neatly) the two modes of knowing and judging. One can know by study and disputation, or one can know from connaturality and affect (*ex quadam connaturalitate et affectu*). John goes beyond Thomas in elaborating the difference between the two. He says that affective knowledge is not simply knowledge stimulated by love. Love, he admits, can make us attend more to learning and can make us apply ourselves more vigorously. It can act as an efficient cause to stimulate the knowing process. If you like mathematics, you will study it more and learn it better. While granting that love can do this, it also does more. In affective knowledge, when the object known is also loved, a formally distinct form of knowing takes place. The affections can "causally provide greater light" by rendering the object known more fully experienced. John admits that this is not easily understood or explained. "What is more occult or more hidden than the interior affections of the will?" he asks. It is far easier, he says, to trace out the workings of purely intellectual knowledge. Still he presses on. In his exposition he reaches for different images than those customarily used to describe more intellectualized knowledge. Affective knowledge is less like seeing and more like "tasting" or "touching." The object that is loved as well as known is somehow "inviscierated" within the knower and somehow experienced from within with an entirely different sense of proportion and congeniality. Affective knowledge is just not the same as "naked" intellection.

Furthermore, John says that the very concept of connaturality implies a permanent and not a transient disposition of the knower. This makes his thought relevant to the discussion of character. He relates affective knowledge to a permanent disposition of the knower engendered by his affective orientation. There is solid insight in this from which modern ethics can profit. Joannes a Sancto Thoma, *Cursus Theologicus*

(Quebeci: Collectio Lavallensis, 1948), a. 3, n. 78, 147; n. 81, 150; n. 82, 151; n. 45, 119; a. 4, n. 15, 168; 169; a. 4, n. 19, 170–71.

33. Richard J. Barnet, *The Economy of Death* (New York: Atheneum, 1969), 25–26.

11. Creativity and Surprise

1. Jared Diamond, *Guns, Germs, and Steel: The Fates of Human Societies* (New York: Norton, 1999), 413.

2. Ibid.

3. See Michael Polanyi, *Personal Knowledge: Towards a Post-Critical Philosophy* (Chicago: University of Chicago Press, 1962), 138, 274–75.

4. Ibid., 218, 230.

5. Ibid., 216.

6. Leonard Shlain, *The Alphabet versus the Goddess: The Conflict between Word and Image* (New York: Viking, 1998).

7. Sophocles, *The Complete Plays of Sophocles*, trans. Sir Richard Claverhouse Jebb (New York: Bantam, 1968), 131.

8. Shlain, *Alphabet versus the Goddess*, 392.

9. Ralph Linton, "The Problem of Universal Values," in Robert F. Spencer, ed., *Method and Perspective in Anthropology: Papers in Honor of Wilson D. Wallis* (Minneapolis: University of Minnesota Press, 1954), 157.

10. Robert J. Bonner and Gertrude Smith, *The Administration of Justice from Homer to Aristotle* (Chicago: University of Chicago Press, 1930), 16.

11. S. Ranulf, *The Jealousy of the Gods and the Criminal Law at Athens* (London: Williams & Norgate, 1934), 157.

12. Aristotle, *Politics* 1254b: 4–6, 12–16.

13. Barbara Ehrenreich, *Blood Rites: Origins and History of the Passions of War* (New York: Henry Holt, 1997), 177–78.

14. See Daniel C. Maguire, *The Horrors We Bless: Rethinking the Just-War Legacy,* Facets (Minneapolis: Fortress Press, 2007), 6–13.

15. Cyril Burt, foreword to Arthur Koestler, *The Act of Creation* (New York: Dell, 1967), 13.

16. Rubem A. Alves, *Tomorrow's Child* (New York: Harper & Row, 1972), 67–68.

17. Jacob Bronowski, *Science and Human Values* (New York: Harper & Row, 1965), 15.

18. Ibid., 13.

19. Ibid., 18.

20. Koestler, *Act of Creation*, 96.

21. Ibid., 123.

22. Ibid., 109.

23. Ibid.. 157.

24. Vaclav Smil, "The Next 50 Years: Fatal Discontinuities," *Population and Development Review* 31, no. 2 (June 2005): 232 n. 19.

25. John R. Platt, *The Excitement of Science* (Boston: Houghton Mifflin, 1962), 64–65.

26. Nicolas Berdyaev, *The Destiny of Man* (New York: Harper & Row, 1960), 136.

27. Loren Eiseley, *The Firmament of Time* (New York: Atheneum, 1960), 4–5.

28. Platt, *Excitement of Science*, 8.

29. Smil, "Next 50 Years," 208. Smil makes this hopeful observation in an article that charts the potential dangers that could all but destroy our species and much of the planet.

30. http://www.swiftsmartveterans.com (June 2, 2009).

31. Quoted in Richard Falk, "The World Speaks on Iraq," *The Nation* 281, no. 4 (August 1–8, 2005): 10.

32. Smil, "Next 50 Years," 206.

33. Quoted in Ronald A. Knox, *Enthusiasm: A Chapter in the History of Religion* (New York: Oxford University Press, 1961), 591.

34. Rollo May, *Love and Will* (New York: Norton, 1969), 123–24.

35. Jonathan Schell, *The Unconquerable World: Power, Nonviolence, and the Will of the People* (New York: Henry Holt, 2003), 216.

36. Henri Bergson, *Two Sources of Morality and Religion* (Garden City, N.Y.: Doubleday, 1956), 74–75.

37. Oscar Wilde, "The Critic as Artist," in *Complete Works of Oscar Wilde* (London and Glasgow: Collins, 1973), 1058.

38. Michel Foucault, *Power/Knowledge: Selected Interviews and Other Writings, 1971–1977* (New York: Pantheon, 1980), 81.

39. Quoted in Koestler, *Act of Creation*, 142.

40. David Hume, who eventually was to be recognized as a major philosophical critic, says that his *Treatise of Human Nature* when published in 1738 "fell deadborn from the press, without reaching such distinction as even to excite a murmur among the zealots." And when he recast and published in 1752 what he considered to be his most important work on morals, "it came unnoticed and unobserved into the world." See A. D. Lindsay, "Introduction to Volume I," in David Hume, *A Treatise of Human Nature* (New York: Dutton, 1964), vii.

41. Jacques Maritain, *Creative Intuition in Art and Poetry* (New York: Meridian, 1955), 188.

42. Quoted in ibid., 187–88.

43. Eamonn Fingleton, "The Creativity Conceit," *The Utne Reader* 148 (July–August 2008): 44.

44. John W. Dixon may well be onto something when he writes in his "The Erotics of Knowing" that "engineering may be the model for the masculine as biology is the model for the feminine." *Anglican Theological Review* 56 (January 1974): 8. By nature and by nurture our distinctive gender experiences affect cognition, requiring complementary cooperation in knowing anything. See Daniel C. Maguire, "The Feminization of God and Ethics," presidential address, *The Annual of the Society of Christian Ethics, 1982*, 1–24; reprinted in Daniel C. Maguire, *The Moral Revolution* (San Francisco: Harper & Row, 1986), 105–21.

45. Jeannine Ouellette, "The Future of Creativity in Our Schools, Our Businesses, and Our Homes," *The Utne Reader* 148 (July–August 2008): 39.

46. Diamond, *Guns, Germs, and Steel*, 159.

47. Ibid., 19–20.

48. Immanuel Kant, *Kritik der Reinen Vernunft*, quoted in Josef Pieper, *Leisure: The Basis of Culture* (New York: New American Library, 1963), 25.

49. The criticism is that of Bernhard Jansen, *Die Geschichte der Erkenntnislehre in der Neueren Philosophie*, quoted in ibid.

50. We should not be too hard on Kant. He did move philosophy and psychology forward. Psychologist Rollo May goes so far as to credit him with the "second Copernican revolution" since he moved psychology and philosophy away from picturing the mind as a passive recipient of information. "Kant held that the mind is not simply passive clay on which sensations write, or something which merely absorbs and classified facts. . . . Kant's revolution lay in making the human mind an active forming participant in what it knows. Understanding, itself, is then constitutive of its world." Rollo May, *Love and Will* (New York: Norton, 1969), 226.

51. Heraclitus in Fragment 112 , quoted by Josef Pieper, *Leisure* (New York: Pantheon, 2000), 26.

52. Ibid.

53. Aristotle, *Metaphysics*, bk. 1, chap. 1, 981b, 22.

54. Aristotle, *Nicomachean Ethics*, bk. 10, chap. 7, 1177b, 5. This leisure, of course, is not just idleness. In his *Leisure: The Basis of Culture*, 41, Pieper describes it as a kind of inner calm that lets things happen. Leisure is a form of silence, of that silence which is the prerequisite of the apprehension of reality: only the silent hear, and those who do not remain silent do not hear. Silence, as it is used in this context, does not mean "dumbness" or "noiselessness"; it means more nearly that the soul's power to "answer" to the reality of the world is left undisturbed.

55. Arnold J. Toynbee, *A Study of History*, vol. 8 (New York: Oxford University Press, 1963), 90. He is speaking of Syria "in the broad sense in which this term had been used in the vocabulary of physical geography, to cover an area bounded by the North Arabian Steppe, the Mediterranean Sea, and the southern escarpments of the Anatolian and Armenian plateaux." The Oxus-Jaxartes Basin is in Central Asia.

56. Ibid., 97.

57. Friedrich Engels, quoted from a manuscript of 1847 in Hannah Arendt, *On Violence* (New York: Harcourt, Brace & World, 1969–1970), 12.

58. A. L. Basham, *The Wonder That Was India: A Survey of the Culture of the Indian Sub-cContinent before the Coming of the Muslims* (London: Sidgwick & Jackson, 1954), 269.

59. Thomas Kuhn, *The Structure of Scientific Revolution* (Chicago: University of Chicago Press, 1966), 91–92. See also Morris R. Cohen and Ernest Nagel, *An Introduction to Logic and Scientific Method* (New York: Harcourt, Brace & World, 1934), 392.

60. H. Richard Niebuhr, *The Responsible Self* (New York: Harper & Row, 1963), 177–78.

61. Ibid., 167.

62. Bronowski, *Science and Human Values*, 69–70.

12. Principles and Their Limits

1. This phrase is that of the poet Stanley Kunitz, quoted in Glenn D. Paige, *The Korean Decision* (New York: Free Press, 1968), 10.

2. Walt Whitman, "Songs of Myself," XLII in *Leaves of Grass*.

3. John Dewey and James H. Tufts, *Ethics*, rev. ed. (New York: Henry Holt, 1932), 304.

4. Moral principles can take various forms: positive (tell the truth, keep promises); negative (don't lie, don't steal); or imperative (thou shalt not commit adultery).

5. See Stanley M. Elkins, *Slavery* (New York: Grosset & Dunlop, 1963), 69.

6. See David Brion Davis, *The Problem of Slavery in Western Culture* (Ithaca, N.Y.: Cornell University Press, 1966), chaps. 3, 4, 7.

7. Quoted in Elkins, *Slavery*, 54.

8. Quoted in Ashley Montague, *The Natural Superiority of Women* (New York: Collier, 1974), 28–29.

9. Immanuel Kant, *Foundations of the Metaphysics of Morals*, trans. Lewis White Beck (New York: Liberal Arts Press, 1959), 18, 19.

10. Immanuel Kant, "On the Supposed Right to Lie from Altruistic Motives," in *Critique of Practical Reason and Other Writings in Moral Philosophy* (Chicago: University of Chicago Press, 1949), 347.

11. Quoted in ibid., 346.

12. Dietrich Bonhoeffer, *Ethics* (New York: Macmillan, 1965), 369 n. 1.

13. Given Kant's theoretical position, it is not surprising that the consequences would talk back and put Kant into this absurd position. Kant's imperative comes from his view of the law of reason. "Reason must regard itself as the author of its principles." The ground of obligation "must not be sought in the nature of man or in the circumstances in which he is placed, but sought *a priori* solely in the concepts of pure reason." Any precept "so far as it leans in the least on empirical grounds . . . may be called a practical rule but never a moral law." Affectivity and feeling are minimized in Kant's view, since "feelings naturally differ so infinitely in degree that they are incapable of furnishing a uniform standard of the good and bad." Kant is a major force behind the downgrading of affectivity in modern ethics. Obviously, affectivity would "contaminate" the abstract world of reason that he was constructing. *Foundations of the Metaphysics of Morals*, 67, 5, 61.

14. E. F. Schumacher, *Small Is Beautiful* (New York: Harper & Row, 1975), 53–54.

15. Ibid., 57.

16. See Jeremy Rifkin, *The End of Work: The Decline of the Global Labor Force and the Dawn of the Post-Market Era* (New York: Putnam's, 1995).

17. Jean Bodin, *On Sovereignty*, ed. Julian H. Franklin (Cambridge: Cambridge University Press, 1992), 108.

18. See Jonathan Schell, *The Unconquerable World* (New York: Henry Holt, 2003), 280–84.

19. Ibid., 349.

20. Ibid., 371.

21. Quoted in ibid., 366.

22. Walter Wink, *Jesus and Nonviolence: A Third Way*, Facets (Minneapolis: Fortress Press, 2003), 1–2.

23. Gene Sharp, *The Politics of Nonviolent Action* (Boston: Sargent, 1973).

24. Schell, *Unconquerable World*, 344.

25. Gidon Gottlieb, *Nation against State* (New York: Council on Foreign Relations, 1993).

26. Reinhold Niebuhr, *Moral Man and Immoral Society* (New York: Scribner's, 1932, [1960]), 88–89.

27. Quoted in ibid., 163.

28. Ralph Linton, "The Problem of Universal Values," in Robert F. Spencer, ed., *Method and Perspective in Anthropology* (Minneapolis: University of Minnesota Press, 1954), 387.

29. Hajime Nakamura, "Unity and Diversity in Buddhism," in Kenneth W. Morgan, ed., *The Path of the Buddha* (New York: Ronald Press, 1956), 387.

30. Aristotle, *Nicomachean Ethics*, bk 5, chap. 10, 1137b. The translation is that of J. A. K. Thomson. The translation of W. D. Ross is: "About some things it is not possible to make a universal statement which shall be correct." See Richard McKeon, ed., *The Basic Works of Aristotle* (New York: Random House, 1941), 1020.

31. Augustine, *De Sermone Dom. In Monte*, Lib. 1, c. 16. The commentator was the conservative Catholic moralist D. Prummer in his *Manuale Theologiae Moralis* ed. 8 (Frigurgi Brisgoviae: Herder, 1935), I, 111.

32. Thomas Aquinas, *Summa Theologiae* I II, q. 94, a. 4, in corp. *Etsi in communibus sit aliqua necessitas, quanto magis ad propria descenditur, tanto magis invenitur defectus.*

33. Ibid., a. 5, ad 2.

34. *Summa Theologiae* I, q. 105, a. 6, ad 2. See also in Aquinas II II, q. 64, a. 5, ad 4; II II, q. 154, a. 2, ad 2; *De Malo*, q. 3, a. 1, ad 17; *De potentia Dei*, q. 1, a. 6, ad 4; *In III Sent.* D. 37, a. 4.

35. As an example of a good principle that is open to exceptions, Thomas gives this: *Things held in trust should be returned upon request.* Normally this is true and applicable. However, if someone came back to claim something that you had held for him in trust for the avowed intention of doing some manifest evil with it, it would be both harmful (*damnosum*) and irrational (*irrationabile*) to conform to the principle. In that case you would be morally justified in keeping what belonged to this person, at least till circumstances changed. *Summa Theologiae* I II, q. 94, a. 4, in corp. There is one more striking point in Thomas in this regard that should be noted. Thomas says that in a sense truth is not the same for all men in matters of behavior: "in speculative things, truth is the same for all men. . . . In matters of behavior, however, truth of practical moral rightness is not the same for all with regards to that which is particular but only with regard to that which is in common." (Ibid.). This is a most notable allowance to the meaningfulness of that which is unique and special and ungeneralizable. If all moral meaning were generalizable, then the truth would be the same for everyone and Thomas's dramatic statement would not be necessary.

36. Joseph Fletcher, *Situation Ethics* (Philadelphia: Westminster, 1966), 164–65. See Harvey Cox, ed., *The Situation Ethics Debate* (Philadelphia: Westminster, 1968).

37. The domino theory is used against mercy death, as I showed in my book *Death by Choice,* updated and expanded ed. (Garden City, N.Y.: Doubleday, 1984). The

objection is reductively utilitarian. The abuse argument implies that even if one exception seems to be a good exception, nevertheless, because of the greatest good of the greatest number, it must be deemed immoral. The contention seems to be not that this exception is abusive and thus wrong, but that it would open the door to abuses. The good in this particular exception is simply written off in view of the alleged requisites of the common good. The *one* is sacrificed for the *many* in a classically utilitarian manner. Clearly, one would not use this argument from predicted abuse in an area where the vested interest of taboo is not present. In fact, a far stronger case could be made to prove that all acts of violence in self-defense and in war are immoral. There the abuses could be historically documented *ad nauseam.* But because these are culturally blessed exceptions, the argument from potential abuse is not used in the way that it is used against mercy death.

38. Stanley Hauerwas, Linda Hogan, and Enda Mc-Donagh, "The Case for Abolition of War in the Twenty-First Century," *Journal of the Society of Christian Ethics* 25, no. 2 (Fall–Winter 2005): 31.

39. He overstates the case when he says: "Scientific knowledge is judgment about things that are universal and necessary . . . and all scientific knowledge follows from first principles." That slights empirical analysis of particulars as modern science would insist. *Nicomachean Ethics,* bk. 6, chap. 6, 1140b, 31.

40. Ibid., bk. 6, chap. 5, 1140b, 9 and 1140a, 27; chap. 7, 1141b, 15.

41. Ibid., bk. 6, chap. 8, 1141a, 14, 15–19.

13. The Role of Authority and the Work of Reason

1. Adam Smith, *The Theory of Moral Sentiments* (New York: Augustus M. Kelley, 1966), 120. Psychologist E. R. Goodenough agrees: "The great majority of men . . . take their patterns of conduct from their society or traditions, get them ready-made as blueprints. . . . This is by no means the attitude of simple and weak minds alone. Often the human mind fears itself, and we shrink from our own thinking." E. R. Goodenough, *The Psychology of Religious Experiences* (New York: Harper & Row, 1968), 272.

2. Ralph H. Major, *A History of Medicine*, vol. 1 (Springfield, Ill.: Charles C. Thomas, 1954), 452.

3. Paul Starr, *The Social Transformation of American Medicine* (New York: Basic, 1982), 4.

4. F. B. McCrea and G. Markle, "Unnecessary Surgery," paper presented at the annual meeting of the American Sociological Association, San Francisco, August 14, 2004, http://www.allacademic.com/meta/p_mla_apa_research_citation/1/0/8/5/9/p108591_index.html (June 4, 2009).

5. Technology enhances authority and extends its reach. Former U.S. Secretary of State Zbigniew Brzezinski writes: "In the technetronic society the trend would seem to be towards the aggregation of the individual support of millions of uncoordinated citizens, easily within the reach of magnetic and attractive personalities effectively exploiting the latest communication techniques to manipulate emotions and control reason." "The Technetronic Society," *Encounter* 30, no. 1 (January 1968): 19.

6. Karl Mannheim, *Ideology and Utopia* (New York: Harcourt, Brace & World, 1963), 10.

7. Aristotle, *Rhetoric*, bk. I, chap. 2, 1356a, 4–5, 10–13.

8. Thomas Aquinas, *Commentary on the Nicomachean Ethics,* bk. 2, lectio 3, trans. C. I. Litzinger (Chicago: Regnery, 1964), 1:126.

9. The Pythagoreans felt that numbers and proportions constituted the basis of reality. This was their dominant metaphor. Since our thought bears the marks of our metaphors, we find that the Pythagoreans took the idea of the mathematical mean and, in ethics, made good behavior the mean between two extremes. The metaphor and its mathematical bias were not useless, but they did introduce a certain abstractness and artificiality that did not always meet the demands of the mysteries of moral meaning. Aristotle credited his use of the golden mean (*Nicomachean Ethics* 1107a 25). Thomas Aquinas followed Aristotle on this. However, both Thomas and Aristotle moved beyond the symbols of mathematics in their ethical epistemology and developed a broader and more elaborate system of ethics. Their devotion to "the mean," however, is strained at times and shows the hazards that beset those who are touched by the long shadow of Pythagoras. The mathematical bias of the Pythagoreans had to give a highly intellectualistic cast to the idea of reason. The mathematical paradigm simply is not conducive to a conception of ethical reason that integrates intellect and affectivity. The Stoic philosophers were also a major influence in the historical understanding of reason in ethics. As Vernon Bourke says to them: "As much as Hegel, the Stoics thought that the world is completely rational in character. There is a reason (logos) for everything that occurs. . . . The Stoics saw all things as interrelated in a comprehensible manner." Vernon J. Bourke, *History of Ethics* (Garden City, N.Y.:

Doubleday, 1968), 1:16. Such a view is not sufficiently hedged by a sense of mystery. And it is precisely this sense of mystery and the modesty it engenders that are sorely lacking in rationalistic thinking and in some presentations of "natural law" ethics. The hubris of rationalism is to think that the mind can take the full measure of the real. Stoic pan-rationalism encourages this. These overdrawn expectations of cosmos and too great a hunger for patterns in Stoic rationalism found their way into much of the ethics of right reason.

10. Aristotle speaks to this kind of rascality. He notes that "someone may say, 'We all aim at what appears to us to be good, but over this appearance we have no control.' How the end appears is determined by the character of the individual." Aristotle, *Nicomachean Ethics*, bk. 3, chap. 5, 1114a, 32. The difficulty is in distinguishing real good from apparent good. Aristotle does well to spotlight the role of character in this. Our impressions about morality resonate within our characterological orientation. This is just fine, and gives us a kind of instinctive divining power for discovering the truly moral—*if* ours is a good character. If not, the good that seems most congenial to us may be only apparent. What makes this so difficult is that no one thinks he or she has a bad character—outside of rare moments of major moral conversion.

11. Michael Polanyi, in his monumental *Personal Knowledge: Towards a Post-Critical Philosophy* (Chicago: University of Chicago Press, 1958), argues for the affective and even creedal aspects of the scientific search, noting how our affections can reach ahead of the mind, as when a researcher stays with a hypothesis even as contrary discouraging data seem to make it implausible only to be vindicated in his hunch. Clearly there is an element of faith in this also. Still, I would argue moral knowledge, affecting our own identity as no other field of knowing does, involves distinctive affective and creedal aspects.

12. Alice Rivlin, U.S. Congress Hearing, Joint Economics Committee, *Thirtieth Anniversary of the Employment Act of 1946—A National Conference on Full Employment* (Washington, D.C.: Government Printing Office, 1976), 276.

13. Josef Pieper writes: "*Reason* includes a reference to reality; indeed it is itself this reference. 'In accord with reason' is in this sense that which is right 'in itself,' that which corresponds to reality itself. The order of reason accordingly signifies that something is disposed in accordance with the truth of real things." *The Four Cardinal Virtues* (New York: Harcourt, Brace & World, 1965), 115–56. Pieper is discussing the meaning of reason in Thomas Aquinas, noting

that in Thomas it is used realistically, not idealistically or rationalistically, that it has none of the connotations of the *ratio* of the Enlightenment, and that it is not spiritualistic. For a fuller idea of Thomas, it is well to look at his idea of *ratio practica*, the role of prudence in ethics and the relationship of prudence to the moral virtues, and to knowledge by way of connaturality.

14. Daniel C. Maguire: *A New American Justice: Ending the White Male Monopolies* (Garden City, N.Y.: Doubleday, 1980; paperback ed., New York: Harper & Row, 1981).

15. This is the origin of the word *university*.

16. F. L. Cross and A. Livingston, eds., *The Oxford Dictionary of the Christian Church* (New York: Oxford University Press, 1974), 1032.

14. Group and Individual Experience: "We-Think" and "I-Think"

1. Dennis Nineham, *Christianity Mediaeval and Modern: A Study in Religious Change* (London: SCM, 1993), 25.

2. Edward O. Wilson, *The Future of Life* (New York: Knopf, 2002), 129.

3. Ibid.

4. Ibid., 189.

5. Joby Warrick, "A Warning of Mass Extinction," *Washington Post*, April 21, 1998.

6. Duane Elgin, *Promise Ahead: A Vision of Hope and Action for Humanity's Future* (New York: William Morrow, 2000), 1–5.

7. Wilson, *Future of Life*, 136.

8. Ibid., 106–7.

9. Psychology and many of the social sciences have stressed the radical degree to which group influences affect us. Anthropologist Clifford Geertz, for example, sees all of our basic talents as dependent upon cultural conditioning. There is no such thing as a human nature independent of culture. Men without culture would not be the clever savages of William Golding's *Lord of the Flies*, thrown back upon the cruel wisdom of their animal instincts; nor would they be the nature's noblemen of Enlightenment primitivism; or even, as classical anthropological theory would imply, intrinsically talented apes who had somehow failed to find themselves. They would be unworkable monstrosities with very few useful instincts, fewer recognizable sentiments, and no intellect; i.e., mental basket cases. Clifford Geertz, "The Impact of the

Concept of Culture," in John R. Platt, ed., *New Visions of the Nature of Man* (Chicago: University of Chicago Press, 1965), 112–13.

10. Quoted in Barbara Ehrenreich, *Blood Rites: Origins and History of the Passions of War* (New York: Henry Holt, 1997), 13.

11. Quoted in ibid., 14.

12. Obery M. Hendricks Jr., "Class, Political Conservatism and Jesus," *Cross Currents* 55, no. 3 (Fall 2005): 307.

13. Ibid., 312.

14. See Michael Zweig, "Six Points on Class," *Monthly Review* 58, no. 3 (July–August 2006): http://www.monthlyreview.org/0706zweig.htm (June 5, 2009).

15. Howard Zinn, *A People's History of the United States: 1492 to Present* (New York: Harper Perennial, 1995), 84.

16. Ibid., 75–76, 249.

17. Ibid., 95.

18. Mary Elizabeth Hobgood, *Dismantling Privilege: An Ethics of Accountability* (Cleveland: Pilgrim, 2000), 94.

19. Ibid., 93.

20. John Raines, "The Room Where I Work Is a Class Room," *Cross Currents* 55, no. 3 (Fall 2005): 365. Comparing Kensington High School in a poor Philadelphia neighborhood to Lower Merion High School on the Philadelphia mainline, Raines reports that the chances of getting a college education are forty times greater for Lower Merion graduates than for Kensington High graduates. Ibid., 369.

21. Reinhold Niebuhr, *Moral Man and Immoral Society* (New York: Scribner's, 1960), 114, 117, 116.

22. *Sweden's News in English*, http://www.thelocal.se/14022/20080829/ (June 5, 2009).

23. Gloria H. Albrecht, *Hitting Home: Feminist Ethics, Women's Work, and the Betrayal of Family Values* (New York and London: Continuum, 2002), 54.

24. Nancy Folbre, *The Invisible Heart: Economics and Family Values* (New York: New Press, 2001), 131–35.

25. Albrecht, *Hitting Home*, 92 n. 15.

26. Ibid., 82.

27. Juliet Schor, *The Overworked American: The Unexpected Decline of Leisure* (New York: Basic, 1991), 30–32.

28. Albrecht, *Hitting Home*, 130 n. 18.

29. Quoted in Lawrence E. Blades, "Employment at Will versus Individual Freedom: On Limiting the Abusive Exercise of Employer Power," *Columbia Law Review* 67 (1967): 1405. Blades is citing *Paine v. Western & A.R.R., 81 Tenn.507*, 519–20 (1884).

30. Joseph Grodin, "Remedy Wrongful Termination by Statute," *California Lawyer* 10, no. 7 (July 1990): 120.

31. David R. Loy, "Pave the Planet or Wear Shoes? A Buddhist Perspective on Greed and Globalization," in Paul F. Knitter and Chandra Muzaffar, eds., *Subverting Greed: Religious Perspectives on the Global Economy* (Maryknoll, N.Y.: Orbis, 2002), 73.

32. Thich Nhat Hanh, *The Heart of Understanding*, quoted in David R. Loy, *Money, Sex, War, Karma: Notes for a Buddhist Revolution* (Boston: Wisdom Publications, 2008), 122.

33. Lucy Dawidowicz, "The Nazi Experience: Origins and Aftermath," *Hastings Center Report* 6, no. 4, special supplement (August 1976): 3.

34. See Daniel C. Maguire, *Death by Choice*, updated and expanded ed. (Garden City, N.Y.: Doubleday, 1984).

35. Henri Bergson, *The Two Sources of Morality and Religion* (Garden City, N.Y.: Doubleday, 1956), 14–15.

36. Ibid.

37. C. Judson Herrick, *Brains of Rats and Man*, quoted in Erich Fromm, *The Anatomy of Human Destructiveness* (New York: Holt, Rinehart & Winston, 1973), 224.

38. Ibid.

39. J. Kashyap, "Origin and Expansion of Buddhism," in Kenneth W. Morgan, ed., *The Path of the Buddha* (New York: Ronald Press, 1956), 16–17.

40. Fromm, *Anatomy of Human Destructiveness*, 224.

41. Ibid., 278.

42. Joseph Ratzinger, "Commentary on the Church in the Modern World," pt. 1, chap. 1, in *Commentary on the Documents of Vatican 2*, vol. 5, gen. ed. Herbert Vorgrimler (New York: Burns & Oates / Herder & Herder, 1969), 134. Emphasis added.

43. Thomas Aquinas, *Summa Theologiae* I II, q. 106, a. 3 et seq.

44. Avery Dulles, S.J., "The Revolutionary Spirit of Thomas Aquinas," *Origins* 4 (February 13, 1975): 543; idem, "Presidential Address: The Theologian and the Magisterium," *Proceedings of the Catholic Theological Society of America* 31 (1976): 235–46.

45. Thomas Aquinas, *In II Pol.*, lects. 6, 8, 13, 15, 17.

46. Asghar Ali Engineer, "Islam, Women, and Gender Justice," in John C. Raines and Daniel C. Maguire, eds., *What Men Owe to Women: Men's Voices from World Religions* (Albany: State University of New York Press, 2001), 121–22.

47. Ibid., 122.

48. Quoted in ibid. 122. Iqbal calls for the application of this today: "The only alternative open to us, then, is to tear off from Islam the hard crust which has immobilized an essentially dynamic outlook on life, and to rediscover the original verities of freedom, equality,

and solidarity with a view to rebuild our moral, social, and political ideas out of their original simplicity and universality."

49. Sa'diyya Shaikh, "Family Planning, Contraception, and Abortion in Islam: Undertaking *Khilafah*," in Daniel C. Maguire, ed., *Sacred Rights: The Case for Contraception and Abortion in World Religions* (New York: Oxford University Press, 2003), 119. See also Azizah al-Hibri, J.D., Ph.D., *Religious and Ethical Perspectives on Population Issues*, a publication of the Religious Consultation on Population, Reproductive Health and Ethics, 2823 N. Summit Avenue, Milwaukee, WI 53211.

50. Josef Pieper, *The Four Cardinal Virtues* (New York: Harcourt, Brace & World, 1965), 28.

15. The Comic and the Tragic in Ethics

1. G. K. Chesterton, *Lunacy and Letters*, ed. Dorothy Collins (New York: Sheed & Ward, 1958), 97.

2. Studies have been done to show the perceptual denial of the incongruous. We develop expectations of what the real has to offer, and we are controlled in our interpretations by those expectations, not by the signals from reality. In one study, subjects were asked to identify a red six of spades from a deck of playing cards. Ninety-six percent of the subjects failed at first to identify the anomalous card for what it was. And it took four times longer to perceive the incongruous cards as it did to identify the normal cards. The conclusion of the researchers was that "for as long as possible and by whatever means available, the organism will ward off the perception of the unexpected, those things which do not fit his prevailing set." J. S. Bruner and L. Postman, "On the Perception of Incongruity," in M. D. Vernon, ed., *Experiments in Visual Perception* (Baltimore: Penguin, 1966), 285–92.

3. Bernard J. F. Lonergan, *Insight: A Study of Human Understanding* (New York: Longmans, Philosophical Library, 1957), 626.

4. Augustine, *City of God*, 14:24. See Daniel C. Maguire, *Whose Church? A Concise Guide to Progressive Catholicism* (New York: New Press, 2008), 7–25.

5. Gordon W. Allport, *The Nature of Prejudice* (Garden City, N.Y.: Doubleday, 1958). See also Daniela Gioseffi, ed., *On Prejudice: A Global Perspective* (New York: Doubleday, 1993).

6. Harvey Mindess, "The Sense in Humor," *Saturday Review,* August 21, 1971, 10.

7. Ibid.

8. Arthur Koestler, *The Act of Creation* (New York: Dell, 1967), 95.

9. Ibid., 59.

10. Beatrice K. Otto, "An Excerpt from *Fools Are Everywhere: The Court Jester around the World,*" *Fooling around the* World (2001) http://www.press.uchicago.edu/Misc/Chicago/640914.html (June 8, 2009). See Beatrice K. Otto, *Fools Are Everywhere: The Court Jester around the World* (Chicago: University of Chicago Press, 2001).

11. Herbert Thurston, "Feast of Fools," in *The Catholic Encyclopedia*, vol. 6 (New York: Robert Appleton Co., 1909); see New Advent, http://www.newadvent.org/cathen/06132a.htm (June 8, 2009).

12. The mind is susceptible to demonic images. Sometimes a word can function as an image that demonically captures a whole history of venom and hate. *Nigger* is a word like that. And Dick Gregory, the prophet-jester, gives an example of what humor can do to relativize that vicious image. He has told hundreds of rollicking audiences that he used that word as the title of one of his books so that whenever his children heard the word, they could say: "Somebody is talking about Daddy's book!" Here Gregory was acting also as an exorcist, driving out the devil that possessed a word.

Humor can go to work also on other demons like the work ethic, male dominance, and the myths of woman, class, and nation. Also, it is not necessary to take on with supine obedience all the imperiously established values of one's profession, class, time, or place. Humor is one of the forces that can bring liberation from the demonic images that come to us from a thousand sources and shackle the mind in disgraceful servitude. Demonic images can easily attach to the most serious things in our life. The more serious things are, however, the more need there is for comic relief.

13. Joseph Grassi, *God Makes Me Laugh: A New Approach to Luke* (Wilmington, Del.: Michael Glazier, 1986), 8.

14. 14, Dr. L. Jolyson West, quoted in *Hastings Center Report* 2, no. 5 (Nov. 1972), 6.

15. Jacques Leclercq, *Christ and the Modern Conscience* (New York: Sheed & Ward, 1963), 263–64.

16. H. Richard Niebuhr, *The Responsible Self* (New York: Harper & Row, 1963), 59–60. Niebuhr comments that suffering is "a subject to which academic ethical theory, even theological ethics, usually pays little attention" (59).

17. Ibid., 59.

18. Though a common enough expression, the notion of national character is imprecise, especially when applied to an incorrigibly pluralistic society such as the United States. More properly it should be said that there are diverse characterological orientations within the American people. Still, there are some general trends that affect most Americans due to those crises of our history and affect all of us more or less, thus justifying this admittedly loose usage. Finding the right symbols to discuss social consciousness is never a wholly successful enterprise.

19. Paul Kennedy, *The Rise and Fall of the Great Powers: Economic Change and Military Conflict from 1500 to 2000* (New York: Random House, 1987), 514–15.

20. Lonergan, *Insight*, 625.

21. Barbara W. Tuchman, "A Nation in Decline? *New York Times Magazine*, September 20, 1987, 58.

22. Jared Diamond, *Guns, Germs, and Steel: The Fates of Human Societies* (New York: Norton, 1999), 40.

16. Conscience and Guilt: The Agenbite of Inwit

1. H. A. Prichard, "Does Moral Philosophy Rest on a Mistake?" *Mind* 21 (1912); reprinted in W. T. Jones, F. Sontag, M. O. Beckner, and R. J. Fogelin, *Approaches to Ethics*, 2nd ed. (New York: McGraw-Hill, 1969), 474.

2. Character is not the same thing as the spontaneously judging moral self that is conscience. The knowing function is primary in conscience; secondary in the denotative meaning of character.

3. Bernard Häring put it this way: Intellect and will "can part ways in their activity, but not without unleashing the most profound grief in the depths in which they are united, not without creating a rift in those very depths. . . . The most agonizing cry wells up from the depth of the soul itself, for as root and source of unity of the powers, it is directly wounded by their dissension. Here is the profound reason for the first elemental agony of conscience . . . a spontaneous unreflecting pain." *The Law of Christ* (Westminster, Md.: Newman, 1961), 143.

4. Rita Nakashima Brock and Rebecca Ann Parker, *Saving Paradise: How Christianity Traded Love of This World for Crucifixion and Empire* (Boston: Beacon, 2008), 6–10.

5. Ibid., 92.

6. Thomas Aquinas calls this skill *solertia*. See *Summa Theologiae* II II, q. 49, a. 4, where he says that *solertia* implies a facile and prompt response to sudden and unexpected situations. (*Solertia est habitus qui provenit ex repentino, inveniens quod convenit*.)

7. Josef Pieper, *The Four Cardinal Virtues* (New York: Harcourt, Brace & World, 1965), 16.

8. Martin Buber, "Guilt and Guilt Feeling," *Cross Currents* 9 (Summer 1958): 202.

9. Thomas Aquinas, *Summa Theologiae* II, q. 10, a. 11 (*Humanum regimen derivatur a divino regimine, et ipsum debet imitari. Deus, autem, quamvis sit imnipotens et summe bonus, permittit tamen aliqua mala fieri in universo, quae probibere posset, ne eis sublatis, maiora mala sequerentur*). (Translated, it reads: "Human government is derived from divine government and should imitate it. God, although all powerful and supremely good, still permits some evils to occur, evils which he could prohibit, lest, with them removed, even greater evils would ensue.")

10. See Henry Davis, *Moral and Pastoral Theology*, vol. 1 (London: Sheed and Ward, 1949), 91–113. All of the so-called manuals of moral theology published in the nineteenth and early twentieth centuries in Catholic moral theology contained a treatment of probabilism.

11. Anouar Majid, *A Call for Heresy: Why Dissent Is Vital to Islam and America* (Minneapolis: University of Minnesota Press, 2007), 215.

12. William Shakespeare, *Hamlet*, act 2, scene 2, lines 315–19.

13. Blaise Pascal, *Pensées* (New York: Washington Square, 1965), no. 434, 127.

14. Robert L. Heilbroner, *An Inquiry into the Human Prospect* (New York: Norton, 1975), 61.

15. Catholic ethics in the past excelled in producing some neuroticizing taboos in the sexual area. Heribert Jone sang in this dismal chorus: "All directly voluntary sexual pleasure is mortally sinful outside of matrimony. This is true even if the pleasure be ever so brief and insignificant. Here there is no lightness of matter. Even the individuals in whom the sex urge is abnormally intense (sexual hyperesthesia) can and must control themselves." Every sexual imagining was full of sin even if the pleasure was "brief and insignificant." Also, the accent is not on harm done but on the pleasure, which was consciously accepted. It is this pleasure that is taboo; hence, there is no need to enter into an analysis of what harm a particular instance of sexual pleasure might do. The guilt is still serious no matter what its effects. Having placed sexual pleasure under taboo, Jone goes on to make the following remarkable classi-

fication: "Because of the varying degrees of influence they may have in exciting sexual pleasure, the parts of the human body are sometimes divided into decent (face, hands, feet), less decent (breast, back, arms, legs), and indecent (sex organs and adjacent parts)." Here again the taboo mentality is present in full vigor. In prosecutorial pursuit of the sexual pleasure that is under taboo, Jone is drawn to using negative value terms to designate the parts of the body most likely to produce that pleasure. This is illustrative of the inability of the taboo mentality to think relationally or with sensitivity to contextual variables. The physical act itself in its simple materiality becomes wrong. With Jone, even the organs that produce the physical phenomenon merit negative judgment. What this celibate scholar missed, of course, was that in a romantic context deft touching of even the "decent" parts can be maximally stimulating. Heribert Jone, *Moral Theology*, "Englished and adapted" by Urban Adelman (Westminster, Md.: Newman, 1955), 146–54.

16. The so-called technical virgin may be used to illustrate taboo. The term is used to refer to a woman who will engage in sexual intimacy even to the point of orgasm but will not have intercourse so as to preserve her "virginity." The taboo mentality shows through here if the abstention from intercourse is not based on fear of pregnancy or some other defensibly realistic consideration, but is rather the result of cultural conditioning that has attached enormous moral prestige to the mere material fact of nonintercourse. The abstention here is not rationally motivated. Such abstention might be rationally argued; in taboo it is not. There is no thought-out evaluation with a resultant decision against intercourse. There is, rather, an almost instinctive withdrawal from this act *regardless of the good or harm that it might do*. This "regardless" is the crux of taboo. The behavior is wrong not because it harms, but because it is forbidden. The forbiddenness comes from without, not from within the situation. The action is not wrong because of the circumstances that orient it more toward disvalue than toward value, but because it is banned.

17. Ayn Rand, *The Virtue of Selfishness: A New Concept of Egoism* (New York: New American Library, 1961).

18. I have written elsewhere about a guilt-avoidance stratagem that I call Imperial Comfort Syndrome (ICS). Empires by definition are exploitative of weaker nations. Those living in the empire center bask in purloined privileges. They become comfortable and indifferent to the exploitation they are wreaking on nations and peoples subject to their siphoning influence. No guilt is felt. All of those problems are *al di la* as the Italians put it—out there somewhere, not our doing or our concern. See Daniel C. Maguire, *The Horrors We Bless: Rethinking the Just-War Legacy*, Facets (Minneapolis: Fortress Press, 2007), 88–89.

19. See Daniel C. Maguire, *Sacred Choices: The Right to Contraception and Abortion in Ten World Religions* (Minneapolis: Fortress Press, 2001), 28–29.

20. *The Nature of the Universe*, sec. 44. This is a Pythagorean treatise spuriously ascribed to Ocellus Lucanus. Quoted in John T. Noonan Jr., *Contraception* (Cambridge: Belknap Press of Harvard University Press, 1965), 47. Stoic influence is seen in this aspect of Pythagorean thought.

21. J. Glenn Gray, *The Warriors: Reflections on Men in Battle* (New York: Harper & Row, 1959), 212.

22. See Winslow T. Wheeler, "The Week of Shame: Congress Wilts as the President Demands an Unclogged Road to War" (Washington, D.C.: Center for Defense Information, January 2003), 17. See also Chalmers Johnson, *The Sorrows of Empire: Militarism, Secrecy, and the End of the Republic* (New York: Henry Holt, 2004).

23. On the criteria for a "just war," see Maguire, *Horrors We Bless.*

24. Jonathan Schell, *The Unconquerable World: Power, Nonviolence, and the Will of the People* (New York: Metropolitan, 2003).

25. Theodore R. Weber, "Guilt: Yours, Ours, and Theirs," *Worldview* 18, no. 2 (February 1975): 15–18.

26. Albrecht Haushofer, "Schuld" (Guilt), quoted and translated by Gray, *Warriors*, 204–5.

> *Doch Schuldig bin ich anders als ihr denkt,*
> *ich musste früher meine Pflicht erkennen*
> *ich musste scharfer Unheil Unheil nennen—*
> *mein Urteil hab ich viel zu lang gelenkt . . .*
> *Ich klage mich in meinem Herzen an:*
> *Ich habe mein Gewissen lang betrogen*
> *Ich hab mich selbst und andere belogen—*
> *Ich Kannte früh des Jammers ganze Bahn*
> *Ich hab gewarnt—nicht hart genug und klar!*
> *Und heute weiss ich, was ich schuldig war . . .*

27. Thomas Aquinas, *Summa Theologiae* II II, q. 61, a. 1 ad 3.

28. Arthur Miller, *Incident at Vichy* (New York: Dramatists Play Service, 1966), 48–49.

29. Derrick A. Bell Jr., "The Real Cost of Racial Equality," *Civil Liberties Review Survey*, Summer 1974, 97.

30. A. L. Basham, *The Wonder That Was India: A Survey of the Culture of the Indian Sub-Continent before the Coming of the Muslims* (London: Sidgwick & Jackson, 1954), 145.

17. The Power of Myth

1. Rollo May refers to the "second Copernican revolution" in modern thought achieved by Immanuel Kant. He writes: "Kant held that the mind is not simply passive clay on which sensations write, or something which merely absorbs and classifies facts. . . . Kant's revolution lay in making the human mind an active, forming participant in what it knows. Understanding, itself, is then constitutive of its world." *Love and Will* (New York: Norton, 1969), 226. This basic insight is one that must be advanced so as to see the specific and varied ways in which the mind is an active participant in what it knows. This participation becomes a hazard when the interpretive aspect of knowing barters away our reality contact and confuses the figment for the fact. This is what happens in the hazard of myth. We can prefer our conceptualization of the reality to the reality itself.

2. See Robert Jewett and John Shelton Lawrence, *Captain America and the Crusade against Evil: The Dilemma of Zealous Nationalism* (Grand Rapids: Eerdmans, 2003). This is a powerful and also a much neglected study of American messianic mythology.

3. Herman Melville, *White-Jacket, or The World in a Man-of-War* (Evanston and Chicago: Northwestern University / Newberry Library, 1970 [1850]), 151.

4. *Congressional Record*, 56th Cong., 1st sess., vol. 33, 711.

5. Quoted in Jewett and Lawrence, *Captain America*, 4.

6. Nathaniel W. Taylor, *Concio ad Clerum: A Sermon Delivered in the Chapel of Yale College, September 10, 1828* (New Haven: Hezekiah Howe, 1828), 22; quoted in William A. Clebsch, *From Sacred to Profane America: The Role of Religion in American History* (New York: Harper & Row, 1968), 32.

7. Quoted in Andrew J. Bacevich, *The New American Militarism: How Americans Are Seduced by War* (New York: Oxford University Press, 2005), 12.

8. George S. Phillips, *The American Republic and Human Liberty Foreshadowed in Scripture* (Cincinnati: Poe & Hitchcock, 1864); quoted in Clebsch, *From Sacred to Profane America*, 189–91.

9. Clebsch, *From Sacred to Profane America*, 191–92.

10. Quoted in Charles A. Beard, *The Idea of National Interest* (New York: Macmillan, 1934), 368.

11. Ibid., 380–83.

12. Quoted in Jewett and Lawrence, *Captain America*, 57.

13. Ibid., 395.

14. George F. Kennan, *American Diplomacy: 1900–1950* (New York: New English Library, 1951), 14.

15. Jewett and Lawrence, *Captain America*, 11.

16. John McCain, "There Is No Substitute for Victory," *Wall Street Journal*, October 26, 2001, A14.

17. Jewett and Lawrence, *Captain America*, 12.

18. See Roland H. Bainton, *Christian Attitudes toward War and Peace: A Historical Survey and Critical Reevaluation* (New York: Abingdon, 1960), 208–10.

19. See Jerome Frank, *Sanity and Survival: Psychological Aspects of War and Peace* (New York: Vintage, 1968), 134–35.

20. The complex myth of woman exercised its blinding influence even in physiology. Thomas Aquinas, for example, relying on Aristotle, wrote, with a view to "particular nature," that woman is something deficient and misbegotten, the result of a lapse in the generative process. His argument is an epic of "male chauvinism." The active strength that is in the sperm of the male would naturally tend to produce something "like unto itself . . . perfect and masculine." Obviously, sperm does not always succeed in doing this, since women are generated. Thomas has several possible reasons for this: it could be due to intrinsic weakness in the active strength of the sperm, or because of some indisposition of this material. Extrinsic causes would also be responsible for the generation of a woman. Thomas, referring to Aristotle, cites the possible causal influence of the humid winds that come in from the south. These might so affect the internal environment that a woman would be conceived instead of a man. Thomas Aquinas, *Summa Theologiae* I, q. 92, a. 1, ad 1 (*Virtus activa quae est in semine maris, intendit producere sibi simile perfectum, secundum masculinum sexum*); notice *masculinum* and *perfectum* are synonymous.

21. Male scholars of religion have joined women scholars in showing the falsehood that became religiously enshrined. See John C. Raines and Daniel C. Maguire, *What Men Owe to Women: Men's Voices from World Religions* (Albany: State University of New York Press, 2001).

22. See Daniel C. Maguire, ed., *Sacred Rights: The Case for Contraception and Abortion in World Religions* (New York: Oxford University Press, 2003.)

23. On the history of "development," see Larry L. Rasmussen, *Earth Community Earth Ethics* (Maryknoll,

N.Y.: Orbis, 1996), 134–37. See also Clive Ponting, *A Green History of the World: The Environment and the Collapse of Great Civilizations* (New York: Penguin, 1991), 139–60. Also see Maria de Lourdes Pintasilo and Paul Harrison, *Caring for the Future: A Radical Agenda for Positive Living*, Report of the Independent Commission on Population and Quality of Life (New York: Oxford University Press, 1996).

24. Edward O. Wilson, *The Future of Life* (New York: Knopf, 2002), 149–50.

25. David C. Korten, *When Corporations Rule the World* (West Hartford, Conn.: Kumarian, 1995), 106, 284.

26. D. Pimentel, R. Harman, M. Pacenza, J. Pecarsky, and M. Pimentel, "Natural Resources and an Optimal Human Population," *Population and Environment* 15, no. 5 (1994): 352.

27. Quoted in Korten, *When Corporations Rule*, 33.

28. Ibid., 85. This came from an internal World Bank memorandum dated December 12, 1991, p. 5.

29. Quoted in Korten, *When Corporations Rule*, 249.

30. Eric Voegelin, *The New Science of Politics* (Chicago: University of Chicago Press, 1952), 111.

31. Ibid., 111–12.

32. Ibid., 113.

33. Jacques Ellul, *The Political Illusion* (New York: Knopf, 1967), 98–108.

34. Ibid., 104.

35. See http://www.kidscount.org; http://www.prb.org; http://www.childtrends.org (June 10, 2009).

36. Sylvester Judd, *A Moral Review of the Revolutionary War, or, Some of the Evils of That Event Considered* (Hallowell, Me.: Glazier, Masters & Smith, 1842), 5.

37. Ibid.

38. Ibid., 4.

39. Ibid., 27.

40. Ibid.

41. Ibid., 39.

42. Ibid., 38–39.

43. Huston Smith, *The Religions of Man* (New York: Harper & Row, 1965), 11.

44. R. R. Palmer, *A History of the Modern World*, 2nd. ed., rev. with collaboration of Joel Colton (New York: Knopf, 1960), 265–66.

18. Obstacles to Right Thinking

1. Ernest Renan, "What Is a Nation?" in Homi K. Bhaba, ed., *Nation and Narration* (New York: Routledge, 1990), 11.

2. On Renan's view of a nation's need for strategic forgetfulness, see Alexis Dudden, "The Politics of Apology between Japan and Korea," in Mark Philip Bradley and Patrice Petro, eds., *Truth Claims: Representation and Human Rights* (New Brunswick, N.J.: Rutgers University Press, 2002), 73.

3. Marilyn B. Young, "Remembering to Forget," 11–21 in ibid.

4. Douglas Strick, "Airing an Ugly Secret," *Washington Post*, October 27, 1999.

5. Young, "Remembering to Forget," 14–15. Multiple other acts of wanton slaughter were committed by Americans but again swallowed up in the fogs and fabrications of war.

6. James Scott, *The Attack on the Liberty: The Untold Story of Israel's Deadly 1967 Assault on a U.S. Spy Ship* (New York: Simon & Schuster, 2009); Marc H. Ellis, *Judaism Does Not Equal Israel* (New York: New Press, 2009); Jimmy Carter, *We Can Have Peace in the Holy Land: A Plan That Will Work* (Simon & Schuster, 2009); Jimmy Carter, *Palestine: Peace Not Apartheid* (New York: Simon & Schuster, 2006). Joel Kovel, a physician and a Jew, in an article entitled "Overcoming Impunity," cites the refusal of Congress to investigate the attack on the USS *Liberty* and also cites the equally uninvestigated killing of Rachel Corrie as she, wearing an orange flack-jacket and "speaking into a bull-horn under a cloudless sky," was run over by an Israeli bulldozer. Ms. Corrie was protesting the destruction of a Palestinian home. Joel Kovel, *The Link* 42, no. 1, January–March 2009: 1–11. On American reticence regarding Israeli policies, see Eric Alterman, "Israel at 60: The State of the State," *The Nation* 287, no. 8 (September 22, 2008): 11–20. He writes: "Israeli writers and intellectuals engage in a discussion about their nation and its problems that is far richer, more nuanced and grounded in reality than that of their American counterparts" (11).

7. A. J. P. Taylor, *The Struggle for the Mastery of Europe* (New York: Oxford University Press, 1954), xxiv.

8. See Jonathan Schell, *The Unconquerable World: Power, Nonviolence, and the Will of the People* (New York: Metropolitan, 2003), 218–19.

9. Ibid., 147.

10. John Adams, *The Works of John Adams*, vol. 10 (Boston: Little, Brown, 1956), 180.

11. Quoted in Jonathan Schell, *Unconquerable World*, 64–65.

12. Richard Hofstadter, *The American Political Tradition* (New York: Vintage, 1954), vii. See Susan George, "A Short History of Neoliberalism," in Francois Houtart

and Francois Polet, eds., *The Other Davos: Globalization of Resistance to the World Economic System* (London: Zed, 2001), 7–16.

13. John Gray, "A Shattering Moment," *JUST Commentary: International Movement for a Just World* 8, no. 10 (2008): 1–2.

14. See Daniel C. Maguire, "Omnipotence in Demise," in *A New American Justice: A Moral Proposal for the Reconciliation of Personal Freedom and Social Justice* (New York: Harper & Row, 1980), 8–25.

15. In the 2008 presidential election, John McCain got more than 4.5 million votes in California, but that is blurred by the winner-take-all approach. Similarly, Barack Obama got 40 percent of the vote in Alabama. This system distorts the actual situation of voters. See editorial in *New York Times*, November 20, 2008, A32.

16. Ross Terrill, "Pax Americana and the Future of Asia," *Cross Currents* 18, no. 4 (Fall 1968): 484.

17. Hannah Arendt, *The Human Condition* (Garden City, N.Y.: Doubleday, 1959), 64.

18. Alexis de Tocqueville, *Democracy in America*, 2 vols., ed. Phillips Bradley (New York: Knopf, 1945), 1:310; 2:8.

19. President Johnson, defending the decision to fight in Vietnam, said in a speech in Beaumont, Texas: "In 1940 with most of Europe in flames, four Democratic senators . . . said that President Roosevelt could negotiate a just peace—that is, with Hitler—if he would only make an effort. Sounds kind of familiar doesn't it? . . . We are not going to be Quislings and we are not going to be appeasers, and we are not going to cut and run. . . . We do believe that if Hitler starts marching across the face of Europe that we ought not wait until the last minute to let him know that might doesn't make right." Quoted in Arthur Schlesinger, *Crisis of Confidence* (Boston: Houghton Mifflin, 1969), 116–17. If that one sentence—"We do believe . . ."—were taken out of the context and one were asked to date it, the date would certainly have to be in the 1930s and not in the mid-1960s. This illustrates the consumptive power of the false analogue.

20. James Barron, "Unnecessary Surgery," *New York Times*, April 16, 1989, A15. "The surgery rate in the United States grew more than twice as fast as the population between 1979 and 1987. By most accounts, it's the highest in the world. For example, studies cited by Lynn Payer in her recent book, 'Medicine and Culture,' show that American women are two to three times more likely to undergo a hysterectomy than women in England. Heart patients here are six times more likely to have a coronary bypass. Yet our more aggressive style of medicine doesn't buy us longer lives: According to the World Health Organization, life expectancy is about the same in the United States as in Western Europe, and Americans are somewhat more likely to die of heart disease than people living in England."

21. Origen, *Fifth Homily on Genesis 4.* See John T. Noonan Jr., *Contraception: A History of Its Treatment by the Catholic Theologians and Canonists* (Cambridge: Harvard University Press, 1956), 77 and 47, 79, 80, 85.

22. Bruce Bagemihl, *Biological Exuberance: Animal Homosexuality and Natural Diversity* (New York: St. Martin's, 1999).

23. As Herbert Marcuse says, "Critical philosophic thought is necessarily transcendent and abstract. Philosophy shares this abstractness with all genuine thought, for nobody really thinks who does not abstract from that which is given, who does not relate the facts to the factors which have made them, who does not—in his mind—undo the facts. Abstractness is the very life of thought, the token of its authenticity." *One Dimensional Man* (Boston: Beacon, 1966), 134. He also adds, however, "There are false and true abstractions. Abstraction is an historical event in an historical continuum. It proceeds on historical grounds, and it remains related to the very basis from which it moves away." If that contact breaks it is illusory.

24. William Shakespeare, *Henry IV*, part 1, act 5, scene 1, lines 126–43.

25. The ought-to-is fallacy of abstractness is often a coping stratagem. Parents of a genetically damaged child, for example, may fail to appreciate what the child is, obsessed as they can be with their stricken hopes of what he might have been. Their abstract conception of what the child should be will overshadow the gentle beauties that may still be there. Lovely forms of personality may even break through the frost of tragic genetic damage and come to blossom. Parents of children afflicted with Down syndrome are now becoming aware that these children need not be relegated into oblivion as though no precious personal life could manifest itself in spite of the serious debits. It would, of course, be abstract in the worst sense to say that the birth of a Down syndrome baby is not normally tragic or that abortion could not be a moral option when amniocentesis discovers an affected fetus. Nevertheless, when

the child is born, the concrete possibilities of the child must be accepted and brought to full potential. The ought in that case is abstract; the child is real.

26. Christopher Flavin and Robert Engelman, "The Perfect Storm," in Worldwatch Institute, *State of the World 2009: Into a Warming World* (New York: Norton, 2009), 5–12.

27. Jean Reith Schroedel, *Is the Fetus a Person? A Comparison of Policies across the Fifty States* (Ithaca, N.Y.: Cornell University Press, 2000), 157.

28. Ibid., 163. "Women's status is consistently lower in antiabortion states than in pro-choice states, indicating that lawmakers in the former are more interested in attacking women's rights than protecting fetal life" (157).

29. Ibid., 157.

30. Ibid., 159.

31. Ibid., 159 n. 23.

32. Samuel Laeuchli, *Power and Sexuality: The Emergence of Canon Law at the Synod of Elvira* (Philadelphia: Temple University Press, 1971).

33. Eduardo Galeano, *Open Veins of Latin America: Five Centuries of the Pillage of a Continent* (New York: Monthly Review Press, 1973, 1997), 5. Regarding Africa, Jacob Olupona writes: "Right from the time of its 'discovery' by the Portugese explorers in the fifteenth century, modern Africa has been subjected to foreign dominance and exploitation of its resources, laying bare its natural riches and human resources." Slavery stole over twenty million of its men and women and exported them. Jacob K. Olupona, "African Religions and Global Issues," in Harold Coward and Daniel C. Maguire, eds., *Visions of a New Earth* (Albany: State University of New York Press, 2000), 176.

34. Pierre Teilhard de Chardin, *The Vision of the Past* (New York: Harper & Row, 1966), 202.

19. Epilogue: Religion, Ethics, and the Social Sciences

1. It would be a mistake to think that "religion" enjoys a universally accepted definition. Chinese scholars, for example, say that there is no word in the rich Chinese lexicon that matches our English *religion*. In the ancient world, as Morton Smith writes, there was not even a "general term for religion." He says that if you want to express what Judaism was about, "the one Hellenistic word which came closest was 'philosophy' or 'the cult of wisdom.'" See his "Pales-tinian Judaism in the First Century," in Moshe David, ed., *Israel: Its Role in Civilization* (New York: Jewish Theological Seminary of America, 1956), 67–81. The central theme of the Bible is "the reign of God." This is a political term. Both Israel and Christianity were at root revolutions in the realm of political economy. Bible scholar Bruce Malina says that "the most significant obstacle" blocking insight into Jesus' mission "is the widespread belief that Jesus and his program were about religion." *The Social Gospel of Jesus: The Kingdom of God in Mediterranean Perspective* (Minneapolis: Fortress Press, 2001), 1, 144.

2. Sam Harris, *The End of Faith: Religion, Terror, and the Future of Reason* (New York: Norton, 2005), 129.

3. Quoted anonymously in Gilbert Murray, *Five Stages of Greek Religion* (Garden City, N.Y.: Doubleday, 1955), 37. The term *religio* has various meanings, including conscientiousness, but is often related to gods and cult and ritual.

4. Ibid.

5. Ibid., 2.

6. See chap. 4 regarding the theory of the triune brain and the differences in right-brain and left-brain functioning and impact.

7. Carl Sagan, Hans Bethe, et al., "An Open Letter to the Religious Community" (1990), available from the National Religious Partnership for the Environment, 1047 Amsterdam Ave., New York, NY 10025.

8. Daniel L. Pals, *Seven Theories of Religion* (New York: Oxford University Press, 1996), 9. As Jack Miles points out in his remarkable book, *God: A Biography* (New York: Knopf, 1995), the God figure confected in the Jewish and Christian Bible became not only the major literary figure in the West, but indeed the very "mirror of the West and a major determinant of its moral and political personality" (4).

9. Douglas Johnston and Cynthia Sampson, eds., *Religion, the Missing Dimension of Statecraft* (New York: Oxford University Press, 1994).

10. Kevin Phillips, *American Theocracy: The Peril and Politics of Radical Religion, Oil, and Borrowed Money in the 21st Century* (New York: Viking, 2006), 102. An example of terrible ideas that got an early grip on Christianity is found in "atonement" through blood and death as a way of explaining the crucifixion of Jesus. This sadomasochistic idea bore baneful progeny in the sacralization of war and in the glorification of suffering and passivity in the face of evil. See Rita Nakashima Brock and Rebecca Ann Parker, *Saving Paradise: How Christianity Traded Love of This World for Crucifixion and Empire* (Boston: Beacon, 2008).

See also Marit Trelstad, ed., *Cross Examinations: Readings on the Meaning of the Cross Today* (Minneapolis: Fortress Press, 2006). On the distortions of biblical data leading to this atonement theory, see Robert Bruce McLaren, *Christian Ethics: Foundations and Practice* (Englewood Cliffs, N.J.: Prentice Hall, 1994).

11. Lynn White Jr., "The Historical Roots of Our Ecologic Crisis," *Science* 155 (March 10, 1967): 1203–07. See James A. Nash, "The Ecological Complaint against Christianity," in *Loving Nature: Ecological Integrity and Christian Responsibility* (Nashville: Abingdon, 1991), 68–92.

12. On the influence of theism and belief in an afterlife on ecological ethics, see Daniel C. Maguire and Larry L. Rasmussen, *Ethics for a Small Planet: New Horizons on Population, Consumption, and Ecology* (Albany: State University of New York Press, 1998), 22–49.

13. Catherine Keller, *On the Mystery: Discerning Divinity in Process* (Minneapolis: Fortress Press, 2008), xi.

14. Jack Nelson-Pallmeyer, *Is Religion Killing Us? Violence in the Bible and the Quran* (New York: Continuum, 2003).

15. Ignatius Jesudasan, *Roots of Religious Violence: A Critique of Ethnic Metaphors* (Delhi, India: Media House, 2007).

16. See Isaac Kramnick and R. Laurence Moore, *The Godless Constitution: The Case against Religious Correctness* (New York: Norton, 1997).

17. Frank Kermode, *The Classic: Literary Images of Permanence and Change* (New York: Viking, 1975), 17–18.

18. See Daniel C. Maguire, *The Moral Core of Judaism and Christianity: Reclaiming the Revolution* (Minneapolis: Fortress Press, 1993), 58–90. I also develop there other characteristics of a classic and apply them to the best of Judaic and Christian literature.

19. Clifford Geertz, *The Interpretation of Cultures* (New York: Basic, 1973), 89.

20. See Pinchas Lapide, *The Sermon on the Mount: Utopia or Program for Action?* (Maryknoll, N.Y.: Orbis, 1986).

21. Elaine Pagels, *Adam, Eve, and the Serpent: Sex and Politics in Early Christianity* (New York: Random House, 1988), xix.

22. Ibid., xx.

23. Ibid., 55, 73.

24. Garry Wills, "Faith and the Race for God and Country," *Sojourners* 15 (March 14, 1988): 4–5.

25. See Eric Hobsbawm, *The Age of Extremes: A History of the World, 1914–1991* (New York: Random House, 1994), 12.

26. See Daniel C. Maguire, *The Horrors We Bless: Rethinking the Just-War Legacy*, Facets (Minneapolis: Fortress Press, 2007), 2–5.

27. James Carroll, "The Bush Crusade," *The Nation* 279, no. 8 (September 20, 2004): 18.

28. M. Douglas Meeks, *God the Economist: The Doctrine of God and Political Economy* (Minneapolis: Fortress Press, 1989), 3.

29. Norman K. Gottwald, quoted in J. Mark Thomas and Vernon Visick, eds., *God and Capitalism: A Prophetic Critique of Market Economy* (Madison: A-R Editions, 1991), 27. Gottwald applies the biblical critique of greed and royalty to American capitalism and concludes: "The most powerful capitalist nation in the world gains the advantage of wealth that is has by 'bleeding' and dominating smaller nations, the majority of whose citizens live in deepening poverty, and at the same time it allows a very large part of its own population to suffer in poverty. Public needs go begging, while a small part of the populace lives in opulence and surfeit of goods. The political leadership is almost totally captive to the ruling economic interest" (26). Gottwald is the premier authority on the political economy of ancient Israel. See his magnum opus, *The Tribes of Yahweh: A Sociology of the Religion of Liberated Israel, 1250–1050 B.C.E.* (Maryknoll, N.Y.: Orbis, 1979).

30. See Daniel C. Maguire, *A Moral Creed for All Christians* (Minneapolis: Fortress Press, 2005), 41–110.

31. Joseph E. Stiglitz, *Globalization and Its Discontents* (New York: Norton, 2002), 12.

32. See Daniel C. Maguire, "Seeking the Path to Adjunct Justice at Marquette University," *Thought and Action* (The NEA Higher Education Journal) 24 (Fall 2008): 47–55.

33. United Nations Development Programme, *Human Development Report 1992* (New York: Oxford University Press, 1992).

34. Jeremy Rifkin, *The End of Work: The Decline of the Global Labor Force and the Dawn of the Post-Market Era* (New York: Putnam's, 1995), 250.

35. Alice Rivlin, U.S. Congress Hearing, Joint Economics Committee, *Thirtieth Anniversary of the Employment Act of 1946—A National Conference on Full Employment* (Washington, D.C.: Government Printing Office, 1976), 276. Mary Evelyn Tucker and John Grim have edited a series at Harvard University Press that is a *tour de force* of positive contributions of the world's major and indigenous religions on the issue of ecology. These include volumes such as *Christianity and Ecology, Buddhism and Ecology*, etc. See also Roger Gottlieb, *The Oxford Handbook of Religion and*

Ecology (New York: Oxford University Press, 2006). Larry L. Rasmussen's *Earth Community Earth Ethics* (Maryknoll, N.Y.: Orbis, 1996) is a veritable *Summa Ecologiae Christianae.*

36. Chun-fang Yu, "Chinese Religions on Population, Consumption, and Ecology," in Harold Coward and Daniel C. Maguire, eds., *Visions of a New Earth* (Albany, N.Y.: SUNY Press, 2000), 162 .

37. See Duane Elgin, *Promise Ahead: A Vision of Hope and Action for Humanity's Future* (New York: William Morrow, 2000), 116–17.

38. See Omid Safi, ed., *Progressive Muslims: On Justice, Gender, and Pluralism* (Oxford: One World Publishers, 2003–2004).

39. Dennis Nineham, *Christianity Mediaeval and Modern* (London: SCM, 1993), 234.

40. Ibid., 41, 80, 91, 102.

41. Ibid., 86.

42. Ibid. 170.

43. Arnold Toynbee, *Change and Habit: The Challenge of Our Time* (New York: Oxford University Press, 1966), 112.

44. Nelson-Pallmeyer, *Is Religion Killing Us?* xv.

45. See Gary Schaub, "Really Soft Power," *New York Times,* January 27, 2009, A29. This would indicate that the worst eruptions of our limbic system where fear abounds are controlling, and the diplomatic work that can be done by the neocortex is slighted on the American moralscape.

46. William Greider, *Secrets of the Temple: How the Federal Reserve Runs the Country* (New York: Simon & Schuster, 1987), 230.

47. 47. Matthew Arnold, see Bartleby.com, "The Study of Poetry," in *Essays English and American 1909–14.*

48. René Dubos, *So Human an Animal* (New York: Scribner's, 1966), 221.

GLOSSARY

Abstinence-only sex ethics. This policy permits no sexual activity outside legal heterosexual marriage. (Chapter 12)

Affirmative action. A term first coined by John F. Kennedy to institute a policy of preferential treatment for previously excluded groups to break up an unjust monopoly. It is a form of empowerment. Thus, there can be preferential admissions to academic programs but not preferential graduation. (Chapters 5, 8, 9)

Altruism. Genuinely caring for the interests and welfare of others, without regard for oneself or one's motivation or benefit in acting morally. (Chapter 3)

Amoral. That which does not fall within the moral ream and which, therefore, cannot be judged morally good or bad. For example, a chemical mixture considered in itself is amoral. However, if the chemical mixture is being introduced into the food chain without examination of dangers, the moral dimension arises because human choice is involved. No conscious human choices are amoral. (Chapter 1)

Anticipatory revisionism. See Pendulum effect.

Apocalypticists. Those who believe in the end of the world and the likely establishment of a new world order based on the triumph of good over evil. (Chapter 1)

Axial Age. The Axial Age developed in several civilizations during the first millennium B.C.E. It involved a stronger sense of transcendence, which included greater tension between that "higher (nonmaterial) world" and this material one. While it included advances in civilization and intellectual life, it also introduced the duality between our immaterial spirit and the corruptions of the flesh, denigrating nature, women, and sex—perhaps because they are associated with death. (Chapter 10)

Character. Character is the embodiment of a person's moral orientation. It is the timbre of a person's ingrained moral quality. It is the moral thrust of the personality that is given its direction from the decisions of our moral history. (Chapter 10)

Collective guilt. See Guilt.

Common good. The *common good* is a term that is both descriptive and normative. It describes the needs and necessities of communal existence, and it implies that we must think of those needs in our pursuit of private goals. We are, as Aristotle said by nature "political" beings, i.e., members of the *polis*, the community. In that sense we are *socialindividuals* with inter-individual moral debts and with debts to the community that bore us and in multiple ways sustains us. (Chapters 1, 5)

Commutative justice. See Justice.

Conscience. The morally conscious self as attuned to moral values and disvalues in the concrete. *Conscience* refers to the individual's (or culture's) actual sensitivity or insensitivity to the worth of persons and the rest of nature. (Chapter 16)

Consequentialism. Teaches that human actions are good or bad primarily or exclusively in terms of their effects or consequences. It neglects the moral significance of all the other circumstances mentioned in the center of the hub of the wheel model of ethics. (Chapter 9)

Corpocracy. A term used to describe the domination of corporations in national government. (Chapter 5)

Courage. The virtue seen as the precondition for all other virtues. It means strength and firmness in the face of challenges and difficulties. (Chapters 1, 13)

Culture. The socialized likes and dislikes, and passions and aversions of people, and these socialized meanings are normally transmitted through symbols. (Chapter 19)

Deontology. Deontological theory holds that certain actions are intrinsically valuable regardless of their consequences. It is sometimes called "duty ethics" or divine command theory. In reality, consequences and teleology are never irrelevant or beyond consideration. (Chapter 6, endnote)

Diplomacy. A nonviolent approach to national and international politics involving the ability to respect others' needs and to make appropriate compromises in the cause of peacemaking. (Chapter 5)

Distributive justice. See Justice.

Domino theory. Other images used to convey the same idea are the wedge, the camel's nose under the tent, the finger out of the dike, the slippery slope, and the parade of horrors. The idea behind these images is that if you allow one exception, others will inevitably follow and moral discernment will be skewed. (Chapter 12)

Double effect, principle of. The principle that analyzes cases where one act had two effects, one good and the other damaging. (Chapter 9).

Egalitarianism. See Equality.

Egoism. In ethics, the theory that morality requires doing what will benefit oneself, or to always act in such a way as is consistent with one's own interests. (Chapter 1)

Emotivism. The view that moral judgments are nothing more than emotional reactions to particular issues and not statements that could be analyzed as true or false. It means that morality is not based on reason. (Chapter 4)

Epistemology. The branch of philosophy that explores the nature and possibility of knowledge or knowing. (Chapter 18)

Equality. Generically it refers to taking every person as of equal value. It is also used in commutative justice

calculations. It is not useful in issues of social or distributive justice where unequal needs require unequal distribution. (Chapter 5)

Ethics. The art/science that seeks to bring sensitivity and method to the discernment of moral values. Ethics can also be described as a dialogue conducted by the moral agent between the moral meaning found in principles and that found in the unique circumstances of the case. Ethics is also described simply as the systematic discussion of morality. (Chapters 1, 6)

Evaluational phase of ethics. That part of the wheel model of ethical method that helps to examine and judge what the reality-revealing questions have uncovered. The spokes of the model spell out the multiple ways available to us personally and socially to evaluate moral matters. They include creative imagination, affectivity, reason and analysis, authority, principles, individual and group experience, comedy, and tragedy. (Chapters 10–15)

Faith. A strong belief or confidence in the truth of some idea or thing, to the point of *knowing* that idea or thing as a result of one's feelings and affectivity. (Chapter 4)

Fallacy. An argument that is not logically valid or a claim that shows incorrect reasoning; a misconception. (Chapters 2, 18)

Fetus, moral status of. This refers to determining when the embryo-fetus attains to personal status. (Chapters 5, 7)

Foundational moral experience (FME). The experience of the value of persons and their environment in nature. It is the grounding of all moral knowledge, moral reasoning, and ethics. The experience is at root an affective faith experience, and it is processual in the sense that it admits of greater or lesser appreciation. It is a faith experience, not in the usual religious sense, but in the sense that we cannot prove the value of persons and of this earth. We *believe* it just as we believe in basic human rights but cannot empirically prove them. What we believe has to be tested by reason, principles, and the other spokes (evaluational processes) of the wheel model. (Chapters 3, 4, 16)

Fundamentalism. In its various manifestations, this describes those who read and interpret religious texts (or constitutions or other documents) in the strictest and most literal of ways. (Chapter 2)

Guilt. A term that describes the state of having transgressed moral boundaries. Guilt is understood in three ways: at the taboo level, something is considered wrong regardless of whether there is resultant harm or unreasonableness; egoistic guilt sees wrongfulness in terms of personal disfigurement, not because of the impact on other persons; realistic guilt is conscious and free behavior (active or passive) that does real, unnecessary harm to persons and/or their environment. The term *collective guilt* is also used. This term is properly employed to describe undue apathy regarding the obligations of social and distributive justice. It is improperly used to imply that a whole people are responsible for certain acts that others have performed, thus denying any personal center of responsibility. (Chapter 16)

Hermeneutics. Methods of interpretation. The importance of the term in this book is to clearly differentiate *descriptive* and *prescriptive* content in sacred texts, which give meaning and interpretation to what is understood as moral or immoral. (Chapter 19)

Hyperfertility. Reproducing beyond the carrying capacity of the ecological environment. (Chapter 1)

Ideology. Broader in meaning than *myth*, an ideology is a systematic way of describing a set of beliefs; it contains a rationalizing and organizing element. (Chapter 17)

Immoral. The opposite of morally good. Often used synonymously with *unethical*. (Chapters 2, 3)

Intuition / Intuitionism. The view that a moral quality is known by direct insight or intuition and not by reasoning and all the other evaluational processes. The moral goodness or badness of a situation is appreciated simply and directly just as one knows the color yellow to be yellow. Intuitionism bypasses the complexity of ethical analysis, assuming that moral knowledge is largely self-evident. Also known as subjectivism. (Chapter 10, 16)

Just war theory. A theory with roots in the Greco-Roman world that stipulates six criteria for declaring war, state-sponsored violence, to be morally justifiable: (1) a just cause; (2) declaration by competent authority; (3) right intention; (4) the principle of discrimination, i.e., of noncombatant immunity; (5) last resort; (6) the principle of proportionality. It is sometimes called "the Catholic just war theory" since it was historically much developed by Catholic thinkers. (Chapters 1, 7, 9)

Justice. Justice is the virtue that renders to each his or her own. *Suum cuique* is the classical Latin expression for justice. Justice ensures that all persons receive their minimal essential due. To deny persons justice is, in effect, to deny their humanity. Justice is the minimal expression of the foundational moral experience (FME): There are three forms of justice, *commutative*, *social*, and *distributive*. Commutative justice renders what is due in relationships between two persons or two social entities. Social justice represents the debts that the individual citizen and social institutions owe to the social whole or the common good. Distributive justice directs the fair allocation of goods, burdens, and duties among the citizens of the community. (Chapters 5, 7)

Moral. Moral can be used as the opposite of *immoral* or as the opposite of *amoral*. In the latter sense it means that

the matter or issue falls within the realm of moral adjudication, as in the expression "This is a moral matter." This means that it is open to moral judgment, whether it will be judged favorably (as moral) or unfavorably (as immoral). (Chapters 1–3)

Myth. A complex of feelings, attitudes, symbols, memories, and experienced relationships through which reality is refracted, filtered, and interpreted. Myth has both positive and negative connotations or meanings. In its positive connotations, myth helps explain or attribute the inexplicable to something else when facts are insufficient or unavailable. In its negative connotations, myth serves to conceal truth or explicitly deceive those who are expected to accept the story or idea. (Chapter 17)

Natural law. An approach to ethics that stresses that an understanding of human nature governs the formulation and applicability of principles and that what is "natural" in a holistic sense tends to determine what should be moral. (Chapter 12)

Obstacles or hazards of moral discourse. Anything that interferes with moral judgment and moral reasoning. The generic hazards are incompleteness and insensitivity. Some of the specific hazards are socially enforced forgetfulness, momentum and the grip of *idee fixe*, mood, false analogy, the ought-to-is fallacy, distracting abstractions, selective virtue, selective memory, the rule of role, and the loss of wonder and awe. (Chapters 17–18)

Ought-to-is fallacy. This fallacy, or mistake in reasoning, leads one to conclude that because a situation *ought* to be a certain way, then the situation *is* that way. It also works in the converse: because things are as they are, they ought to be as they are. (Chapter 18)

Pacifism. A commitment to nonviolence that may be absolute or may allow for instances of self-defense. (Chapter 1)

Pendulum effect. The tendency in social thought to swing from one extreme to the other. Good ethics seeks anticipatory revisionism to avoid the currents of extremism. (Chapter 12)

Policing paradigm. A principle in contemporary ethics derived from the Charter of the United Nations. It says that war is never justified unless it is waged defensively and collectively under the supervision of the United Nations in a context of the restraints of law that characterize the use of force by internal national policing. It is the opposite of the vigilante approach to war whereby a nation will set out on its own to vindicate its rights. It puts the same restraints on war that are put on police. See also War. (Chapters 1, 7)

Positivism. A reductionist theory holding that truth can be known only through scientific and empirical means. (Chapters 3, 12)

Probabilism. The basis for using one's conscience to determine what is or is not moral. Deriving from the Catholic ethical tradition, probabilism supports dissent from an official teaching where there is reasonable debate over that moral teaching, making it subject to doubt; as a doubtful moral teaching, it cannot oblige as if it were certain. Thus, in the face of a formidable consensus of authority, an individual can still dissent from that authority's teaching, given that there are *probable* reasons for holding different moral positions. (Chapter 16)

Principles. Generalizations about what is morally good or bad. Sometimes stated declaratively, as in "Promise keeping is good," and sometimes stated imperatively, as in "Thou shalt not kill." Moral principles are more or less open to exceptions. The exceptions are reasonable and have equal moral standing with the principles. (Chapter 12)

Profanation, sense of. The moral shock and horror that we feel when persons and/or our terrestrial environment are abused or offended. It is the shock and withdrawal we feel when the value of life is debased. (Chapter 10)

Propaganda. This term refers to those uses of information which attempt to influence opinion or behavior, and its import is that it hides one's real agenda behind some kind of abstraction or misinformation. (Chapter 18)

Proportionality, principle of. Since ethics always weighs and balances values and disvalues amid the complexities of life, this principle can be considered the master principle in ethics. Basically it seeks to do more good than harm. It is one of the principles of the "just war theory," since a war that does more harm than good is collective murder. (Chapters 9, 10)

Reasonable versus Rationalistic. "Reasonable" connotes an openness to reality and being, with a kind of balance and thoroughness; having good contact with reality and fairness. "Rationalistic" signifies here an (intellectually dishonest) attempt to confine reality to narrow understandings, even when evidence and reasons require further openness and explanation. (Chapter 13)

Relativism. The viewpoint that says that what we call "morally good" is merely socially approved custom. Relativism holds that right and wrong depend on the cultural setting, that there is no objective morality to which all peoples could appeal. Ethical relativism does not exist in a pure state, but it does pervade much thinking in formal ethics and in the popular "do your own thing" culture. It often appears under the mantle of the lubricious term *postmodern*. (Chapter 2)

Religion. The response to the sacred which includes broad understandings of spirituality and the divine, and the response is seen in a set of narratives, symbols, practices, beliefs and institutions. (Chapter 19)

Rights. Claims that you can make or insist on against others. These claims carry obligations on the part of others. There are two main sources of rights: earned entitlements, as a result of some action, and need, as a result of one's nature or situation. (Chapter 5)

Sacred. Not limited to institutionalized religion, it is something which is extraordinary and often beyond the natural realm (in a religious sense), and which is considered holy or deserving of deep reverence or respect (as in the case of both religious and non-religious examples, such as with legal systems). (Chapter 19)

Sanctity of life. A broadly used term to denote the supreme value of life. Primarily an expression of valuation of the dignity and worth of persons. The term is used by extension to refer to the value of all forms of life in this interdependent biosphere. (Chapter 3)

Secular. Not specifically connected to religion or spiritual matters, and sometimes seen as outright rejecting of religion and religious considerations. (Chapter 19)

Situation ethics. A theory holding that moral obligation is dictated by the situation alone. This theory is suspicious of absolutes or hard-and-fast rules or principles. The term is sometimes used negatively as an excessively permissive approach to ethics. Others use it to insist on a sensitivity to situational differences. It is also sometimes called "contextualism." (Chapters 6, 12)

Social justice. See Justice.

Speciesism/speciests. This involves granting different value or more or fewer rights to certain beings based on the species to which they belong, generally according more to human beings than to animals and other living things. (Chapter 5)

Spirituality. A response to the sacredness of life that may or may not involve a belief in a divine being. (Chapter 1)

Subjectivism. See Intuitionism.

Supreme sacrifice. Offering one's life for the welfare of others. It is the most dramatic expression of the foundational moral experience, and it is revered in the literature of most cultures. (Chapter 3)

Suum cuique. A Latin term that literally means "to each his or her own" and is the core meaning of justice. See Justice. (Chapter 5)

Taboo. Treating certain actions as wrong regardless of the circumstances. (Chapter 16)

Utilitarianism. Utilitarianism is not a full theory of ethics but is rather a short-circuited effort to define the good as that which achieves the greatest good for the greatest number. Utilitarianism is totalitarian in thrust for all of its democratic pretensions. It provides for a tyranny of the majority and does not provide for the necessary and natural tension between the private and the common good, between minority good and majority good. The theory is tied to Jeremy Bentham and John Stuart Mill, and most ethics book give it more consideration than is its due. (Chapters 2, 9, 16)

Velleity. *Velleity* comes from the Latin *vellem*, meaning "I would like." *Volition* comes from the Latin *volo*, referring to what you really will. Velleity refers to what you would fully and honestly will were things more to your liking and less taxing. Many apparent volitions are actually velleities since they lack the will to follow through. (Chapter 8)

Volition. See Velleity.

War. State-sponsored violence. (Chapters 1, 7, 9)

INDEX